P9-EMO-208

Cape Town & the Garden Route

"All you've got to do is decide to go
and the hardest part is over.

So go!"

TONY WHEELER, COFOUNDER – LONELY PLANET

THIS EDITION WRITTEN AND RESEARCHED BY

Simon Richmond
Lucy Corne

Contents

Left: District Six Museum (p77)

Above: V&A Waterfront (p99)

Right: Abseilers on Table Mountain (p28 & p88)

Welcome to Cape Town & the Garden Route

The Mother City, home to soaring Table Mountain, golden beaches and bountiful vineyards, is an old pro at capturing people's hearts.

Natural Wonders

Table Mountain National Park defines the city. The flat-topped mountain is the headline act, but there are many other equally gorgeous natural landscapes within the park's extensive boundaries. Cultivated areas, such as the historic Company's Gardens, Kirstenbosch Botanical Gardens and Green Point Park, also make exploring the city a pleasure. Follow the lead of locals by taking full advantage of the abundant outdoor space. Learn to surf; go hiking or mountain biking; tandem paraglide off Lion's Head; abseil off the top of Table Mountain – these are just a few of the many activities on offer.

Design Delights

The World Design Capital 2014 is in the process of using innovative design to transform the city. It's already one good-looking metropolis, from the brightly painted facades of the Bo-Kaap and the bathing chalets of Muizenberg to the Afro-chic decor of its restaurants and bars, and the striking street art and innovation incubators of The Fringe and Woodstock. The shack communities of the Cape Flats are a sobering counterpoint, but even in these deprived suburbs there are enterprising projects that put food from organic market gardens on tables, or stock gift shops with attractive souvenirs.

Proudly Multicultural

Christian, Muslim, Jewish, Hindu and traditional African beliefs coexist in this proudly multicultural city. Given South Africa's troubled history, such harmony has been hard won and remains fragile: practically everyone has a fascinating, sometimes heartbreaking story to tell. It's a city of determined pioneers – from the Afrikaner descendants of the original Dutch colonists and the majority coloured community to the descendants of European Jewish immigrants and more recent Xhosa (isiXhosa) migrants from the Eastern Cape. They all bring unique flavours to Cape Town's rich Creole melting pot.

Beyond the City

Wrenching yourself away from the magnetic mountain and all the delights of the Cape Peninsula is a challenge, but within an hour you can exchange urban landscapes for the charming towns, villages and bucolic estates of Winelands destinations such as Stellenbosch and Franschhoek. Hermanus is a prime whale-watching location and also a base from which to organise shark-cave diving. Further afield, the delights of the Garden Route unfold with more inspiring scenery to be viewed on thrilling drives down the coast and over mountain passes.

Why I Love Cape Town

By Simon Richmond, Author

Mother Nature surpassed herself when crafting the Mother City. Whether jogging along Sea Point Promenade, climbing up Lion's Head in the dawn light, clambering over giant boulders at Sandy Bay or driving the amazing coastal roads down to Cape Point, I never fail to feel my spirits soar as I take in the breathtakingly beautiful vistas. You don't need to break a sweat; sipping wine on a historic farm in Constantia or enjoying a picnic at an outdoor concert in Kirstenbosch Botanical Gardens are equally memorable ways to commune with Cape Town's great outdoors.

For more about our authors, see p288.

V&A Waterfront (p99), with Table Mountain (p28 & p88) as a backdrop

Cape Town's
Top 10

Table Mountain (p28)

1 Whether you take the easy way up and down on the revolving cableway or put in the leg work and climb, attaining the summit of Table Mountain is a Capetonian rite of passage. Weather permitting, your rewards are a panoramic view across the peninsula and a chance to experience something of the park's incredible biodiversity. Schedule time for a hike – the park's 24,500 hectares include routes to suit all levels of fitness and ambition, from gentle ambles to spot *fynbos* (literally 'fine bush', primarily proteas, heaths and ericas) to the five-day, four-night Hoerikwaggo Trail.

◉ *Table Mountain National Park*

Robben Island (p102)

2 A World Heritage site, the former prison on Robben Island is a key location in South Africa's long walk to freedom. Nelson Mandela and other Freedom struggle heroes were incarcerated here, following in the tragic footsteps of earlier fighters against the several colonial governments that ruled over the Cape. Taking the boat journey here and the tour with former inmates provides an insight into the country's troubled history and a glimpse of how far it has progressed on the path to reconciliation and forgiveness. CHURCH ON ROBBEN ISLAND

◉ *Green Point & Waterfront*

DENNIS STONE/LATITUDESTOCK / GETTY ©

3

5

Kirstenbosch Botanical Gardens

(p118)

3 There's been European horticulture on the picturesque eastern slopes of Table Mountain since Jan van Riebeeck's time in the 17th century, but it was British imperialist Cecil Rhodes, owner of Kirstenbosch Farm and surrounding properties, who really put the gardens on the map when he bequeathed the land to all Capetonians. Today it is a spectacular showcase for the thousands of plant species in the Cape floral kingdom (also a World Heritage site) and a brilliant venue for outdoor summer concerts.

◉ *Southern Suburbs*

District Six Museum *(p77)*

4 The desolate inner city plots of District Six – for decades left barren after they were cleared during apartheid – are coming back to life, with construction of thousands of new homes scheduled for the next three to five years. To understand the history of what was destroyed and how this impacted the lives of the former residents and on all of Cape Town, a visit to this illuminating, moving museum is a must. In the museum's annex, another interesting permanent exhibition traces the development of soccer on the Cape.

◉ *East City Corridor*

V&A Waterfront

(p99)

5 Cape Town's top sight in terms of visitor numbers, the V&A Waterfront is big, busy and in a spectacular location, with Table Mountain as a backdrop. There's a pirate's booty of consumer opportunities, from chic boutiques to major department stores, plus plenty of cultural and educational experiences, including walking tours of its well-preserved heritage buildings and public sculptures, and the excellent Two Oceans Aquarium, a firm family favourite. Be sure to schedule a harbour cruise, too – preferably at sunset.

◉ *Green Point & Waterfront*

Cape of Good Hope (p131)

6 The spectacular journey out to Cape Point, the tip of the peninsula protected within Table Mountain National Park, is a trip you're going to want to make: rugged cliffs shoot down into the frothing waters where the Atlantic and Indian Oceans mingle; giant waves crash over the enormous boulders at Africa's most southwesterly point; and the Flying Dutchman Funicular runs up to the old lighthouse for more views. Afterwards you can relax on lovely beaches such as the one at Buffels Bay, lapped by the slightly warmer waters of False Bay.

⊙ *Simon's Town & Southern Peninsula*

Franschhoek (p156)

7 Franschhoek is the smallest – but for many the prettiest – Cape Winelands town. Nestled in a spectacular valley, Franschhoek bills itself as the country's gastronomic capital, and you won't find too many people arguing. You'll certainly have a tough time deciding where to eat – the main road is lined with top-notch restaurants, some of them among the best in the country. The surrounding wineries likewise offer excellent food and no shortage of superb wine. Add a clutch of art galleries and some stylish guesthouses and it really is one of the loveliest towns in the Cape. BOSCHENDAL WINERY (P157)

⊙ *Day Trips & Wineries*

6

Bo-Kaap (p57)

8 Painted in vivid colours straight out of a packet of liquorice allsorts, the jumble of crumbling and restored heritage houses and mosques along the cobblestoned streets of the Bo-Kaap are both visually captivating and a storybook of inner-city gentrification. A stop at the Bo-Kaap Museum is recommended to gain an understanding of the history of this former slave quarter; also try Cape Malay dishes at one of the area's several restaurants, or stay in the homes turned into guesthouses and hotels, including the lovely antique-filled Dutch Manor.

⊙ *City Bowl, Foreshore, Bo-Kaap & De Waterkant*

Surfing along the Garden Route (p172)

9 The Garden Route is known for its outdoor pursuits, both terrestrial and on the water. The coast between Mossel Bay and Plettenberg Bay boasts some of the Western Cape's best surf, whether you're a pro or just starting out. Herold's Bay and Victoria Bay, near George, are particularly pretty spots to catch a wave and offer excellent beaches for nonsurfing travel companions. In Victoria Bay you can try a beginner lesson or rent a board and join the experts on a more challenging day trip.

🏃 *The Garden Route*

Kalk Bay (p129)

10 This delightful False Bay fishing village – named after the kilns that produced lime from seashells, used for painting buildings in the 17th century – offers an abundance of antique, arts and craft shops, great cafes and restaurants, plus a lively daily fish market at its harbour. A drink or meal at institutions such as the Brass Bell pub or Live Bait restaurant, practically as close to the splashing waters of False Bay as you can get without swimming, are fine ways to pass time.

👁 *Simon's Town & Southern Peninsula*

What's New

Artisan Food & Goods Markets

The roaring success of the Neighbourgoods Market has sparked a craze for weekly gourmet, crafts and design goods markets across the Cape. Spend a weekend shuttling from the grooving Blue Bird Garage (p140), in Muizenberg on Friday night to the relaxed City Bowl Market (p94) in Gardens on Saturday morning and the buzzy Bay Harbour Market (p113) in Hout Bay on Sunday – each offer a subtly different grazing and shopping experience.

Babylonstoren

An elegantly reimagined wine and fruit estate with a blissful garden of edible and medicinal plants, splendid restaurant, lovely hotel, irresistible tasting room/deli/bakery and thoughtfully designed cellar tour. (p162)

Green Point Urban Park

Great play areas – one for toddlers, another for older children – are part of this inventively laid-out park, which also showcases biodiversity and the area's original wetlands. (p103)

The Kitchen

Not to be confused with The Test Kitchen (another fab addition to the local gourmet scene), Karen Dudley's slick catering operation is the toast of Woodstock, and the choice of Michelle Obama. (p80)

Studio 7

Grab one of the limited tickets for this super intimate living room venue in Sea Point where you can catch acoustic performances by top-notch musical talents. (p114)

Casa Labia Cultural Centre

Once home to an Italian count and his family, this beautifully restored villa in Muizenberg houses a cultural centre, restaurant and branch of the arts and crafts store Africa Nova. (p133)

Tintswalo Atlantic

The only luxury lodge within Table Mountain National Park is gorgeously designed with a secluded position at the base of Chapman's Peak on the edge of Hout Bay. (p195)

2014 World Design Capital

Head to The Fringe, one of the regeneration areas targeted under Cape Town's award-winning plans to use design to improve the lives of its citizens (p79).

Microbrew Beers

Jack Black, Darling Brew and Triggerfish are among the local craft beer makers whetting the whistle of Capetonian real ale fans. Sample many of them at Banana Jam. (p125)

Art in the Forest

Browse the ceramic goodies at this stunning gallery space overlooking Constantia, all sold in aid of the charity Light from Africa Foundation. (p127)

For more recommendations and reviews, see **lonelyplanet.com/south-africa/cape-town**

Need to Know

Currency
South African rand (R)

Language
English, Afrikaans, Xhosa

Visas
Australian, UK, US and most Western European citizens can get a 90-day entry permit on arrival; see p242.

Money
ATMs widely available; credit cards accepted at most businesses, but some smaller food places, including weekly markets are cash-only.

Mobile Phones
South Africa uses the GSM digital standard; check compatibility with your phone provider. Local SIM cards are easy to buy.

Time
South Africa Standard Time (GMT/UTC plus two hours)

Tourist Information
The head office of Cape Town Tourism (☎021-426 4260; www.capetown.travel; cnr Castle & Burg Sts, City Bowl; ☺8am-6pm daily Oct-Mar, 9am-5pm Mon-Fri, 9am-1pm Sat & Sun Apr-Sep) is centrally located and there are plenty of satellite offices around the city including one at the airport.

Your Daily Budget

Budget less than R500
➡ Dorm bed R150

➡ Gourmet burger R50

➡ Local beer R15

➡ Hiking in Table Mountain National Park Free

➡ Shared taxi ride from City Bowl to Camps Bay R10

Midrange R500–2000
➡ Hotel R800-1200

➡ Township/cultural tour R350-650

➡ Kirstenbosch Summer Sunset Concert ticket R100

➡ Meal with wine at Waterfront restaurant R200–400

Top end R2000 plus
➡ Hotel R3000–5000

➡ Meal at Aubergine R500–1000

➡ Full-day gourmet wine tour R1700

➡ Thirty-minute helicopter flight R2500

➡ Three-hour cruise on luxury yacht R28,500

Advance Planning

Two months before Book Robben Island tour; reserve table at The Test Kitchen; and train for hiking in Table Mountain National Park.

Three weeks before Book township/cultural tour; check listings for theatre shows and for Kirstenbosch Summer Sunset Concerts.

One week before See what gigs and club events are coming up; buy online tickets for Table Mountain Cableway.

Useful Websites

➡ **Webtickets** (www.webtickets.co.za) For booking Robben Island, Table Mountain Cableway, concert, event and theatre tickets.

➡ **Cape Town Magazine** (www.capetownmagazine.com) Online magazine with its finger on Cape Town's pulse.

➡ **Lonely Planet** (www.lonelyplanet.com) Destination information, hotel bookings, travellers forum and more.

WHEN TO GO

December through February brings warm, dry weather and lively festivals. Winter (Jun-Aug) is wet, cool and windy. Neither season experiences extremes of temperature.

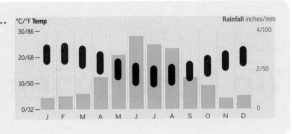

Arriving in Cape Town

➡ **Cape Town International Airport** MyCiTi bus to Cape Town Train Station is R53 (cash only); the Backpacker Bus shared minivan taxi is R180 to city centre hotels and hostels; a private taxi is around R200.

➡ **Cape Town Train Station** Long distance trains and buses arrive at this centrally located terminal; a taxi ride to most central locations will be under R50.

➡ **V&A Waterfront Jetty 2 or Duncan Dock** Where international cruise ships dock.

For much more on arrival, see p234.

Getting Around

Contact the Transport Information Centre ✆0800 656 463 for timetables.

➡ **Car Hire** Budget around R300 per day hire and R300 for a tank of petrol.

➡ **City Sightseeing Cape Town** Two hop-on, hop-off routes, useful for an orientation of the city; see p25.

➡ **Public buses** Handy for city centre and Atlantic Coast routes.

➡ **Cape Metro Rail** For trips to Southern Suburbs, False Bay and Stellenbosch.

➡ **Shared minibus taxis** Useful from City Bowl along Atlantic Coast to Sea Point.

➡ **Private Taxis** Many firms with rates from R10 per kilometre. Book to be sure of a pick up.

For much more on getting around, see p234.

Sleeping

There are plenty of budget backpackers, charming guesthouses and five-star pamper palaces, but reserve well in advance, especially if visiting during school holidays from mid-December to the end of January. All places will slash their rates from May to October in the quiet winter season. Rates usually include VAT of 14% and often the 1% tourism promotion levy. Also check whether secure parking is included in your hotel rate, otherwise you could be charged anything up to R50 per day extra to park your car.

Useful Websites

SA Venues (www.sa-venues. com) Online booking agency with a wide range of options across the Cape.

Cape Town Tourism (www. capetown.travel) Offers accommodation bookings and occasional special deals, but only recommends its members.

Lonely Planet (www.lonely planet.com) Expert author reviews, user feedback, and booking engine.

For much more on sleeping, see p187.

CAPE TOWN'S MICROCLIMATES

Pack a raincoat and umbrella so you're prepared to deal with 'four seasons in one day'. The peninsula's geography creates microclimates, so you can be basking in the sun on one side of the mountain and sheltering from chilly rain and winds on the other. It is no accident that Newlands is so lush in comparison to Cape Point – the former receives four times as much rain annually as the latter.

Top Itineraries

Day One

Gardens & Surrounds (p86)

 Skip the line at the kiosk by printing a web-ticket for the **Table Mountain cableway**; it's a little cheaper, too. The revolving car provides 360-degree views as you ascend this mesmerising 60-million-year-old mountain. From the upper cableway station it's about an hour's round-trip hike to the 1088m summit at Maclear's Beacon.

> **Lunch** Catch the local vibe at Jason Bakery (p64) or Lola's (p65).

City Bowl, Foreshore, Bo-Kaap & De Waterkant (p52)

 Having had a postprandial stroll through the **Company's Gardens**, and browsed the craft stalls in **Greenmarket Square**, head uphill into the old Cape Malay quarter the **Bo-Kaap**, where cobblestoned streets are lined with brightly painted houses. There's more good shopping here in stores such as **Haas**, **Monkeybiz** and **Streetwires**. Continue over into the gay-friendly **De Waterkant** for more prettily restored cottages and the buzzing malls of the Cape Quarter.

> **Dinner** Book for culinary delights at the secluded Roundhouse (p111).

Sea Point to Hout Bay (p108)

 Catching the sunset, cocktail in hand, is a must whether it be from along **Sea Point's promenade** or the strip of touristy restaurants and cafe-bars lining picturesque **Camps Bay**.

Day Two

East City Corridor (p75) & City Bowl, Foreshore, Bo-Kaap & De Waterkant (p52)

 Learn about the city's troubled past at the **District Six Museum**. Join the 11am tour of the 350-year-old **Castle of Good Hope**, then watch the noon key ceremony. Across the road is the handsome Old Town Hall.

> **Lunch** The Kitchen (p80) offers delicious food fit for First Ladies.

East City Corridor (p75)

Check out contemporary galleries such as **Stevenson**, as well as the abundant street art. In nearby Salt River there's more art at **What If the World** in a converted old synagogue, and the fabulous collection of emporia at the **Old Biscuit Mill**: if it's Saturday don't miss the **Neighbourgoods Market** that happens here, offering the cream of the region's artisan food purveyors and product designers.

> **Dinner** Wakame (p103) serves good seafood with water views.

Green Point & Waterfront (p97)

More than just a mega-shopping mall, the **V&A Waterfront** is worth exploring for its carnival atmosphere, well-preserved Victorian architecture and the chance to join a harbour cruise. It's also where you board the boat out to World Heritage–listed **Robben Island**, for which you should book ahead.

Day Three

Southern Suburbs (p116)

 Explore the beautiful **Kirstenbosch Botanical Gardens**, covering some 500 hectares of the eastern slopes of Table Mountain, to learn more about the richly endowed Cape floral kingdom. A wander around lovely **Wynberg Village**, packed with old thatched-roof cottages, is also a pleasure. Alternatively, admire the paintings in the **Irma Stern Museum**.

> **Lunch** Picnic on the lawn at **Buitenverwachting** (p120).

Southern Suburbs (p116)

Spend a blissful afternoon exploring the wineries on the Constantia Valley Wine Route. Target the historic ones such as **Groot Constantia**, with its beautifully restored homestead and wine cellar, and **Klein Constantia**, producer of Napoleon's favourite tipple. **Steenberg Vineyards** has an excellent contemporary tasting room and tapas restaurant, not to mention delicious wines.

> **Dinner** Tuck into top-quality pizza at **Massimo's** (p112).

Sea Point to Hout Bay (p108)

Motor over Constantia Neck, dropping by the hidden ceramics gallery **Art in the Forest**, if it's not too late in the day. Enjoy the view of Hout Bay, beer in hand, from the deck of the **Chapman's Peak Hotel** or beachside pub **Dunes**. If it's Friday night, there will be live music and tasty eats at the **Bay Harbour Market**.

Day Four

Simon's Town & Southern Peninsula (p129)

 Time to explore the peninsula's deep south. Take the Atlantic Coast route, including spectacular Chapman's Peak Drive, past Noordhoek's broad sweep of sand and the surfing hot spots of Kommetjie and Scarborough to the very southeastern tip of Africa within the **Cape Point** section of Table Mountain National Park.

> **Lunch** Meeting Place (p139) in Simon's Town offers fine food.

Simon's Town & Southern Peninsula (p129)

Also part of the park is **Boulders**, home to a thriving colony of super cute African penguins who waddle around and over the giant boulders that give this secluded False Bay beach area its name. The historic naval yard of **Simon's Town** is just up the road; take a cruise around the harbour or potter in its antique and gift stores.

> **Dinner** Kalk Bay (p137) has many appealing seafood restaurants..

Simon's Town & Southern Peninsula (p129)

Continue around False Bay to charming **Kalk Bay**, an old fishing village packed with more great places to find arty buys and tasty nibbles. Freshen up with a dip in one of the sea pools here or in nearby **St James**. Muizenberg's cosy the **Melting Pot** offers live music, as does the **Blue Bird Garage Food & Goods Market** on Friday nights.

If You Like...

Beaches

Muizenberg Colourful Victorian chalets, warm(ish) water and fun surfing. (p133)

Clifton No 3 Where the gay community leads, the rest follow. (p110)

Buffels Bay Tranquil with sweeping views across False Bay and a sea pool for swimming. (p131)

Sandy Bay The nudist beach also has amazing giant rock formations to explore. (p111)

Noordhoek Magnificently broad, overlooked by Chapman's Peak and with a shipwreck in the sand. (p136)

Long Surfers rate the waves off this idyllic and aptly named swathe of sand. (p137)

Viewpoints

Table Mountain Sweeping vistas across the city and peninsula. (p88)

Bloubergstrand Picture-perfect view of Table Mountain north of the city. (p145)

Cape of Good Hope Walk to just above the Cape's original lighthouse. (p136)

Chapman's Peak Drive Take in the elegant sweep of horseshoe-shaped Hout Bay. (p110)

Signal Hill Hear the canon fire and look out over the Waterfront. (p62)

Mouille Point Stroll the promenade around to Sea Point at sunset. (p103)

FRANS LEMMENS / LONELY PLANET IMAGES ©

Bathing huts at Muizenberg Beach (p133)

Free Attractions

V&A Waterfront Buskers, outdoor events, seals, historic buildings, public artworks and the comings and goings of the harbour. (p99)

Table Mountain National Park No charge for hiking the myriad trails on the main mountain, up Lion's Head or along Signal Hill. (p88)

Company's Gardens Relax or stroll through these historic gardens, marvelling at ancient trees and pretty flower beds. (p55)

Graffiti Art District Six and Woodstock are dotted with impressive large-scale works. (p79)

Green Point Park Enjoy the lovely eco-legacy of World Cup 2010 at this new park showcasing biodiversity. (p103)

Nelson Mandela Gateway Learn about the Freedom struggle and life in the prison before heading to Robben Island. (p102)

Artistic Collections

South African National Gallery Fascinating exhibitions and a great gift shop are found in this elegant building. (p91)

Michaelis Collection Old masters and new works in the Old Town House on Greenmarket Square. (p58)

Stevenson Major commercial gallery for contemporary artists with interesting thematic exhibitions. (p84)

Irma Stern Museum Former home of the pioneering expressionist artists, with a lovely garden. (p123)

Casa Labia Beautifully restored interiors at this Muizenberg villa

turned into an arts and cultural space. (p137)

Ellerman House Fabulous collection of old and new South African works at this exclusive hotel. (p196)

Historical Insights

District Six Museum Shines a light on the destroyed multicultural inner city area. (p77)

Bo-Kaap Museum Learn about the Cape Malay community's lives in this colourful district. (p57)

Slave Lodge Exhibits on the history of slaves and their descendants. (p59)

South African Museum Lots of natural history, fine examples of San rock art and an African Cultures Museum. (p91)

South African Jewish Museum Traces the routes of Jewish migration and settlement in the country, and has a section on the Holocaust. (p90)

Prestwich Memorial Ossuary and information about the mass graves of slaves, ne'er-do-wells and the poor discovered on the site. (p62)

Hidden Gems

6 Spin Street Herbert Baker–designed building with impressive site-specific contemporary artworks. (p61)

Rust en Vreugd Elegant 18th-century mansion and garden in the midst of the city. (p91)

Art in the Forest Ceramics gallery and art complex overlooking Constantia valley. (p127)

Roundhouse Join the chickens for lunch on the lawn overlooking Camps Bay. (p111)

For more top Cape Town spots, see
➡ Eating (p32)
➡ Drinking & Nightlife (p35)
➡ Entertainment (p37)
➡ Shopping (p39)
➡ Sports & Activities (p41)
➡ GLBT (p43)
➡ Wineries (p45)

PLAN YOUR TRIP IF YOU LIKE...

Tintswalo Atlantic Not staying at this luxe lodge? Call to see if you can visit for dinner. (p195)

Enmasse Thai massage the modern way, in a historic building tucked away in Gardens. (p96)

The Luxe Life

Status Luxury Vehicles Cruise Cape Town's roads in a top marque convertible, or have a chauffer drive it for you. (p236)

Charter a private yacht Plenty to choose from at the V&A Waterfront, including the Cape Grace's *Spirit of the Cape*. (p195)

Cape Town Diamond Museum Learn the story of the world's most precious gem then go shopping for bling. (p101)

Stefania Morland Pick up an elegant outfit from this designer, whose workshop lies behind the racks of silky dresses. (p95)

Mount Nelson Hotel Not a guest? Come for afternoon tea, the Librisa Spa or the Planet bar and restaurant. (p193)

Delaire Graff Estate Enjoy the Winelands using this ultraluxurious estate as your base. (p151)

Month by Month

January

Expect packed hotels and restaurants, crowds at the beaches and traffic on main coastal roads. Some restaurants, cafes and shops close for the first week or so of the month.

🎭 Cape Town Minstrel Carnival

Tweede Nuwe Jaar, 2 January, is when the satin- and sequin-clad minstrel troupes traditionally march through the city for the Kaapse Klopse (Cape Minstrel Carnival) from Keizersgracht St, along Adderley and Wale Sts to the Bo-Kaap. Throughout January into early February there are Saturday competitions between troupes at Athlone Stadium. (www.capetown-minstrels.co.za)

🏇 J&B Met

At Kenilworth Race Course, South Africa's richest horse race, with a jackpot of R1.5 million, is a time for big bets and even bigger hats. Generally held on the last Saturday in January. (www.jbmet.co.za)

February

Check for classical concerts at the Cape Town International Summer Music Festival. Also note that the city goes into lock down for the opening of parliament in the first week of February – avoid anything but essential travel on that day.

☆ Design Indaba

This creative convention, bringing together the varied worlds of fashion, architecture, visual arts, crafts and media, is held at the end of February and early March, usually at the Cape Town International Convention Centre, and proceeded by a two-week film festival at the Labia. (www.designindaba.com)

March

The cultural calendar cranks up with a series of arts and music festivals. Cyclists take over the streets (and many of the city's hotels) for the Pick 'n' Pay Cycle Tour; forget driving around town on the day of the event.

☆ Infecting the City

Cape Town's squares, fountains, museums and theatres are the venues for this innovative performing arts festival featuring artists from across the continent. (http://infectingthecity.com/2012)

🏃 Cape Argus Pick 'n' Pay Cycle Tour

Held on a Saturday in the middle of March, this is the world's largest timed cycling event, attracting more than 30,000 contestants. The route circles Table Mountain, heading down the Atlantic Coast and along Chapman's Peak Dr. (www.cycletour.co.za)

🎭 Cape Town International Jazz Festival

Cape Town's biggest jazz event, attracting big names

from both South Africa and overseas, is usually held at the Cape Town International Convention Centre at the end of March. It includes a free concert in Greenmarket Sq. (www.capetownjazzfest.com)

🌟 Toffie Pop Cultural Conference & Festival

Three-day event focusing on pretty much anything connected with contemporary pop culture. The same organisers launched the Toffie Food Festival (held in September) in 2011. (www.toffie.co.za)

April

The weather starts to chill from now through early October so bring warmer clothes and be prepared for rainy, blustery days.

☆ Just Nuisance Great Dane Parade

No, this is not an April Fools' joke. Every 1 April a dog parade is held through Jubilee Sq in Simon's Town to commemorate Able Seaman Just Nuisance, the Great Dane who was a mascot of the Royal Navy during WWII. (www.simonstown.com/tourism/nuisance/nuisance.htm)

🏃 Old Mutual Two Oceans Marathon

Held early April, this 56km marathon kicks off in Newlands on Main Rd and follows a similar route to the Pick 'n' Pay Cycle Tour around Table Mountain. It generally attracts about 9000 competitors. (www.twooceansmarathon.org.za)

May

Acoustic concerts are held every Sunday from mid-May to the end of October at the Kirstenbosch Botanical Gardens' Silver Tree Restaurant (see www.sanbi.org.za for details).

🌟 Franschhoek Literary Festival

As if you need any further reason to visit this delightful Winelands town, along comes this literary festival which attracts the cream of locally based and expat South African writers. (www.flf.co.za)

🍴 Good Food & Wine Show

Cape Town goes gourmet with this four-day event held at the Cape Town International Convention Centre. (www.goodfoodandwineshow.co.za)

July

Winter in Cape Town can be very blustery and wet so it's not the best season for outdoor activities

🔒 Cape Town Fashion Week

Fashionistas line the catwalks to spot the hottest local designers' work and pick up on the latest trends. (www.afisa.co.za)

September

South Africa's creative community comes out to play in the Mother City during this month when Creative Week (www.creativeweekct.co.za) happens around the same

time as the Loerie Awards, recognising regional creative excellence.

🌟 Nando's Comedy Festival

Catch some of South Africa's top comedians at this festival, held over several weeks at a range of venues across the city including the Baxter Theatre. (www.comedyfestival.co.za/main_arena.php)

☆ Out of the Box

The International Association of Puppetry SA (UNIMA SA) organises this nine-day puppetry festival in early September, which brings in puppeteers from around the world as well as screening documentaries and holding workshops. (www.unima.za.org)

🌟 Cape Town International Kite Festival

Held in mid-September, in support of the Cape Mental Health Society, this colourful gathering of kite enthusiasts at Zandvlei, near Muizenberg, is big, entertaining and for a good cause. (www.capementalhealth.co.za/kite.index.htm)

October

🏃 Outsurance Gun Run

Starting from Beach Rd in Mouille Point, this popular half-marathon (21km) is the only time that the Noon Gun on Signal Hill gets fired on a Sunday – competitors try to finish the race before the gun goes off. (www.outsurance.co.za/gunrun)

November

Beat the Christmas rush; Cape Town can be lovely in the spring.

☆ Old Mutual Summer Sunset Concerts

Start of the Sunday afternoon concerts at Kirstenbosch Botanical Gardens, which run through until April. Anything from arias performed by local divas to a funky jazz combo. There's always a special concert for New Year's Eve, too. (www.oldmutual.co.za/music)

December

Top holiday season; book well ahead for tickets for popular attractions. New Year's Eve is busy, with fireworks at the Waterfront.

✵ Obs Arts Festival

South Africa's biggest street festival takes over the suburb of Observatory on the first weekend of December. (http://obsarts.org.za)

☆ Adderley St Christmas Lights

Join the thousands that turn out for the concert in front of Cape Town Railway Station followed by a parade along illuminated Adderley St; also a night market from around 17 to 30 December.

☆ Mother City Queer Project

There's always a wacky fancy dress theme to this massive gay-friendly dance party. (www.mcqp.co.za)

(Top) Racing in the J&B Met, South Africa's richest horse race, at Kenilworth Race Course
(Bottom) Carnival minstrels

With Kids

Soft sand beaches, the mountain and its myriad activities, wildlife spotting, the carnival atmosphere of the Waterfront and much more: Cape Town takes the prize as a lekker (Afrikaans for brilliant) location for family vacations.

Animals, Birds & Sea Life

Check out the local marine life at the excellent Two Oceans Aquarium (p107); birds and monkeys at Hout Bay's World of Birds (p111) or the wetland reserve of Intaka Island (p145); a happy-footed African penguin colony at Boulders; wild ostriches, baboons and dassies at Cape Point; and the shy hippos at Rondevlei Nature Reserve (p134). Farm animals live at Oude Molen Eco Village (p145) and at Imhoff Farm (p136), where you can arrange camel rides!

Interesting Museums

Science and technology is made fun at the Cape Town Science Centre (p79), where there's usually some special activity scheduled. The South African Museum (p91) offers a giant whale skeleton and star shows at the attached planetarium. The Castle of Good Hope (p54), with its battlements, museums and horse and carriage rides, is an entertaining visual history lesson.

Beaches & Boats

There's no shortage of beaches, with those on the False Bay side of the peninsula lapped by warmer waters than those on the Atlantic Coast. Good choices include Muizenberg, St James, or lovely Buffels Bay at Cape Point.

Boat tours (p101) are abundant; Tommy the Tugboat and the Jolly Roger Pirate Boat at the V&A Waterfront; cruises from the harbours at Simon's Town and Hout Bay.

Shopping & Eating

Toy and kids' clothing stores are found at all the major shopping malls. For an excellent selection of secondhand items, a play area and kids' yoga, visit Merry Pop Ins (p73). The Book Lounge (p83) has a great kids' book section and story readings.

Weekly markets, including Neighbourgoods (p83), City Bowl (p94) and Blue Bird Garage (p140), have play areas and kid-friendly food. For fish and chips try the Waterfront, Hout Bay and Simon's Town.

Playgrounds & Parks

There are two inventively designed playgrounds at Green Point Park. Mouille Point (p103) has a big play area, toy train, maze and golf-putting course. Sea Point Promenade (p110) features the outdoor baths of the pavilion. In Vredehoek, there's a good playground right outside Deer Park Café (p92). The amusement park Ratanga Junction (p146) offers thrill rides for teens as well as plenty for smaller kids. There are also several indoor play spaces, including Roly Polyz (p74).

Need to Know

Information

➡ **Cape Town Kids** (www.capetownkids.co.za).

➡ **Child Mag** (www.childmag.co.za)

Babysitting

➡ **Childminders** (☎083-254 4683; www.childminders.co.za)

➡ **Super Sitters** (☎021-552 1220; www.supersitters.net)

Like a Local

The extremes of wealth in Cape Town mean there's a vast difference in the life of a typical resident in Crossroads vs Clifton. However, there are opportunities for visitors to experience all aspects of the city with insight and sensitivity to local communities, whatever their circumstances.

Weekly Shopping

Capetonians love their markets. Joining the centuries old Trafalgar Square flower market and the bric-a-brac and antique vendors at Milnerton Flea Market are a trendy breed of artisan food and designer goods and crafts markets. Neighbourgoods – the original – is still the best, although it's so busy each Saturday you may prefer the less frenetic City Bowl Market. Muizenberg locals love to gather on Friday nights for the bash at Blue Bird Garage (with great live jazz) while the inhabitants of Hout Bay do the same at the Bay Harbour Market, which is also very popular during the day on Saturday and Sunday.

Outdoor Activities

Capetonians take full advantage of the magnificent national park in the midst of their city. Groups of friends gather for weekly hikes (set your alarm to join the 6am Wednesday hike up Lion's Head, for example), sunbathing on the beaches, or picnics in the parks. At Kirstenbosch Botanical Gardens or De Waal Park, don't pass up the chance to attend one of the vibey Sunday concerts held throughout the summer.

Surfing has a huge following; if you don't know how to surf, there are several operations ready to teach you in Muizenberg; the more ambitious could enquire about kiteboarding from the experts flying off the waves in Table Bay each weekend. And yachties will always be welcome to join in the Wednesday afternoon races at the Royal Cape Yacht Club.

Township Experiences

Finding out about life in Cape Town's disadvantaged townships and the blighted suburbs of the Cape Flats is easier than you may think. There are plenty of township and cultural tours, but for a more immersive experience consider staying at one of several guesthouses in the townships (they're all run by wonderful women), eating at a restaurant such as the buzzy braai (barbecue) joint Mzoli's or heading to a classy sheeben such as Kefu's. A night dancing at Galaxy or listening to jazz at Swingers will show you how the coloured community likes to chill.

Parties & Performances

All Capetonians love a *jol* (party) and preferably one that involves dressing up! The Mother City Queer Project (MCQP) in December and the Cape Minstrel Carnival and subsequent competitions in January and February are the biggest bashes of this nature. Other regularly hosted themed parties and events include raucous **Renegade Bingo** (www.facebook.com/rbingo) and **Unsolved Mystery** (bepartofthemystery.yolasite.com) murder-mystery dinners.

Attending a book launch at the Book Lounge or a concert at intimate spaces such as Studio 7, the Mahogany Lounge or Alma Café are other entertaining ways to rub shoulders with locals.

Tours

If you're short on time, have a specific interest, or desire some expert help in seeing Cape Town, there's a small army of tour guides and companies waiting to assist you. Topics of interest run from sex and slavery to food and wine via local flora and fauna.

Hair salon in Khayelitsha, Cape Flats

ADRIAN VAN ZANDERBERGEN / LONELY PLANET IMAGES ©

Lonely Planet's Top Choices

City Sightseeing Cape Town (⏲021-511 6000; www.citysightseeing.co.za; adult/child one day R140/70, two day R250/150) These hop-on, hop-off buses, running two routes, are perfect for a quick orientation with commentary available in 16 languages. The open-top double-deckers also provide an elevated platform for photos. Buses run at roughly half-hourly intervals between 9am and 4.30pm with extra services in peak season. They also offer a **canal cruise** (R20) with five stops between the Waterfront and the Cape Town International Convention Centre.

Coffeebeans Routes (Map p262; ⏲021-424 3572; www.coffeebeansroutes.com; tours R650) The concept – hooking up visitors with interesting local personalities, including musicians, artists and gardeners – is fantastic. Among innovative programs is their Friday night reggae safari trip to Marcus Garvey, a Rastafarian settlement in Philippi, for a night.

Awol Tours (⏲021-418 3803; www.awoltours. co.za) Discover Cape Town's cycle lanes on this superb city bike tour (three hours, R300, daily) from Awol's Waterfront base. Other pedalling itineraries including the Winelands, Cape Point and the township of Masiphumelele – a great alternative to traditional township tours. They also offer guided hikes on Table Mountain (R950).

Sex and Slaves in the City (⏲021-785 2264; www.capetownwalks.com; tour R150) Learn about the contribution of slaves to Cape Town's history on this hilarious, actor-led two-hour tour around the city centre. The same company also arranges literary themed walks on Long St with a local author and hikes on Table Mountain.

Uthando (⏲021-683 8523; www.uthandosa.org; R650) The extra cost of these township tours is because half the money goes towards the social upliftment projects that the tours visit and is specifically designed to support. Usually four or so projects are visited and could be anything from an organic farm to an old folks' centre.

City Tours

See p101 for details of a walking tour around the Waterfront.

Good Hope Adventures (⏲021-510 7517; goodhopeadventures.com; 3-5hr tours R250-500) Go underground on these fascinating walking tours (not for the claustrophobic), as you explore the historic tunnels and canals that run beneath the city. You'll need to be wearing old shoes and clothes and have a torch.

Cape Town on Foot (☑021-462 2252; www.wanderlust.co.za; tour R150) Walking tours leav-ing from Cape Town Tourism's office on Burg St at 11am Monday to Friday and 10am on Saturday.

Day Trippers (☑021-511 4766; www.daytrippers.co.za) Many of this long-established outfits' tours include the chance to go cycling.

Township & Cultural Tours

You may have qualms about visiting the desperately poor townships and suburbs under the guise of tourism. However, the best tours provide a clearer understanding of the Mother City's split nature and the challenges faced by the vast majority of Capetonians in their daily lives. They also reveal that these lives, while undoubtedly deprived, are not uniformly miserable and that there are many inspiring things to see and do and people to meet.

Half-day tours are generally sufficient, with full-day itineraries tacking on a trip to Robben Island for which you don't need a guide (however, if individual Robben Island tickets are sold out this may be one way for you to get there). Township tours usually involve travel in a car or small coach, but there are also walking and cy-cling tours, if you'd prefer.

Apart from the following, also see p146 for details of Greenpop's tree planting trips.

Andulela (☑021-790 2592; www.andulela.com) Creative, responsible tourism company that offers a variety of cultural, culinary and wildlife themed tours.

Cape Capers Tours (☑083 358 0193, 021-448 3117; www.tourcapers.co.za) Award-winning guide Faizel Gangat leads a band of informative guides to the townships, with tours concentrating either on Langa (R390) or the Cape Care Route (R690), highlighting some of the city's standout com-munity and environmental projects.

Vamos (☑072 499 7866; www.vamos.co.za; walking/cycling tours R200/250) Young Langa-based guide Siviwe Mbinda (www.townshiptour scapetown.co.za) is one of the cofounders of this company, offering two to three hour walking and cycling tours around Langa. Itineraries often in-clude a performance by the Happy Feet gumboot dance troupe that Siviwe established.

Dinner@Mandela's (☑021-790 5817, 083 471 2523; www.dinneratmandelas.co.za; tour R225) A highly recommended alternative or addition to daytime township tours is this evening tour and dinner combination at Imizamo Yethu, which runs Monday and Thursday from 7pm with pick ups in the city centre. The meal, which includes African traditional dishes and is veggie-friendly, is held at Tamfanfa's Tavern and is preceded by lively African dancing and a choir singing.

Township Tours SA (☑083 719 4870; www.suedafrika.net/imizamoyethu; tour R85) Afrika Moni can guide you on a two-hour walking tour of Imizamo Yethu (it's on the blue line of the City Sightseeing Cape Town bus), including a visit to a *sangoma* (traditional medicine practitioner, usu-ally a woman), a drink of homebrew at a shebeen (an unlicensed drinking establishment), a look at some art projects and the township museum. Bookings essential.

Imivuyo Touring (☑072-624 4211; www.imivuyo.co.za) As well as a township itinerary, Imivuyo offers tours to the Winelands and around the city.

Transcending History Tours (☑084 883 2514; http://sites.google.com/site/capeslaver outetours) Lucy Campbell is the go-to academic for these tours that offer a deeper insight into the rich and fascinating indigenous and slave history of the Cape.

Mountain-bike touring, Cape Town–style

Nature Tours

For hiking tours in Table Mountain National Park see p30. Walking tours can also be arranged around the Rondevlei Nature Reserve (p134).

Apex Shark Expeditions (☎021-786 5717; www.apexpredators.com) Shark-watching trips from Simon's Town – so you don't have to schlep out to Gansbaai. There's no cage involved: should you choose, you can go snorkel with the big fish. They also specialise in trips to see the pelagic birds – an awesome sight of thousands of sea birds including up to seven species of albatross.

Birdwatch Cape (☎072-635 1501; www. birdwatch.co.za) Offers informative tours pointing out the many unique species of the Cape bird kingdom.

Winery Tours

African Story (☎073-755 0444; www. africanstorytours.com; R545) Full-day tours including wine, cheese and chocolate tastings at four estates in the Stellenbosch, Franschhoek and Paarl regions.

Bikes 'n Wines (☎074-186 0418; http://bikesn wines.com; R495) The cost of this 9km cycle tour around wineries in the Stellenbosch region includes the train from Cape Town.

Easy Rider Wine Tours (☎021-886 4651; www.stumbleinnstellenbosch.hostel.com; R400) Reliable Stellenbosch-based operation. The day kicks off with a cellar tour and includes visits (usually) to Boschendal and Fairview as well as a few other estates.

Gourmet Wine Tours (☎021-705 4317, 083 229 3581; www.gourmetwinetours.co.za; half/ full day tours from R1100/1700) Stephen Flesch, a former chairman of the Wine Tasters Guild of South Africa, has over 35 years of wine-tasting experience and runs tours to the wineries of your choice.

Vine Hopper (☎021-882 8112; R170) A hop-on/ hop-off bus with two routes each covering six estates, the Hopper departs hourly from Stellenbosch Tourism where you can buy tickets.

Vineyard Ventures (☎021-434 8888; www. vineyardventures.co.za; R500) This long-running specialist wine-tour company can customise a wine tour to your needs or suggest places to visit off the beaten track.

Wine Desk at the Waterfront (☎021-418 0108; www.winedesk.co.za; R395-850) Departing from the V&A Waterfront Information Centre and offering customised or pre-packaged tours taking in a different selection of wineries each day.

Wine Flies (☎021-423 2444; www.wineflies. co.za; R545) Fun trips taking in four to five estates and including cellar and vineyard walking tours, cheese, olive and chocolate tasting.

Table Mountain National Park

Covering about 73% of the Cape Peninsula, Table Mountain National Park stretches from Signal Hill to Cape Point. Apart from hiking, the park is a venue for activities including abseiling, mountain biking, rock climbing, paragliding, bird and wildlife watching, snorkelling and diving.

Penguins on Boulders Beach (p137)

The Park's Highlights

➡ Spend a night sleeping at one of the **tented camps** (p30) and hiking some, if not all, of the Hoerikwaggo Trail.

➡ Ride the **cableway** (p88) and enjoy the view from the top of the mountain without the slog.

➡ Paddle with a colony of African penguins at **Boulders** (p137).

➡ Journey to Africa's most southwestern tip at **Cape Point** (p131).

➡ Climb **Lion's Head** (p96) for an awesome view over Table Bay and down the Twelve Apostles.

➡ Go mountain biking in **Tokai Forest** (p123) or **Silvermine** (p133)

Hikes Galore

There are scores of routes on Table Mountain alone, covering everything from easy strolls to extreme rock climbing. Entrance fees have to be paid for the Boulders, Cape of Good Hope, Ouderkraal, Silvermine and Tokai sections of the park, but otherwise the routes are freely open. Signage is improving, but it's far from comprehensive and even with a map it's easy to get lost; read the safety tips below before setting off, and consider hiring a guide.

Popular Routes

Platteklip Gorge (p88) is the most straightforward route up the mountain, but if you want less of a slog then the Pipe Track is preferable but takes roughly double the time. Climbing Lion's Head, and the walk from the upper cableway station to Maclear's Beacon, the highest point of the mountain, are both easily achievable.

Possibilities for overnight treks include the two-day, one-night, 33.8km Cape of Good Hope Trail (p131) and the five-day, four-night, 80km Hoerikwaggo Trail running the full length of the peninsula from Cape Point to the upper cableway station.

Safety First

Just because Table Mountain National Park is on the doorstep of the city doesn't make this wilderness area, extending

FOCUS ON NATURE /ISTOCK ©

above 1000m, any less dangerous and unpredictable. Hardly a week goes by without some accident or fatality on the mountain, often due to a climbing expedition gone wrong. More people have died on Table Mountain than on Mt Everest. Mountain fires have also claimed their victims, and muggings on the slopes of Table Mountain and Lion's Head are, unfortunately, not rare events.

There are 50 staff patrolling the park but it covers such a large area they cannot be everywhere, so be well prepared before setting off. Even if taking the cableway to the summit, be aware that the weather up top can change very rapidly. The main emergency numbers are ☑086 110 6417 to report fires, poaching, accidents and crime, and ☑021-948 9900 for Wilderness Search and Rescue.

Hiking Tips

➡ Hike with long trousers. Much of the *fynbos* (literally 'fine bush', primarily proteas, heaths and ericas) is tough and scratchy. There's also the seriously nasty blister bush (its leaves look like those of continental parsley); if you brush against this plant cover the spot immediately – exposure to sunlight activates the plant's toxins which can leave blisters on your skin that may refuse to heal for years.

➡ Tell someone the route you're planning to climb and take a map (or better still, a guide).

➡ Stick to well used paths and don't be tempted to take shortcuts.

➡ Take plenty of water, some food, weatherproof clothing and a fully charged mobile phone.

➡ Wear proper hiking boots or shoes and a sun hat.

➡ Don't climb alone – park authorities recommend going in groups of four.

➡ Don't leave litter on the mountain.

➡ Don't make a fire on the mountain – they're banned.

Table Mountain National Park by Area

Table Mountain (p91) The park's main attraction is here; climb it, or ride the cableway to within easy walking distance of the summit.

Lion's Head (p96) An easier climb than the main

Table Mountain NP

mountain and providing 360-degree views of the mountain, coastline and city.

Signal Hill (p62) Home of the Noon Gun; access by car from Kloof Nek Rd or on foot from Bo-Kaap or Sea Point.

Ouderkraal (p111) A picnic area and popular dive site on the Atlantic coast.

Back Table (p124) Follow the old bridle path up the back of Table Mountain from Constantia Nek to the series of reservoirs.

Kirstenbosch (p118) The gardens themselves are managed separately but adjoin sections of the park: hike up the mountain along Skeleton Gorge or Nursery Ravine, or join the contour path that connects across to Constantia Nek through the Cecilia Plantation.

Tokai Forest (p123) A popular shady picnic site with an arboretum and hiking, mountain biking and horseriding trails.

Silvermine (p133) In the middle of the Southern Peninsula this section of the park offers board-walks alongside a river and the reservoir, as well as treks to caves and magnificent view points.

Boulders (p137) Sheltered sandy coves on False Bay and a reserve protecting a colony of 2800 African penguins.

Cape of Good Hope (p131) The peninsula's tip is protected by this 7750-hectare reserve, including the most southwestern point of Africa.

Guided Walks

As well as the companies listed below, **Abseil Africa** (Map p264; ☑021-424 4760; www. abseilafrica.co.za; R595), **Awol Tours** (☑021-418 3803; www.awoltours.co.za) and **Downhill Adventures** (p96) have guides to lead you around the mountain and park.

Venture Forth (☑021-554 3225, 086 110 6548; www.ventureforth.co.za) Excellent guided hikes and rock climbs with enthusiastic, savvy guides. Outings (around R500 per person) are tailored to individual requirements and aim to get you off the beaten track.

Walk in Africa (☑021-785 2264; http://walkinafrica.com) Steve Bolnick, an experienced and passionate safari and mountain guide, runs this company. Their flagship hike is the five-day, four-night Mountain in the Sea trail (R14,000 per person) that runs from Platteklip Gorge to Cape Point, partly following the Hoerikwaggo Trail.

South African Slackpacking (☑082 882 4388; www.slackpackersa.co.za) Registered nature guide Frank Dwyer runs this operation, which offers day and multiday hikes in the national park.

Table Mountain Walks (☑021-715 6136; www.tablemountainwalks.co.za) Offers a range of guided day hikes in different parts of the park, from ascents of Table Mountain to rambles through Silvermine (from R450).

Christopher Smith (☑071-270 6081; fauna. flora7@gmail.com) The National Park–trained freelance guide is a personable, knowledgeable chap who has plenty of experience guiding along the Hoerikwaggo Trail and other routes.

Accommodation in the Park

Private camping in the park is banned so if you want to sleep close to nature your choices are either one of the creatively designed 'tented camps' or the park's self-catering cottages. Bookings can be made online (http://sanparks.org.za/parks/table_mountain/tourism/accommodation. php/tented) or by phone (☑021-422 2816; ☺7.30am-4pm Mon-Fri).

Tented Camps

These camps have been designed to blend in with nature, using materials gathered from the park. The 'tents' are canvas, army camp types, protected by wooden structures and housing comfortable beds. The bathroom facilities at all are excellent, as are the fully equipped communal kitchen and braai (barbecue) areas. You can drive to within relatively easy hiking reach of each. The rates are R440 per twin bedded units; bedding can be provided for R80 per person extra, if you don't have your own.

Orange Kloof Perhaps the best, tucked away in a beautiful area near Constantia Nek and providing direct access to the last strand of Afromontane forest in the park.

Silvermine In a breezy location near the reservoir in the Silvermine section of the park.

Slangkop Near the lighthouse at Kommetjie, beneath a forest of rare, indigenous milkwood trees and decorated with the bones of a whale that washed up on the beach in 2006.

Smitswinkel The only camp to offer en suite

bathrooms in its tents, this location is steps from the entrance to the Cape of Good Hope section of the park. Note that it does get windy here.

Cottages

The park's self-catering cottages encompass purpose built and renovated buildings, all in lovely spots and most of which you can drive to. Linens are provided. Bookings for cottages within Cape of Good Hope National Park can also be made on ☎021-780 9240.

Platteklip Wash House (Deer Park, Vredehoek; 1-4 people R800, extra adult/child R400/200; Ⓟ) The old wash houses on the park's edge have been converted into some very stylish accommodation. The decoration in the living room includes pieces by top Capetonian craftspeople, while outside there's a *bomah* (a sunken campfire circle) and hammocks to settle into.

Overseers Cottage (De Villiers Reservoir, Back Table; 1-6 people R1980, extra adult/child R330/165). You'll need to hike to the only place atop Table Mountain that you can stay the night. Consisting of two cottages sleeping up to 16, the accommodation is decorated in a smart, contemporary style, with a comfortable lounge heated by an open fire – very welcome when night falls or the weather changes for the worse.

Wood Owl Cottage (Tokai Plantation; 1-3 people R740, extra adult/child R290/145) Sleep in the heart of Tokai at this elegantly restored, fully furnished former forester's cottage with three bedrooms sleeping up to six. The open-plan kitchen and living room has a fireplace and there's a separate TV room. It's ideal for a family.

Eland & Duiker Cottages (Cape of Good Hope; 1-4 people R805, extra adult/child R172/86) Sleeping up to six people each and located at the northern section of the reserve. The outdoor showers are a nice feature.

Olifantsbos (Cape of Good Hope; 1-6 people R2640, extra adult/child R290/145) Escape from it all at this pretty whitewashed cottage with an isolated position just steps from the beach and the pounding waves of the Atlantic. Together with its annex, it sleeps a maximum of 12 people.

Wild Cards

Providing unlimited access to South Africa's national parks for a year are various types of Wild Cards (www.wildcard.co.za).

NEED TO KNOW

Information Centres
➡ **Table Mountain National Park Head Office** (☎021-701 8692; Shop A1, Westlake Square, cnr Westlake Dr & Steenberg Rd, Westlake; ◷8am-3pm Mon-Fri)

➡ **Boulders Visitor Centre** (☎021-786 5787; 1 Kleintuin Rd, Seaforth, Simon's Town; ◷8am-4pm)

➡ **Buffelsfontein Visitor Centre** (☎021-780 9204; Cape of Good Hope; ◷8am-4pm)

➡ **Tokai Forest Office** (☎021-712 7471; Tokai Rd, Tokai; ◷8am-1pm & 2-4pm Mon-Fri)

Maps
➡ **Slingsby Maps** (www.slingsbymaps.com)

Hiking Clubs
➡ **Cape Union Mart Hiking Club** (www.cumhike.co.za)

➡ **Trails Club of South Africa** (www.trailsclub.co.za)

➡ **Mountain Club of South Africa** (http://cen.mcsa.org.za)

International visitors must purchase the All Parks Cluster card (individual/couple/family R340/560/700). South African citizens and Cape Town residents can buy My Green Card (R85), which allows 12 entries per year to any of Table Mountain National Park's pay points. Either card can be bought at the park's information centres.

Books

➡ *Mountains in the Sea: Table Mountain to Cape Point* (John Yeld)

➡ *Best Walks in the Cape Peninsula* (Mike Lundy; www.hikecapetown.co.za)

➡ *A Walking Guide for Table Mountain* (Shirley Brossy)

➡ *Table Mountain Classics* (Tony Lourens)

➡ *Table Mountain Activity Guide* (Fiona McIntosh)

Eating

It's a wonder that all those Capetonians look so svelte on the beach because this is one damn delicious city to dine in. The best of Cape Town's restaurants and cafes are on a par with those of other far larger and more cosmopolitan cities, and there's a wonderful range of cuisines to sample, including local African and Cape Malay concoctions, and superb seafood fresh from the boat.

Seafood Galore

There are many types of fish here that you're unlikely to find at home, such as kingklip or snoek – a very meaty, mackerel-on-steroids type of fish that is delicious barbecued (or 'braaied' as they say in these parts). Watch out for the many small bones, though. If you see 'line fish' advertised it means the catch of the day. There's also deliciously fresh cray-fish and *perlemoen* (abalone).

Before ordering, make sure what you're eating isn't on the endangered list. The **Southern African Sustainable Seafood Initiative** (SASSI; www.wwfsassi.co.za) helps to educate consumers and allow them to enjoy seafood in a responsible and sustainable manner. Visit the website to download a handy wallet card and booklet that tells you more about the conservation status of local seafood supplies. If you're at a restaurant, you can also text the name of the fish to ☎ 079 499 8795 to get an instant answer on its status.

Cape Malay Cuisine

This intriguing mix of Malay and Dutch styles originated in the earliest days of Euro-pean settlement and marries pungent spices with local produce. It can be stodgy and on the sweet side for some people's tastes, but is still well worth trying.

The Cape Malay dish you'll come across most often is *bobotie,* usually made with lightly curried minced beef or lamb topped with savoury egg custard, and served on a bed of turmeric-flavoured rice with a dab of chutney on the side. Some sophisticated versions of *bobotie* use other meats and even seafood.

There is a variety of *bredies* – pot stews of meat or fish, and vegetables. *Dhaltjies* (chilli bites) are very moreish deep-fried balls of chickpea-flour batter mixed with potato, coriander and spinach. Mild curries are popular and are often served with *rootis,* similar to Indian roti bread but doughier. Also taking a cue from Indian cooking are *samosas:* triangular pockets of crisp fried pastry enclosing a spicy vegetable filling. Meat lovers should try *sosaties,* which is a Cape Malay–style kebab.

Traditional desserts include *malva* pud-ding, a delicious sponge traditionally made with apricot jam and vinegar, and brandy pudding (true Cape Malay cuisine – strongly associated with the Muslim community – contains no alcohol). Also try *koeksusters,* a heavy doughnut dipped in syrup.

African & Afrikaner Cuisine

The staple for most blacks in the township restaurants is rice or mealie *pap* (maize porridge), often served with a fatty stew. It isn't especially appetising, but it's cheap. The same goes for the *smilies* (sheep's heads) that you'll see boiled up and served on the streets. Other dishes include *samp* (a mix-ture of maize and beans), *imifino* (mealie meal and vegetables) and *chakalaka* (a tasty fry-up of onions, tomatoes, peppers, garlic, ginger, sweet chilli sauce and curry powder).

Grilled meats, seasoned and sauced on the braai (barbecue), is a dish that cuts across the colour bar as well as being the keystone of traditional Afrikaner cuisine. The Voor-trekker heritage comes out in foods such as biltong (deliciously moreish dried beef and venison) and rusks, perfect for those long journeys into the hinterland. *Boerewors* (spicy sausage) is the traditional sausage and plenty of recipes make use of game; some include venison, which will be some type of buck.

Where to Eat

With both the sea and fruitful farmlands on hand, you can be assured of fresh, top-quality ingredients. There are places to suit practically everyone's taste and budget, from fabulous delis and organic food markets to temples of haute cuisine. Fast-food options are common and include **Nandos** (www.nandos.co.za), which purveys spicy Portuguese-style peri peri chicken and the **Vida e Caffé** (www.vidaecaffe.com) cafe chain. Many bars serve excellent food. Wine estates can also offer excellent restaurants or pre-packed picnics. There are halaal and kosher restaurants, as well as several good vegetarian and vegan cafes.

Eating by Neighbourhood

➡ **City Bowl, Foreshore, Bo-Kaap & De Waterkant** Most options are clustered in City Bowl and De Waterkant, with a scattering of Cape Malay cafes in the Bo-Kaap.

➡ **East City Corridor** Join the boho and student set along Lower Main Rd in Observatory or discover all the new cafes in Woodstock and Salt River.

➡ **Gardens & Surrounds** Kloof St has many good places to eat, several with great views of Table Mountain.

➡ **Green Point & Waterfront** Prime waterfront dining, but choose carefully at the Waterfront where prices are inflated and quality isn't always up to scratch.

➡ **Sea Point to Hout Bay** Sea Point's dining scene goes from strength to strength. Camps Bay's beachside dining usually comes at a premium.

➡ **Southern Suburbs** Best for picnics in Kirstenbosch or the wine farms of Constantia, where there are also some very classy restaurants.

➡ **Simon's Town & Southern Peninsula** Kalk Bay is great for seafood fresh off the boat in the harbour.

➡ **Cape Flats & Northern Suburbs** Traditional African food at township restaurants and roadside braais.

NEED TO KNOW

Price Ranges

In our listings the following price ranges represent the cost of a meal (not including drinks):

$	less than R100
$$	R100-250
$$$	more than R250

Opening Hours

Many restaurants and cafes are closed Sunday.

➡ **Cafes** 7.30am-5pm Mon-Fri, 8am-3pm Sat

➡ **Restaurants** 11.30am-3pm, 6-10pm Mon-Sat

Reservations

Where a telephone number is listed, reservations are recommended, particularly for Friday or Saturday nights. For top places such as the Test Kitchen reserve at least a month in advance.

Guides & Blogs

➡ **Rossou Restaurants** (www.rossouwsrestaurants.com) Independent reviews and sprightly criticism of Cape Town's restaurant scene.

➡ **Eat Out** (www.eatout.co.za) Online reviews and annual print magazine guide with Cape Town and Western Cape reviews.

➡ **Eat Cape Town** (www.eatcapetown.co.za)

➡ **Once Bitten** (oncebitten.co.za)

➡ **Relax With Dax** (www.relax-with-dax.co.za)

BYO

Most restaurants are licensed, but some allow you to bring your own wine for little or no corkage. Call ahead to check.

Smoking

Smoking in restaurants is permitted only if there is a separate room where smokers are seated.

Tipping

10% is standard, more if service is very good.

Lonely Planet's Top Choices

Bombay Brasserie (p62) Feasts fit for the Mughals and maharajas at the Taj's fine dining Indian.

Bizerca Bistro (p62) Contemporary French bistro food, brilliant service.

Dear Me (p64) Brilliant showcase for freshly sourced local produce.

Roundhouse (p111) Gourmet delights by night, dazzling view of Camps Bay by day.

The Kitchen (p80) Fabulous cafe with the First Lady's seal of approval.

Pot Luck Club & The Test Kitchen (p80) Double taste sensation whammy from top chef Luke Dale-Roberts and his talented team.

Best By Budget

$
Casa Labia (p137)
Charly's Bakery (p81)
The Dog's Bollocks (p92)
Maria's (p92)

$$
Olympia Café & Deli (p138)
La Boheme (p111)
Wakame (p103)
Hemelhuijs (p65)

$$$
Aubergine (p92)
La Colombe (p124)
Savoy Cabbage (p64)
Foodbarn (p138)

Best Cuisine

African
Africa Café (p64)
Addis in Cape (p64)
Mzoli's (p146)
Lelapa (p147)

Cape Malay
Biesmiellah (p66)
Noon Gun Tearoom & Restaurant (p66)
Gold (p64)
Jonkershuis (p125)

Italian
La Perla (p112)
95 Keerom (p64)
Massimo's (p112)
A Tavola (p124)

Asian & Indian
Masala Dosa (p65)
Kyoto Sushi Garden (p92)
Chandani (p80)
Willoughby & Co (p104)

Vegetarian & Vegan
Closer (p138)
Deer Park Café (p92)
O'ways Teacafe (p125)
Sophea Gallery & Tibetan Teahouse (p139)

Best Deli Cafes
Giovanni's Deli World p104)
Melissa's (p92)
Newport Market & Deli (p104)
Bread, Milk & Honey (p65)

Best Gourmet Cafes
Café Neo (p104)
Manna Epicure (p92)
Lazari (p92)
River Café (p124)

Best Seafood
Fish on the Rocks (p112)
Willoughby & Co (p104)
Live Bait (p138)
Fisherman's Choice (p104)

Drinking & Nightlife

Cape Town didn't become known as the 'Tavern of the Seven Seas' for nothing. There are scores of bars – with stunning views of either beach or mountain – in which to sip cocktails, fine wines or craft beers. If strutting your stuff on the dance floor is more your thing, then there's bound to be a club to suit.

Join the *Jol*

The busy nights are Wednesday, Friday or Saturday when you'll see how the locals like to party, or *jol*, as they say here. It's not all about drinking and dancing. Cape Town's nightlife embraces cabaret and comedy venues, and live music gigs from jazz to rap. For more about the city's performing arts scene see p37.

What to Drink

There are abundant opportunities to sample the Cape's wines in bars, restaurants and at the cellar door: for more on wine see p45 and p229. Cocktails are also popular, the best mixologists incorporating local flavours and artisan spirits in their liquid creations.

European beermaking at the Cape also has a long history with Pieter Visagle said to have first brewed ale on the banks of the Liesbeek River in 1658. At Newlands Brewery, major brands such as Castle and Black Label are pumped into barrels and 750ml (quart) and 330ml (dumpy) bottles. Another popular mass-market brand is Windhoek, brewed in Namibia.

Microbrewing is booming. Joining old timers such as **Mitchells** (www.mitchellsbrewery.com) and **Birkenhead** (www.birkenhead.co.za) are **Jack Black** (www.jackblackbeer.com), **Old Everson Cider** (www.eversonwine.co.za), **Darling Brew** (www.darlingbrew.co.za), **Triggerfish** (www.facebook.com/triggerfishbrewer?sk=info) and **Camelthorn** (camelthornbrewing.wordpress.com). Beer lovers should mark their calendar for the **Cape Town Festival of Beer** (capetownfestivalofbeer.co.za) at the end of November.

Clubbing

Cape Town's club scene is firmly plugged into the global dance network, so expect star appearances by international DJs. Trance parties, such as Vortex (www.intothevortex.co.za) and Alien Safari (http://aliensafari.net), held outdoors an hour or so from the city centre, happen through summer; check the respective websites for details or make some enquiries at backpacker hostels.

Drinking & Nightlife by Neighbourhood

→ **City Bowl & De Waterkant** (p52) Pumping nightlife on upper Long St, Bree St and around De Waterkant.

→ **East City Corridor** (p75) Clubs in the Fringe and borders of District Six; student/boho hangouts in Observatory.

→ **Gardens & Surrounds** (p86) Kloof St and Kloof Nek Rd are the hip hangouts.

→ **Green Point & Waterfront** (p97) Drinks with either harbour, bay or stadium views.

→ **Sea Point to Hout Bay** (p108) See and be seen at trendy Camps Bay; relax in more laid-back Sea Point and Hout Bay.

→ **Southern Suburbs** (p116) Established pubs around Newlands and historic wine estates in Constantia.

→ **Southern Peninsula** (p129) The Brass Bell and Polana allow you to enjoy drinks within reach of crashing waves.

→ **Cape Flats & Northern Suburbs** (p143) Jazz and dance clubs in Athlone or beer and pizza with a view of Table Mountain at Bloubergstrand.

PLAN YOUR TRIP DRINKING & NIGHTLIFE

NEED TO KNOW

Opening Hours

➡ **Bars** Noon-midnight, but some stay open much later.

➡ **Clubs** 8pm-4am, but most places don't really get going until well after midnight.

Cover Charges

Club admission charges from R20 to R100 depending on event.

Tipping

It's the norm to tip 10% to bartenders.

Event Tickets

➡ **Computicket** (www.computicket.com)

➡ **Webtickets** (www.webtickets.co.za)

Facts

➡ The alcohol content of beer is around 5% – stronger than UK or US beer.

➡ It's OK to drink the tap water.

Information

➡ **Mail & Guardian** (www.theguide.co.za)

➡ **Tonight** (www.iol.co.za/tonight)

➡ **Cape Town Magazine** (www.capetownmaga zine.co.za).

➡ **The Next 48 Hours** (www.48hours.co.za)

➡ **Playground.sa.co. za** (www.playgroundsa.co.za)

➡ **Thunda.com** (www.thunda.com)

Lonely Planet's Top Choices

&Union (p67) Quaffable craft beers, ethically sourced meats, ping pong, coffee and cupcakes.

Waiting Room (p67) Catch the breeze and view over Long St from this grooving attic and rooftop bar.

Amadoda (p81) Boogie down with Cape Town's black diamonds at this township-style braai/shebeen in Woodstock.

Banana Jam (p125) Go-to bar for local craft beer enthusiasts, plus tasty Caribbean food.

Brass Bell (p139) Classic Kalk Bay pub, so close to the water you could jump in from your seat.

Espressolab Microroasters (p81) Global coffee blends treated with the same respect as fine wines at this dedicated roastery in the Old Biscuit Mill

Best for Sea Views

Polana (p139)

Dunes (p113)

Tobago's (p105)

Grand Café & Beach (p105)

Skebanga's Bar (p139)

Blue Peter (p147)

Best Hotel Bars

Planet (p93)

Twankey Bar (p68)

Bascule (p105)

Vista Bar (p105)

Salt (p113)

Leopard Bar (p113)

Best for Wine

Caveau (p68)

Fork (p68)

W Tapas Bar (p105)

Cape Point Vineyards (p139)

Caveau at the Mill (p126)

Best for Stylistas

Tjing Tjing (p67)

Don Pedro (p81)

Harbour House (p105)

Martini Bar (p126)

The Bungalow (p112)

Julep Bar (p68)

Best for Beers

The Power & The Glory/Black Ram (p93)

Saints (p93)

Mitchell's Scottish Ale House & Brewery (p105)

Forrester's Arms (p126)

Perseverance Tavern (p93)

Fireman's Arms (p69)

Best for Coffee

Escape Caffe (p67)

Bean There (p68)

Haas (p69)

Truth (p82)

Yours Truly (p68)

Best for Clubbing

Trinity (p69)

Assembly (p82)

Vinyl Digz (p68)

Crew (p69)

Decodance (p113)

St Yves (p113)

Entertainment

Rappers and comediennes performing in a mix of Afrikaans and English; a cappella township choirs and buskers at the Waterfront; theatre on the streets and old churches; intimate performances in suburban living rooms – the Mother City dazzles with a diverse and creative range of entertainment, with live music a particular highlight.

All that Jazz

Many world-renowned jazz artists began their careers in Cape Town. The free-flowing nature of this genre is well suited to the relaxed, cosmopolitan nature of the city. Although there are few permanent jazz venues, it's a rare night that there's not a jazz jam somewhere in the city; check www.capetownjazz.com for details.

All other forms of live music can be enjoyed here, too. The line up for the celebrated Sunday-afternoon concerts at Kirstenbosch reads like a who's who of the South African music scene, skipping right across the genres. Big rock music festivals include **Rocking the Daisies** (www.rockingthedaisies.com), a three-day event held in October.

Dance & Theatre

Capetonians also love dance. Apart from the **City Ballet** (www.capetowncityballet.org.za) there's also **Jazzart Dance Theatre** (www.jazzart.co.za), South Africa's oldest modern dance company, and the **Cape Dance Company** (www.capedancecompany.co.za) and associated Cape Youth Dance Company, made up of talented youths aged from 13 to 23. Shows can be seen at Artscape and the Baxter Theatre which, along with The Fugard, form a trinity of top performing arts venue. Smaller theatres, such as the Kalk Bay Theatre, Theatre on the Bay and the various studios at University of Cape Town Hiddingh Campus in Gardens, also thrive.

Comedy & Cinema

Capetonian comedians whose shows you should keep an eye out for include TV star **Marc Lottering** (www.marclottering.com); **Mark Sampson** (www.samp.co.za), who has played at the Edinburgh Fringe Festival; and **Kurt Schoonraad** (www.kurt.co.za), who headlines at the Jou Ma Se Comedy Club.

Big multiplexes, run by **Ster Kinekor** (www.sterkinekor.com) and **Nu Metro** (www.numetro.co.za; various locations), show the latest international releases, as well as a decent selection of art-house movies. The Fugard's Bioscope screens digital broadcasts of shows by the Bolshoi, Royal Opera House and Royal Ballet.

Entertainment by Neighbourhood

➡ **City Bowl, Foreshore, Bo-Kaap & De Waterkant** Artscape, classical concerts at the Old Town Hall and events at bars and clubs along Long St.

➡ **Green Point & Waterfront** Cape Town Stadium for concerts by international stars; the Waterfront for free music and other entertainment.

➡ **East City Corridor** The Fugard Theatre and live gigs at the Assembly and Mercury Live.

➡ **Southern Suburbs** Shows at the Baxter Theatre and outdoor concerts at Kirstenbosch Botanical Gardens.

NEED TO KNOW

Tickets

➡ **Computicket** (online. computicket.com/web)

➡ **Webtickets** (www. webtickets.co.za)

Information

➡ **What's On!** (www. whatson.co.za)

➡ **The Next 48 Hours** (www.48hours.co.za)

➡ **Mail & Guardian** (www.theguide.co.za)

➡ **Tonight** (www.iol. co.za/tonight)

➡ **Cape Town Magazine** (www.capetownmaga zine.co.za).

Free Tickets

Free tickets available every Friday for events via Webtickets (www. webtickets.co.za).

Readings

Book launches and readings at Book Lounge and Kalk Bay Books. Poetry performances at A Touch of Madness on Monday, the Melting Pot on Tuesday and the Verses at iBuyambo Music & Art Exhibition Centre on the last Wednesday of the month.

Film Festivals

➡ **Encounters** (www. encounters.co.za) International documentary film festival in June.

➡ **Out in Africa: SA International Gay & Lesbian Film Festival** (www.oia.co.za) Gay-themed films in March, July & October.

➡ **Winter Classic Film Festival** (www.thefu gard.com) Classic world cinema in July.

Lonely Planet's Top Choices

Baxter Theatre (p126) Premier theatre and performing arts complex in a striking 1970s building.

The Fugard (p82) Vibrant addition to city's arts, theatre and cinema scene in a converted church.

Labia (p94) A haven for world cinema fans with several screens across two locations.

Assembly (p82) Live music and DJ performance space hosting popular and cutting edge music.

Old Mutual Summer Sunset Concerts at Kirstenbosch (p22) A lineup of top South African musical talent in beautiful outdoor surroundings.

Best for Theatre

Artscape (p70)

Kalk Bay Theatre (p140)

Theatre in the District (p83)

Maynardville Open-Air Theatre (p126)

Theatre on the Bay (p113)

Intimate Theatre (p94)

Best for Music

Bands & Big Acts

Cape Town International Convention Centre (p70)

Cape Town Stadium (p103)

Zula Sound Bar (p70)

Mercury Live & Lounge (p82)

Acoustic Sets

Studio 7 (p114)

Alma Café (p126)

Tagore (p82)

Waiting Room (p67)

Melting Pot (p140)

Jazz & African

Mahogany Lounge (p94)

Swingers (p148)

Harvey's (p112)

Asoka (p94)

iBuyambo Music & Art Exhibition Centre (p70)

Mama Africa (p70)

Classical

Cape Town City Hall (p70)

Artscape (p70)

St George's Cathedral (p59)

Casa Labia (p137)

Best for Movies

Cavendish Nouveau (p127)

Cinema Nouveau (p106)

Pink Flamingo (p70)

Cine 12 (p113)

Best Spoken Word

Book Lounge (p83)

A Touch of Madness (p82)

Kalk Bay Books (p141)

iBuyambo Music & Art Exhibition Centre (p70)

House of Joy (p83)

Best Cabaret & Comedy

Jou Ma Se Comedy Club (p82)

Stardust (p126)

Obz Café (p82)

Zula Sound Bar (p70)

Evita se Perron (p168)

Shopping

Bring an empty suitcase because the chances are that you'll be leaving Cape Town laden with booty. The World Design Capital 2014 offers up an irresistible range of products, including traditional African crafts, ceramics, fashion, fine wines and contemporary art. You'll also find antiques and curios from all over Africa, but shop carefully as there are many fakes among the originals.

World Design Capital

Local designers will be under the international spotlight with Cape Town the World Design Capital for 2014. A selection goes on show at the annual Design Indaba and at events such as **The Fringe Handmade** (http://thefringe.org.za), as well as the many weekly markets and designer collective spaces.

Capetonian artists are also a very talented bunch working in a variety of media including ceramics. Look out for pieces by **Barbara Jackson** (www.barbarajackson.co.za) and **Clementina van der Walt** (www.clementina.co.za) whose super colourful pots take their inspiration from the geometric patterns of Zulu and Ndebele beadwork, and traditional African basketry, pottery and textiles.

Ethical & Edible

Township-produced crafts might be made from recycled items such as tin cans and plastic bottles. Proceeds from sales may go towards helping people struggling with poverty, or towards supporting projects to deal with health issues such as HIV/AIDS or education. Established brands include **Wola Nani** (www.wolanani.co.za) specialising in picture frames and papier-mâché bowls; **KEAG** (www.keag.org.za) who recycle plastic into colourful ornaments; and the painted tin art of **Umlungu** (www.umlungu.co.za).

Edible goodies can also be purchased at delis such as Melissa's or at the popular artisan food markets. Fine wines are available at hundreds of vineyards.

Fashion Rules

For up-and-coming designers, scout the boutiques on Long and Kloof Sts. Local designers of note include **Maya Prass** (www.mayaprass.com), known for her use of boldly feminine colours, textures and patterns; Amanda Laird Cherry, whose designs can be found in the Big Blue boutiques; Themba Mngomezulu, of **Darkie** (www.darkieclothing.com) streetwear label; and Stefania Morland and her daughter Sasha. See also p72.

Shopping by Neighbourhood

➡ **City Bowl** Long St offers up an eclectic retail mix; Greenmarket Sq has a good craft market.

➡ **Gardens & Surrounds** Kloof St has several fashion boutiques, galleries and gift stores.

➡ **Waterfront** Victoria Wharf mall and plenty of other retail action in Cape Town's premier shopping destination.

➡ **Sea Point** If you're based in the area, Main Rd is convenient for everyday essentials.

➡ **Southern Peninsula** Kalk Bay offers a brilliant mix of crafts, antique and fashion boutiques.

Lonely Planet's Top Choices

Old Biscuit Mill (p83) Fabulous retail and Saturday's Neighbourgoods Market.

The Fringe Arts (p94) Representing almost 100 South African artists and designers.

Kalk Bay Modern (p140) The cream of Capetonian artistic creativity from fine art to jewellery and fabrics.

African Music Store (p71) CDs and DVDs to provide memories of a highly musical city.

Sobeit (p140) A modern curiosity shop housing the studios of wax artists, graphic and furniture designers and jewellery makers.

NEED TO KNOW

Opening Hours

➡ **Shops** 8.30am-5pm Mon-Fri, 8.30am-1pm Sat

➡ **Malls** 9am-9pm daily

Bargaining

When buying handicrafts from street hawkers, and at some market stalls, bargaining is expected; it's not a sophisticated game, so don't press too hard.

Taxes & Refunds

VAT of 14% is included in prices. Foreign visitors can reclaim some of their VAT expenses on departure.

Events

➡ **Design Indaba** (www. designindaba.com) Local and international designers across media swap ideas and show products in March.

➡ **Fashion Week** (www. afisa.co.za) Held in July; South Africa's top designers run their new looks down the catwalk.

➡ **Rondebosch Potters Market** (www.ceramics -sa-cape.co.za) Second last Saturday of March and November.

Best for Fashion

Stefania Morland (p95)

Merchants on Long (p71)

Solveig (p106)

Habits (p127)

Bluecollarwhitecollar (p95)

Grant Mason Originals (p94)

Best for Ceramics

Africa Nova (p73)

Art in the Forest (p127)

Clementina Ceramics (p83)

Imiso Ceramics (p83)

Pottershop (p141)

Best for Contemporary Art

Stevenson (p84)

What If the World (p84)

Goodman Gallery Cape (p84)

AVA Gallery (p73)

Erdmann Contemporary & Photographers Gallery (p73)

South African Print Gallery (p84)

Best for Crafts

Design Afrika (p83)

Red Rock Tribal (p140)

Mogalakwena (p71)

African Image (p71)

Pan African Market (p71)

Kirstenbosch Craft Market (p127)

Best Weekly Markets

Neighbourgoods Market (p83)

Hout Bay Craft Market (p113)

Blue Bird Garage (p140)

City Bowl Market (p94)

Bay Harbour Market (p113)

Milnerton Flea Market (p149)

Best for Books

Book Lounge (p83)

Clarke's Bookshop (p71)

Kalk Bay Books (p141)

Quagga Art & Books (p141)

Best Recycled & Ethical

Heath Nash (p84)

Montebello (p127)

Streetwires (p73)

Monkeybiz (p73)

Umlungu (p84)

Philani Nutrition Centre (p149)

Best Food & Wine

Vaughan Johnson's Wine & Cigar Shop (p106)

Honest (p71)

Porter Estate Product Market (p127)

Melissa's (p92)

Wine Concepts (p95)

Best for Design

Church (p71)

Ashanti (p83)

LIM (p95)

Tribal Trends (p71)

Recreate (p84)

Field Office (p85)

Best Shopping Malls

Victoria Wharf (p105)

Cape Quarter (p74)

Cavendish Square (p127)

Canal Walk (p148)

Gardens Centre (p95)

Sports & Activities

Want to get active? You've come to the right place. Cape Town is a nirvana for the adventure sport enthusiast, with operators lining up to ensure you don't go home without having experienced an adrenaline rush. Capetonians are also avid sports fans – attending a football, rugby or cricket game is highly recommended.

Getting Active

With wind-whipped waves and Table Mountain on hand, surfing, hiking and rock climbing are hugely popular and can easily be organised. For more extreme adventures, such as shark-cage diving or paragliding, you'll need to travel out of the city or wait for the ideal weather conditions.

It's not all about thrill-seeking: the Mother City is also a fabulous location for golf, a bike ride or a canter along the beach on horseback. Luxury spas are found at many of the city's top hotels and there are plenty of gyms.

Spectator Sports

SOCCER

In terms of drawing crowds, the biggest game on the Cape is soccer (football, known locally as *diski*). Cape Town has two teams in the national Premier Soccer League (www.psl.co.za): Santos (www.santosfc.co.za) and Ajax Cape Town (www.ajaxct.com). If either of these teams is playing the nation's top soccer teams, the Kaizer Chiefs and the Orlando Pirates (both based in Jo'burg), you'll have to fight for tickets, which start at R40. The season runs from August to May with matches played at either Cape Town Stadium or Athlone Stadium.

CRICKET

Capetonians have a soft spot for cricket, hardly surprising given the attractiveness of Sahara Park Newlands where all top national and international games are played. The game was the first of the 'whites-only' sports to wholeheartedly adopt a nonracial attitude, and development programs in the townships have paid dividends; hailing from Langa is Thami Tsolekile, who played three test matches for South Africa as wicket-keeper. Cape Cobras (www.capecobras.co.za) is the local team.

RUGBY

Rugby (union, not league) is the traditional Afrikaner sport. Games are held at the Newlands Rugby Stadium with the most popular matches those in the Super 14 tournament, in which teams from South Africa, Australia and New Zealand compete from late February until the end of May.

HORSE RACING

Cape Town has two courses: Kenilworth, which has two tracks, and **Durbanville** (☏ 021- 700 1600), northeast of the city. Races are held Wednesday and Saturday.

Sports & Activities by Neighbourhood

➡ **Gardens & Surrounds** (p96) Hiking, climbing and abseiling in Table Mountain National Park.

➡ **Sea Point to Hout Bay** (p115) Swimming at Sea Point or off Clifton's beaches, diving at Ouderkraal or kayaking at Hout Bay.

➡ **Southern Suburbs** (p128) Watching cricket and rugby at Newlands and hiking up the mountain from Kirstenbosch.

➡ **Southern Peninsula** (p141) Surfing at Muizenberg and Kommetjie, horse riding at Noordhoek, kayaking at Simon's Town and cycling at Cape Point.

➡ **Northern Suburbs** (p149) Head here to windsurf and kite-surf, sandboard and skydive.

NEED TO KNOW

Contacts & Information

➡ **Pedal Power Association** (www.pedalpower.org.za)

➡ **South African Rugby Union** (www.sarugby.net)

➡ **TASKS: The African Sea Kayak Society** (www.tasks.co.za).

➡ **The Soccer Pages** (www.thesoccerpages.com).

➡ **Wavescape Surfing South Africa** (www.wavescape.co.za)

➡ **Western Province Cricket** (www.wpca.org.za)

➡ **Western Province Golf Union** (www.wpgu.co.za).

Cycling Events

➡ **Cape Argus Pick 'n' Pay Cape Cycle Tour** (www.cycletour.co.za) Held on a Saturday in early March; with more than 30,000 entrants each year it's the largest bicycle race in the world.

➡ **The Absa Cape Epic** (www.cape-epic.com) An eight-day event with a Western Cape route that changes each year.

Tickets

➡ **Computicket** (http://online.computicket.com/web)

➡ **Webtickets** (www.webtickets.co.za)

Lonely Planet's Top Choices

Hiking in Table Mountain National Park (p29) Hire a guide so you don't get lost, and learn more about the fabulous Cape floral kingdom.

Abseil Africa (p89) Dangle from a rope off the edge of Table Mountain and take in the view.

Downhill Adventures (p96) Offering a range of adrenaline-fuelled activities, from mountain biking to surf safaris.

Cape Town Stadium (p103) If there's no soccer game or concert on at this giant open air arena, there are tours you can take around the structure.

Sea Kayak Simon's Town (p141) Paddle out of Simon's Town harbour and along False Bay, keeping an eye out for African penguins.

Shark Cage Diving (p170) Several outfits in Cape Town can get you down to Gansbaai, where the bulk of these man-faces-shark adventures happen.

Best Sports Venues

Sahara Park Newlands (p128)

Kenilworth Race Course (p128)

Newlands Rugby Stadium (p128)

Athlone Stadium (p149)

Best for Swimming

Sea Point Pavilion (p115)

Long St Baths (p74)

Kalk Bay sea pool (p137)

Buffels Bay sea pool (p131)

Best Spa

Enmasse (p96)

Librisa Spa (p96)

Angsana Spa (p197)

Arabella Spa (p190)

Best Aerial Adventures

Cape Town Tandem Paragliding (p96)

Hopper (p107)

Huey Helicopter Co (p107)

Skydive Cape Town (p149)

Best for Sailing

Royal Cape Yacht Club (p74)

Waterfront Boat Company (p101)

Yacoob Tourism (p101)

Ocean Sailing Academy (p107)

Simon's Town Boat Company (p136)

Duiker Island Cruises (p111)

Best for Diving

Two Oceans Aquarium (p100)

In the Blue (p115)

Pisces Divers (p142)

Table Bay Diving (p107)

Best Golf

Mowbray Golf Club (p149)

Metropolitan Golf Club (p107)

Milnerton Golf Club (p149)

Logical Golf Academy (p85)

Best for Surfing & Windsurfing

Gary's Surf School (p142)

Roxy Surf Club (p142)

Sunscene Outdoor Adventures (p142)

Windswept (p149)

 # GLBT

Africa's pinkest city is a glam-to-the-max destination that any gay, lesbian, bisexual and transgender (GLBT) traveller should have on their bucket list. Size queens shouldn't dis De Waterkant, the official queer precinct; it may be tiny but it's welcoming to everyone, from Cape Town's finest drag queens to leathered-up muscle Marys.

GLBT Rights

Skin colour wasn't the only thing that got you into trouble in South Africa during apartheid. Gay male erotic contact was illegal. (Female same sex conduct was never illegal: as in other formerly British colonies such activities were considered simply unthinkable!)

That all changed with democracy. South Africa was the first country in the world to enshrine gay and lesbian rights in its constitution. There's an equal age of consent and GLBT peeps are legally entitled to marry.

Sadly the queer lifestyle is not embraced by traditional black South African cultures. In 2011, Human Rights Watch (www.hrw.org) released a damning report on the continuing discrimination and violence suffered by black lesbians and transgender men in townships and rural areas.

Gay Language

Moffie, the local term for a homosexual, comes from the Afrikaans word for glove. It's also the title of the leader of a performance troupe in the Cape Minstrel Carnival. These flamboyantly dressed and acting guys wear gloves and are often gay. Among gays, *moffie* has come to be used like 'queer' – in an affirmative way to repudiate its negative connotations.

During apartheid gays also developed a code language, called 'Gayle', in which women's names stand in for certain words. For example, a 'Cilla' is a cigarette; 'Priscilla', police; 'Beaulah', beautiful; 'Hilda', ugly; and 'Griselda', gruesome. If you hear someone talking about 'Dora' in a bar, you'll know they're after a drink (they could also be calling someone a drunk!). *Gayle – The Language of Kinks and Queens* by Ken Cage includes a dictionary of the most popular code words.

Festivals & Events

Cape Town Pride (http://capetownpride.org) End of Feburary and early March; in De Waterkant.

Out in Africa: SA International Gay & Lesbian Film Festival (www.oia.co.za) March, July and October; in Cape Town.

Pink Loerie Mardis Gras & Arts Festival (www.pinkloerie.co.za) April; in Knysna.

Miss Gay Western Cape (www.missgay.co.za) November; beauty pageant in Cape Town.

MCQP (www.mcqp.co.za) December; fancy dress dance party in Cape Town.

GLBT by Neighbourhood

➡ **De Waterkant** (p52) This compact 'gaybourhood' offers the full party from disco and drag to leather and near naked barmen. At its cruisiest on a Friday and Saturday night.

➡ **Sea Point to Hout Bay** (p108) Sea Point has long had a gay vibe; Clifton No 3 is the beach for the beautiful, Sandy Bay for nudists.

➡ **Gardens & Surrounds** (p86) Inner city 'hoods with a sprinkling of GLBT-run and friendly guesthouses, cafes and restaurants.

NEED TO KNOW

Information

➡ *The Pink Map* (www. mapsinfo.co.za)

➡ *Pink South Africa* (www.pinksa.co.za)

➡ Gaynet Cape Town (www.gaynetcapetown. co.za)

➡ Mamba (www.mam baonline.com)

➡ Girl Ports (www. girlports.com/lesbi antravel/destinations/ cape_town)

➡ Cape Town.tv (www. capetown.tv)

Magazines & Newspapers

➡ *Alice* (www.alicemag azine.co.za)

➡ *Pink Tongue* (www. pinktongue.co.za)

➡ *Out Africa Magazine*

Support

Triangle Project (☏021-448 3812; www.triangle. org.za)

Movies

➡ *Skoonheid* (Beauty) Oliver Hermanus's Afrikaans-language drama won the Gay Palm at Cannes in 2011.

➡ *Darling! The Pieter-Dirky Uys Story* (http:// pdudarlingmovie.word press.com) Documentary about the national acting icon and AIDS activist.

➡ *The World Unseen* A lesbian love story set in 1950s Cape Town.

➡ *Glitterboys & Ganglands* Insightful documentary that goes behind the scenes of the annual Miss Gay Western Cape beauty pageant.

Lonely Planet's Top Choices

Glen Boutique Hotel (p196) Glam Sea Point digs hosting monthly 'Shame' pool parties.

Crew Bar (p69) The most happening of De Waterkant's late night clubs with muscular bar men.

Beaulah Bar (p69) Fun club for the girls – but welcoming to the boys too.

Deon Nagel's Gat Party (p147) Experience a gay old dance, Afrikaans style.

Clifton No 3 (p110) See and be seen on the cruisiest of Clifton's quartet of beaches.

Beefcakes (p66) Burger bar with campy bingo, drag shows and topless muscular boy waiters.

Best GLBT Stays

De Waterkant House (p191)

Amsterdam Guest House (p194)

Colette's (p199)

Huijs Haerlem (p196)

Best GLBT Friendly Bars

Alexander Bar & Café (p67)

Amsterdam Action Bar (p69)

Bubbles (p69)

Bar Code (p69)

Best GLBT Friendly Eats

Savoy Cabbage (p64)

Lazari (p92)

Cafe Manhattan (p69)

La Petite Tarte (p66)

Wineries

With over 200 wine farms within a day's drive, Cape Town is the natural hub for touring the Western Cape's Winelands. This is where South Africa's wine industry – in 2010 the eighth-largest in the world – began back in the 17th century; for more about the history of wine at the Cape see p229.

Growing Industry

Scores of new wine producers join the industry each year, and while many are content to remain as micro-wineries, honing their wines to perfection, others are seeking to capitalise on the industry's popularity by adding museums, restaurants, accommodation, walking trails and other attractions. We review the more notable of these, along with vineyards that are renowned for their fine wines.

Wine Varieties

Reds Regular pinotage, a cross between pinot noir and cinsaut, which produces a very bold wine, is the Cape's signature grape. Together with other robust red varieties such as shiraz (syrah) and cabernet sauvignon, it's being challenged by lighter blends of cabernet sauvignon, merlot, shiraz and cabernet franc, which are closer in style to bordeau.

Whites The most common variety of white wine is chenin blanc. In the last decade or so, more fashionable varieties such as chardonnay and sauvignon blanc have been planted on a wide scale. Other widely planted whites include colombard, semillon and sweet muscats. Table whites, especially chardonnay, once tended to be heavily oaked and high in alcohol, but lighter, more fruity whites are now in the ascendancy. For good sauvignon blancs, look to wineries in the cooler regions of Constantia, Elgin and Hermanus.

Sparkling Méthode Cap Classique (MCC) is the name that South Africa's wine industry has come up with for its champenoise-style wines: many are as good as, or even better than, the real thing.

Fortified The Worcester region is the country's leading producer of fortified wines, including port, brandy and South Africa's own *hanepoot*. This dessert wine is made from the Mediterranean grape variety known as muscat of Alexandria to produce a sweet, high-alcohol tipple for the domestic market.

Wineries by Region

➡ **Constantia** (www.constantiavalley.com; p121) South Africa's oldest wine farm area with nine wineries on the route, all within 30 minutes' drive of the city centre.

➡ **Durbanville** (www.durbanvillewine.co.za; p148) Around 20 minutes' drive north of the city centre, this coastal region offers 12 vineyards.

➡ **Stellenbosch** (www.wineroute.co.za; p151) The first region to promote a 'wine route', it remains South Africa's largest, with more than 200 wineries and five sub-routes to follow.

➡ **Franschhoek** (www.franschhoekwines.co.za; p156) Ideal for those who like to drink rather than sip and spit because several wineries are within walking or cycling distance of the town centre.

➡ **Paarl** (www.paarlwine.co.za; p160) Another centuries-old vine-growing region, particularly known for its shiraz and viognier.

Planning Your Wine Tour

Just starting out? Heed the following and you'll never be caught confusing your *vin rouge* with your vanity.

Starting Off Call ahead to any estates you want to visit to make sure they're open and not too crowded (some get very busy from December to February). Allow around an hour for tasting at each estate. It's worth joining at least one cellar tour; these can be fascinating. Appoint a designated driver. For those

NEED TO KNOW

Reading Up

Platter's South African Wine Guide
(www.wineonaplatter.com) The definitive
guide to the nation's wines, providing
tasting notes on thousands of locally
produced drops to which it awards star
ratings.

Top 100 SA Wines (www.top
100sawines.com) An annual book and
ongoing website.

Courses

The Cape Wine Academy (☎021-889
8844; www.capewineacademy.co.za)
Runs wine-appreciation courses in Stellenbosch, Cape Town and other locations
around the Western Cape.

Fynbos Estate (www.fynbosestate.
co.za) Hands-on winemaking courses
(one day R450 per person) in the Paardeberg mountains, 15km outside Malmesbury, an hour's drive from Cape Town.

Shopping

There are several wine shops in Cape
Town with excellent selections, including
Vaughan Johnson's Wine & Cigar Shop
and Wine Concepts.

Other Wine Regions

If you have more time, the following
wine-growing regions are all within a
day's drive of Cape Town.

➡ **Robertson** (www.robertsonwineval
ley.com)

➡ **Tulbagh** (www.route62.co.za)

➡ **Darling** (www.darlingtourism.co.za/
wineartdetail.htm)

➡ **Hemel en Aarde** (http://hermanus.
com/winetasting.mv)

➡ **Elgin** (www.elginvalley.co.za)

Brandy

The Western Cape Brandy Route links up
distilleries at 14 wineries; for more information contact the South African Brandy
Foundation (☎021-882 8954; www.
sabrandy.co.za).

without their own wheels, there are plenty of tours
of the Winelands (p25).

Tasting Many (but not all) cellars will charge you
for tasting – usually a little, sometimes a lot, and
often refundable with a minimum purchase. You
might get to take home the logo-carrying glass
you tasted from – it saves them the washing up,
and gives you a souvenir. Usually the server (who
could even be the winemaker at a small family
winery) will guide you through the range, starting
with whites (dry then less dry), moving through
reds, then on to sweet and fortified wines. To get
the most out of it all, give the wine a deep sniff,
then swirl a little round your mouth – then spit
that out in the spittoon provided (save swallowing
for the ones you really like). Drain the glass before
moving on, but don't bother rinsing – better a
stray drop of different wine than dilution!

Ageing Producers will usually sell their wine soon
after it's bottled, and most of it is then ready to
drink. Even many serious red wines these days are
designed to give youthful pleasure – though an
estate may recommend waiting a year or longer
to get the benefit of mature flavours. Good restaurants will often sell particular reds and whites
after some bottle ageing.

Buying Intercontinental delivery is expensive, so
check the cost before buying a crate. Wine prices
vary hugely, of course: there's a big bulge between
R50 and R150 for good reds and whites, and an
increasing number of grand wines going for much
higher than that.

Lonely Planet's Top Choices

Babylonstoren (p162) New wines and artisan food on a magnificently reimagined estate with amazing culinary garden.

Solms-Delta (p157) Excellent museum, inventive wines, local music, indigenous garden and a beautiful riverside picnic area.

Boschendal (p157) Historic estate, stunning location, posh nosh and picnics.

Buitenverwachting (p120) The blissful picnics on this old Constantia estate are complemented by luscious wines.

Vergelegen (p154) Handsome heritage building, rose gardens and a revamped restaurant.

Fairview (p160) Great value wine and cheese tasting, plus tower-climbing goats!

Best for Tastings

Klein Constantia (p120)

L'Avenir (p153)

Meerlust Estate (p154)

Steenberg Vineyards (p120)

La Motte (p157)

Best for Sparkling Wine

Steenberg Vineyards (p120)

Villiera (p151)

Haute Cabrière (p158)

Laborie Cellar (p161)

Best for Food

Constantia Uitsig (p120)

Steenberg Vineyards (p120)

La Motte (p157)

Tokara (p152)

Waterkloof (p154)

Best for Families

Groot Constantia (p119)

Blaauwklippen (p153)

Spier (p153)

Villiera (p151)

Backsberg (p161)

Best for Views

Durbanville Hills (p148)

Delaire Graff Estate (p151)

Mont Rochelle (p157)

Landskroon (p162)

Warwick Estate (p151)

Waterkloof (p154)

Best for Accommodation

Delaire Graff Estate (p151)

Grande Provence (p158)

Chamonix (p157)

Spier (p153)

L'Avenir (p153)

Best off the Beaten Track

Ntida (p148)

Groote Poste (p168)

Bouchard Finlayson (p169)

Elgin Wine Route (p167)

Eagle's Nest (p120)

Best for Art

Glen Carlou (p162)

Grande Provence (p158)

Tokara (p152)

La Motte (p157)

Explore Cape Town & the Garden Route

CAPE TOWN'S
TOP SIGHTS

Neighbourhoods at a Glance

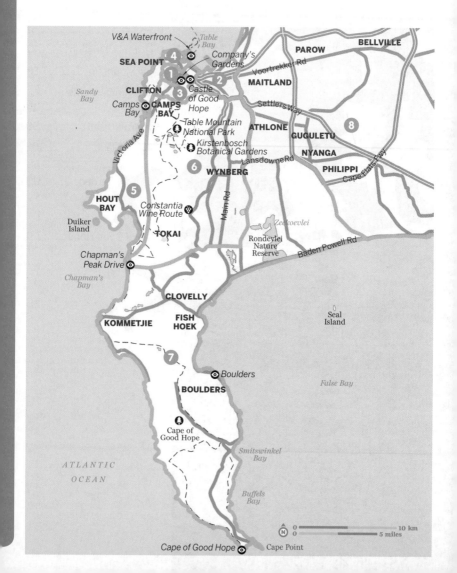

V&A Waterfront
Table Bay
PAROW
BELLVILLE
Company's Gardens
SEA POINT
Voortrekker Rd
MAITLAND
Sandy Bay
CLIFTON
Castle of Good Hope
Settlers Way
Camps Bay
CAMPS BAY
Table Mountain National Park
ATHLONE
GUGULETU
Victoria Ave
Kirstenbosch Botanical Gardens
NYANGA
Lansdowne Rd
PHILIPPI
WYNBERG
Cape Flats Hwy
HOUT BAY
Constantia Wine Route
Main Rd
Duiker Island
Zeekoevlei
TOKAI
Rondevlei Nature Reserve
Baden Powell Rd
Chapman's Peak Drive
Chapman's Bay
CLOVELLY
Seal Island
KOMMETJIE
FISH HOEK
False Bay
Boulders
BOULDERS
Cape of Good Hope
ATLANTIC OCEAN
Smitswinkel Bay
Buffels Bay
0   10 km
0   5 miles
Cape of Good Hope
Cape Point

❶ City Bowl, Foreshore, Bo-Kaap & De Waterkant

The City Bowl, where the Dutch first set up shop, includes many historic sights and businesses. Landfill created the Foreshore district in the 1940s and 1950s, now dominated by Duncan Dock and the convention centre. Tumbling down Signal Hill are the colourfully painted houses of the Bo-Kaap and, to the northeast, Cape Town's pink precinct De Waterkant, a retail and party hub. **p52**

❷ East City Corridor

No tfar from the City Bowl is the creative industries' enclave that's been dubbed The Fringe. Next door, the empty plots of District Six are set to be developed in the coming years. Woodstock and Salt River continue to attract the attention of developers and the art set, but are yet to fully gentrify. Bohemian rules at Observatory near Cape Town University. **p75**

❸ Gardens & Surrounds

From the cluster of museums at the south end of the Company's Gardens up the slopes of Table Mountain is the wider area known as Gardens. Small neighbourhoods within here include Tamboerskloof, Oranjezicht, Higgovale and Vredehoek – all desirable residential suburbs with views of Table Bay and immediate access to Table Mountain. Kloof St and Kloof Nek Rd are the main retail strips. **p86**

❹ Green Point & Waterfront

Green Point's common includes a new park and the Cape Town Stadium, built for the 2010 World Cup. Fronting Table Bay is the V&A Waterfront shopping, entertainment and residential development, commonly known simply as the Waterfront, as well as the residential Mouille Point. **p97**

❺ Sea Point to Hout Bay

Sea Point blends into ritzier Bantry Bay and Clifton before culminating in the prime real estate of Camps Bay. After here, urban development is largely curtailed by the national park until you reach delightful Hout Bay, which has good access to both the city and the vineyards of Constantia. **p108**

❻ Southern Suburbs

The lush eastern slopes of Table Mountain are covered by the areas known collectively as the Southern Suburbs. Here you'll find Kirstenbosch Botanical Gardens, the rugby and cricket grounds of Newlands, the centuries old vineyards of Constantia and the shady forests of Tokai. **p116**

❼ Simon's Town & Southern Peninsula

On the False Bay side of the peninsula are the charming communities of Muizenberg, Kalk Bay and Simon's Town, plus the penguins living at Boulders. More wildlife and incredible landscapes are protected within the national park at Cape Point. On the Atlantic coast side, Kommetjie is beloved by surfers and the broad beach at Noordhoek by horse riders. **p129**

❽ Cape Flats & Northern Suburbs

The vast black townships and poor coloured suburbs southeast of Table Mountain are known collectively as the Cape Flats. Cheek by jowl with Langa, but a world apart, is the formerly white-only garden suburb of Pinelands. North along Table Bay lie Milnerton and Bloubergstrand. **p143**

City Bowl, Foreshore, Bo-Kaap & De Waterkant

CITY BOWL | FORESHORE | BO-KAAP | DE WATERKANT

Neighbourhood Top Five

1 Learn about the history of Cape Town at the **Castle of Good Hope** (p54), the 17th-century pentagonal stone fortress built by the Dutch that once guarded Table Bay.

2 Explore the cobbled streets of the rainbow-painted **Bo-Kaap** (p57).

3 Wander the lush, historic **Company's Gardens** (p55).

4 Shop and party along **Long Street** (p58), lined with grand Victorian buildings.

5 Browse the daily craft market on cobbled **Greenmarket Square** (p58).

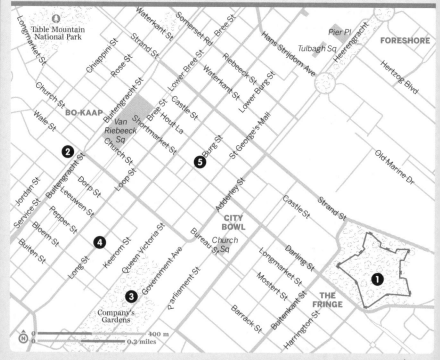

For more detail of this area, see Map p264 and p268 ➡

Explore City Bowl, Foreshore, Bo-Kaap & De Waterkant

The City Bowl, bordered by Buitenkant St to the southeast, Buitengracht St to the northwest, and Orange St and Annandale Rd to the south, is the Mother City's commercial and historical heart, home to the castle and garden set out by the original Dutch settlers, as well as the nation's parliament and newest skyscrapers. During the day it bustles with colourful street life, from the art and souvenir stalls lining the length of St George's Mall to the flower sellers of Trafalgar Pl off Adderley St. You'll most likely spend at least a couple of days looking around the sights in this part of town, and a night or two on Long St.

Other parts of the City Bowl turn deathly quiet come nightfall, though this is slowly changing as more and more old office blocks and commercial buildings are transformed into swanky apartments. New buildings are also planned for the Foreshore, the bleak swathe of reclaimed land between Strand St and Table Bay, including an extension to the Cape Town Convention Centre, and the 150m-tall Portside, Cape Town's first post-apartheid skyscraper.

Further to the west, up the slopes of Signal Hill, is the Bo-Kaap, a predominantly Muslim area of brightly painted houses where time is measured by the regular calls to prayer from the suburb's many mosques. Immediately to its northeast is De Waterkant, a chic, party-district personality much favoured by Cape Town's gay community.

Local Life

➡ **Markets** Buy a bunch of roses or proteas from the flower vendors at Trafalgar Place flower market (p60).
➡ **Party** Bar hop along Bree St on Thursday night between &Union, Clarke's and Jason Bakery when the latter opens late for pizza and beer (p64).
➡ **Parades** Cheer on the marchers in the Cape Town Minstrel Carnival parades on New Year's Eve and 2 January (p20).

Getting There & Away

➡ **Walk & Cycle** Fine as there's lots of street security. There are dedicated cycle routes, too, but motorists sometimes block them.
➡ **Bus** Golden Acre Bus Terminal is next to the Grand Parade. MyCiTi bus routes connect the hub of Civic Centre with Gardens, De Waterkant and the Waterfront.
➡ **Shared Taxis** Plenty of these stop on Strand St and Long St.
➡ **Train** Cape Metro Rail trains and long-distance buses terminate at Cape Town Train Station.

Lonely Planet's Top Tip

At the south end of St George's Mall near a slab of the Berlin Wall, the **Earth-Fair Food Market** (www.earthfairmarket.co.za; ◷11am-4pm Thu) is a good place to buy artisan food products or grab a healthy lunch; if it's raining it moves inside Mandela Rhodes Place.

Best Places to Eat

➡ Bombay Brasserie (p62)
➡ Bizerca Bistro (p62)
➡ Dear Me (p64)
➡ Africa Café (p64)
➡ Savoy Cabbage (p64)

For reviews, see p62 ➡

Best Places to Drink

➡ Waiting Room (p67)
➡ Alexander Bar & Café (p67)
➡ &Union (p67)
➡ Tjing Tjing (p67)

For reviews, see p67 ➡

Best Places to Shop

➡ Africa Nova (p73)
➡ Streetwires (p73)
➡ Church (p71)
➡ African Music Store (p71)
➡ Monkeybiz (p73)
➡ Merchants on Long (p71)

For reviews, see p71 ➡

TOP SIGHTS
CASTLE OF GOOD HOPE

The blue-stone-walled pentagonal castle is the nation's oldest colonial building, dating from between 1666 and 1679. It replaced the original 1652 clay and timber fort built by VOC (Vereenigde Oost-Indische Compagnie; Dutch East India Company) Commander Jan van Riebeeck. Before the Foreshore district was created in the 1940s, the sea lapped up to the walls.

The Layout

The castle is very well protected with defensive bastions jutting out from its five corners. Climb up to and around these to take in the fort's layout and for the view across the Grand Parade. Along the Leerdam Bastion, as well as on the approach to the main entrance gate over the moat, fly the six national flags commemorating who has been in power during the castle's history.

Across the fort's centre and around its walls are various buildings, some of which continue to be used by the military. You can peep into the torture chamber, see a replica of the forge and a reconstruction of the 18th-century bakery (Het Bakhuys) and Dolphin Pool, so called because of the ornate dolphin fountain at its centre.

The Museums

The interesting **Castle Military Museum** (Map p264) occupies the castle's original bayside entrance. Inside you can see examples and vivid paintings of all the different military uniforms down the centuries as well as a very good exhibition on the Anglo-Boer War, and a shop selling military memorabilia.

A large chunk of the **William Fehr Collection** (www.iziko.org.za/static/page/william-fehr-collection) of oil paintings, furniture, ceramics, metal and glassware is displayed at the castle. Temporary exhibitions on a range of more contemporary themes are also held here. Fronting this building is a beautifully restored 18th-century balcony with pediment bas-relief created by the German sculptor, Anton Anreith.

Next door is the **Secunde's House** (Map p264), which once housed the Cape's vice governor and was the administrative heart of Cape Town during VOC control. There's no original furniture here but the rooms are designed to reflect what they would have looked like during the 17th, 18th and 19th centuries. Restoration has revealed some the house's original wall paintings.

Ceremonies, Tours & Events

A traditional key ceremony is performed at 10am and noon from Monday to Friday, followed by the firing of a cannon. On public holidays, volunteer guides from the Canon Association of South Africa hold public demonstrations of how to fire a canon.

Included in the admission fee are **guided tours** (⊙11am, noon & 2pm Mon-Sat); extra are hour-long **horse and carriage rides** (☑021-704 6908; www.ctcco.co.za; adult/child R150/50; ⊙10.30am, 12.45pm & 2.45pm) for which bookings are essential.

Special outdoor events and held occasionally in the castle, including the Cape Town Military Tattoo (www.capetattoo.co.za) one weekend in November.

DON'T MISS

⇒ Walking the fortifications
⇒ Castle Military Museum
⇒ William Fehr Collection
⇒ Traditional military ceremonies

PRACTICALITIES

⇒ Map p264
⇒ ☑021-787 1249
⇒ www.castleofgoodhope.co.za
⇒ Main entrance off Buitenkant St, City Bowl
⇒ adult/child R28/12, Sun adult/child R20/5
⇒ ⊙9am-4pm
⇒ ⓟDarling St side of Castle
⇒ ⓠGolden Acre Bus Terminal

TOP SIGHTS
COMPANY'S GARDENS

What was once the vegetable patch for the Dutch East India Company (VOC) is now a verdant escape in the heart of the city, where many locals can be found relaxing on the lawns in the shade of centuries-old trees. The primary focus is the Public Garden but many other interesting buildings and landmarks are found around the Garden's main pedestrian thoroughfare Government Ave.

DON'T MISS

➡ Public Garden
➡ De Tuynhuis
➡ Delville Wood Memorial
➡ National Library of South Africa
➡ Centre for the Book

PRACTICALITIES

➡ Map p264
➡ Government Ave, City Bowl
➡ Admission free
➡ ⊙Public Garden 7am-7pm
➡ 🚊Government Ave or Dorp

The Garden's History

The Company's Garden began to be cultivated in April 1652 as soon as the VOC's first officials arrived at the Cape. *Grachten* (irrigation channels) were dug to lead water from the streams that flowed down Table Mountain and these eventually determined the shape not only of the garden but also the city's original streets and boundaries. By the end of the 17th century, pathways, fountains and even a menagerie had been established in the area.

It was during the 19th century that the gardens began to take on the shape that they have today. Chunks of the grounds were carved off for buildings including St Georges Cathedral, the Houses of Parliament and the South African Museum. In 1848 the lower part of the area became a public Botanical Garden and in the 1920s the construction of the Delville Wood Memorial radically changed the upper part of the Garden close to the South Africa Museum.

The Public Garden

Planted with a fine collection of botanical specimens, including frangipanis, African flame trees, aloes and roses, the **Public Garden** is the area's highlight. The oldest recorded specimen is a Saffron pear tree, in the region of 300 years old and still bearing fruit.

The Delville Wood Memorial honours the 2000-plus South African soldiers who fell during a five-day WWI battle. The ensemble's elements include Alfred Turner's sculptures of Castor and Pollux, representing the unity of British and Boer soldiers, Anton van Wouw's statue of General Henry Lukin (who gave the order to advance on Delville Wood) and a WWI artillery gun.

EATING

Shaded by giant old Eucalyptus trees and many red umbrellas, the **Garden Tea Room** (Public Garden; mains R40-100; ◔8am-5pm) is a pleasant spot to grab simple refreshments, including a beer.

The squirrels that scamper around were imported from North America by the politician and mining magnate Cecil Rhodes. A bronze **statue** of Rhodes was erected in 1908 on a plinth carved with the phrase 'Your hinterland is there' as the Imperialist points towards the heart of the continent. Other things to discover here include a small aviary; a fake 'slave bell' erected in 1911; a herb and succulent garden; a rose garden designed in 1929; and the Chalet, a public lavatory on the Queen Victoria St side of the Garden, dating from 1895 and still in use.

Along Government Avenue

The original Company's Garden was bisected by the oak-lined Government Avenue, which has entrances off Wale St between St George's Cathedral and the Houses of Parliament, and Orange St. Along here, peer through ornate gates at the **De Tuynhuis** (The Garden House), a handsome building originally constructed in 1700 as a visitor's lodge. From the front gate you'll just about be able to make out the VOC's monogram on the pediment – as close as you'll get since De Tuynhuis is now an official office of South Africa's president, and off-limits to tourists. The design of the parterre garden dates from 1788 and was recreated in the 1960s.

Further south along Government Ave you'll pass the South African National Gallery and Great Synagogue and the tree-shaded, grassy lawns of the Paddocks where game animals were once kept. The only animals here now are made of plaster – the lions created by Anton Anreith in 1805 that grace the Lioness Gateway just behind the South African Museum.

Surrounding Buildings & Statues

The **National Library of South Africa** (◔9am-5pm Mon-Fri) facing the north end of the Garden, is a neoclassical building based on the Fitzwilliam Museum in Cambridge, UK, and holds a copy of nearly every document published in South Africa. Exhibitions are held here; enter to admire the central rotunda.

The library's annex, the **Centre for the Book** (62 Queen Victoria St; ◔8am-4pm Mon-Fri), is housed in a grand domed building to the east of the park, first opened in 1913. It also has a beautiful central reading room and is sometimes used for concerts.

Two **statues of Jan Smuts**, former general and prime minister (1870–1950), stand at opposite ends of Government Ave. The more attractive and abstract one by Sydney Harpley is in front of the South African National Gallery. When unveiled in 1964, though, a storm of protest resulted in the more traditional second statue by Ivan Mitford-Barberton beside the Slave Lodge.

TOP SIGHTS
BO-KAAP

Literally meaning 'Upper Cape, the Bo-Kaap, with its vividly painted low-roofed houses strung along narrow cobbled streets, is one of the most-photographed sections of the city. Initially a garrison for soldiers in the mid-18th century, this is where freed slaves started to settle after emancipation in the 1830s.

Centre of Muslim Life
The Cape Malay people built many mosques in the Bo-Kaap including in 1789, the **Auwal Mosque** (34 Dorp St). The oldest place of Islamic worship in South Africa was established by Iman Abdullah Kadi Salaam, an Indonesian prince who served time on Robben Island where he wrote a copy of the Koran from memory.

Bo-Kaap Museum
Drop by the small but interesting **Bo-Kaap Museum** (www.iziko.org.za/museums/bo-kaap -museum; 71 Wale St; adult/child R10/free; ⏰10am-5pm Mon-Sat), which provides some insight into the lifestyle of a 19th-century Cape Muslim family, and a somewhat idealised view of Islamic practice in Cape Town. The most interesting exhibit, although it lacks decent captions, is the selection of black-and-white photos of local life displayed in the upstairs room.

Picturesque Streets
Photos from the 1950s show that the Bo-Kaap didn't used to be so well kept; the bright paint jobs are actually a post-democracy development. In parts of the Bo-Kaap poverty remains evident and away from the main streets it is not safe to walk around at night. By day the area is a pleasure to explore, with the most picturesque streets being Chiappini, Rose and Wale; drop by the atmospheric **Atlas Trading Company** (94 Wale St) where the pungent smell of over 100 different herbs, spices and incense perfumes the air.

DON'T MISS
➡ Chiappini St
➡ Rose St
➡ Bo-Kaap Museum
➡ Atlas Trading Company
➡ Auwal Mosque

PRACTICALITIES
➡ Map p264
➡ 🚇Dorp

◉ SIGHTS

City Bowl & Foreshore

CASTLE OF GOOD HOPE CASTLE
See p54

FREE **COMPANY'S GARDENS** GARDENS
See p55

LONG STREET SHOPPING, ARCHITECTURE
Map p264 (Long Street, City Bowl; 🚇Dorp)
This busy commercial and nightlife thoroughfare, partly lined with Victorian-era buildings featuring lovely wrought-iron balconies, once formed the border of the Muslim Bo-Kaap. Along it you'll find several old mosques, including the **Palm Tree Mosque** (185 Long St), dating from 1780, as well as the **SA Mission Museum** (40 Long St; admission free; ☺9am-6pm Mon-Fri), the oldest Mission church in South Africa.

By the 1960s, the street had fallen into disrepute and it remained that way until the late 1990s, when savvy developers realised the street's potential. The most attractive section runs from the junction with Buitensingel St north to around Strand St. Whether you come to browse the antique shops, secondhand bookshops or the streetwear boutiques, or party at the host of bars and clubs that crank up at night, a stroll along Long St is an essential element of a Cape Town visit.

**MICHAELIS COLLECTION
AT THE OLD TOWN HOUSE** MUSEUM
Map p264 (www.iziko.org.za/museums/michaelis-collection-at-the-old-town-house; Greenmarket Sq, City Bowl; admission R10; ☺10am-5pm Mon-Sat; 🚇Longmarket) On the south side of Greenmarket Sq is the beautifully restored Old Town House, a Cape rococo building dating from 1755 that was once City Hall. It now houses the impressive art collection of Sir Max Michaelis. Dutch and Flemish paintings and etchings from the 16th and 17th centuries (including works by Rembrandt, Frans Hals and Anthony van Dyck) hang side by side with contemporary works – the contrasts between old and new are fascinating. The cool interior is a relief from the buzzing market outside, while the **Scotch Coffee House** (☺7am-4.30pm Mon-Fri, 8am-3pm Sat) in the leafy courtyard

behind is worth considering for a drink or light lunch.

**GREENMARKET
SQUARE** ARCHITECTURE, MARKET
Map p264 (Greenmarket Sq, City Bowl; 🚇Longmarket) This cobbled square is Cape Town's second-oldest public space after the Grand Parade and hosts a lively and colourful daily crafts and souvenir market. Apart from the Old Town House, it's also surrounded by some choice examples of art deco architecture. On the corner of Shortmarket St is **Namaqua House**; the cafe Baran's here has a wrap-around balcony providing a great view over the square. **Kimberley House** (34 Shortmarket St) is built of sandstone and decorated with an attractive diamond-theme design. Fronting onto the square, **Market House** is the most elaborately decorated building of all and has majestic stone-carved eagles and flowers on its facade as well as balconies. Next door, the dazzling-white **Protea Insurance Building** was built in 1928 and renovated in 1990. Opposite is **Shell House**, once the South African headquarters of Shell and now housing a hotel and restaurant.

**GOLD OF AFRICA
BARBIER-MUELLER MUSEUM** MUSEUM
Map p264 (📞021-405 1540; www.goldofafrica.com; 96 Strand St, City Bowl; adult/child R35/25; ☺9.30am-5pm Mon-Sat; 🚇Castle) A third of the world's gold is produced in South Africa. In this glitzy museum, based in the historic Martin Melck House (dating from 1783), gorgeous gold jewellery from across the continent is displayed. There are some stunning pieces, mostly from West Africa, with lots of background information. The shop is worth a browse for interesting gold souvenirs, including copies of some of the pieces in the museum. Return in the evening for the good Gold restaurant or to take the night tour of the museum (adult/child R60/40), which includes a glass of wine with flakes of gold leaf and for which you need to book.

CHURCH ST MARKET, MONUMENTS
Map p264 (Church St, City Bowl; 🚇Longmarket) The pedestrianised portion of this street, between Burg and Long Sts, hosts a **flea market** (☺8am-3pm Mon-Sat) and has several art galleries. At the Burg St end *The Purple Shall Govern* memorial is a piece of graphic art by Conrad Botes commemorating a 1989 anti-apartheid march. Outside the

AVA Gallery is the *Arm Wrestling Podium* by Johann van der Schijff.

FREE **HOUSES OF PARLIAMENT**   PARLIAMENT

Map p264 (☎021-403 2266; www.parliament.gov.za; Parliament St, City Bowl; ☺tours 9am-noon Mon-Thu, 9am-noon & 2-4pm Fri; ☐Dorp) A tour around parliament is fascinating, especially if you're interested in the country's modern history. Opened in 1885, the hallowed halls have seen some pretty momentous events; this is where British Prime Minister Harold Macmillan made his 'Wind of Change' speech in 1960, and where President Hendrik Verwoerd, architect of apartheid, was stabbed to death in 1966. Call ahead and present your passport to gain entry.

SLAVE LODGE   MUSEUM

Map p264 (www.iziko.org.za/museums/slave-lodge; 49 Adderley St, City Bowl; adult/child R20/10; ☺10am-5pm Mon-Sat; ☐Dorp) This museum, mainly devoted to the history and experience of slaves and their descendants in the Cape, also has artefacts from ancient Egypt, Greece, Rome and the Far East on the 1st floor.

One of the oldest buildings in South Africa, dating back to 1660, the Slave Lodge has a fascinating history in itself. Until 1811 the building was home, if you could call it that, to as many as 1000 slaves, who lived in damp, insanitary, crowded conditions; up to 20% died each year. The slaves were bought and sold just around the corner on Spin St.

From the late 18th century the lodge was used as a brothel, a jail, a mental asylum, a post office, a library and the Cape Supreme Court until 1914. The walls of the original Slave Lodge flank the interior courtyard, where you can find the tombstones of Cape Town's founder, Jan van Riebeeck, and his wife, Maria de la Queillerie. The tombstones were moved here from Jakarta where Van Riebeeck is buried.

MUTUAL HEIGHTS   ARCHITECTURE

Map p264 (cnr Parliament & Darling Sts, City Bowl; ☐St George's) Clad in rose- and gold-veined black marble and decorated with one of the longest continuous stone friezes in the world (designed by Ivan Mitford-Barberton and chiselled by master stonemasons the Lorenzi brothers), Mutual Heights is the most impressive of the City Bowl's collection of art deco structures. Commissioned by the Old Mutual financial company, this was once not only the tallest structure in Africa bar the Pyramids, but also the most expensive.

Unfortunately the building's opening in 1939 was eclipsed by the start of WWII. Additionally, its prime position on the Foreshore was immediately made redundant when the city decided to extend the land 2km further into the bay. Old Mutual started moving its business out of the building to Pinelands in the 1950s. Made into apartments and renamed Mutual Heights in 2002, it kicked off a frenzy among developers to convert similarly long-neglected and empty city-centre office blocks. Much of the building's original detail and decoration has been preserved, including the impressive central banking space (sadly not open for general viewing).

ST GEORGE'S CATHEDRAL   CHURCH

Map p264 (www.stgeorgescathedral.com; 1 Wale St, City Bowl; ☐Dorp) Designed by Sir Herbert Baker at the turn of the 19th century, its official name is the Cathedral Church of St George the Martyr in Cape Town. However, it's more commonly known as St George's Cathedral, or the People's Cathedral, since this was one of the few places of worship that was open to people of all races during apartheid. Archbishop Desmond Tutu presided here and made the cathedral a focus of opposition to the Afrikaner regime – something you can learn more about if you look around the exhibition in the Memory & Witness Centre in the Crypt, where you'll also find the good Café St George. The Cathedral remains a beacon of hope through its HIV/AIDS outreach program – note the Cape Town AIDS quilt hanging above the north door. Classical concerts are sometimes held here; see the website for details as well as times of daily services.

CHURCH SQUARE   CHURCH, MONUMENTS

Map p264 (Church Sq; ☐Dorp) So named because this is where you'll find **Groote Kerk** (www.grootekerk.org.za; Church Sq, City Bowl; admission free; ☺10am-2pm Mon-Fri, services 10am & 7pm Sun; ☐Dorp), the mother church of the Dutch Reformed Church (Nederduitse Gereformeerde Kerk; NG Kerk). Go inside to see the mammoth organ and ornate Burmese teak pulpit, carved by master sculptors Anton Anreith and Jan Graaff. The building's otherwise an architectural mishmash with parts dating from the 1704 original and other bits from 1841. Facing

START **CAPE TOWN TOUR-ISM, CORNER CASTLE & BURG STS, CITY BOWL**

END **CHURCH SQ**

DISTANCE **1.5KM**

DURATION **ONE HOUR**

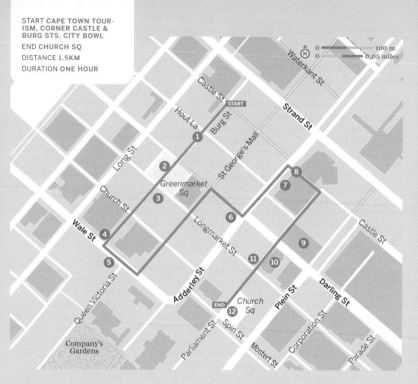

Neighbourhood Walk
Art & Architecture Walk

A building boom in Cape Town during the 1930s resulted in the city centre having a remarkable number of grand art deco buildings. This walk takes you past some of the key buildings. At 24 Burg St is ① **New Zealand House**, designed by WH Grant in a style known as Cape Mediterranean. Ahead is ② **Greenmarket Square**, which hosts a daily crafts and souvenir market. Three quarters of the buildings surrounding the square hail from the 1930s, the main exception being the ③ **Old Town House**, completed in 1761.

Exit the square on Burg St and continue to the junction with Wale St where the ④ **Waalburg Building** has a facade decorated with bronze and Table Mountain–stone panels depicting scenes of South African life. Opposite is the ⑤ **Western Cape Legislature**, its grey bulk enlivened by stone-carved animal heads.

Turn into St George's Mall and continue to Shortmarket St, where a right turn will bring you to the junction with Adderley St.

Here is the ⑥ **First National Bank**, completed in 1913, and one of the final projects of Sir Herbert Baker: pop inside to see some of the bank's original fittings. Head up Adderley St, past the grand Edwardian ⑦ **Standard Bank** and turn right into ⑧ **Trafalgar Place**, home to Cape Town's flower sellers.

At the end of the alleyway is the ⑨ **General Post Office**. Much of the ground floor has been taken over by market stalls. Look above them to discover colourful painted panels of Cape Town scenes.

Emerge onto Darling St to face ⑩ **Mutual Heights**. At the crossing of Parliament and Longmarket Sts is ⑪ **Mullers Opticians**, one of the most beautifully preserved art deco shopfronts in the city. A few steps further along Parliament St will bring you to ⑫ **Church Square** to see Groote Kerk, the mother church of the Dutch Reformed Church, facing the old National Building.

LOCAL KNOWLEDGE

ART AT 6 SPIN STREET

Apart from housing the restaurant 6 Spin Street and the Cape Town Democracy Centre, the building at this address is also home to a couple of site-specific art installations. Inside the main vaulted hall of the 1902 building, designed by Sir Herbert Baker, hangs Brendhan Dickerson and Petra Keinhorts' bronze-and-stainless-steel mobile sculpture *In The Balance*. This elegant piece speaks to many issues around democracy, such as how to balance competing interests.

The rear seminar room is dominated by Ed Young's *Arch*, a remarkable piece composed of a life-size model of Archbishop Desmond Tutu swinging from a chandelier and a text mural on the wall, the words of which change according to the artist's whims and the promises, slogans and issues of South African politics. It's both a fun and thought-provoking tribute to the much-loved Tutu.

the church from the other side of the square is the handsome old National Mutual Building, parts of which date to 1905; it now houses the Iziko Social History Centre.

In the square itself stands a **statue of Jan Hendrik**, one-time editor of the *Zuid Afrikaan* newspaper and a key figure behind the drafting of the 1909 South African constitution, as well as the **Slavery Memorial** – 11 low, black granite blocks engraved with the names of slaves or words relating to slavery, resistance and rebellion. It's a somewhat abstract memorial but at least more obvious than the circular plaque in the traffic island on adjacent Spin St that marks the location of the **Slave Tree** under which slaves were sold until emancipation in 1834.

GRAND PARADE & AROUND   SQUARE

Map p264 (Darling St, City Bowl; 🚌Golden Acre Bus Terminal) A prime location for Cape Town's history, the Grand Parade is where the Dutch built their first fort in 1652; slaves were sold and punished; crowds gathered to watch Nelson Mandela's first address to the nation as a free man after 27 years in jail from the balcony of the Old Town Hall; and the official FIFA fan park for the 2010 World Cup was set up. A market is held on part of the square which is also used for parking.

Facing the parade, the city has allotted R7 million for the renovation of the grand Edwardian **Cape Town City Hall** (Map p264), now used occasionally for music and cultural events. Nearby Drill Hall, dating from 1889 and where Queen Elizabeth II celebrated her 21st birthday, has been sensitively restored and turned into the city's **Central Library** (Darling Street, City Bowl; ⊙9am-8pm Mon, 9am-6pm Tue-Thu, 8.30am-5.30pm Fri, 9am-2pm Sat).

KOOPMANS-DE WET HOUSE   MUSEUM

Map p264 (www.iziko.org.za/museums/koopmans-de-wet-house; 35 Strand St, City Bowl; adult/child R10/free; ⊙10am-5pm Mon-Fri; 🚉St George's) Step back two centuries from 21st-century Cape Town when you enter this classic example of a Cape Dutch townhouse, furnished with 18th- and early-19th-century antiques. It's an atmospheric place with ancient vines growing in the courtyard and floorboards that squeak just as they probably did during the times of Marie Koopmans-de Wet, the socialite owner after whom the house is named.

LUTHERAN CHURCH   CHURCH

Map p264 (98 Strand St, City Bowl; ⊙10am-2pm Mon-Fri; 🚉Castle) Converted from a barn in 1780, the first Lutheran church in the Cape has a striking pulpit, perhaps the best created by the master German sculptor Anton Anreith, whose work can also be seen in Groote Kerk and at Groot Constantia. Go to the room behind the pulpit to see the collection of old Bibles.

HERITAGE SQUARE   ARCHITECTURE

Map p264 (www.heritage.org.za/heritage_square _project.htm; 90 Bree St, City Bowl; 🅿; 🚉Longmarket) This beautiful collection of Cape Georgian and Victorian buildings was saved from the wrecking ball in 1996. The complex includes the Cape Heritage Hotel, and the wine bar, deli and restaurant Caveau, plus a courtyard where you'll find a grape vine that has been growing here since the 1770s, making it the oldest such vine in South Africa. It still produces grapes from which wine is made. Appropriately the square is also home to the tasting room of **Signal Hill Wines** (http://winery.

synthasite.com; ⊙11am-6pm Mon-Fri, noon-4pm Sat), South Africa's only city based winery.

Bo-Kaap & De Waterkant

BO-KAAP NEIGHBOURHOOD

See p57.

FREE **SIGNAL HILL & NOON GUN** HILL

off Map p264 (Military Rd, Bo-Kaap; P) Separating Sea Point from the City Bowl, Signal Hill provides magnificent views from its 350m-high summit, especially at night. Once also known as Lion's Rump, as it is attached to Lion's Head by a 'spine' of hills, it is officially part of Table Mountain National Park. To reach the summit by road head up Kloof Nek Rd from the city and take the first turn-off to the right at the top of the hill.

Signal Hill was the early settlement's lookout point, and it was from here that flags were hoisted when a ship was spotted, giving the citizens below time to prepare their goods for sale and dust off their tankards.

At noon, Monday to Saturday, a cannon known as the **Noon Gun** is fired from the lower slopes of Signal Hill; you can hear it all over town. Traditionally, this allowed the burghers in the town below to check their watches. It's a stiff walk up here through the Bo-Kaap – take Longmarket St and keep going until it ends. The **Noon Gun Tearoom & Restaurant** (off Map p264) is a good place to catch your breath; a gate behind the restaurant is usually unlocked around 11.30am, beyond which it's another minute's walk to where to the canon is fired.

FREE **PRESTWICH MEMORIAL & PRESTWICH MEMORIAL GARDEN** MEMORIAL

Map p268 (cnr Somerset & Buitengracht Sts, De Waterkant; ⊙8am-6pm Mon-Fri, 8am-2pm Sat & Sun; ▣Prestwich) When construction of new apartments started in 2003 along nearby Prestwich St, many skeletons were uncovered – these were the unmarked graves of the unfortunate slaves and others executed by the Dutch in the 17th and 18th centuries on what was then known as Gallows Hill. The bones were exhumed and this memorial building, with an attractive facade of Robben Island slate, was created. It includes an ossuary, excellent interpretive displays (including a replica of the remarkable 360-degree panorama of Table Bay painted by Robert Gordon in 1778) and a branch of the coffee shop Truth.

In the memorial garden outside you can see the outline of tram tracks – horse-drawn trams once used to run past here along Somerset and down through Sea Point to terminate in Camps Bay – as well as a collection of quirky statues by Capetonian artists, including the rainbow arch *It's Beautiful Here* by Heath Nash and the *Full Cycle Tree* by KEAG.

✕ EATING

There's no shortage of places to eat in the city centre, with cafes plentiful around both Greenmarket Sq and St George's Mall. Note that many places are closed on Sundays. The Cape Quarter is the nexus around which De Waterkant's dining scene revolves. The Bo-Kaap has a few dining options up its sleeves, too; locals swear by the takeaway grilled chicken and other meats served up by the guy near the corner of Rose and Wale Sts.

City Bowl & Foreshore

TOP CHOICE **BOMBAY BRASSERIE** INDIAN $$

Map p264 (☑021-819 2000; www.tajhotels.com; Wale St, City Bowl; mains R150, 4-course menu R395; ⊙6-10.30pm Mon-Sat; P; ▣Dorp) Far from your average curry house, the Taj's main restaurant, hung with glittering chandeliers and mirrors, is darkly luxurious. Chef Harpreet Kaur's cooking is creative and delicious, and the presentation spot on, as is the service. Go on a spice journey with the four-course tasting menu.

TOP CHOICE **BIZERCA BISTRO** FRENCH, CONTEMPORARY $$

Map p268 (☑021-418 0001; www.bizerca.com; 15 Anton Anreith Arcade, Jetty St, Foreshore; mains R110-150; ▣Convention Centre) French chef Laurent Deslandes and his South African wife Cyrillia run this fantastic bistro – the atmosphere is contemporary and relaxed, and the expertly prepared food is bursting with flavour. Menu items, chalked up on a blackboard, are explained at the table by the knowledgeable waiters.

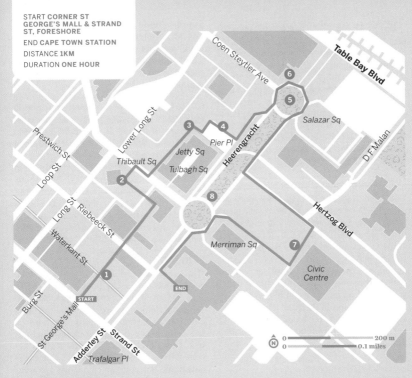

Coen Steytler Ave

Table Bay Blvd

Salazar Sq

D F Malan

Prestwich St

Lower Long St

Pier Pl

Heerengracht

Jetty Sq

Thibault Sq

Tulbagh Sq

Loop St

Long St

Riebeeck St

Hertzog Blvd

Waterkant St

Merriman Sq

Civic Centre

START

END

Burg St

St George's Mall

Adderley St Strand St

Trafalgar Pl

0   200 m
0   0.1 miles

Neighbourhood Walk
Foreshore Public Art Walk

The Foreshore isn't big on sightseeing, but on this walk you can explore around the concrete towers and plazas and take in sculptures both old and new.

On pedestrianised St George's Mall, opposite Waterkant St, is Brett Murray's quirky statue **1** **Africa**. This African-curio bronze statue, sprouting bright-yellow Bart Simpson heads, is typical of Murray's satirical style and caused much public debate on its unveiling in 2000.

At the end of St George's Mall turn left into Thibault Square surrounded by some the Foreshore's oldest skyscrapers including the ABSA Centre. In the square you can view **2** **Mythological Landscape**, a steel and bronze piece by John Skotnes that celebrates diversity.

Cross Mechau St and continue towards **3** **Jetty Square** where a school of steel sharks by Ralph Borland respond to passersby by swivelling on their poles.

Around the corner **4** **Pier Place** is scattered with the lifelike statues of people by Egon Tania.

In the middle of the roundabout at the Foreshore end of Heerengracht is a statue of the Portuguese sailor **5** **Bartholomeu Dias**, the first European recorded to have rounded the Cape of Good Hope in 1488. Across the road, beside the Cape Town International Convention Centre is the 8m-tall, red-painted man **6** **Olduvai** by Gavin Younge, a piece inspired by the Rift Valley and great lakes of East Africa.

Return towards the city down Heerengracht, detouring left on Hertzog Blvd. Near the Civic Centre is Edoardo Villa's **7** **The Knot**, which looks like a giant red paper clip bent out of shape. Back on Heerengracht, opposite Cape Town Train Station, are statues of **8** **Jan van Riebeeck and Maria de la Queillerie**, the first Dutch boss of Cape Town and his wife. This is apparently the spot where they stepped ashore in 1652.

TOP CHOICE **DEAR ME** CONTEMPORARY, DELI **$$**

Map p264 (☑021-422 4920; www.dearme.co.za; 165 Longmarket St, City Bowl; mains R100; ☺7am-4pm Mon-Fri, 7-10pm Thu; ☎; ☐Longmarket) High-quality ingredients, creatively combined and served by gracious staff in a pleasant playful space where pot plants dangle from the ceiling – what more could you wish for? Well they have a deli and bakery section, too. Reservation for their excellent Thursday-night gourmet dinners (3/5 courses R210/310) is essential.

TOP CHOICE **AFRICA CAFÉ** AFRICAN **$$**

Map p264 (☑021-422 0221; www.africacafe.co.za; 108 Shortmarket St, City Bowl; set banquet R245; ☺cafe 8am-4pm Mon-Fri, 10am-2pm Sat; restaurant 6.30-11pm Mon-Sat; ☐Longmarket) Touristy, yes, but still one of the best places to sample African food. Come with a hearty appetite as the set feast comprises some 15 dishes from across the continent, of which you can eat as much as you like. A wonderful new addition is their daytime cafe specialising in wheat-free baked goodies and a variety of tasty 'raw' foods including salads and cassava.

TOP CHOICE **SAVOY CABBAGE** MODERN SOUTH AFRICAN **$$**

Map p264 (☑021-424 2626; www.savoycabbage.co.za; 101 Hout Lane, City Bowl; mains R110-165; ☺noon-2.30pm Mon-Fri, 7-10.30pm Mon-Sat; ☐Longmarket) The long-running Savoy Cabbage remains a great place for inventive cooking, and gives diners the chance to try local game meats, like eland and springbok. The tomato tart is legendary.

6 SPIN ST RESTAURANT INTERNATIONAL **$$**

Map p264 (☑021-461 0666; www.6spinstreet.co.za; 6 Spin St, City Bowl; mains R75-160; ☺8.30am-10pm Mon-Fri, 6pm-10pm Sat; ☐Dorp) Robert Mulders' brings his personable restaurant skills and famous double-baked cheese soufflé to the elegant surrounds of this Sir Herbert Baker–designed building. You might also try Moroccan lamb with couscous or linefish roasted with a garlic crust.

JASON BAKERY BAKERY, CAFE **$**

Map p264 (www.jasonbakery.com; 185 Bree St, City Bowl; mains R50; ☺7am-3.30pm Mon-Sat; ☐Bloem) Good luck at securing a seat at this super-popular street-corner cafe that makes splendid breakfasts and sandwiches as well serving decent coffee, &Union beers and MCC bubbles by the glass and bottle. Good job that it has a take-away counter. Check them out on Thursday and Friday nights when they often stay open later for pizzas and drinks.

GOLD CAPE MALAY, AFRICAN **$$**

Map p264 (☑021-421 4653; www.goldrestaurant.co.za; 96 Strand St, City Bowl; set menu R250; ☺cafe 9am-4pm, restaurant 6.30-11pm; ☐Castle) Based inside the Gold of Africa Barbier-Mueller Museum, the main deal here is the evening set meal and show, which can include a *djembe* drumming session (R85 extra) at 6.30pm. The well-cooked, eat-as-much-as-you-like, Cape Malay and African cuisine buffet is complemented by a life-sized Malian puppet show.

95 KEEROM ITALIAN **$$**

Map p264 (☑021-422 0765; www.95keerom.com; 95 Keerom St, City Bowl; mains R60-120; ☺12.30-2pm Mon-Fri, 7pm-10.30pm Mon-Sat; ☐Bloem) Bookings are essential for this chic Italian restaurant, with an olive tree the centrepiece of the 1st floor. Chef-patron Giorgio Nava lays on the Italian accent with a trowel in his table-side presentations, but you can't fault his splendid pasta. If it's full, as it often is, meat lovers might want try Nava's premium steak restaurant **Carne SA** (Map p264; www.carne-sa.com) opposite.

ADDIS IN CAPE ETHIOPIAN **$**

Map p264 (☑021-424 5722; www.addisincape.co.za; 41 Church St, City Bowl; mains R75-90; ☺noon-2.30pm & 6.30-10.30pm Mon-Sat; ☎; ☐Longmarket) Sit at a low basket-weave table and enjoy tasty Ethiopian cuisine served traditionally on plate-sized *injera* (sourdough pancakes), which you rip up and use to eat with instead of cutlery. Also try their home-made *tej* (honey wine) and authentic Ethiopian coffee.

ROYALE EATERY GOURMET BURGERS **$**

Map p264 (☑021-422 4536; www.royaleeatery.com; 279 Long St, City Bowl; mains R60-70; ☺noon-11.30pm Mon-Sat; ☐Bloem) Gourmet burgers are grilled to perfection here; downstairs is casual and buzzy while upstairs is a restaurant where you can book a table. For something different try the Big Bird ostrich burger.

MASALA DOSA
INDIAN $

Map p264 (☏021-424 6772; www.masaladosa. co.za; 167 Long St, City Bowl; mains R40-85; ⏱noon-4.30pm & 6-10.30pm Mon-Sat; 🚇Dorp) Bollywood chic rules at this colourful South Indian cuisine outpost serving decent *dosas* (lentil pancakes) and *thalis* (set meals with a variety of curries). Get a group of eight together and the owner will run a cooking class (R350 per person) on the weekend.

CLARKE'S
AMERICAN $

Map p264 (☏021-422 7648; 133 Bree St, City Bowl; mains R30-50; ⏱8am-6pm Mon-Tue, 8am-2pm Wed-Thu, 8am-3pm Sat; 🚇Dorp) A focus of the Bree St hipster scene is this convivial spot with counter seating that pays homage to the US diner tradition. They do breakfast dishes, such as grilled cheese sandwiches and huevos rancheros, all day and reubens and pork belly sandwiches from lunch, as well as burgers and mac and cheese.

BIRDS CAFÉ
INTERNATIONAL $

Map p264 (127 Bree St, City Bowl; mains R40-70; ⏱7am-5pm Mon-Fri, 8am-3pm Sat; 🚇Longmarket) The sophisticated, rustic style (think milk-bottle crate seats in a grand old Dutch building) of this delightful cafe matches its artisanal food, including delicious homemade pies, strudels and chunky scones.

LOLA'S
INTERNATIONAL $

Map p264 (www.lolas.co.za; 228 Long St, City Bowl; mains R30-40; ⏱7am-9pm Mon-Sat, 7.30am-4pm Sun; 🕾; 🚇Bloem) Old Lola has traded her hippy veggie past for a trendier look and meatier menu. The vibe remains relaxed and the breakfasts, including sweetcorn fritters and eggs Benedict, are still good. Linger over a drink and watch Long St's passing parade.

FRIEDA'S ON BREE
INTERNATIONAL $

Map p268 (www.friedasonbree.co.za; 15 Bree St, Foreshore; mains R30-40; ⏱6.30am-3.30pm Mon-Fri; 🕾; 🚇Prestwich) Hung with paper lanterns and plastered with technicolour Indian posters, jumble-sale chic is the look at this huge, convivial cafe. It does a fine line in sandwiches, salads and comfort food, including lasagne. Check the website for regular evening events here such as **tango dancing** (R30; 6-8.30pm Tue), or the deep house club night **Svetbox** (R40; ⏱9pm-3am Fri).

HEMELHUIJS
INTERNATIONAL $$

Map p268 (021-418 2042; www.hemelhuijs.co.za; 71 Waterkant St, Foreshore; mains R60-120; 🕾; 🚇Prestwich) Part of the **Freeworld Design Centre** (www.freeworlddesigncentre.com; a showroom for a paint company that occasionally hosts interesting events such as a food-related movie nights or a designer goods market), Hemelhuijs is a quirkily decorated space – think deer heads with broken crockery and a mosaic made from toast – showcasing the art and culinary creations of Jacques Erasmus. The inventive food is delicious and includes lovely fresh juices and daily bakes.

KEENWÄ
PERUVIAN $

Map p268 (021-419 2633; www.keenwa.co.za; 50 Waterkant St, Foreshore; mains R50-100; 🕾; 🚇Prestwich) Avoiding the clichés of pan pipes and ponchos, owner German de la Melena offers up the tangy, refreshing cuisine and drinks of his home country at this stylish restaurant bar. The ceviche (fish cured in lime juice and chilli) is served three ways. Their balcony bar is a good spot to sample a pisco sour.

BREAD, MILK & HONEY
SANDWICHES, SALADS $

Map p264 (10 Spin St, City Bowl; mains R30-50; ⏱6.30am-4pm Mon-Fri; 🚇Dorp) The spirited debate of politicos and bureaucrats from nearby parliament rings through this smart family-run cafe. The menu is delicious: the cakes and desserts are especially yummy and they have a pay-by-weight daily lunch as well as plenty of stuff to go.

SABABA
MIDDLE EASTERN, MEDITERRANEAN $

Map p264 (www.sababa.co.za; 231 Bree St, City Bowl; mains R30-50; ⏱7am-5pm Mon-Wed & Fri, 7am-9pm Thu, 9am-2pm Sat; 🚇Buitensingel) Spotlessly white space serving delicious falafel sandwiches, salads, sweets and drinks; it's the larger, newer outpost of an operation that has been successfully going in Sea Point's Piazza St John for years. They stay open late on Thursday, when it can turn into a bit of a party.

SOUTH CHINA DIM SUM BAR
CHINESE $

Map p264 (289 Long St, City Bowl; mains R30-50; ⏱noon-3pm Tue-Fri, 6-11pm Tue-Sun; 🚇Buitensingel) No frills for sure, and the service can be very slow, but the food – succulent dumplings, savoury noodles, spring rolls and homemade iced teas, is authentic and worth the wait. The decor – packing-crate stools, tattered Bruce Lee posters – has a rustic, Asian cafe charm.

SKINNY LEGS & ALL
GOURMET CAFE $

Map p264 (www.skinnylegsandall.co.za; 70 Loop St, City Bowl; mains R50-60; ☺7am-4pm Mon-Fri, 8.30am-2pm Sat; 🚌Castle) Doreen Southwood's painted bronze *Dancers* dangle from the ceiling at the back of this elegant cafe serving very good renditions of standards made with top-quality ingredients. Their chicken and avo sandwich is the business.

CAFÉ ST GEORGE
SANDWICHES, SALADS $

Map p264 (St George's Cathedral, Wale St, City Bowl; mains R35-45; ☺9am-5pm Mon-Fri, 9am-3pm Sat, 10am-2pm Sun; 🚌Dorp) There's at least one hot dish of the day, usually a Cape Malay treat, at this peaceful cafe occupying part of the cathedral's vaulted stone crypt. Breakfast is served all day and they also do good sandwiches and tempting homemade cakes.

CAFÉ MOZART
INTERNATIONAL $

Map p264 (www.themozart.co.za; 37 Church St, City Bowl; mains R35-50; ☺7am-5pm Mon-Fri, 8am-3pm Sat; 🛜; 🚌Longmarket) Sample food from their 'table of love' and pay by weight, or order a coffee and sandwich at this charming cafe with streetside tables amid the daily flea market. Inside upstairs is a lovely quiet space like your great aunt's parlour in which to net surf and catch up on emails on your laptop.

CRUSH
SANDWICHES $

Map p264 (www.crush.co.za; 100 St George's Mall, City Bowl; mains R20-30; ☺7am-5pm Mon-Fri, 9am-3pm Sat; 🚌Longmarket) Offering freshly squeezed juices, smoothies and tasty wraps that prove healthy eating need not be boring.

Bo-Kaap & De Waterkant

BEEFCAKES
BURGERS $

Map p268 (☎021-425 9019; www.beefcakes.co.za; 40 Somerset Rd, De Waterkant; burgers R55-85; ☺11am-10pm Mon-Sat, 6pm-10pm Sun; 🛜; 🚌Buitengratch) Pink flamingos, feather boas, fairylights, topless barmen – yup, this burger bar camps it up nicely and is a fave *jol* (party) for groups who come to play bitchy bingo on Tuesday or enjoy the professional drag shows on Wednesday and Thursday (do not miss Odidiva, the fierce first lady of Capetonian drag; she's usually appears on Wednesday). Friday and Saturday nights it's for the boys only. The burgers? They're fine but that's not what you really come for.

NOON GUN TEAROOM & RESTAURANT
CAPE MALAY $

off Map p264 (273 Longmarket St, Bo-Kaap; mains R70-100; ☺10am-4pm, 7-10pm Mon-Sat; 🅿) High on Signal Hill, this is a fine place to sample Cape Malay dishes such as *bobotie* (curried mince pie topped with egg custard), curries and *dhaltjies* (deep-fried balls of chickpea-flour batter mixed with potato, coriander and spinach).

BIESMIELLAH
CAPE MALAY, INDIAN $

Map p264 (www.biesmiellah.co.za; cnr Wale & Pentz Sts, Bo-Kaap; mains R66-76; ☺noon-10pm Mon-Sat) Seldom big on atmosphere, Biesmiellah nonetheless offers authentic and spicy Cape Malay and Indian food in a room decorated with tapestries of Mecca. It's all halal and no alcohol is served.

ANATOLI
TURKISH $$

Map p268 (☎021-419 2501; www.anatoli.co.za; 24 Napier St, De Waterkant; meze R35-40, mains R75-120; ☺7-10.30pm Mon-Sat; 🚌Buitengracht) You can always rely on this atmospheric Turkish joint that's a little piece of Istanbul in Cape Town. Make a meal out of their delicious meze, both hot and cold, or try their kebabs.

LOADING BAY
LEBANESE $

Map p268 (☎021-425 6320; 30 Hudson St, De Waterkant; mains R50; ☺7am-5pm Mon, 7am-9pm Tue-Fri, 8am-4pm Sat; 🚌Buitengratch) Hang with De Waterkant style set at this low-key 'luxury cafe', serving Lebanese-style nibbles such as *manoushe* (flat bread) sandwiches and *spedini* (kebabs). There's an attached boutique offering menswear fashion lines from overseas labels. Make a booking for their Thursday evening burger nights – the patties, both premium beef and vegetarian, are top grade.

LA PETITE TARTE
CAFE $

Map p268 (☎021-425 9077; Shop A11, Cape Quarter, 72 Waterkant St, De Waterkant; mains R30-50; ☺8.30am-4.30pm Mon-Fri, 8.30am-2.30pm Sat; 🅿; 🚌Buitengracht) Fancy teas and delicious homemade, sweet and savoury French-style tarts are served at this adorable cafe on the Dixon St side of the Cape Quarter.

LOCAL KNOWLEDGE

LOVING CAPE TOWN'S COFFEE CULTURE

Cape Town's in the midst of a coffee crush with digital odes to the roasted bean including **I Love Coffee** (ilovecoffee.co.za) and **From Coffee With Love** (fromcoffeewithlove.wordpress.com), a blog written by Lameen Abdul-Malik, the English-Nigerian owner of **Escape Caffe**. Almost certainly the only Nobel Peace Prize laureate to run a coffee shop, Lameen was part of the International Atomic Energy Agency team that shared the prize in 2005. While working for the agency Lameen helped set up the first cancer disease hospital in Lusaka, Zambia and in the process spent much time passing through Cape Town, where he settled with his family in 2009 and turned his passion for coffee into a new career. When he gets time off from Escape, this 'fussy' coffee drinker prefers the brews from **Espressolab Microroasters** (p81). 'They source some of the best beans in the world,' says Lameen. 'In terms of their commitment and attention to detail they are very serious about coffee; their main outlet in the Old Biscuit Mill is not a place to hang out, but you can get your fix there or at the **Loading Bay** (p66) and **Dear Me** (p64), which also serve Espressolab's coffee.' Lameen also tips **Bean There** (p68) for their fair trade coffees and **Tashas** (p125) for their desserts and giant food servings.

DRINKING & NIGHTLIFE

City Bowl & Foreshore

TOP CHOICE &UNION
BEER, CAFE

Map p264 (www.andunion.com; 110 Bree St, City Bowl; ⊗noon-midnight; 🅿🛜; 🚃Longmarket) To the rear of St Stephen's Church, this cool hangout specialises in imported craft beers – seven types all bottled – and, in summer, has ping pong and the occasional live gig. They also pride themselves on their ethically sourced meats used in tasty sandwiches, hot dogs and braais (barbequed meats). The cupcakes are pretty damn good, too.

TOP CHOICE WAITING ROOM
DJ, BAR

Map p264 (273 Long St, City Bowl; cover R20 Fri & Sat; ⊗6pm-2am Mon-Sat; 🚃Bloem) Climb the narrow stairway beside the Royale Eatery to find this totally hip bar decorated in retro furniture with DJs spinning funky tunes. Climb even further and you'll eventually reach the roof deck, the perfect spot from which to admire the city's glittering night lights.

ALEXANDER BAR & CAFÉ
GAY, COCKTAIL BAR

Map p264 (http://alexanderbar.co.za; 76 Strand St, City Bowl; ⊗11am-1am Mon-Sat; 🚃Castle) Playwright Nicholas Spagnoletti and software engineer Edward van Kuik are the driving duo behind this fun, eccentric space in a gorgeous heritage building. Pick up the antique telephones on the tables to chat with fellow patrons, place an order at the bar or send a telegram to someone you might have your eye on.

TJING TJING
BAR

Map p264 (www.tjingtjing.co.za; 165 Longmarket St, City Bowl; 4pm-late Tue-Fri, 6.:30pm-late Sat; 🛜; 🚃Longmarket) This slick rooftop bar, perched above the restaurant Dear Me, is a stylish hangout for cocktails and wine. The interior is like a chic barn with exposed beams, a photo mural of Tokyo and a scarlet lacquered bar. Check the website for details of special events including Together, a monthly meetup of Capetonian creatives, and **wine tastings** (⊗5-7pm Wed).

ESCAPE CAFFE
COFFEE

Map p264 (http://escapecaffe.wordpress.com; Manhattan Place, 130 Bree St, City Bowl; ⊗7am-4pm Mon-Fri; 🚃Dorp) Coffee connoisseur Lameen Abdul-Malik serves all his coffees with a double shot; for the truly caffeine addicted there's his Sleep Suicide: a double espresso plus a French press coffee. As well as the java, there are good freshly made sandwiches and divine cheesecakes.

FORK
TAPAS, WINE

Map p264 (☏021-424 6334; www.fork-restaurants.co.za; 84 Long St, City Bowl; tapas R25-55; ⊙noon-11pm Mon-Sat; ☐Longmarket) Whether you just want to graze on a few tapas-style dishes or cobble together a full meal, this super-relaxed venue is the business, serving inventive if not strictly Spanish nibbles with excellent wines, many by the glass.

BEAN THERE
COFFEE

Map p264 (www.beanthere.co.za; 58 Wale St, City Bowl; ☐Dorp) Not much other than Fair Trade coffees from across Africa and a few sweet snacks are served in this ultra chic cafe, which has space to spread out and a relaxed vibe despite all the caffeine flowing around.

YOURS TRULY
CAFE

Map p264 (www.yourstrulycafe.co.za; 175 Long St, City Bowl; ☐Dorp) Inspirational sayings in bold, graphic, white-on-black lettering cover the wall at this cute cafe-cum-art gallery. You don't need to hang around as there's a street-side serving hatch – although it's nice if you do as their sandwiches are good and there is a shoe-cleaning service.

DELUXE COFFEEWORKS
COFFEE

Map p264 (25 Church St, City Bowl; ☐Longmarket) Providing the city centre's groovsters with their daily caffeine fix is this tiny cafe with what looks like a giant kit model for a Vespa hanging on the wall. Ask the baristas if you can have one of the burlap coffee bags as a souvenir.

TWANKEY BAR
COCKTAIL BAR

Map p264 (www.tajhotels.com; Taj Hotel, cnr Adderley & Wale Sts, City Bowl; ⊙3-11pm Mon-Thu, 3pm-2.30am Fri & Sat; ☐Dorp) For those not familiar with the conventions of British theatre, this stylish and far-from-draggy bar is named after pantomime dame Widow Twankey. They mix a mean cocktail and have super fresh oysters and other tasty bar snacks. An elegant option for quiet drinks in the centre of the city.

JULEP BAR
COCKTAIL BAR

Map p264 (Vredenburg Lane, City Bowl; ⊙5pm-2am Tue-Sat; ☐Bloem) Occupying the ground floor of a former brothel, this hidden gem, a favourite with local hipsters, will set you apart from the riff-raff on nearby Long St.

MARVEL
DJ BAR

Map p264 (236 Long St, City Bowl; ⊙1pm-4am; ☐Bloem) Stuffed as a sardine, Marvel is a fantastic bar where cool kids of all colours rub shoulders (not to mention practically everything else). If you can, grab one of the cosy booths at the front, or linger on the pavement and enjoy the foot-tapping grooves from the DJ.

NEIGBOURHOOD
RESTAURANT, BAR

Map p264 (www.goodinthehood.co.za; 163 Long St, City Bowl; ☐Dorp) At this relaxed bar and casual restaurant, styled after British gastropubs, the colour divide of Cape Town melts away. Their long balcony is good place to cool off or keep tabs on Long St.

CAVEAU
RESTAURANT, WINE BAR

Map p264 (☏021-422 1367; www.caveau.co.za; Heritage Sq, 92 Bree St, City Bowl; ⊙7am-11.30pm Mon-Sat; ☐Longmarket) Cape Town should have more wine bars like this excellent one at Heritage Sq. It has a decent selection of local drops and very good food from both its restaurant and deli, which you can enjoy al fresco in the courtyard or on a raised terrace on Bree St. They also have a branch in Newlands, **Caveau at the Mill** (p126).

VINYL DIGZ
CLUB

Map p264 (www.facebook.com/VinylDIGZ; 113 Loop St, City Bowl; admission R20; ⊙1pm-1am; ☐Dorp) This rooftop dance party that happens every other Saturday is a more casual bring-and-buy LP record swapmeet during the afternoon with braai available too. As the sun sets, the grooving to classic soul and R&B from the '60s onwards starts and the very chilled, mixed crowd make it one of the best dance events in Cape Town.

THE LOOP
CLUB

Map p264 (www.theloopnightclub.co.za; 161 Loop St, City Bowl; cover R50, VIP area R80; ☐Bloem) Brightly coloured outside and roomy inside, this latest entry to Cape Town's hip club scene can be worth checking out depending on the DJ they have playing. Everything and anything is promised music-wise.

Bo-Kaap & De Waterkant

CREW BAR
GAY, CLUB

Map p268 (www.crewbar.co.za; 30 Napier St, De Waterkant; cover R20 Fri & Sat; 🖳Buitengracht) The best place for gays and the gay friendly to dance the night away – it helps that they have hunky bar dancers dressed only in skimpy shorts and glitter. Downstairs it's hands in the air to the latest pop and dance anthems, while upstairs (usually only open weekends) the beats are harder and more eclectic.

TRINITY
CLUB, RESTAURANT

off Map p268 (www.trinitycapetown.co.za; 15 Bennett St, De Waterkant; cover R50-150; 🖳Buitengracht) Occupying an enormous warehouse space, one part decorated with an organ salvaged from an old church, Trinity offers a state-of-the art dance club with the one of the most sophisticated sound systems in South Africa, as well as bars and an all day restaurant serving sushi, pizza and burgers. Naturally, big name DJs play here, but also look out for events such as live jazz on Tuesdays and, once a month, a jazz orchestra band playing in the main hall.

BEAULAH BAR
LESBIAN

Map p268 (www.beaulahbar.co.za; 30 Somerset Rd, De Waterkant; cover R20; 🖳Buitengracht) This fun bar and dance venue, up a floor from the street, has a devoted crowd of young boys and girls who are always ready to bop to the DJ's poppy tunes. It's one of the pink precinct's few lesbian-oriented venues but not exclusively so.

BUBBLES BAR
DRAG SHOW

Map p268 (www.facebook.com/pages/Bubbles-Bar/170161596362850; 125A Waterkant St, De Waterkant; 🖳Buitengracht) The divas of Cape Town's flourishing drag scene and their admirers – who seem to number many hunky lesbians – gather to pout, lip-sync, sashay and occasionally (gasp!) actually sing at this cosy, bubbly bar. Depending on the crowd it can be hoot, but beware the open mike karaoke which can get aurally ugly.

AMSTERDAM ACTION BAR
GAY

Map p268 (www.amsterdambar.co.za; 10-12 Cobern St, De Waterkant) The action is mainly on the upper level where dark rooms and cubicles provide a venue for punters to dabble in whatever or whomever they fancy. At ground level, an older gay set tends to gather, the street-side balcony being a popular spot to smoke and watch the comings and goings. There's a pool table in the nonsmoking area.

BAR CODE
GAY

Map p268 (www.leatherbar.co.za; 18 Cobern St, De Waterkant; ⊘10pm-3am Sun-Thu, 10pm-4am Fri & Sat; 🖳Buitengracht) Leather and latex daddies and their acolytes gather at this small bar with a equally cosy dark room upstairs. Check the website to make sure you're dressed (or undressed) appropriately for whatever theme is on that night, otherwise you might not be let in.

CAFE MANHATTAN
GAY, RESTAURANT

Map p268 (🕿021-421 6666; www.manhattan.co.za; 74 Waterkant St, De Waterkant; ⊘9.30am-2am; 🛜; 🖳Buitengracht) Give thanks to the far-sighted proprietor of Cafe Manhattan since he kick-started the gay quarter a decade or so ago by opening this popular bar and restaurant. Check out the area's human traffic from its wrap-around deck.

FIREMAN'S ARMS
PUB

Map p268 (🕿021-419 1513; 25 Mechau St, De Waterkant; 🖳Buitengracht) Here since 1906, the Fireman's is likely to be around for quite a while longer. Inside, the Rhodesian and old South African flags remain pinned up alongside a collection of firemen's helmets and old ties. Come to watch rugby on the big-screen TV, grab some seriously tasty pizza or down a lazy pint or two.

HAAS
COFFEE

Map p264 (www.haascollective.com; 67 Rose St, Bo-Kaap; ⊘7am-5pm Mon-Fri, 8am-3pm Sat & Sun; 🛜; 🖳Longmarket) Both a cafe and a very appealing arty gift and interior decor shop, Haas is the stylish contemporary face of the Bo-Kaap. They serve their house-roasted single origin and blended versions of coffee, as well as tasty bakes and meals. Slump in one of their comfy street-side sofas and ponder whether to splash out on the pricey civet coffee made from very specially procured beans.

ORIGIN & NIGIRO
COFFEE, TEA

Map p268 (www.originroasting.co.za; 🕿021-421 1000; 28 Hudson St, De Waterkant; ⊘7am-5pm Mon-Fri, 9am-2pm Sat & Sun; 🛜; 🖳Buitengracht) Apart from great coffee their traditional bagels are pretty awesome. Book ahead for their coffee and tea appreciation courses (R200). At the rear the caffeinated buzz gives way to the zen calm of Nigiro's tea salon where you can sample scores of the leaf or have a traditional Taiwanese tea ceremony (R125).

 ## ⭐ ENTERTAINMENT

ARTSCAPE
THEATRE
Map p268 (☎021-410 9800; www.artscape.co.za; 1-10 DF Malan St, Foreshore; P; ☐Foreshore) Consisting of three different-sized auditoriums (including the studio On The Side), this behemoth is the city's main arts complex. Theatre, classical music, ballet, opera and cabaret shows – Artscape offers it all. The desolate area means it's not recommended to walk around here at night; there's plenty of secure parking though.

CAPE TOWN CITY HALL
MUSIC, EVENTS
Map p264 (www.creativecapetown.net/cape-town-city-hall; Darling St, City Bowl; P; ☐Golden Acre Bus Terminal) One of the several venues where the **Cape Philharmonic Orchestra** (www.cpo.org.za), South Africa's 'orchestra for all seasons', plays concerts. The CPO has been working hard to ensure its musicians reflect the ethnic breakdown of the Western Cape more closely. To this end it has formed the Cape Philharmonic Youth Orchestra and the Cape Philharmonic Youth Wind Ensemble, with around 80% of members coming from disadvantaged communities. The auditorium has very good acoustics that are also taken advantage of by local choirs.

CAPE TOWN INTERNATIONAL CONVENTION CENTRE
CONCERTS, EVENTS
Map p268 (CTICC; ☎021-410 5000; www.cticc.co.za; 1 Lower Long St, Foreshore; P; ☐Convention Centre) Since opening for business in 2003, the R582 million CTICC has barely paused for breath, packing in a busy annual program of musical performances, exhibitions, conferences and other events such as the Cape Town International Jazz Festival and Design Indaba. There are plans to extend the CTICC towards Artscape, almost doubling its size and making it an environmentally friendly building. Step inside the main entrance to admire the giant relief sculpture in the main hall, *Baobabs, Storm-clouds, Animals and People* – a collaboration between Brett Murray and the late San artist Tuoi Steffaans Samcuia of the !Xun and Khwe San Art and Cultural Project.

ZULA SOUND BAR
MUSIC, COMEDY
Map p264 (☎021-424 2442; www.zulabar.co.za; 98 Long St, City Bowl; admission from R30; ☐Longmarket) Progress from the cafe and bar fronting the street to the performance spaces at the back. The line up includes a range of hip local bands, DJs and comedy every Monday night.

IBUYAMBO MUSIC & ART EXHIBITION CENTRE
MUSIC
Map p268 (☎082 569 9316; 11 Bree St, Foreshore; ☺noon-midnight daily; ☐Prestwich) This 'art gallery with a twist' is worth trying for its eclectic evening events and performances, which range from the monthly Verses spoken-word nights to regular Saturday evening gigs by Dizu Plaatjies and the iBuyambo Ensemble playing traditional African music. Sunday is jazz night.

PINK FLAMINGO
CINEMA
Map p264 (☎021-423 7247; www.granddaddy.co.za; 38 Long St, City Bowl; tickets R60 or R120 ☐Castle) From as early as August to as late as April, the Grand Daddy Hotel's rooftop trailer park of Airstream caravans is the venue for this al-fresco cinema screening old school classics, usually on Monday evenings. The regular 'old school' ticket gets you entrance plus a bag of popcorn and welcome drink; for R120 they throw in a gourmet picnic. It's small, so bookings are required.

MAMA AFRICA
LIVE MUSIC
Map p264 (☎021-426 1017; www.mamaafrica restaurant.co.za; 178 Long St, City Bowl; diner/non diner R10/15; ☺6.30pm-2am Mon-Sat; ☐Bloem) Live marimba and other swinging African sounds fuel the atmosphere at this eternally popular tourist venue, where you can dine on a range of game dishes (mains R100). Bookings are essential on weekends, otherwise squeeze into a spot by the bar.

MARIMBA
JAZZ
Map p268 (☎021-418 3366; www.marimbasa.com; Cape Town International Convention Centre, cnr Coen Steytler Ave & Heerengracht Blvd, Foreshore; diner/nondiner R20/30; ☐Convention Centre) Yes, there is a marimba band playing occasionally at this slick Afro-chic venue. The food is good and music sets typically

kick off around 8pm from Thursday to Saturday, but call first to check as they often host special events.

 SHOPPING

City Bowl & Foreshore

TOP CHOICE AFRICAN MUSIC STORE   MUSIC
Map p264 (www.africanmusicstore.co.za; 134 Long St, City Bowl; ☐Dorp) The range of local music here, including all top jazz, kwaito (a form of township music), dance and trance recordings, can't be surpassed; and the staff are knowledgeable about the music scene. You'll also find DVDs and other souvenirs.

TOP CHOICE CHURCH   DESIGN, GIFTS
Map p264 (http://churchgifts.blogspot.com; 12 Spin St, City Bowl; ☐Dorp) 'Seek and ye shall find' is the mantra of this gift shop that's worth visiting if only for its incredible window and shop displays – all the work of the design collective The President, who also organise the Toffie pop culture and food festivals. You can buy designer perfumes, wooden sunglasses, posters, magazines and local fashion and food items here.

MERCHANTS ON LONG   FASHION, GIFTS
Map p264 (www.merchantsonlong.com; 34 Long St, City Bowl; ☐Castle) This 'African salon store', in one of Long Street's more beautiful buildings and boasting a terracotta art nouveau facade, is a gallery of top contemporary design – from fashion to stationery – sourced from across the continent. Among the choice goodies on display are the all-natural perfumes, made using pure oils and essences, of Cape Town-based **Frazer Parfum Gallery & Laboratory** (www.frazerparfum.com). There's also a cafe.

AFRICAN IMAGE   ARTS & CRAFTS
Map p264 (www.african-image.co.za; cnr Church & Burg Sts, City Bowl; ☐Longmarket) There's a fab range of new and old crafts and artefacts at reasonable prices, including the funky, colourful pillow covers and aprons of Shine Shine. You'll find a lot of township crafts here, as well as wildly patterned shirts.

MOGALAKWENA   ARTS & CRAFTS
Map p264 (www.mogalakwena.com; 3 Church St, City Bowl; ☐Longmarket) This attractive gallery displays colourful stitched panels depicting rural scenes as well as other Pedi crafts from the Limpopo province. They make charming gifts.

PAN AFRICAN MARKET   ARTS & CRAFTS
Map p264 (www.panafrican.co.za; 76 Long St, City Bowl; ☐Longmarket) A microcosm of the continent, with a bewildering range of arts and crafts. There's also the cheap cafe Timbuktu, with seating on the balcony overlooking Long St, and a tailor and music shop packed into the three floors.

TRIBAL TRENDS   ARTS & CRAFTS
Map p264 (Winchester House, 72-74 Long St, City Bowl; ☐Longmarket) Attractively set out emporium of all things African, tribal and crafty, from across the continent. They support local artists who sell some of their bead work and jewellery here.

CLARKE'S BOOKSHOP   BOOKS
Map p264 (www.clarkesbooks.co.za; 199 Long St, City Bowl; ☐Dorp) Recently moved into smaller premises, Clarke's still stocks the best range of books on South Africa and the continent, and has a great secondhand section. If you can't find what you're looking for here, it's unlikely to be at the many other bookshops along Long St (although there's no harm in browsing).

IMAGENIUS   ARTS & CRAFTS
Map p264 (www.imagenius.co.za; 117 Long St, City Bowl; ☐Longmarket) Set over three levels, this treasure-trove of modern African design offers an eclectic range, including ceramics, beachwear, jewellery and super-cute buckskin baby booties. There are stylish gift cards, boxes and wrapping, too.

LUCKY FRIDAY   T-SHIRTS, CRAFTS
Map p264 (www.luckyfriday.co.za; 43 Long St, City Bowl; ☐Castle) A very groovy little shop stocking a great range of unusual South African souvenirs from Electric Zulu print T-shirts and cute Bokkie shoes to African music CDs.

COMMUNE.1   GALLERY
Map p264 (www.commune1.com; 64 Wale St, City Bowl; ☐Dorp) Greg Dale's gallery, in a building that was once a mortuary, is devoted to sculpture and installations. Also here are

LOCAL KNOWLEDGE

URBAN STREET FASHION

Sam Walker, a fashion buyer for Woolworths, is the editor of **Pop Ya Collar** (www.popyacollar.co.za), a blog focused on South African fashion. 'It's a laid back, do what you like look,' says Walker of Capetonian style. 'In summer, it's all about cut-off denim shorts, kaftans and espadrilles – perfect for the beach. If the trend is to wear animal print, the Capetonian way is to wear just a hint of it – to interpret the style.' In Walker's little black book are the following:

Best Capetonian Designers
Malcolm Klûk (p73) for girls who want wedding dresses as well as a dress to wear at a wedding; and I love anything by Jenny le Roux (p127) who does beautiful kaftans and dresses with different shapes and colours – her designs are stunning!

Best Shopping Spots
The **Old Biscuit Mill** (p83) on Saturday, where you'll find designers such as Christopher Strong whose clothes you can find in boutiques along Long St such as **Merchants on Long** (p71), which also promotes African fashion and jewellery.

Best Boutiques
Just go into **Mungo & Jemima** (p72): you will always find something that will suit you. The range at **Peach** (p114) is absolutely beautiful, and **House of Fashion** (p73) is every girl's dream, with racks of clothes all colour coded.

the furniture and interior designs of **Liam Mooney** (www.liammooney.co.za) and the delicious handmade chocolates of **Honest** (www.honeschocolate.co.za), made with no dairy or added sugar and with wrappers illustrated by local artists.

MEMEME FASHION
Map p264 (www.mememe.co.za; 121 Long St, City Bowl; ☺9.30am-6pm Mon-Sat; ⬚Longmarket) A forerunner of the funky boutiques blooming along Long St, Mememe was started by award-winning sculptor and fashion designer Doreen Southwood in 2001. It's a showcase for young Capetonian designers and labels such as Cherry Clair, Pink Ant and Adam & Eve.

MUNGO & JEMIMA FASHION
Map p264 (www.mungoandjemima.com; 108 Long St, City Bowl; ⬚Longmarket) It may sound like a kid's puppet show, but this cute boutique showcases pretty clothes for adults by local labels such as Holiday and Coppelia.

OLIVE GREEN CAT JEWELLERY
Map p264 (www.olivegreencat.com; 77 Church St, City Bowl; ☺9.30am-5pm Mon-Fri; ⬚Longmarket) At the studio of Philippa Green and Ida-Elsje, you'll find the work of two talented young jewellery designers, both of whom are catching international attention.

Green's signature pieces are her chunky Perspex cuffs, hand-stitched with patterns and graphic text, while Elsje specialises in delicate earrings and necklaces. They also collaborate on the striking Situ range of diamond jewellery.

PRINS & PINS JEWELLERS JEWELLERY
Map p264 (www.prinsandprins.com; 66 Loop St, City Bowl; ⬚Castle) This old Cape Dutch–style house makes for a suitably salubrious venue for stocking up on some of South Africa's mineral wealth in wearable form.

SKINZ ACCESSORIES
Map p264 (www.skinzleather.co.za; 86 Long St, City Bowl; ⬚Longmarket) If you want a little something made from exotic leather or animal skins – think zebra, springbok, crocodile and ostrich – then this is your place. It does regular cowhide leather too, but doesn't that sound boring compared to purple-dyed crocodile?

SKINNY LA MINX CRAFT
Map p264 (www.skinnylaminx.com; 201 Bree St, City Bowl; ⬚Bloem) The print designs of Heather Moore, on cotton and cotton linen mix, can be found in several other shops, but here you can view the full range plus purchase cloth by the metre.

MERRY POP INS
CHILDRENSWEAR, TOYS

Map p264 (www.merrypopins.co.za; 201 Bree St, City Bowl; ☐Bloem) Stocking a quality selection of pre-loved kids' clothes, toys and furniture. The selection of stuff for newborns to 10 year olds is impressive and they also have a small cafe and an area downstairs where they hold kids' yoga classes.

DOKTER & MISSES /DAVID WEST
FASHION, FURNITURE

Map p264 (www.dokterandmisses.com; 113 Long St, City Bowl; ☐Longmarket) A very cool combo of unisex fashion, made in the city by David West out of lovely natural fibres such as linen and organdie, and the functional, stylish furniture and decor of Dokter & Misses.

HOUSE OF FASHION
FASHION

Map p264 (www.houseoffashion.co.za; 153 Loop St, City Bowl; ☐Dorp) Really a member's club, but they'll let you look around once to get an idea – and having seen how gorgeous a set up it is, with beautiful one-off pieces from top global designers, you may well be tempted to sign up. A fashion stylist is on hand to provide direction and advice.

AVOOVA
CRAFTS

Map p264 (www.avoova.com; 97 Bree St, City Bowl; ☐Longmarket) Stocking the beautiful ostrich eggshell–decorated accessories made by Avoova – each one is a unique piece. You'll also find Masai beadwork from Kenya here and a few other carefully selected crafts.

LONG STREET ANTIQUE ARCADE
ANTIQUES

Map p264 (127 Long St, City Bowl; ☐Dorp) Browse the booths in this compact arcade, offering a range of antiques and bric-a-brac, and you're likely to find something of interest, from dusty old books and pieces of silverware to art and furniture. There are plenty more antique shops on Long St if you can't find what you're looking for here.

KLÛK & CGDT
FASHION

Map p268 (kluk.co.za; 47 Bree St, Foreshore; ☐Prestwich) The showroom and atelier of Malcolm Klûk (once an apprentice to John Galianno) and Christiaan Gabriel Du Toit are combined here. Expect haute couture, with similarly haute prices, and some more affordable prêt-à-porter pieces.

ERDMANN CONTEMPORARY & PHOTOGRAPHERS GALLERY
GALLERY

Map p264 (www.erdmanncontemporary.co.za; 63 Shortmarket St, City Bowl; ◷10am-5pm Tue-Fri, 10am-1pm Sat; ☐Longmarket) As well as representing the fine work of many top South African photographers, this gallery shows drawings by Lien Botha and Conrad Botes.

AVA GALLERY
GALLERY

Map p264 (www.ava.co.za; 35 Church St, City Bowl; ☐Longmarket) Exhibition space for the nonprofit Association for Visual Arts (AVA), which shows some very interesting work by local artists.

Bo-Kaap & De Waterkant

⭐TOP CHOICE AFRICA NOVA
ARTS & CRAFTS

Map p268 (www.africanova.co.za; Cape Quarter, 72 Waterkant St, De Waterkant; ◷9am-5pm Mon-Fri, 10am-5pm Sat, 10am-2pm Sun) One of the most stylish and desirable collections of contemporary African textiles, arts and crafts. You'll find potato-print fabrics made by women in Hout Bay, Karin Dando's mosaic trophy heads, Jordaan's handmade felt rock cushions (which look like giant pebbles) and a wonderful range of ceramics and jewellery. They also have a smaller branch at Casa Labia in Muizenberg.

⭐TOP CHOICE STREETWIRES
ARTS & CRAFTS

Map p268 (www.streetwires.co.za; 77 Shortmarket St, Bo-Kaap; ☐Longmarket) The motto is 'anything you can dream up in wire we will build'. And if you visit this social project designed to create sustainable employment and see the wire sculptors at work, you'll see what that means! It stocks an amazing range, including working radios and chandeliers, life-sized animals and artier products such as the Nguni Cow range, which you'll also find sold at upmarket craft shops such as Africa Nova.

MONKEYBIZ
ARTS & CRAFTS

Map p264 (www.monkeybiz.co.za; 43 Rose St, Bo-Kaap; ◷9am-5pm Mon-Fri, 9am-1pm Sat; ☐Longmarket) Colourful beadwork crafts, made by local township women, are Monkeybiz's super successful stock in trade. The shop also has funky jewellery and gifts by other quirky Capetonian designers. Profits are reinvested back into community services such as soup kitchens and a burial fund for artists and their families.

BARAKA
GIFTS

Map p268 (Shop 13A, Cape Quarter, Dixon St, De Waterkant; ☺10am-5.30pm Mon-Fri, 10am-3.30pm Sat, 11am-3.30pm Sun) Baraka means 'blessing' in Arabic and co-owner Gavin Terblanche has an eclectic eye for what works as a gift or quirky piece of home decor. Products include handmade leather journals and photo albums by his own company Worlds of Wonder (www.worldsofwonder.co.za).

CAPE QUARTER

Map p268 (www.capequarter.co.za;27 Somerset Rd, De Waterkant; ☺9am-6pm Mon-Fri, 9am-4pm Sat, 10am-2pm Sun; P; ☐Buitengracht) Now split over two adjacent locations the Cape Quarter's newer, larger block is anchored by a snazzy branch of the supermarket **Spar** (☺7am-9pm Mon-Sat, 8am-9pm Sun), handy if you're self-catering in one of the area's cottages or flats. There's also a lively food and goods market held on the upper floors every Sunday from 10am to 3pm. At other times, browse the many interesting shops here, including **Lou at the Quarter** (www.louharvey.co.za) offering the plasticised and washable fabric designs of Durban-based Lou Harvey; the monochrome aesthetic of clothing and homewears at **Nap Living** (www.napliving.co.za); and **Boutique Township** (www.township.co.za) with fair trade clothes made entirely in Africa – their designs inspired by the colours of township life.

SPORTS & ACTIVITIES

LONG ST BATHS
SWIMMING

Map p264 (cnr Long & Buitensingel Sts, City Bowl; adult/child R13/7.50; ☺7am-7pm; ☐Buitensingel) Dating from 1906, these nicely restored baths, featuring painted murals of city-centre life on the walls, are heated and very popular with the local community. The separate Turkish steam baths (R42) are a great way to sweat away some time, especially during the cooler months. Women are admitted from 9am to 6pm Monday, Thursday and Saturday, and from 9am to 1pm on Tuesday; men from 1pm to 7pm on Tuesday, from 8am to 7pm on Wednesday and Friday, and from 8am to noon on Sunday.

ROYAL CAPE YACHT CLUB
SAILING

off Map p268 (☎021-421 1354; www.rcyc.co.za; Duncan Rd, Foreshore) Races known as the 'Wags' are held every Wednesday afternoon at the club. Get here at 4.30pm if you want to take part; otherwise it's a 5.30pm start. Anyone with sailing knowledge can participate – you'll be assigned to a boat.

ROLY POLYZ
PLAY CENTRE

Map p268 (www.rolypolyz.co.za; 8 Bree St, Foreshore; adult/child free/R40; ☺10am-5pm daily) Huge indoor jungle gym and kids activity centre with a cafe serving healthy kids' food.

East City Corridor

DISTRICT SIX | THE FRINGE | WOODSTOCK | SALT RIVER | OBSERVATORY

Neighbourhood Top Five

1 Learn about Cape Town's troubled past at the **District Six Museum** (p77), which is aimed as much *for* the people of the destroyed inner city as it is about them.

2 Browse the **Old Biscuit Mill** (p83) for retail therapy and gourmet eats.

3 Discover South African artists at galleries such as **Stevenson** (p84) and **What If The World** (p84).

4 Enjoy top class theatre and digital movie events at the **Fugard** (p82).

5 Admire the dazzling **street art** (p79) brightening up the Fringe, District Six and Woodstock.

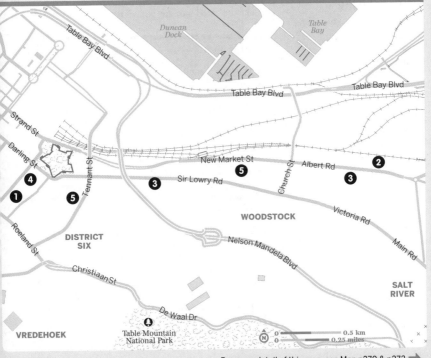

For more detail of this area, see Map p270 & p272 ➡

Lonely Planet's Top Tip

Observatory is the Cape Town apex of alternative lifestyles. The **Holistic Lifestyle Fair** (Map p272; http://holisticlifestylefair.yolasite.com; Observatory Community Centre, cnr Station & Lower Main Rds; ⊙10am-4pm) is held here on the first Sunday of the month.

 Best Places to Eat

➡ The Kitchen (p80)
➡ Pot Luck Club & The Test Kitchen (p80)
➡ Chandani (p80)
➡ Hello Sailor (p81)
➡ Charly's Bakery (p81)

For reviews, see p80 ➡

Best Places to Drink

➡ Espressolab Microroasters (p81)
➡ Amadoda (p81)
➡ Don Pedro (p81)
➡ Truth (p82)

For reviews, see p81 ➡

Best Places to Shop

➡ Old Biscuit Mill (p83)
➡ Neighbourgoods Market (p83)
➡ Book Lounge (p83)
➡ Ashanti (p83)
➡ Design Afrika (p83)

For reviews, see p83 ➡

Explore East City Corridor

East of the City Bowl are a string of working-class and industrial suburbs that are regenerating and partly gentrifying. The process is a patchy, controversial one and has long been so – this is where you'll find the empty lots of District Six, a multicultural area destroyed during apartheid.

Closest to the city, the area dubbed 'The Fringe' is set to be a showcase hub of Cape Town's successful bid to become World Design Capital 2014. Moving eastwards, Woodstock and Salt River continue their upwardly mobile trajectory, with the Woodstock Industrial Centre, the Woodstock Foundry and Salt Circle Arcade among the latest big redevelopments following in the wake of the phenomenal Old Biscuit Mill. The opening of several major and minor Cape Town galleries, joining pioneers such as Greatmore Studios, has put the region on the art-lovers' map; it's also the canvas for the city's most striking street.

Further east is Observatory, named after the first Royal Observatory established nearby in 1820; the site remains the headquarters of the South African Astronomical Observatory. Commonly known as 'Obs', the suburb has long been a bohemian, racially mixed area, even during apartheid. It's popular with students attending the nearby University of Cape Town and the Medical School at Groote Schuur Hospital. Several good backpacker hostels and lively, inexpensive restaurants make it a `good base for budget travellers.

Local Life

➡ **Markets** Neighbourgoods (p83) every Saturday is the big one, but also look out for occasional designer-goods markets in The Fringe.

➡ **Cafes** Elbow your way into The Kitchen (p80) or Charly's Bakery (p81) or chill in less hectic spots such as the Field Office (p85).

➡ **Books** Broaden your intellectual horizons and be entertained by one of many fascinating readings and book launches at the Book Lounge (p83).

Getting There & Away

➡ **Walk** Fine from the City Bowl to The Fringe, and during daylight around the main roads of Woodstock and Salt River. Proceed with caution at night.

➡ **Bus & Shared Taxis** City buses and shared minibus taxis plough the route between the city and Observatory along Sir Lowry and Victoria Rds.

➡ **Train** Cape Metro trains stop at Woodstock, Salt River and Observatory.

TOP SIGHTS
DISTRICT SIX MUSEUM

If you only have time to visit one museum in Cape Town, make it this one, based in two heritage buildings. The museum celebrates the once lively multiracial area that was reclassified a whites-only zone in the 1960s and subsequently destroyed as the 60,000 inhabitants were forcibly removed. The *Digging Deeper* exhibition in the main building, formerly the Methodist Mission Church, includes reconstructions of home interiors, photographs, recordings and testimonials, all of which build an evocative picture of a shattered but not entirely broken community.

Noor Ebrahim's Story

The best way to understand the events of District Six is to speak with the staff, all of whom have heartbreaking stories. 'I used to live at 247 Caledon St,' begins museum guide Noor Ebrahim, pointing at the map covering the museum's floor.

Noor's grandfather came to Cape Town in 1890 from Surat in India. An energetic man who had four wives and 30 children, he built up a good business making ginger beer. Noor's father was one of the old man's sons to his first wife, a Scot called Fanny Grainger, and Noor grew up in the heart of District Six. 'It was a very cosmopolitan area. Many whites lived there – they owned the shops. There were blacks, Portuguese, Chinese and Hindus all living as one big happy family.'

'We didn't know it was going to happen,' remembers Noor of the 1966 order declaring District Six a white area under the Group Areas Act. 'We saw the headlines in the paper and people were angry and sad but for a while little happened.' Then in 1970 the demolitions started and gradually the residents moved out.

DON'T MISS

➡ Floor Map of District Six
➡ *Digging Deeper* exhibition
➡ *Fields of Play* exhibition

PRACTICALITIES

➡ Map p270
➡ ☏021-466 7200
➡ www.districtsix. co.za
➡ 25A Buitenkant St, District Six
➡ adult/child R20/5, with Sacks Futeran Building R25/10
➡ ⊙9am-2pm Mon, 9am-4pm Tue-Sat
➡ ⊠Golden Acre Bus Terminal

READING UP

Recalling Community in Cape Town (eds Ciraj Rassool & Sundra Posalendis) An illustrated account of the now-destroyed District Six area and how its memory was kept alive by those who once lived there.

The area gets its name from being the sixth municipal area of the city to be designated in 1867. In the 1960s it was renamed Zonnebloem (meaning 'Sunflower' in Afrikaans).

WALKING TOURS

Speak to staff about arranging a walking tour of the old District Six with a former resident (R90 per person, a minimum of 10 people). Many township tours also start at the museum, where the history of the apartheid era pass laws, which regulated where people were allowed to live based on their race, are explained.

'Buckingham Palace', District Six (Richard Rive) Eloquent tales about the inhabitants of five houses in the heart of District Six.

Noor's family hung on until 1976, when they were given two weeks to vacate the house that his grandfather had bought some 70 years previously. By that time they'd seen families, neighbours and friends split up and sent to separate townships determined by their race. They'd prepared by buying a new home in the coloured township of Athlone.

Noor will never forget the day he left District Six. 'I got in the car with my wife and two children and drove off, but only got as far as the corner before I had to stop. I got out of the car and started to cry as I saw the bulldozers move in immediately. Many people died of broken hearts.'

Sacks Futeran Building

A block north of the main museum is its annex, occupying part of the **Sacks Futeran Building** (15 Buitenkant St, District Six; admission adult/child R25/10 inc District Six Museum; ⊙9am-2pm Mon, 9am-4pm Tue-Sat). For many generations the Futeran family traded soft goods and textiles from these premises, and before that part of the building was the Buitenkant Congregational Church. It now houses two fascinating permanent exhibitions: *Fields of Play* on the history and development of soccer on the Cape; and *Offside* about the soccer relationship between South Africa and the UK over the last century, focusing on experiences of racism in both countries.

The Future of District Six

Since democracy, there have been promises to rebuild the 42-hectare site, but it has been slow going. The District Six Beneficiary Trust (www.districtsix.za.org) formed to register land claims and handle the issues and processes of resettlement. However it wasn't until December 2011 that a financial commitment to the tune of R7 billion was given by local government to have 1500 homes rebuilt by February 2015 and a total of 5000 by 2019, when it's hoped the area will have some 20,000 inhabitants. Plans include the revival of Hanover St, once District Six's commercial spine. However, it will be impossible for everyone to return to where they once lived because buildings such as the Cape Peninsula University of Technology now occupy large chunks of the area.

To get an idea of what District Six was like, you could explore (in daytime and preferably in company) the area around Chapel St, north of the raised Nelson Mandela Blvd; here you'll find the Theatre in the District and Trafalgar Park, which contains the remains of the French Redoubt, one of a series of defensive positions built by the Dutch East India Company (VOC) in 1871 to protect the Cape against a British attack.

TOP SIGHTS
DISTRICT SIX MUSEUM

⊙ SIGHTS

The shows at the Woodstock commercial galleries listed in the shopping section of this chapter are worth a look even if you have no intention of buying the art displayed.

DISTRICT SIX MUSEUM MUSEUM
See p77.

FREE SUBSTATION 13 STREET ART
Map p270 (Canterbury St, District Six; ⬚Golden Acre Bus Terminal) The beautification of this electricity substation building is just the start of many planned upgrades for the innovative district dubbed The Fringe. The colourful murals were partly designed and painted by Mak1one (aka Maxwell Southgate) who also decorated the facade of Charly's Bakery opposite, and whose distinctive street art can be spotted at several other locations around town including District Six and Long St. The substation stands on the District Six side of the boundary with The Fringe, so that is the theme the wall murals take. At the time of research it was still a work in progress but there are plans to make the art work as interactive as possible with the community by having a 'Before I Die' wall, where people can inscribe their dreams and wishes, and an area where recipes of traditional Cape dishes can be recorded.

FREE I ART WOODSTOCK STREET ART
Map p270 (btwn Gympie St & Hercules St, Woodstock, ⬚Woodstock) Much of the fabulous street art in this sketchy grid of streets off Albert Rd was created during a collaborative project between **a word of art** (www.a-word-of-art.co.za) and Adidas Originals in 2011. Guided tours can be arranged via Ricky Lee Gordon, aka the mural artist Freddy Sam (www.freddysam.com) whose 'a word of art' residency project is based in the nearby **Woodstock Industrial Centre**. Freddy Sam's work includes the beautiful mural of Zimbabwean immigrants Juma and Willard facing onto Albert Rd.

CAPE TOWN SCIENCE CENTRE MUSEUM
Map p272 (⬚021-300 3200; www.ctsc.org.za; 370B Main Rd, Observatory; admission R40; ⊙9am-4.30pm daily; ⓟ; ⬚Observatory) The opening of this fun hands-on science centre was delayed slightly in 2011 when it was discovered that the building it occupies is a rare Cape Town example of the work of Modernist architect Max Policansky. The original bones of the architecture have largely been preserved and the revived space is a great place to bring kids for attractions such as the giant gyroscope (R5 extra), a room full of Lego, and a replica of the Soyuz capsule that returned South African tech billionaire Mark Shuttleworth to earth after his trip to the International Space Station.

LOCAL KNOWLEDGE

DISTRICT SIX STREET ART

Driving east out of the city along Nelson Mandela Blvd or De Waal Dr, you won't miss several giant pieces of street art decorating the sides of buildings. The following are well worth getting closer to so you can admire the work from a stationary position:

Land & Liberty (Map p270; Keizersgracht, District Six) One of the most recent works by the prolific street artist Faith47 (www.faith47.com) is this eight-story tall mother with a baby strapped to her back pointing up towards Lion's Head.

African Woman With TV (Map p270; Picket Post 59-63 block, corner of Cauvin Rd and Christiaan St, District Six) Another work by Faith47, this sassy mama balances a couple of kids in one hand and a portable TV on her head like a pitcher of water. Behind her is a streetscape of the old District Six.

Refugee Rights (Map p270; Keizersgracht, District Six) Park by the Holy Cross Church and walk across the wasteland to view this striking collaborative work commissioned by the Human Rights Media Centre.

Freedom Struggle Heroes (Map p270; Darling St, District Six) Portraits of Nelson Mandela, Steve Biko, Cissie Gool and Imam Haron, painted as if their faces were carved into the side of Table Mountain. Nearby on the corner of Tennant St you'll find more street art, including a proud-looking Masai woman.

HEART OF CAPE TOWN MUSEUM   MUSEUM
Map p272 (☎021-404 1967; www.heartofcape
town.co.za; Old Main Bldg, Groote Schuur Hospital, Main Rd, Observatory; overseas visitor R176,
South African adult/student R88/44; ☉guided
tours 9am, 11am, 1pm & 3pm; ℗; ℝObservatory)
Capetonians are very proud that their city
was the first place in the world where a
successful heart transplant operation was
carried out (never mind that the recipient
died a few days later). This museum allows you to see the very theatre in Groote
Schuur Hospital where history was made
in 1967. The displays have a fascinating Dr
Kildare–quality to them, especially given
the heartthrob status of Dr Christiaan Barnard at the time. The only way to visit the
museum is by booking on to a tour; for R50
extra transfers to and from your hotel can
be arranged. To reach the hospital from Observatory station, walk west along Station
Rd for about 10 minutes.

FREE **GREATMORE STUDIOS**   ART STUDIOS
Map p270 (☎021-447 9699; www.greatmoreart.
org; 47-49 Greatmore St, Woodstock; ☉9am-5pm
Mon-Fri) The pioneer of the Woodstock art
scene, Greatmore Studios was set up in
1998 to provide studio space for local artists. Some of the 12 studios are reserved for
visiting overseas artists, with the idea of
providing skills transfer and cross-cultural
stimulation of ideas and creativity. Visitors
are welcome to stroll around the studios
and there are occasionally group exhibitions held here.

THE BIJOU   ART STUDIOS
Map p272 (178 Lower Main Rd, Observatory;
ℝObservatory) Very occasionally the artists
who now work in this fabulous art-deco
building, once a cinema, open up their studios to the public. In the past it's coincided
with the **Observatory Art Walk** (www.face
book.com/events/153184148113303) in early
December. Even if the studios themselves
aren't open, the building is still worth a
look for art deco aficionados.

FREE **THE BANK**   DESIGN STUDIOS
Map p270 (71 Harrington St, The Fringe; ℝGold-
en Acre Bus Terminal) If you'd like to flick
through the weighty, illustrated bid book
that helped secure Cape Town the title of
World Design Capital 2014, it's on public
display in the lobby of this building. Once a
branch of Barclays Bank (hence the name)

it now houses various design studios and
freelance designers.

EATING

**The three main dining strips to zone in
on are Woodstock's Roodebloem Rd,
Salt River's Albert Rd and Lower Main Rd
in Observatory. Also mark your calendar
with a big red cross for Saturday's
brunch fest at the Neighbourgoods
Market.**

TOP CHOICE **THE KITCHEN**   SALADS, SANDWICHES $
Map p270 (www.karendudley.co.za; 111 Sir Lowry
Rd, Woodstock; sandwiches & salads R50-60;
☉8.30am-4pm Mon-Fri; ℝWoodstock; ☑) Over
all the swanky restaurants in town, it was
this little charmer that Michelle Obama
chose for lunch, proving the First Lady has
excellent taste. Tuck into plates of divine
salads, rustic sandwiches made with love,
and sweet treats with tea served from china
teapots.

TOP CHOICE **POT LUCK CLUB
& TEST KITCHEN**   CONTEMPORARY $$
Map p270 (☎021-447 0804; http://thetestkitch
en.co.za/info.html; Shop 104 A, Old Biscuit Mill,
375 Albert Rd, Salt River; Pot Luck Club mains R55-
140; Test Kitchen 3/5 courses R375/470; ☉Pot
Luck Club 6-10pm Tue-Sat; Test Kitchen 12.30-
2.30pm, 7-10pm Tue-Sat; ℗; ℝWoodstock) Make
reservations well in advance for dinner at
either of these side-by-side operations – un-
der the stewardship of top chef Luke Dale-
Roberts – that have brought fine creative
dining to the wilds of Salt River. Pot Luck
is the more affordable of the two serving
delicious tapas-style plates designed to be
shared; we defy you not to order a second
plate of the smoked beef with truffle-café-
au-lait sauce.

CHANDANI   INDIAN, VEGETARIAN $
Map p270 (☎021-447 7887; www.chandani.
co.za; 85 Roodebloem Rd, Woodstock; mains
R55-70; ☉11.30am-3pm & 6.30-10.30pm Mon-
Sat; ☑) This appealing Indian restaurant
is one of the tastiest places on Roodebloem
Rd. There's a great selection of dishes for
vegetarians including favourites such as
aloo gobi (potato and cauliflower) and *dal
makani* (black lentils in a creamy tomato
sauce).

HELLO SAILOR
BISTRO **$**

Map p272 (📞021-448 2420; www.hellosailorbistro.co.za; 86 Lower Main Rd, Observatory; mains R50; ☺8.30am-11pm Mon-Fri, 9am-11pm Sat & Sun; 📮Observatory) A tattooed mermaid in a round portrait on the wall looks down on the tattooed patrons of this slick new bistro serving comfort food – burgers, salads, pastas – all done well and affordably. The opening times refer to food; the bar here can kick on until 2am on the weekend.

CHARLY'S BAKERY
BAKERY, CAFE **$**

Map p270 (www.charlysbakery.co.za; 38 Canterbury St, The Fringe; baked goods R12.50-20; ☺8am-5pm Tue-Fri, 8.30am-2pm Sat; 🅿; 📮Golden Acre Bus Terminal) The fabulous female team here, stars of the reality TV series *Charly's Cake Angels,* make – as they say – 'mucking afazing' cupcakes and other baked goods. In a heritage building that is as colourfully decorated as one of their cakes, the team have recently added a shop upstairs to sell cupcake-inspired T's, cushions, soft toys, aprons and the like.

QUEEN OF TARTS
CAFE **$**

Map p272 (📞021-448 2420; 213 Lower Main Rd, Observatory; mains R45-70; ☺8am-4pm Mon-Fri, 8am-2.30pm Sat; 📮Observatory) The image of a young Queen Elizabeth II gazes out over customers from a cake tin at this charming cafe decorated like your granny's kitchen. The sweet and savoury tarts and other confections are delish and can also be bought at the Neighbourgoods Market.

THE DELI
SALADS, SANDWICHES **$**

Map p270 (190 Sir Lowry Rd, Woodstock; mains R40; ☺8am-4pm Mon-Fri, 8am-1pm Sat; 📮Woodstock; 🖉) The Kitchen too busy? Don't sweat it – there's an equally appealing, fresh, wholesome food operation across the road run by ex-Brits Nicky and Carlos. Unlike the Kitchen, it's open Saturday morning.

SUPERETTE
CAFE, DELI **$**

Map p270 (www.superette.co.za; 218 Albert Rd, Woodstock; mains R50; ☺9am-4pm Mon-Fri, 9am-2pm Sat; 📮Woodstock) From the same guys behind the gallery What if the World and the organisers of the Neighbourgoods Market comes this laid-back, tastefully turned out and oh-so-trendy neighbourhood cafe – a barometer of the gentrification of Woodstock. Try their all-day breakfast sandwich or baked goods made with natural sugars.

CAFÉ GANESH
AFRO-INDIAN **$**

Map p272 (38B Trill Rd, Observatory; mains R40-70; ☺6-11.30pm Mon-Sat; 📮Observatory) Sample *pap* (maize porridge) and veg, grilled springbok or lamb curry at this funky hang-out, squeezed into an alley between two buildings. Junkyard decor and matchbox-label wallpaper create that chic-shack look.

ARTISAN BAKER
BAKERY, CAFE **$**

Map p270 (www.artisanbaker.co.za; 399 Albert Rd, Salt River; mains R50; ☺7.30am-4pm Mon-Fri, 8am-3pm Sat; 📮Salt River) If for nothing else, drop by the Artisan Baker to sample excellent homemade pies – perfectly crusty pastry packed with fillings such as lemon chicken, beef in chocolate and chilli sauce, or pork and cider. They also do their own burgers, cassoulet, breads and jams.

🍷 DRINKING & NIGHTLIFE

TOP CHOICE AMADODA
BAR, BRAAI

Map p270 (www.amadoda.co.za; 1-4 Strand St, Woodstock; ☺5pm-midnight Tue-Thu, noon-2am Fri & Sat, 1pm-midnight Sun) Pulling off a township braai (barbecue; menus start at R30) and shebeen atmosphere, is this slickly decorated venue, tucked away down a side road beside the railway tracks, that attracts an racially mixed crowd. The juke box is stacked with African, jazz and house music tracks; it's worth checking out late on a weekend evening when patrons start to boogie.

TOP CHOICE ESPRESSOLAB
MICROROASTERS
COFFEE

Map p270 (espressolabmicroroasters.com; Old Biscuit Mill, 375 Albert Rd, Woodstock; ☺8am-4pm Mon-Fri, 8am-2pm Sat; 🅿; 📮Woodstock) Geek out about coffee at this lab staffed with passionate roasters and baristas. Their beans, which come from single farms, estates and co-ops from around the world, are packaged with tasting notes such as found for fine wines.

DON PEDRO
RESTAURANT-BAR

Map p270 (📞021-447 6125; http://donpedros.co.za; 113 Roodebloem Rd, Woodstock; ☺4pm-midnight Tue-Sat) Madame Zingara has sprinkled her magic across this old place and created a romantic boudoir suitable for all the Don's 'beautiful wives'. Torch singers belt out numbers from beside the self-playing piano and the menu is equally retro. Of course, they still do a wide range of Don Pedros – liqueur coffees made with ice cream.

TRUTH
COFFEE

Map p270 (www.truthcoffee.com; 36 Buitenkant St, The Fringe; ⊘6am-midnight) Occupying a 16,000 sq metre-space is this self-described 'steampunk roastery and coffee bar', the new HQ of the coffee company that also has a branch at the Prestwich Memorial.

WOODSTOCK LOUNGE
CAFE, BAR

Map p270 (www.woodstocklounge.co.za; 70 Roodebloem Rd, Woodstock; ⊘noon-midnight Mon-Sat) Wall-sized prints of black and white photos of old Woodstock provide some visual relief at this white box cafe-bar that's part of the area's renaissance. There are pretty good pizzas to go with Jack Black on tap and TV screens and comfy sofas to watch sport.

QUE PASA
DANCE CLUB

Map p270 (www.quepasa.co.za; 15A Caledon St, The Fringe; cover from R30; ⬛Golden Acre Bus Terminal) Dance classes and dance parties, usually on Saturday, are held at this long-running Latin and salsa dance studio. On Sunday nights they host a tango salon.

☆ ENTERTAINMENT

TOP CHOICE FUGARD
THEATRE

Map p270 (☎021-461 4554; www.thefugard.com; Caledon St, The Fringe; ⬛Golden Acre Bus Terminal) Named in honour of Athol Fugard, South Africa's best-known living playwright, this very impressive arts centre has already attracted the likes of acting knights Ian McKellan and Anthony Sher, with more stars on the way. The former Congregational Church Hall has been skilfully transformed to contain two stages, the largest theatre also doubling up as a 'bioscope' (a fancy word for a digital cinema where top international dance and opera performances are screened); tickets include a glass of bubbly.

TOP CHOICE ASSEMBLY
LIVE MUSIC

Map p270 (www.theassembly.co.za; 61 Harrington St, The Fringe; cover R30-50; ⬛Golden Acre Bus Terminal) In an old furniture assembly factory, this live music and DJ performance space has made its mark with an exciting, eclectic line-up of both local and international artists.

JOU MA SE COMEDY CLUB
COMEDY CLUB

Map p272 (www.kurt.co.za/jmscc; River Club, Liesbeek Parkway, Observatory; tickets R80; ⊘8.30pm Thu; ⬛Observatory) The title means 'Your mother's ***!' but you don't need to understand Afrikaans slang to get the jokes of funny guy Kurt Schoonraad and his pals at this laugh-a-minute comedy club, one of the best of several such shows in the city.

MERCURY LIVE & LOUNGE
LIVE MUSIC

Map p270 (www.mercuryl.co.za; 43 De Villiers St, District Six; admission R20-40) Cape Town's premier rock venue plays host to top South African bands and overseas visitors. The sound quality is good and if you don't like the band, there's always the DJ bar Mercury Lounge, below, and the Shack bar, next door.

TAGORE
LIVE MUSIC

Map p272 (☎021-447 8717; 42 Trill Rd, Observatory; ⊘5pm-midnight; ⬛Observatory) Candles, cosy nooks and crannies, and avant-garde music set the scene at this tiny cafe-bar, a favourite with the Obs alternative set. There's no cover for the sets that usually kick off at 9.30pm Wednesday, Friday and Saturday. Do sample their food, made to traditional Zulu recipes by the lovely Tobekele.

TOUCH OF MADNESS
SPOKEN WORD

Map p272 (☎021-448 2266; www.touchofmadness.co.za; 12 Nuttall Rd, Observatory; ⊘noon-late Mon-Sat, 7pm-late Sun; ⬛⬛; ⬛Observatory) This long-running bar and restaurant, which dubs itself a 'Victorian quaffery', offers an eclectic art-house atmosphere, dressed up in purple with lace trimmings. Wannabe poets should check out the Monday night open-mike poetry fests starting at 8pm.

OBZ CAFÉ
LIVE MUSIC

Map p272 (☎021-448 5555; www.obzcafe.co.za; 115 Lower Main Rd, Observatory; admission R20-50; ⬛Observatory) As if the human theatre of Lower Main Rd wasn't enough, inside this spacious cafe-bar is a separate performance space where you can catch all manner of music shows and burlesque shows.

THEATRE IN THE DISTRICT THEATRE

Map p270 (☑079 770 4686; www.theatreinthedistrict.co.za; Chapel St, District Six) The original St Philip's Church, built in 1885, is one of the few surviving remnants of District Six. It now serves as a community theatre and arts project base. From October through to April come here on Monday night to see *Woza Cape Town,* a highly energetic production by a talented bunch of youngsters combining dance, song, poetry and a little drama. The show starts at around 7.15pm; arrive an hour earlier if you want to also eat the pre-show Cape Malay meal.

MAGNET THEATRE THEATRE

Map p272 (☑021-448 3436; www.magnetheatre.co.za; Unit 1, The Old Match Factory, cnr St Michaels & Lower Main Rds, Observatory; tickets R50; ☐Observatory) This National Lottery–funded project works with youngsters on a variety of performance and theatre projects. Some of their shows have won awards at festivals in South Africa and overseas.

HOUSE OF JOY SPOKEN WORD, MUSIC

Map p272 (☑021-447 9844; emmanence@gmail.com; 6 Lower Trill Rd, Observatory; tickets R30; ☐Observatory) Usually on the last Sunday of the month Emma and Kolade turn their home, tucked away on the west side of the train line, into the venue for this afternoon event – perhaps a poetry reading or some folk music. There's food and drink and it's a very relaxed, arty vibe.

 SHOPPING

TOP CHOICE OLD BISCUIT MILL SHOPPING CENTRE

Map p270 (www.theoldbiscuitmill.co.za; 373-375 Albert Rd, Salt River; ℙ; ☐Salt River) A one-time biscuit factory is home to a very appealing collection of arts, craft, fashion and design shops, as well as places to eat and drink. Favourites include **Clementina Ceramics** (http://clementina.co.za) and **Imiso Ceramics** (http://imisoceramics.co.za/) for ceramics; colourful craft store **Heartworks** (www.heartworks.co.za); the rustic emporium **Karoo Moon Country Store** and quirky interior design emporium **Abode** (www.abode.co.za); **Cocofair** (www.cocoafair.com), Africa's

only organic bean-to-shop chocolate factory; **Kat Van Duinen** (http://katvanduinen.com) for lovely clothes and distinctive handbags; and the fantastic **Mü & Me** (www.muandme.net), the design studio and shop for Daley Muller who creates super-cute graphic art for cards, wrapping paper, stationery and kids' T-shirts.

TOP CHOICE NEIGHBOURGOODS MARKET MARKET

Map p270 (www.neighbourgoodsmarket.co.za; 373-375 Albert Rd, Salt River; ☉9am-2pm Sat; ℙ; ☐Salt River) An area used as a car park during the week at the Old Biscuit Mill morphs into this fabulous weekly event, the first and still the best of the artisan goods markets that are now common across the Cape. Food and drinks are gathered in the main area where you can pick up groceries, gourmet goodies or just graze, while the separate Designergoods area hosts a must-buy selection of local fashions and accessories.

TOP CHOICE BOOK LOUNGE BOOKS

Map p270 (☑021-462 2425; www.booklounge.co.za; 71 Roeland St, The Fringe; ☉9.30am-7.30pm Mon-Fri, 8.30am-6pm Sat, 10am-4pm Sun) Mervyn Sloman has been practically canonised by local booklovers for creating this heavenly bookshop that has become the hub of Cape Town's literary scene, thanks to its great selection of titles, comfy chairs, simple cafe and program of events. There are up to three talks or book launches a week, generally with free drinks and nibbles, and readings for kids on the weekend. Also look for the handmade Elizabethan bags and brooches here made from recycled pieces of fabric and other found objects.

ASHANTI FABRICS, CRAFTS

Map p270 (www.ashantidesign.com; 133-135 Sir Lowry Rd, Woodstock; ☐Woodstock) Baskets, mats, lamp shades, pillows, bags and cushions are among the many rainbow-coloured products on sale, gathered from across Africa at this great artisan design shop. Often no two pieces are alike. You can also buy their fabrics by the metre.

DESIGN AFRIKA ARTS & CRAFTS

Map p270 (www.designafrika.co.za; 42 Hares Ave, Woodstock; ☉9am-5pm Mon-Fri) Weaving designs across Africa is Binky Newman's slogan for this marvellous, hidden-away emporium of arts and crafts gathered from remote corners of the continent. Come for traditional fabrics, metalware, carved wood items and tribal artefacts.

SOUTH AFRICAN
PRINT GALLERY
ART GALLERY

Map p270 (www.printgallery.co.za; 109 Sir Lowry Rd, Woodstock; ◎9.30am-4pm Tue-Fri, 10am-1pm Sat; ▣Woodstock) Of all the galleries clustered along this strip of Sir Lowry Rd, this one specialising in prints by local artists – both well established and up-and-coming – is most likely to have something that is both affordable and small enough to fit comfortably in your suitcase for transport home.

STEVENSON
ART GALLERY

Map p270 (www.stevenson.info; 160 Sir Lowry Rd, Woodstock; ◎9am-5pm Mon-Fri, 10am-1pm Sat; ▣Woodstock) Exhibitions at this well-respected gallery have included the humorous, subversive work of Anton Kannemeyer, also known as Joe Dog, creator of the darkly satiric comic Bitterkomix with Conrad Botes, who is also represented here. You can also browse pieces of the distinctive ceramic art of Hylton Nel.

WHAT IF THE WORLD
ART GALLERY

Map p270 (www.whatiftheworld.com; 1 Argyle St, Woodstock; ◎10am-4.30pm Tue-Fri, 10am-3pm Sat; ▣Woodstock) A new expanded base in an old synagogue and associated buildings for this gallery, which can be credited with kicking Capetonian creativity up the backside. Drop by to witness the unruly forces of young South African art. Also on the site is the furniture and interior design shop of **Gregor Jenkins** (www.gregorjenkin.com) and – in the works – a bakery.

GOODMAN GALLERY CAPE
ART GALLERY

Map p270 (www.goodman-gallery.com; 3rd fl, Fairweather House, 176 Sir Lowry Rd, Woodstock; ◎9.30am-5.30pm Tue-Fri, 10am-4pm Sat; ▣Woodstock) A big gun of the Jo'burg art world, the Goodman Gallery was one of the few to encourage artists of all races during apartheid. They represent luminaries like William Kentridge and Willie Bester, as well as up-and-coming artists. The entrance is around the back of the building.

BLANK PROJECTS
ART GALLERY

Map p270 (www.blankprojects.com; 113-115 Sir Lowry Rd, Woodstock; ◎10.30am-4pm Tue-Fri, 10.30am-1pm Sat; ▣Woodstock) By their own confession this is 'not a normal gallery'. Rather think of it as a project space for shows which can be highly conceptual and avant garde.

RECREATE
INTERIOR DESIGN, FURNITURE

Map p270 (www.recreate.za.net; 368 Albert Rd, Salt River; ▣Salt River) Extraordinary re-purposed furniture and lighting by Katie Thompson – think suitcases turned into chairs, crockery as lamp stands and fridge magnets made from computer keyboard letters. Around the back continue your interior design adventures at **Vamp** (www.vamp furniture.co.za) where you may also be able to pick up original framed Trechtikoff prints.

UMLUNGU
CRAFTS

Map p272 (www.umlungu.co.za; 4 Bowden Rd, Observatory; ◎8am-4pm Mon-Fri; ▣Observatory) Quirky and colourful hand-painted metal fridge magnets and other decorative pieces are the prime range of this craft operation – they're sold at many craft shops and markets across the city but this is main distribution centre. Recycled materials also go into other gifts such as wire radios and plastic chickens.

MNANDI TEXTILES
& DESIGN
CLOTHING, TEXTILES

Map p272 (90 Station Rd, Observatory; ▣Observatory) Mnandi sells cloth from all over Africa as well as clothing printed with everything from ANC election posters to animals and traditional African patterns. You can also have clothes tailor-made. The Xhosa women and Desmond Tutu cloth dolls (R290) are adorable.

HEATH NASH
INTERIOR DESIGN

Map p270 (☎021-447 5757; www.heathnash.com; 2 Mountain Rd, Woodstock; ◎8.30am-5pm Mon-Thu, 8.30am-4pm Fri) Give the international hit of the Cape Town arts-and-crafts scene a call before visiting his Woodstock studio, in an unmarked building off Victoria Rd. Here you'll find his full range of fab Flowerball shades made from recycled plastics, wire-work fruit bowls, candelabra and coat racks, plus new products in the making.

WOODHEAD'S
LEATHER GOODS

Map p270 (www.woodheads.co.za; 29 Caledon St, The Fringe; ▣Golden Acre Bus Terminal) If you're after a full hide – cow, buffalo, antelope, zebra etc – head over to these savvy guys who've been catering to Cape Town's leather trade since 1867. They also stock locally made flip flops, hide boots, bags and belts.

AFRICAN HOME   CRAFTS
Map p270 (www.africanhome.co.za; 41 Caledon St, The Fringe; ◷8.30am-5pm Mon-Fri) There's an appealing range of fair-trade crafts on sale here, including striking white-beaded mirror and picture frames.

BLANK {SPACE}   STATIONERY, PRINTS
Map p270 (http://blankspace.co.za/; 71 Roeland St, The Fringe; ◷1-6pm Tue-Fri, 10am-1pm Sat) Not so blank after all, this cute shop sells limited-edition art prints, stationary and wrapping paper – perfect for wrapping a gift from the Book Lounge next door.

BROMWELL   BOUTIQUE MALL
Map p270 (www.thebromwell.co.za; 250 Albert Rd, Woodstock; ◷9am-5pm daily; 🚉Woodstock) This stylish collection of vendors selling exotic artefacts, fashions, accessories, art and decor is huddled together in the spruced up old Bromwell Hotel, dating back to the 1930s. Following the Woodstock redevelopment blueprint to the T, there's a cafe, bakery and deli on the ground floor.

WOODSTOCK FOUNDRY   SHOPPING CENTRE
Map p270 (160 Albert Rd, Woodstock; 🚉Woodstock) This renovation project of a heritage building has resulted in a handsome complex of design studios and shops built around the cast metal foundry Bronze Age (www.bronzeageart.com). Tenants include: the quirky interior design store O.live; furniture designed by John Vogel (www.vogeldesign.co.za); jewellery in brass, silver and gold by Dear Rae; the street art of Selah; and West Street Café, serving all day breakfasts, and promising live folk, blues and jazz music shows on Saturday nights.

SALT CIRCLE ARCADE   SHOPPING CENTRE
Map p270 (19 Kent Rd, Salt River; 🚉Salt River) Providing competition for the Old Biscuit Mill is this new development across the road. Tenants so far include **Karizma Décor & Design** (www.karizmadecor.co.za),

Henry Garment Archaeology (garmentarchaeology.blog.com) – essentially well edited pre-loved clothing; **Cloth** (www.louisdesigns.com) for designer shirts; and **Ma Mère Maison** confectioners and bakers. A Saturday market is also scheduled for the central courtyard.

FIELD OFFICE   INTERIOR DESIGN
Map p270 (www.fieldoffice.co.za; 37 Barrack St, The Fringe; 🚉Golden Acre Bus Terminal) This spacious 'coffice' (a cafe with wi-fi where people often bring their laptops and work for the day) also doubles as the showroom for furniture and lighting designers **Pedersen & Lennard** (www.pedersenlennard.co.za) as well as the canvas and leather bags of **Chapel** (www.store.chapelgoods.co.za), which are also sold at the Old Biscuit Mill's Saturday market.

INTSANGU   FASHION
Map p272 (intsangu.com; 111 Lower Main Rd, Observatory; 🚉Observatory) Dreadlocked dude Sizwe Shangase, from Durban, displays his unisex streetwear designs in this narrow shop, more an alleyway than a boutique. The brand name means 'dope' in Nguni.

🏃 SPORTS & ACTIVITIES

CITY ROCK   CLIMBING
Map p272 (📞021-447 1326; www.cityrock.co.za; cnr Collingwood & Anson Rds, Observatory; ◷9am-9pm Mon-Thu, 9am-6pm Fri, 10am-6pm Sat & Sun; 🚉Observatory) This popular indoor climbing gym offers climbing courses (from R190), and hires out and sells climbing gear. A day pass for the climbing wall is R85.

LOGICAL GOLF ACADEMY   GOLF
Map p272 (📞021-448 6358; www.logicalgolf.co.za; River Club, Liesbeek Parkway, Observatory; 🚉Observatory) Behind the River Club is this driving range and golf school where you can perfect your swing. A 90-minute lesson is R550.

Gardens & Surrounds

Neighbourhood Top Five

1 Ride the revolving cableway up **Table Mountain** then walk across the top to the summit at Maclear's Beacon or abseil off the edge (p88).

2 View the nation's best visual art at the **South African National Gallery** (p91).

3 Discover all about South Africa's Jewish immigrants at the **South African Jewish Museum** (p90).

4 Graze at the relaxed **City Bowl Market** (p94) on Saturday.

5 Climb **Lion's Head** (p96) for a panoramic view of the city and coast.

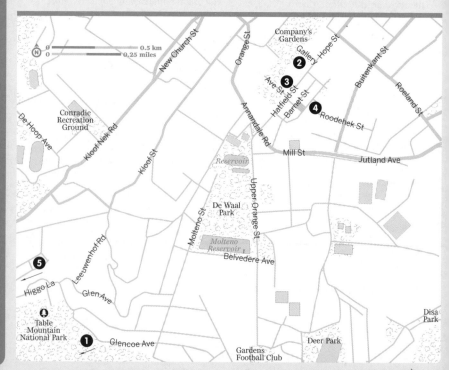

For more detail of this area, see Map p274 ➡

Explore Gardens & Surrounds

Taking its name from the Company's Gardens, the City Bowl end of this mountainside region is where you'll find some of Cape Town's premier museums. Further up the slopes are desirable residential areas, home to some of the city's most appealing and individual accommodation options, not least of which is the leafy compound of the famous Mount Nelson Hotel.

It goes without saying that the area is dominated by the massive bulk of Table Mountain and the adjacent rocky humps of Lion's Head and Devil's Peak. You'll hardly be able to keep your eyes off the mountain, especially when the famous tablecloth of cloud is tumbling off its summit – usually in the late afternoon. Climbing it more than repays the effort but, if that's not on the cards, then there's always the cableway.

Kloof St, the Gardens' commercial spine, is perfect for leisurely strolls with its collection of individual boutiques, restaurants and lively bars. West and up Signal Hill you'll find the suburb of Tamboerskloof, while Oranjezicht lies to the east behind De Waal Park. Windblasted Vredehoek is further to the east towards Devil's Peak (it's marked by the trio of residential blocks officially called Disa Park, but more commonly known as the 'tampon towers'), while Higgovale, sheltered from the wind, is to the west.

Local Life

➡ **Concerts** The Friends of De Waal Park arrange a season of free Sunday-afternoon concerts in the park's bandstand (p91).

➡ **De-stress** Enjoy a clothed, oil-free massage at contemporary styled Enmasse (p96).

➡ **Movies** Catch the latest flick and art-house gems at the Labia, the neighbourhood's cinema (p94).

Getting There & Away

➡ **Bus** MyCiTi buses run from the Foreshore and City Bowl up to the Gardens Centre; there are plans to extend routes up Kloof Nek Rd, too.

➡ **Shared taxi** These shuttle up Kloof St to Kloof Nek Rd and over to Camps Bay before returning to the City Bowl.

➡ **Walk** It's easy enough to walk between the main sights of lower Gardens, but be prepared for quite a workout if you plan on hiking up to the lower cableway.

Lonely Planet's Top Tip

Bertram House and Rust en Vreugd are a couple of small museums in the Gardens area that you are likely to have to yourself. The former is the city's last remaining example of a Georgian-style red brick house while the latter has a lovely formal garden and some beautiful watercolour and print art works.

 Best Places to Eat

➡ Maria's (p92)
➡ Manna Epicure (p92)
➡ Woodlands Eatery (p92)
➡ Aubergine (p92)
➡ The Dog's Bollocks (p92)

For reviews, see p92 ➡

Best Places to Drink

➡ Planet (p93)
➡ The Power & The Glory/Black Ram (p93)
➡ Saints (p93)
➡ Perseverance Tavern (p93)

For reviews, see p93 ➡

Best Places to Shop

➡ City Bowl Market (p94)
➡ The Fringe Arts (p94)
➡ Grant Mason Originals (p94)
➡ Stefania Morland (p95)
➡ Bluecollarwhitecollar (p95)
➡ LIM (p95)

For reviews, see p94 ➡

GARDENS & SURROUNDS

MARK KARRASS / CORBIS ©

TOP SIGHTS
TABLE MOUNTAIN

About 600 million years in the making, and a canvas painted with the rich diversity of the Cape floral kingdom, Table Mountain is truly iconic. Its flat-topped outline, attended by the outcrops of Devil's Peak to the east and Lion's Head to the west, is so distinctive it was used by astronomers to name the Mensa ('Table') constellation of stars. You can admire the mountain – voted one of the world's New7Wonders of Nature (www. new7wonders.com) in 2011 – from multiple angles around the city, but you really can't say you've visited Cape Town until you've stood on top of it.

DON'T MISS
➡ Cableway
➡ Maclear's Beacon
➡ Abseil Africa
➡ Dassies

PRACTICALITIES
Lower cableway station off Map p274
➡ www.sanparks.org/parks/table_mountain
➡ Climbing & hiking free; cableway charges apply

Table Mountain Cableway

Riding the **cableway** (☎021-424 8181; www.tablemountain.net; Tafelberg Rd; adult one-way/return R100/195, child R50/95; ⊙8.30am-7pm Feb-Nov, 8am-10pm Dec & Jan) up Table Mountain is a no-brainer; the views from the revolving car and the summit are phenomenal. Once you are at the top there are souvenir shops, a good cafe and some easy walks to follow.

Departures are every 10 minutes in high season (December to February) and every 15-20 minutes at all other times, but the cableway doesn't operate when it's dangerously windy (call in advance to see if it's operating), and there's obviously little point going up if you are simply going to be wrapped in the cloud known as the 'tablecloth'. The best visibility and conditions are likely to be first thing in the morning or in the evening.

Climbing the Mountain

In 1503 Portuguese navigator Admiral Antonio de Saldanha bagged the title of 'first white guy to climb Table Mountain'; he named it 'Taboa do Cabo' (Table of the Cape) although the Khoe-san, the Cape's original inhabitants, knew it as 'Hoerikwaggo' meaning

'Mountain of the Sea'. Visitors have been climbing the mountain ever since and there's a range of ways you can ascend from Gardens.

None of the routes up are easy, but the 3km-long Platteklip Gorge route, accessed from Tafelberg Rd, is at least straightforward. It's very steep and you should reckon on it taking you about 2½ hours to reach the upper cableway station at a steady pace. Be warned that the route is exposed to the sun, so climb as early in the morning as possible and bring plenty of water and sunblock.

Another possibility, recommended for very experienced climbers only, is the India Fenster route that starts from directly behind the lower cableway station and heads straight up. The hikers you see from the cableway, perched like mountain goats on apparently sheer cliffs, are taking this route.

Climbing Around the Mountain

There's no need to climb to the top of the mountain to get brilliant views. A short hike up behind the lower cableway station will bring you to the Contour Path, running a fairly level way eastwards around Devil's Peak to the King's Blockhouse and, eventually, Constantia Nek.

The Pipe Track runs along the west side of the mountain towards the Twelve Apostles and provides stunning coastal views; the path was originally constructed to carry water along a pipe from Disa Gorge on Table Mountain's Back Table to the Molteno Reservoir in Oranjezicht. This route is best walked in the early morning, before the sun hits this side of the mountain. The Kasteelspoort Path off the Pipe Track is an alternative way to the top of the mountain.

On Top of Mountain

Concrete paths lead from the upper cableway station to the restaurant, shop and various terraces. These are easy enough to stroll around without a guide, and from them you may even be able to spot the dassie, a large hamster-like creature who – believe it or not – is related to the elephant. Free volunteer-guided walks across Table Mountain's plateau run at 10am and noon daily from beside the upper cableway station.

To reach the mountain's 1088m summit you'll need to go a bit further along the track to Maclear's Beacon, a distance of around 5km, which should take one hour for the round trip. Don't attempt this route if there's low cloud or mist on the mountain as it's very easy to lose your way.

DISCOUNTS

There's a 10% discount on cableway tickets if you book online. The voucher, valid for 14 days from your nominated day of use, allows you to skip the line at the ticket counter.

The 112m drop off the top of Table Mountain with Abseil Africa (Map p264; ☏021-424 4760; www. abseilafrica.co.za; R595) is a guaranteed adrenaline rush. Don't even think of tackling it unless you've got a head (and a stomach) for heights. Take your time, because the views are breathtaking. Tag on a guided hike up Platteklip Gorge for R250.

EATING & SLEEPING

Near the upper cableway station, the self-serve **Table Mountain Café** offers tasty deli items and meals, compostable plates and containers, and good coffee. They also sell wine and beer, so there's no need to cart your bottle up the slopes to toast the view. Camping isn't allowed on the mountain. Should you wish to spend the night up here, the only option is to book into the self-catering accommodation at the Overseers Cottage (p31).

GARDENS & SURROUNDS TABLE MOUNTAIN

TOP SIGHTS
TABLE MOUNTAIN

TOP SIGHTS
SOUTH AFRICAN JEWISH MUSEUM

This imaginatively designed museum incorporates the beautifully restored Old Synagogue (1863). Downstairs is a partial re-creation of a Lithuanian *shtetl* (village); many of South Africa's Jews fled this part of Eastern Europe during the pogroms and persecution of the late 19th and early 20th centuries. The permanent exhibition *Hidden Treasures of Japanese Art* showcases a collection of exquisite *netsuke*, carved pieces of ivory and wood. There are also temporary exhibitions that are usually worth seeing.

Your ticket also entitles you to watch the fascinating 25-minute documentary *Nelson Mandela: A Righteous Man* in the building across the courtyard from the museum's exit. Upstairs the **Cape Town Holocaust Centre** (www.holocaust.org.za; admission free; ☺10am-5pm Sun-Thu, 10am-2pm Fri) packs a lot in with a considerable emotional punch. The history of anti-Semitism is set in a South African context with parallels drawn to the local struggle for freedom.

Also within the compound is the functioning and beautifully decorated **Great Synagogue** (guided tours free; ☺10am-4pm Sun-Thu), a 1905 building in neo-Egyptian style; a good gift shop; and the kosher **Café Riteve**, a pleasant spot for a snack. You need photo ID to be able to enter the compound.

DON'T MISS
....
➡ Old Synagogue
➡ Great Synagogue
➡ Cape Town Holocaust Centre
➡ *Nelson Mandela: A Righteous Man* video

PRACTICALITIES
....
➡ Map p274
➡ ☎021-465 1546
➡ www.sajewishmuseum.co.za
➡ 88 Hatfield St, Gardens
➡ adult/child R40/free
➡ ☺10am-5pm Sun-Thu, 10am-2pm Fri
➡ 🚌Government Avenue

◉ SIGHTS

TABLE MOUNTAIN   MOUNTAIN
See p88.

**SOUTH AFRICAN
JEWISH MUSEUM**   MUSEUM
See p90.

**SOUTH AFRICAN
NATIONAL GALLERY**   GALLERY
Map p274 (www.iziko.org.za/museums/south
-african-national-gallery; Government Ave,
Gardens;adult/child R20/free; ⊙10am-5pm Tue-
Sun; ☐Government Avenue) The impressive
permanent collection of the nation's premier art space harks back to Dutch times
and includes some extraordinary pieces.
But it's often contemporary works, such
as the *Butcher Boys* sculpture by Jane Alexander, looking like a trio of *Lord of the
Rings* orcs who have stumbled into the gallery, that stand out the most. Also check out
the remarkable teak door in the courtyard,
carved by Herbert Vladimir Meyerowitz,
with scenes representing the global wan-
derings of the Jews; his carvings also adorn
the tops of the door frames throughout the
gallery. There's also a good shop with some
interesting books and gifts.

SOUTH AFRICAN MUSEUM   MUSEUM
Map p274 (☎021-481 3330; www.iziko.org.za/
museums/south-african-museum; 25 Queen Victoria St, Gardens; adult/child R20/10, Sat by donation; ⊙10am-5pm; ☐Michaelis) South Africa's
oldest museum may be showing its age but
it does contain a wide and often intriguing
series of exhibitions, many on the country's
natural history. The best galleries are the
newest, showcasing the art and culture
of the area's first peoples, the Khoekhoen
and San, and including the famous Linton
Panel, an amazing example of San rock art.
There's an extraordinary delicacy to the
paintings, particularly the ones of graceful
elands. Also worth looking out for are the
startlingly lifelike displays in the African
Cultures Gallery of African people (cast
from living subjects); the terracotta Lyden-
burg Heads, the earliest-known examples of
African sculpture (AD 500–700); a 2m-wide
nest of the sociable weaver bird, a veritable
avian apartment block, in the Wonders of
Nature Gallery; and the atmospheric Whale
Well, hung with giant whale skeletons and
models and resounding with taped recordings of their calls.

PLANETARIUM   PLANETARIUM
Map p274 (☎021-481 3900; www.iziko.org.
za/museums/planetarium; 25 Queen Victoria
St, Gardens; adult/child R25/10; ⊙10am-5pm;
☐Michaelis) The displays and star shows
at the Planetarium, attached to the South
African Museum, unravel the mysteries of
the southern hemisphere's night sky. Call or
check the website for times of daily shows
using images caught by the Southern African Large Telescope in the Karoo (which
has the largest aperture of any telescope
in the world); there's a kids' show at noon
daily.

RUST EN VREUGD   GALLERY, GARDEN
Map p274 (www.iziko.org.za/museums/rust-en
-vreugd; 78 Buitenkant St, Gardens; admission by
donation; ⊙9am-5pm Mon-Fri; ☐Gardens) This
delightful mansion, dating from 1777–78
and fronted by a period-style garden re-created in 1986 from the original layout, was
once the home of the state prosecutor. It
now houses part of the Iziko William Fehr
collection of paintings and furniture (the
major part is in the Castle of Good Hope);
you may see detailed lithographs of Zulus
by George Angus and a delicately painted
watercolour panorama of Table Mountain
from 1850, by Lady Eyre.

BERTRAM HOUSE   MUSEUM
Map p274 (www.iziko.org.za/museums/bertram
-house; cnr Orange St & Government Ave, Gardens;
adult/child around R5/R2; ⊙10am-5pm Mon-Sat;
☐Government Avenue) A minor diversion if
you're at this end of the Company's Gardens
is to drop by the only surviving Georgian-
style brick house in Cape Town, dating from
the 1840s. Inside it's decorated appropriately to its era with Regency-style furnishings and displays of 19th-century English
porcelain.

DE WAAL PARK   PARK
Map p274 (Camp St, Gardens; ☐Government
Avenue) Named in honour of Christiaan de
Waal, a former mayor of Cape Town, this
park opened in 1895 and is planted with
several species of exotic and flowering trees.
The bandstand in its centre was made in
Glasgow and was originally brought to the
city for the 1904–5 Cape Town Exhibition at
Green Point. It's a community park, much
patronised by dog owners and families who
live in the area. Between late November and
early April a series of free Sunday afternoon

concerts, usually starting around 3pm, are held in the bandstand.

EATING

TOP CHOICE MARIA'S
GREEK $

Map p274 (☑021-461 3333; Dunkley Sq, Barnet St, Gardens; mains R50-90; ⊙11am-10.30pm Mon-Fri, 5.30-10.30pm Sat; P; 🚇Government Avenue) There a few places more romantic or relaxing for a meal than Maria's on warm night, when you can tuck into classic Greek meze and dishes such as moussaka on rustic tables beneath the trees in the square.

MANNA EPICURE
CONTEMPORARY, BAKERY $

Map p274 (☑021-426 2413; 151 Kloof St, Gardens; mains R40-110; ⊙9am-6pm Tue-Sat, 9am-4pm Sun) Come for a deliciously simple breakfast or lunch, or for late-afternoon cocktails and tapas on the veranda of this white-box cafe. The freshly baked breads alone – coconut, or pecan and raisin – are worth dragging yourself up the hill for.

WOODLANDS EATERY
PIZZA, BURGERS $

Map p274 (☑021-801 5799; 2 Deer Park Dr West, Vredehoek; mains R60-70; ⊙5pm-10.30pm Tue-Thu, noon-midnight Fri-Sun) Having got the shabby chic look of mismatched furniture and quirky art down to a T, Woodlands also delivers on its comfort-food menu of gourmet pizzas, burgers and the like. Wash it all down with craft beers and ciders.

AUBERGINE
CONTEMPORARY $$$

Map p274 (☑021-465 4909; www.aubergine.co.za; 39 Barnet St, Gardens; mains R200, 3/4/5 courses R375/455/565; ⊙noon-2pm Wed-Fri, 5-10pm Mon-Sat; 🚇Government Avenue) Harald Bresselschmidt is one of Cape Town's most consistent chefs, producing creative yet unfussy dishes. Service and ambiance are equally impeccable. It's a good pre-theatre option as from 5 to 7pm they serve drinks and a selection of smaller dishes from their dinner menu. Look out for wine events at their new venture **Auslese** (Map p274; www.auslese.co.za; 115 Hope St, Gardens).

DOG'S BOLLOCKS
BURGERS $

Map p274 (6 Roodehek St, Gardens; burgers R50; ⊙5-10pm Mon-Sat; 🚇Gardens) One-man-band Nigel Wood tosses just 30 premium patties per night in this alleyway operation, so get there early if you want to sample some of the best burgers in Cape Town. They come with a variety of sauces and, if you're lucky, a bowl of his nachos, as well as Nige's wine in a tube. There's no elegant way to eat these beefy blockbusters but they're well worth getting your fingers sticky for.

SOCIETI BISTRO
FRENCH, CONTEMPORARY $

Map p274 (☑021-424 2100; http://societi.co.za; 50 Orange St, Gardens; mains R90-100; ⊙noon-11pm Mon-Sat; 🚇Michaelis) Dine in the courtyard garden, with Table Mountain views, or in the atmospheric, brick-walled and wine-rack covered interior on unfussy bistro dishes that are well prepared and proficiently served. Offers a decent selection of wines by the glass, as well as artisanal beers and spirits. Check their website for details of their cooking courses and sister establishment in Tokai.

KYOTO SUSHI GARDEN
JAPANESE $$

Map p274 (☑021-422 2001; 11 Lower Kloofnek Rd, Tamboerskloof; mains R80-130; ⊙6-11pm Mon-Sat) Beechwood furnishings and subtle lighting lend a Zen-calm air to this superior Japanese restaurant, owned by an LA expat but with an expert chef turning out sushi and sashimi. Their prawn noodle salad is excellent as is their Asian Mary cocktail.

LAZARI
INTERNATIONAL, GREEK $

Map p274 (☑021-461 9895; cnr Upper Maynard St & Vredehoek Ave, Vredehoek; mains R30-50; ⊙7.30am-4pm Mon-Fri, 8am-2.30pm Sat & Sun; 🛜; 🚇Gardens) Few proprietors nwork as hard as Chris Lazari to be friendly to their customers who, understandably, are a loyal bunch. It's buzzy, gay-friendly and great for brunch or an indulgent moment over coffee and cake. Check out the local art for sale.

DEER PARK CAFÉ
INTERNATIONAL, VEGETARIAN $

Map p274 (☑462 6311; 2 Deer Park Dr West, Vredehoek; mains R50-70; ⊙8am-9pm; 🛜🚼) Another good reason for schlepping up the mountain is to visit this relaxed cafe, fronting a kid's playground. The chunky wooden furniture gives it the feel of a big nursery, but the tasty food is anything but child's play. There're some great vegetarian options and a kids menu. The last Wednesday of the month they serve a vegan menu from 6pm.

MELISSA'S
INTERNATIONAL, DELI $

Map p274 (www.melissas.co.za; 94 Kloof St, Gardens; mains R50-70; ⊙7.30am-7pm Mon-Fri, 8am-

7pm Sat & Sun) Pay by weight for the delicious breakfast and lunch buffets (R17.50 per 100g) then browse the grocery shelves for picnic fare or gourmet gifts. Other branches in Newlands (corner Kildare Ln & Main St) and Victoria Wharf at the Waterfront.

FAT CACTUS
MEXICAN $

Map p274 (☎021-422 5022; www.fatcactus.co.za; 5 Park Rd; mains R70-100; ☺11am-11pm; ▣Michaelis) This much loved Mexican operation – its original location in Mowbray is still going strong – brings its fine fajitas and margaritas to town, living up to its mantra of 'always open, always cooking'.

LIQUORICE & LIME
INTERNATIONAL, DELI $

Map p274 (☎021-423 6921; 162 Kloof St, Gardens; sandwiches R38-50; ☺7am-4pm Mon-Fri, 7am-5pm Sat & Sun) Pause at this convivial gourmet deli on your way from climbing up or down Table Mountain or Lion's Head. The French toast with grilled banana is yummy and they have baked goods and sandwiches.

DAILY DELI
INTERNATIONAL, DELI $

Map p274 (☎021-426 0250; 13 Brownlow Rd, Tamboerskloof; mains R25-55; ☺8am-10pm; ☎) Locals swear by the breakfast and coffee at this cute whitewashed cottage with an iron-lace fringe veranda and street tables; it doubles up as a mini-deli for all of life's culinary essentials. Try their homemade ginger beer and dishes such as *bobotie* (delicately flavoured curry with a topping of beaten egg baked to a crust) or lasagne.

SAIGON
VIETNAMESE $

Map p274 (☎021-424 7669; cnr Kloof Rd & Camp St, Gardens; mains R65-110; ☺noon-2.30pm Sun-Fri, 5-10.30pm daily) There's a sushi bar at this smart restaurant with a view of Table Mountain, but they mainly serve Vietnamese cuisine. The rice-paper rolls are well made and you can't go wrong with a steaming bowl of beef noodle pho. A popular showstopper is the mixed seafood hotplate, flambéed at the table.

🍷 DRINKING & NIGHTLIFE

PLANET
COCKTAIL BAR

Map p274 (☎021-483 1864; Mount Nelson Hotel, 76 Orange St, Gardens; ℗; ▣Government Avenue) Isn't that Rod Stewart on the sofa? Drinks at the old Nellie's cool silver-coated champagne and cocktail bar can be a star-studded affair. Join the smart set to enjoy some 250 different bubblies and 50-odd alcoholic concoctions. The restaurant is also worth considering for a special occasion, including the chance to sample a gourmet vegan degustation menu.

THE POWER & THE GLORY/ BLACK RAM
CAFE, BAR

Map p274 (13B Kloof Nek Rd, Tamboerskloof; ☺cafe 8am-10pm, bar 5pm-late Mon-Sat) The coffee and food (pretzel hot dogs, crusty pies and other artisan munches) are good but it's the smoky, cosy bar that packs the trendsters in, particularly on Thursday to Saturday nights.

SAINTS
CRAFT BEER

Map p274 (www.saintsburgerjoint.co.za; 84 Kloof St, Gardens) They serve gourmet burgers (doesn't everywhere in Cape Town these days?) but what we like is their range of Camelthorn craft beers, which you can sample in 100mL tasting glasses (R6 or four for R22) before deciding which pint to go for. Also a nice touch: the lyrics of 'Stairway to Heaven' painted on the stairs.

PERSEVERANCE TAVERN
PUB

Map p274 (www.perseverancetavern.co.za; 83 Buitenkant St, Gardens; ☺4pm-2am Mon, noon-2am Tue-Sat, 11am-8pm Sun) This convivial heritage-listed pub, which is affectionately known as Persies and has been around since 1808, was once Cecil Rhodes' local. There are beers on tap and you can order decent pub grub, such as fish and chips (R55).

BLAKES
BAR, CLUB

Map p274 (www.blakesbar.co.za; 189 Buitengracht St, Tamboerskloof; ☺5pm-2am Tue-Thu, noon-3am Fri-Sun; ▣Buitensingel) Sip a glass of wine or a cocktail and nibble on canapés and tapas while you enjoy panoramic views of Table Mountain and Lion's Head from this trendy cocktail bar, restaurant and club, with a wide outdoor deck and 12m-long bar.

RICK'S CAFÉ AMERICANE
BAR, RESTAURANT

Map p274 (www.rickscafe.co.za; 2 Park Lane, Gardens; ☺noon-2am Mon-Sat; ☎; ▣Michaelis) No Sam to 'play it again', but everything else looks like it could be straight from *Casablanca* (including the famous neon sign) at this movie-themed bar and restaurant.

Wear a fedora and make like Bogie and Bergman.

ASOKA
RESTAURANT, BAR

Map p274 (www.asokabar.co.za; 68 Kloof St, Gardens) Pronounced 'ashoka', a Zen-mellow vibe pervades this groovy Asian restaurant-bar with a tree growing in the middle of it. The jazz quintet the Restless Natives have become a regular feature of Tuesday nights (performances from 8pm), while on other nights DJs play suitably chilled sounds.

RAFIKI'S
RESTAURANT, BAR

Map p274 (www.rafikis.co.za; 13B Kloof Nek Rd, Tamboerskloof; 🐾) This bar's 35m-long, wrap-around balcony, with views out to Table Bay, continues to draws the crowds. It's a super-relaxed, mainly white-faced place, and serves pizzas and half-kilo buckets of prawns and mussels.

VAN HUNKS
RESTAURANT, BAR

Map p274 (www.vanhunks.co.za; cnr Kloof & Upper Union St, Gardens) Ponder the legend of Van Hunks who challenged the devil to a smoking match atop the peak you can see clearly from this establishment's deck. It's a good spot to watch the comings and goings along Kloof St, and if you're hungry some Cape Malay dishes are thrown amid the rest of the international menu.

⭐ ENTERTAINMENT

TOP CHOICE LABIA
CINEMA

Map p274 (www.labia.co.za; 68 Orange St, Gardens; tickets R35; 🔲Michaelis) This lifeline to the nonmainstream movie fan is named after the old Italian ambassador and local philanthropist Count Labia. It is Cape Town's best cinema in terms of price and programming. The African Screen program is one of the rare opportunities you'll have to see locally made films; check the website for session times. Also check out what's playing at the two-screen Labia on Kloof, in the Lifestyles on Kloof centre (see p96) around the corner.

MAHOGANY LOUNGE
JAZZ CLUB

Map p274 (📞079-679 2697; www.facebook.com/MahoganyRoom; 79 Buitenkant St, Gardens; one/two sets R60/100; ☺7pm-2am Wed-Sat) Next to Diva's Pizza, this tiny jazz club aims to recreate the atmosphere of Ronnie

Scott's and Village Vanguard. It's run by hard-core jazz cats who take their music seriously and who also have the connections to get top-class talent on the stage. Bookings are essential for their two sets a night, starting at 8.30pm and 10.30pm.

INTIMATE THEATRE
THEATRE

Map p274 (📞021-480 7129; University of Cape Town Hiddingh Campus, Orange St, Gardens; 🅿; 🔲Michaelis) This 75-seater venue is the pick among the three stages that can be found at the University of Cape Town's drama department. Read the reviews before going to see the productions, which can widely vary in quality and content. The improv show Theatresports plays here every Monday at 8.30pm.

 ## SHOPPING

TOP CHOICE THE FRINGE ARTS
ART, CRAFTS

Map p274 (www.thefringearts.co.za; 99B Kloof St, Gardens) You're sure to find a unique gift or item for yourself at this creative boutique representing almost 100 South African artists and designers, ranging from ceramics and jewellery to prints and bags. Check to see if they are still running their pop-up shop at the Waterfront which stocks more African-themed designs.

CITY BOWL MARKET
MARKET

Map p274 (www.citybowlmarket.co.za; 14 Hope St, Gardens; ☺9am-2pm Sat; 🔲Gardens) Based in a lovely old building with a lofty hall and outside garden areas, this is the Gardens' best Saturday morning hangout with a very chilled vibe. The market sells fresh produce and plenty of delicious nibbles and drinks from freshly made salads and sandwiches to craft beers and fruit juices. There's a fashion store downstairs and occasionally they have a larger selection of fashion vendors.

GRANT MASON ORIGINALS
SHOES

Map p274 (g-mo.co.za; 18 Roeland St, Gardens) Grant Mason uses beautiful fabrics from the ends of rolls and swatch books to create his one-off shoes and boots. No animal products are used in their construction. This is his atelier and showroom, and he also has a stall at the Saturday market at the Old Biscuit Mill. In the same building you'll find the workshops of other designers, including the well-crafted leather goods of **Urban Africa** (www.urbanafrica.co.za).

STEFANIA MORLAND   FASHION

Map p274 (stefaniamorland.com; Shop 2, 15 Orange St, Gardens; Michaelis) Gorgeous gowns and more casual wear under the ready-to-wear Shana brand are made from silks, linens and other natural fibres at this chic showroom and atelier. There are a handful of pieces for men, too, as well as accessories such as shoes and jewellery.

BLUECOLLARWHITECOLLAR   FASHION

Map p274 (www.bluecollarwhitecollar.co.za; Lifestyles on Kloof, 50 Kloof St, Gardens; P; Michaelis) Designer Paul van der Spuy and business partner Adrian Heneke offer a wonderful selection of tailored shirts – formal (white collar) and informal (blue collar). Recently added to the range are T-shirts and shorts. Also find them at the Old Biscuit Mill Saturday market.

LIM   HOMEWARES

Map p274 (www.lim.co.za; 86A Kloof St, Gardens) Although the shop's name is an acronym for 'less is more', this interior design shop has been so successful that they have had to add more room by expanding into the neighbouring house. Wander through the rooms admiring the stylish, pared-back selection of homewares, including fashion accessory items made from buckskin.

73 ON KLOOF   FASHION

Map p274 (73 Kloof St, Gardens; Michaelis) On one side of this boutique you'll find clothes such as shirts, shorts and trousers by Adriaan Kuiters (www.adriaankuiters.com) for men, as well as accessories such as canvas and leather bags and belts. On the other is something for the girls from Take Care. Designs for either range share the same clean-line, monochrome aesthetic.

MANTIS PRINTS   HOMEWARES

Map p274 (021-461 9919, 083 242 7888; www.mantisprints.co.za; 33 Breda St, Oranjezicht; 9am-1pm Sat & by appointment) Ena Hesses's distinctive, natural, hand-printed fabrics made into cushions and bags are sold in several shops as well as used as furnishings at guesthouses. At her home shop you can buy her printed cloth by the metre or as ready-made cushions, robes and table-wear.

JEWISH SHELTERED EMPLOYMENT CENTRE   TOYS, GIFTS

Map p274 (jsec.org.za; 20 Breda St, Oranjezicht; Gardens) 'Ability rather than disability' is the creed of this admirable organisation that helps create meaningful employment for physically and mentally challenged members of Cape Town's Jewish community. There's both a shop and a charming kosher cafe **Coffee Time** (8am-3.30pm Mon-Thu, 8am-2.30pm Fri) at the centre, where you can buy beautifully made toys such as rag dolls and wooden playthings, as well as other colourful weaving, needlework and woodwork gifts.

WINE CONCEPTS   WINE

Map p274 (wineconcepts.co.za; Lifestyles on Kloof, 50 Kloof St, Gardens; 10am-7pm Mon-Wed, 10am-8pm Thu & Fri, 9am-5pm Sat; P; Michaelis) You'll get expert advice on a broad range of local wines at this small but appealing cellar. Free wine tastings are held on Friday evening and Saturday from 11am to 2pm. There's also a branch in Newlands (corner Kildare Rd & Main St).

MR & MRS   FASHION, HOMEWARES

Map p274 (mrandmrs.co.za; 98 Kloof St, Gardens) A tasteful selection of fashion, gifts and homewares from both South African and international designers. The choices of products reflect the owners' travels through Indonesia, Argentina and India.

DARK HORSE   BAGS, FURNISHINGS

Map p274 (www.dark-horse.co.za; 83 Kloof Nek Rd, Tamboerskloof) Designer Lise du Plessis works out of this studio/shop halfway up to the lower cableway station on Table Mountain. The schlep is worth it for her handcrafted bags in canvas and leather, including iPad and computer cases, cushions, belts, jewellery and other interior decor pieces.

GARDENS CENTRE   MALL

Map p274 (www.gardensshoppingcentre.co.za; Mill St, Gardens; P; Gardens) A handy, well-stocked mall covering all the bases with good cafes (including an internet cafe), bookshops, Pick 'n' Pay and Woolworths supermarkets, a Flight Centre and a Cape Union Mart for camping and outdoor adventure gear.

GARDENS & SURROUNDS SHOPPING

LIFESTYLES ON KLOOF
MALL

Map p274 (50 Kloof St, Gardens; P; Michaelis) Apart from the businesses already mentioned, you'll find fashion and footwear boutiques, Exclusive Books, Woolworths, Wellness health food and chemists (www. wellnesswarehouse.com), Postnet and a branch of the Labia cinema, here.

MABU VINYL
BOOKS, MUSIC

Map p274 (www.mabuvinyl.co.za; 2 Rheede St, Gardens; 9am-8pm Mon-Thu, 9am-7pm Fri, 9am-6pm Sat, 11am-3pm Sun; Michaelis) New and secondhand LPs, CDs, DVDs, comics and books are bought, sold and traded at this reputable shop. It's the place to hunt for independently released CDs by local artists.

SPORTS & ACTIVITIES

TOP CHOICE DOWNHILL ADVENTURES
ADVENTURE ACTIVITIES

Map p274 (021-422 0388; www.downhilladventures.com; cnr Orange & Kloof Sts, Gardens; activities from R595; Buitensingel) This adrenaline-focused company offers a variety of cycling trips as well as sandboarding out at Atlantis and a surf school. Options include a thrilling mountain-bike ride down from the lower cable station on Table Mountain, mountain biking in the Tokai Forest, or a pedal through the Constantia Winelands and the Cape of Good Hope. You can also hire bikes here (R160 per day).

LION'S HEAD
HIKE

(Signal Hill Rd, Tamboerskloof; P) It was the Dutch who coined the term Lion's Head (Leeuwen Kop) for the giant nipple-like outcrop that overlooks Sea Point and Camps Bay. The main access is from the road leading to the top of Signal Hill just off Kloof Nek Rd, although there are also hiking routes up from the Sea Point side. It takes about 45 minutes to cover the 2.2km-hike from Kloof Nek to the 669m summit and it is deservedly popular. A lot of people do it as an early-morning constitutional and it's a ritual to go up and watch the sun go down on a full-moon night. The moonlight aids

the walk back down, although you should always bring a torch (flashlight) and go with company.

ENMASSE
MASSAGE

Map p274 (021-461 5650; www.enmasse.co.za; 123 Hope St, Gardens; 60 min massage R385; 8am-10pm; Gardens) Enter around the back via Gate 2, Schoonder Rd, to find this contemporary de-stressing experience in a historic building that was once a hotel. Aiming to make Thai style and Shiatsu massage a less inhibiting experience, you wear loose white cotton clothing (provided by enmasse) and no oils are used. Stay as long as you like afterwards, relaxing in their tea salon and enjoying any of their 49 different blends of teas.

LIBRISA SPA
SPA

Map p274 (021-483 1550; www.librisa.co.za; Mount Nelson Hotel, 76 Orange St, Gardens; 9am-8pm Mon-Sat; P) A beautifully remodelled Victorian house, decorated in dusky pinks and beige with weeping cherry-blossom murals and a soothing fountain, is the spacious premises of this idyllic spa. There are 10 treatment rooms and afterwards you can relax in the glass conservatory or in private saunas with outdoor plunge pools.

MOUNTAIN CLUB OF SOUTH AFRICA
CLIMBING

Map p274 (021-465 3412; http://mcsacapetown.co.za; 97 Hatfield St, Gardens; Government Avenue) This club, which can recommend guides to serious climbers, also has a climbing wall (R5); call them to check on opening times for the public.

CAPE TOWN TANDEM PARAGLIDING
PARAGLIDING

(076-892 2283; www.paraglide.co.za) Feel like James Bond as you paraglide off Lion's Head, land near the Glen Country Club and then sink a cocktail at Camps Bay. This is one of several outfits through whom novices can arrange a tandem paraglide where you're strapped to an experienced flyer who takes care of the technicalities. Make enquiries on your first day in Cape Town as the weather conditions have to be right.

Green Point & Waterfront

Neighbourhood Top Five

1 Journey to **Robben Island** (p102), once an infamous prison, now a cultural history museum site, where you can see the cells in which Mandela and other Freedom-struggle heroes spent time.

2 Eyeball all kinds of sea life, including sharks, at the **Two Oceans Aquarium** (p100).

3 Explore the V&A Waterfront on a **walking tour** (p101) and stand next to statues of the Nobel Laureates.

4 Learn about biodiversity at beautiful **Green Point Urban Park** (p103) and take a tour around **Cape Town Stadium** (p103).

5 Sail into Table Bay on one of the many **harbour cruises** (p101) from the Waterfront.

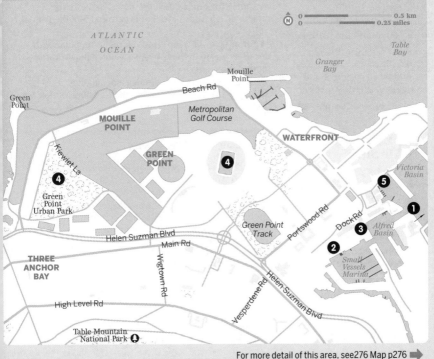

For more detail of this area, see276 Map p276 ➡

Lonely Planet's Top Tip

The restaurant at Cape Town Hotel School (p104) is one of the city's secret seaside dining spots, with vistas straight onto Granger Bay. In the garden you can also see the base of the original Mouille Point Lighthouse.

 Best Places to Eat

➡ Wakame (p103)
➡ Willoughby & Co (p104)
➡ Café Neo (p104)
➡ Nobu (p104)
➡ El Burro (p104)
➡ Giovanni's Deli World (p104)

For reviews, see p103 ➡

 Best Places to Drink

➡ Bascule (p105)
➡ Vista Bar (p105)
➡ Harbour House (p105)
➡ W Tapas Bar (p105)
➡ Tobago's (p105)
➡ Mitchell's Scottish Ale House & Brewery (p105)

For reviews, see p105 ➡

Best Places to Shop

➡ Victoria Wharf (p105)
➡ Waterfront Craft Market & Wellness Centre (p106)
➡ Vaughan Johnson's Wine & Cigar Shop (p106)
➡ Solveig (p106)
➡ Cape Union Mart Adventure Centre (p106)

For reviews, see p105 ➡

GREEN POINT & WATERFRONT

Explore Green Point & Waterfront

It's easy to see why the V&A Waterfront, commonly called the Waterfront, is Cape Town's top tourist attraction, drawing more visitors than the cableway ride to the top of Table Mountain. A textbook example of how to best redevelop a declining dock area, the atmosphere here is always buzzing and there's plenty to do, not least of which is making a trip out to Robben Island, the infamous prison island that is now a thought-provoking museum. Ten hotels are located around the Waterfront so it might even end up being the base for your stay in the city.

The outcrop of largely open land, west of the Waterfront, is Green Point, where you'll find Cape Town Stadium and an excellent new municipal park – both legacies of the 2010 World Cup. As well as being the name of the actual point, Green Point is also the name of the surrounding suburb, which includes rocky Mouille Point, right on the Atlantic coast and an atmospheric place for a seaside stroll or sunset cocktails and a meal. If the shopping and dining at the Waterfront isn't for you, there's also a retail and restaurant cluster along Main Rd between Braemar and York Rds.

Local Life

➡ **Constitutionals** Catch the sunset and evening breeze on a leisurely stroll or jog around Mouille Point (p103).
➡ **Shop** Victoria Wharf (p105) is just as popular with locals as it is with tourists. Also, catch a movie at the multiplex.
➡ **Delis** Grab a coffee, a sandwich or supplies at Giovanni's Deli World (p104) or the Newport Market & Deli (p104), both local institutions.

Getting There & Away

➡ **Walk/Cycle** The pedestrian Fan Walk, created for the 2010 World Cup, provides easy, safe walking or cycling access to and from the city.
Bus MyCiTi buses shuttle from the city to stops at Stadium, Granger Bay, Breakwater and Waterfront. Two Oceans Aquarium is also the start/finish point of tours on the City Sightseeing Cape Town buses (Map p276; www.citysightseeing.co.za).
➡ **Boat** City Sightseeing Cape Town offer a riverboat service along the canals linking the Waterfront to the Cape Town International Convention Centre.

TOP SIGHTS
V&A WATERFRONT

When redevelopment of the 19th-century Victoria and Alfred Docks began in the late 1980s prospects did not look bright for the project or, for that matter, South Africa in the dying days of apartheid. Flash forward two decades and the V&A Waterfront is a dazzling beacon of success for the rainbow nation, attracting 23 million visitors a year to its glitzy mix of retail and touristic entertainment. Adding greatly to the carnival atmosphere is the fact that the Waterfront remains a working harbour and that much of its historic fabric has been preserved.

Evolution of the Waterfront

It was the Dutch who first built in this area of Table Bay as early as 1726 with the Chavonnes Battery. In June 1858 a storm wrecked over 30 vessels in the bay, reinforcing the need to create Cape Town's first proper harbour. This began in 1860 with Queen Victoria's second son Prince Alfred on hand for the ceremonial duties. The first basin constructed was named after him, the second after his mother, hence the Victoria and Alfred Docks.

By the mid-20th century maritime trade in Cape Town had outgrown these docks. Once Duncan Dock had been constructed further west along the Foreshore, the V&A area fell into disuse and creeping decay. The dock's rebirth as the V&A Waterfront began in the late 1980s and is still ongoing: upcoming projects include the redevelopment of the Clocktower precinct and the old Grain Silo into a state-of-the-art, eco-friendly building; and the Polaris Climate Change Observatory (www.polarfoundation.org) to be built on Collier Jetty by 2014.

DON'T MISS

➡ Two Oceans Aquarium
➡ Chavonnes Battery Museum
➡ Nobel Square
➡ Harbour cruises
➡ Historical walking tourV&A Waterfront

PRACTICALITIES

➡ Map p276
➡ ☎021-408 7600
➡ www.waterfront. co.za
➡ Information Centre; Dock Rd
➡ ⊙Information Centre 9am-6pm daily
➡ ▣Breakwater & Waterfront

EATING & SLEEPING

For reviews of some of the best places to stay at the Waterfront see p194, and for reviews of places to eat and drink, turn to p103 and p105.

The Waterfront's wharves are too small for modern container vessels and tankers, but the Victoria Basin is still used by tugs, harbour vessels of various kinds and fishing boats. In the Alfred Basin you'll see ships under repair and seals splashing around and lazing on the giant tyres that line the docks – a favourite spot for them are the jetties behind the Two Oceans Aquarium.

FIREWORKS

The annual fireworks display on 31 December is one of the Waterfront's biggest events; book well in advance for seats at restaurants with views of the outdoor spectacular.

Two Oceans Aquarium

The excellent **Two Oceans Aquarium** (☎021-418 3823; www.aquarium.co.za; Dock Rd; adult/child R105/50; ☺9.30am-6pm) is one of the Waterfront's top attractions. It features denizens of the deep from the cold and the warm oceans that border the Cape Peninsula, including ragged-tooth sharks. There are seals, penguins, turtles, an astounding kelp forest, and pools in which kids can touch sea creatures. Qualified divers can get in the water for a closer look (R595 including dive gear). Get your hand stamped on entry and you can return any time the same day.

Chavonnes Battery Museum

Along with the Castle of Good Hope, the Dutch built a series of fortifications around Table Bay. The **Chavonnes Battery Museum** (☎021-416 6230; www.chavonnesmuseum.co.za; Clock Tower Precinct; adult/child R25/10; ☺9am-4pm Wed-Sun) houses the remains of an early 18th century cannon battery. Although they had been partly demolished and built over during the construction of the docks in 1860, an excavation of the site in 1999 revealed the remains. You can walk around the entire site and get a good feel for what it was originally like. It's staffed by costumed enthusiasts who like to shoot off a real cannon in front of the museum on Sunday at noon.

Nobel Square & Around

Here's your chance to have your photo taken with Desmond Tutu and Nelson Mandela. In **Nobel Square** larger-than-life statues of both men, designed by Claudette Schreuders, stand beside those of South Africa's two other Nobel Prize winners – Nkosi Albert Luthuli and FW de Klerk. Also here is the *Peace and Democracy* sculpture by Noria Mahasa, which symbolises the contribution of women and children to the struggle. It's etched with pertinent quotes by each of the great men.

Nearby, next to Robinson Dry Dock, is another mammoth piece of public art. Standing 18m-tall, **Elliot the Cratefan**, made from 42,000 red plastic Coca Cola crates, was designed by Porky Hefer for the 2010 World Cup. It's scheduled to come down at the end of 2012 but has become such a defining image at the Waterfront that it might stay longer.

Maritime Centre

Stocked with model ships and a model of Table Bay harbour, made in 1885 by prisoners and warders of Breakwater Prison (another redeveloped part of the Waterfront site), the small **Maritime Centre** (www.iziko.org.za/museums/maritime-centre; 1st fl, Union-Castle House, Dock Rd; adult/child R10/free; ☺10am-5pm) also houses the **John H Marsh Maritime Research Centre** (rapidttp.co.za/museum), a resource for those interested in South Africa's maritime history. The main exhibition at the centre is about the ill-fated voyage of the *Mendi,* which sank in the English Channel in 1917 taking 607 black troops to a watery grave.

Diamond Museum

Cape Town has a gold museum so it's only natural that it should also have a **Diamond Museum** (www.capetowndiamondmuseum.org; 1st fl, Clock Tower Shopping Centre; admission R50, free with voucher downloaded from website; ⊙9am-9pm). Really an extended sales pitch for the bling on sale in the attached Shimansky jewellers, the displays have nonetheless been put together with some style and imagination. There's no obligation to buy and you can learn a lot about diamonds and how their discovery contributed to the wealth of South Africa. The guided tours are led by one of the sales staff who will point out replicas of famous rocks such as the Hope and the Taylor-Burton diamonds. Turn up between 8am and 5pm and you'll be able to see craftspeople at work in the attached factory.

Historical Walking Tour

One of the best ways to get an insight into the history of the Waterfront and its development, as well as make sense of this sprawling site, is to sign up for a **historical walking tour** (⊘bookings 021-408 7600; adult/child R50/20, minimum 4 people). Starting at the Chavonnes Battery Museum these 45-minute tours take you past buildings and sights such as the Clock Tower from where the harbour master used to control the comings and goings in the docks; Robinson Dry Dock, one of the oldest of its kind in the world and still in use today; the Breakwater Prison where you see carvings made by the prisoners in the slate walls; and the Time Ball Tower previously used to signal the time to ships in the bay.

Harbour Cruises

See Table Mountain as mariners of yore did on a cruise into Table Bay:

Waterfront Boat Company (⊘021-418 5806; www.waterfrontboats.co.za; Shop 5, Quay 5) Offers a variety of cruises, including highly recommended 1½-hour sunset cruises (R220), on its handsome wood-and-brass-fitted schooners *Spirit of Victoria* and *Esperance.* A jet-boat ride is R500 per hour.

Yacoob Tourism (⊘021-421 0909; www.ytourism.co.za; Shop 8, Quay 5) Among the several trips that this company runs are those on the *Jolly Roger Pirate Boat* (adult/child from R100/50) and *Tommy the Tugboat* (adult/child R50/25), both perfect for families. Adults may prefer their *Adrenalin* speed-boat jaunts or a cruise on the catamarans *Ameera* and *Tigress.*

Helicopter Tours

Another adventurous activity that can be arranged at the Waterfront is a flight over the peninsula in a helicopter. Two outfits offering these tours are:

Hopper (⊘021-419 8951; www.thehopper.co.za; Shop 6, Quay 5; R600; ℗; ▣Waterfront) Single bookings are accepted for this helicopter operation with tours starting from a 15-minute flight over either Sandy Bay or out to the Twelve Apostles.

Huey Helicopter Co (⊘021-419 4839; www.thehueyhelicopterco.co.za; East Pier Rd, Waterfront; from R2200; ℗; ▣Waterfront) To add to the exhilaration, this ex-Vietnam US Marine Corps Huey chopper, which takes off from the Watefront, flies with open doors for that authentic *Apocalypse Now* experience. Standard tours last 20 minutes and take you towards Hout Bay and back; the hour long tour gets you down to Cape Point.

TOP SIGHTS
V & A WATERFRONT

TOP SIGHTS
ROBBEN ISLAND

Some 12km out in Table Bay, this flat island, just 2km by 4km, may look like a pleasant place with its neat village of stone buildings and white church steeple, however, to the prisoners who were incarcerated here from the early days of VOC *(Vereenigde Oost-Indische Compagnie; Dutch East India Company)* control right up until 1996, it was nothing short of hell. Now a museum and UN World Heritage site, Robben Island's best known involuntary resident was Nelson Mandela and for this reason alone it is one of the most popular pilgrimage spots in all of Cape Town.

The Tour

The island can only be visited on a tour that starts with a 30-minute ferry journey from Nelson Mandela Gateway at the Waterfront. The two-hour tours are typically led by former inmates and include a walk through the old prison (with an obligatory peek into Mandela's cell). There's also a bus ride around the island with commentary on the various places of note, such as the lime quarry in which Mandela and many others slaved, the prison house of Pan African Congress (PAC) leader Robert Sobuke, and the church used during the island's stint as a leper colony.

Cell Stories

If you're lucky, you'll have about 10 minutes to wander around on your own. The guides may suggest checking out the African Penguin colony near the landing jetty or the karamat (Muslim shrine), but a better alternative is to return to the prison's A section to view the remarkable exhibition *Cell Stories*. In each of 40 isolation cells is an artefact and story from a former political prisoner: chess pieces drawn on scraps of paper, a soccer trophy, a Christmas card from an abandoned wife. It's all unbelievably moving. This is not part of the regular tour, but there's nothing to stop you slipping away to see it should you find the guide's commentary or the crowds not to your liking.

Booking Tickets

While we highly recommend going to Robben Island, a visit here is not without its drawbacks. One hurdle can be getting a ticket – in peak times these can sell out for days in advance. Problems with the island's management has also led to its boats sometimes being out of commission and, as occurred in November 2011, to some of the staff going on strike. Reserve well in advance via the web. Another strategy is to book a ticket in conjunction with a township tour – some operators have access to blocks of tickets not available to the public.

At the Quayside

Even if you don't make it to the island there are still things to see at the Waterfront. The **Nelson Mandela Gateway** (admission free; ☺9am-8.30pm) has a small museum with displays that focus on the struggle for freedom. Also preserved as a small museum is **Jetty 1** (admission free; ☺7am-9pm), the departure point for Robben Island when it was a prison.

DON'T MISS

⇒ Nelson Mandela's Cell

⇒ *Cell Stories* exhibition

⇒ Nelson Mandela Gateway

⇒ Jetty 1

PRACTICALITIES

⇒ off Map p276

⇒ ☎021-413 4220

⇒ www.robben-island.org.za

⇒ adult/child R230/120

⇒ ☺ferries depart Nelson Mandela Gateway at 9am, 11am, 1pm & 3pm weather permitting, and return at the conclusion of each tour.

⇒ 🚌Breakwater

GREEN POINT & WATERFRONT

SIGHTS

V&A WATERFRONT
NEIGHBOURHOOD

The V&A Waterfront includes the following sights: Two Oceans Aquarium (p100), Chavonnes Battery Museum (p100), Nobel Square (p100), Maritime Centre (p100) and Diamond Museum (p101).

ROBBEN ISLAND
MUSEUM

See p102.

TOP CHOICE CAPE TOWN STADIUM
STADIUM

Map p276 (☏021-417 0101; Granger Bay Blvd, Green Point; tours adult/child R45.60/17.10; ☉tours 10am, noon & 2pm Tue-Sat; P; 🚉Stadium) Shaped like a giant, traditional African hat and wrapped with a Teflon-mesh membrane designed to catch and reflect natural light, this stadium is Cape Town's most striking piece of contemporary architecture. Built at a cost of R4.5 billion, the stadium regularly seats 55,000, down from the 68,000 capacity for the 2010 World Cup. It's the homeground of the soccer team Ajax Cape Town and has been used for big pop concerts by the likes of Coldplay, U2 and the Eagles. The hour-long tours will take you behind the scenes into the VIP and press boxes as well as the teams' dressing rooms. Across from the new stadium is a section of the old Green Point Stadium: there are plans to use the grounds here for a new running and cycling track.

GREEN POINT URBAN PARK
PARK

Map p276 (Bay Rd, Green Point; ☉7am-7pm daily; P; 🚉Stadium) One of the best things to come out of the redevelopment of Green Point Common for the 2010 World Cup is this park and biodiversity garden. Streams fed from Table Mountain's springs and rivers water the park, which has three imaginatively designed areas – People & Plants, Wetlands, and Discovering Biodiversity – that along with educational information boards act as the best kind of outdoor museum.

As well as the many types of *fynbos* (literally 'fine bush', primarily proteas, heaths and ericas) and other indigenous plants, you can see an example of the kind of structure that the Khoe-san used to live in and spot beautifully made beaded animals, insects and birds among the flower beds. There's plenty of space for picnics with bril-

liant views of the stadium, Signal Hill and Lion's Head, and two kids' play parks – one for toddlers and one for older kids. Guided tours (adult/child R34.20/17.10) of the park can be arranged through the Cape Town Stadium.

GREEN POINT LIGHTHOUSE & MOUILLE POINT
LIGHTHOUSE, PARK

Map p276 (100 Beach Rd, Mouile Point; adult/child R16/8; ☉10am-3pm Mon-Fri; P) Often mistakenly called Mouille Point Lighthouse (the remains of which are in the grounds of the nearby Cape Town Hotel School), this red and white candy-striped beacon dates back to 1824 and is a striking landmark. You can take a self-guided tour inside.

Outside on the grassy common beside the Mouille Point Promenade are a variety of attractions that will appeal to families, including a good **kids' playground**; **The Blue Train** (R10; ☉9am-6pm daily), a child-size loco and carriages; a **maze** (adult/child R22/11; ☉10.30am-6pm) made of scrappy looking New Zealand pine trees which claims to be 'the third largest in the world!'; and **Putt-Putt Golf** (R14; ☉9am-10pm).

CAPE MEDICAL MUSEUM
MUSEUM

Map p276 (Portswood Rd; R10; ☉9am-4pm Mon-Fri; P; 🚉Stadium) The *Disease and History* exhibit at this quirky museum details in length (with some gruesome photographs) the history of major diseases in the Cape, from scurvy to HIV/AIDS. Less horrific are a re-created Victorian doctor's room and pharmacy.

EATING

It's natural that you'll want to dine with an ocean view while in Cape Town. The Waterfront's plethora of restaurants and cafes fit the bill nicely, although it's essentially a giant tourist trap. Alternatives are available a short walk away in Green Point and Mouille Point.

TOP CHOICE WAKAME
SEAFOOD, ASIAN $$

Map p276 (☏021-433 2377; www.wakame.co.za; cnr Beach Rd & Surrey Pl; mains R70-120; ☉noon-11.30pm) Tucking into Wakame's salt-and-pepper squid or sushi platter while gazing at the glorious coastal view is a wonderful way to pass an afternoon. On the second level they specialise in Asian dumplings and sunset cocktails, when their deck can get packed.

TOP CHOICE WILLOUGHBY & CO
SEAFOOD, JAPANESE $

Map p276 (☏021-418 6115; www.willoughbyand co.co.za; Shop 6132, Victoria Wharf, Breakwater Blvd, Waterfront; mains R60-70; ⊙deli 9.30am-8.30pm, restaurant noon-10.30pm; ℗; ⬚Waterfront) Commonly acknowledged as one of the better places to eat at the Waterfront – with long queues to prove it. Huge servings of sushi are the standout from a good-value, fish-based menu at this casual eatery inside the mall.

TOP CHOICE CAFÉ NEO
GREEK, CAFE $

Map p276 (☏021-433 0849; 129 Beach Rd, Mouille Point; mains R50-70; ⊙7am-7pm; ☏) This favourite seaside cafe has a relaxed vibe and pleasingly contemporary design. Check out the big blackboard menu while sitting at the long communal table inside or from a seat on the deck overlooking the red-and-white lighthouse.

NOBU
JAPANESE $$$

Map p276 (☏021-431 5111; www.noburestau rants.com; One & Only Cape Town, Dock Rd, V&A Waterfront; mains R200-400, set dinners from R190; ⊙6-11pm daily; ℗; ⬚Breakwater) This branch of the upmarket global Japanese chain, a fixture of the One & Only since it opened, is a smooth running operation. The chefs turns out expert renditions of Nobu Masahisa's signature ceviches and cod in miso sauce, along with the expected sushi and tempura, best sampled in the good-value set meals. The soaring dining hall offers a New York metro buzz, while the more intimate bar upstairs is a nice spot to work your way through their extensive sake menu.

EL BURRO
MEXICAN $

Map p276 (☏021-433 2364; www.elburro.co.za; 81 Main Rd, Green Point; mains R50-70; ⊙noon-10.30pm; ℗; ⬚Stadium) On the upper floor of the Exhibition Building, with a balcony providing views of Cape Town Stadium, this is one stylish donkey, the decor a bit more chic than your average Mexican joint, the menu more inventive. Supplementing the usual tacos and enchiladas are traditional dishes such as chicken mole poblano.

GIOVANNI'S DELI WORLD
CAFE, DELI $

Map p276 (103 Main Rd, Green Point; mains R20-40; ⊙7.30am-8.30pm) Bursting with flavoursome products, Giovanni's can make any sandwich you fancy, which is ideal for a picnic if you're on your way to the beach. The pavement cafe is a popular hangout.

CAPE TOWN HOTEL SCHOOL
CONTEMPORARY $

Map p276 (☏021-440 5736; Beach Rd, Mouille Point; mains R60-100; ⊙11.30am-2.30pm, 6.30pm-9.30pm Mon-Sat, noon-2.30pm Sun; ℗) The dining room is elegantly decorated in shades of grey and silver and the outdoor patio looks straight onto Granger Bay. Enthusiastic students train here as chefs and waiters so be prepared to cut some slack on quality; we found the experience pleasant and the food very tasty and nicely presented on our visit. Their Sunday buffet is R110 per person.

MISS K
INTERNATIONAL $

Map p276 (www.missk.co.za; Shop 1, Winston Place, 65 Main Rd; mains R35-50; ⊙8am-4.30pm Tue-Sat, 8.30am-1pm Sun) We dare you to resist Miss K's decadent desserts. It's a good option for breakfast, too with a variety of fancy egg dishes.

NEWPORT MARKET & DELI
INTERNATIONAL, DELI $

Map p276 (www.newportdeli.co.za; 47 Beach Rd, Mouille Point; mains R50-60; ⊙6.30am-9pm) Grab a smoothie, power blend or caffeinated beverage plus sandwiches and deli goods to enjoy along Mouille Point prom or in Green Point Park. There's a sit down cafe too with plenty of outdoor tables.

FISHERMAN'S CHOICE
SEAFOOD $

Map p276 (Quay 5, Waterfront; fish & chips from R70; ⊙9am-9pm; ℗; ⬚Breakwater) Fish and chips for breakfast? It's possible at this harbourside joint, one of the best value places for a fresh fry up at the Waterfront with the bonus of a brilliant view of Table Mountain. Order at the counter and your choice of fish and sides will be brought to your table.

MELISSA'S
INTERNATIONAL, DELI $

Map p276 (www.melissas.co.za; Shop 6195, Victoria Wharf, Breakwater Blvd, Waterfront; mains R40-70; ⊙9am-9pm; ℗; ⬚Waterfront) Attractive branch of this top notch deli with lovely eats and a pay-by-weight buffet table for breakfast and lunch.

GREEN POINT & WATERFRONT EATING

DRINKING & NIGHTLIFE

GREEN POINT & WATERFRONT DRINKING & NIGHTLIFE

BASCULE
TOP CHOICE

BAR

Map p276 (☏021-410 7097; www.capegrace.com; Cape Grace, West Quay Rd, Waterfront; ⏰noon-2am) Over 450 varieties of whisky are served at the Grace's sophisticated bar, and there're still a few slugs of the 50-year-old Glenfiddich (just R18,000 a tot) left. Make a booking for one their whisky tastings (R175 or R220) in which you can try six drams, three of which are paired with food. Outdoor tables facing onto the marina are a pleasant spot for drinks and tasty tapas.

VISTA BAR
TOP CHOICE

COCKTAIL BAR

Map p276 (http://capetown.oneandonlyresorts. com; One&Only Cape Town, Dock Rd, Waterfront; ⏰noon-1am; P; ☐Breakwater) The luxe hotel's bar offers plush surrounds and a perfectly framed view of Table Mountain. It's a classy spot for afternoon tea (R145; ⏰2.30pm-5.30pm) or a creative cocktail including classics with a local twist.

HARBOUR HOUSE
BAR, RESTAURANT

Map p276 (☏021-418 4744; Quay 4, Waterfront; ⏰noon-10pm; P; ☐Breakwater) The Kalk Bay institution makes its debut at the Waterfront with a good restaurant on the ground floor and even better sushi and lounge bar on the upper deck – just the spot for a chilled glass of wine at sunset.

GRAND CAFÉ & BEACH
BAR, RESTAURANT

Map p276 (☏072 586 2052; www.grandafrica. com; Granger Bay Rd, off Beach Rd, Granger Bay; ⏰noon-11pm; P; ☐Granger Bay) Sand was imported to created the private beach for this oh-so-chic bar and restaurant operating out of a former warehouse. Locals love to gather on weekends here to enjoy the laid-back vibe, rather than the so-so food. DJs kick in later at night. There's a good gift shop here, too.

W TAPAS BAR
CAFE, WINE BAR

Map p276 (☏021-415 3411; Woolworths, Victoria Wharf, Breakwater Blvd, Waterfront; ⏰9am-9pm; P; ☐Waterfront) Tucked away on the top floor of Woolworths, with a sweeping view across the harbour, is this modern, uncrowded wine bar where you can sample the best of the department store's selection of local drops along with tapas platters of charcuterie, seafood or vegetarian dips (R65-95).

ALBA LOUNGE
COCKTAIL BAR

Map p276 (☏021-425 3385; www.albalounge. co.za; 1st fl, Hildegards, Pierhead, Waterfront; ⏰5pm-2am; P; ☐Breakwater) The views across the harbour are grand from this contemporary-designed cocktail bar where the drinks are inventive and there's a roaring fire in winter to add to that inner alcohol glow.

TOBAGO'S
COCKTAIL BAR

Map p276 (☏021-441 3000; Radisson Blu Hotel Waterfront, Beach Rd, Mouille Point; ⏰6.30am-10.30pm; P) Walk through the hotel to the spacious deck bar with a prime Table Bay position. It's a great place to enjoy a sunset cocktail and you can take a stroll along the breakwater afterwards.

MITCHELL'S SCOTTISH ALE HOUSE & BREWERY
PUB

Map p276 (www.mitchellsbreweries.co.za; East Pier Rd, Waterfront; ⏰11am-2am; P; ☐Breakwater) Check all airs and graces at the door of South Africa's oldest microbrewery (est. 1983 in Knysna) serving a variety of freshly brewed ales and good-value meals. Their 'Old Wobbly' packs an alcoholic punch.

BELTHAZAR
RESTAURANT, WINE BAR

Map p276 (☏021-421 3753; www.belthazar. co.za; Shop 153, Victoria Wharf, Breakwater Blvd, Waterfront; P; ☐Waterfront) Claiming to be the world's biggest wine bar, Belthazar offers 600 different South African wines, around 250-odd of which you can get by the (Riedel) glass. The restaurant specialises in top-class Karan beef and it also does plenty of seafood dishes, too.

SHOPPING

The bulk of the Waterfront's hundreds of shops and stalls are in Victoria Wharf, although there are a few interesting shops in the smaller Alfred Mall. The Clock Tower Precinct was being redeveloped at the time of research.

VICTORIA WHARF
TOP CHOICE

SHOPPING MALL

Map p276 (Breakwater Blvd, Waterfront; ⏰9am-9pm; P; ☐Waterfront) All the big names of South African retail, including Woolworths,

WATERFRONT ENTERTAINMENT

The Waterfront's **Market Square** is a focus for much free entertainment including buskers and various musical and dance acts. Apart from the giant electronic screen showing videos, the amphitheatre acts as a platform for up-and-coming artists, and there are always live shows from 5pm to 6pm on Saturday and Sundays. Mainstream movies are screened in at the Numetro Multiplex in the Victoria Wharf mall, and art-house offerings at the Ster Kinekor Cinema Nouveau in the same complex.

CNA, Pick n' Pay, Exclusive Books and Musica, plus international luxury brands, are represented at this appealing mall, one of Cape Town's best. Attached to it is the **Red Shed Craft Workshop**, a permanent market focused on local crafts, including ceramics, textiles and jewellery.

TOP CHOICE WATERFRONT CRAFT MARKET & WELLNESS CENTRE
ARTS & CRAFTS
Map p276 (Dock Rd, Waterfront; ⊙9.30am-6pm; P; ☐Breakwater) Also known as the Blue Shed, this eclectic arts and crafts market harbours some great buys. Seek out the colourful textile products of Ikamva Labantu; and Township Guitars, which makes and sells the all-electric township 'blik' guitars made from oil cans, wood and fishing wire (from R2000). In the Wellness Centre section you'll find various holistic products and can have a massage.

TOP CHOICE VAUGHAN JOHNSON'S WINE & CIGAR SHOP
WINE
Map p276 (www.vaughanjohnson.co.za; Market Sq, Dock Rd, Waterfront; ⊙9am-6pm Mon-Fri, 9am-5pm Sat, 10am-5pm Sun; P; ☐Breakwater) Selling practically every South African wine of repute you could wish to buy (plus a few more from other countries); it's also open, unlike most wine sellers, on Sundays.

SOLVEIG
FASHION
Map p276 (www.solveigoriginals.co.za; Albert Mall, Dock Rd, Waterfront; ⊙9am-9pm; P; ☐Breakwater) Stocking highly original, colourful and distinctively South African fashions – mainly for women but with a few jackets for men – accessories and lovely rag dolls.

CAPE UNION MART ADVENTURE CENTRE
OUTDOOR GEAR
Map p276 (www.capeunionmart.co.za; Quay 4, Waterfront; ⊙9am-9pm; P; ☐Waterfront) This emporium is packed with backpacks, boots, clothing and practically everything else you might need for outdoor adventures, from a hike up Table Mountain to a Cape-to-Cairo safari. There's also smaller branches in **Victoria Wharf**, as well the Gardens Centre and Cavendish Square.

NAARTJIE
CHILDREN'S CLOTHING
Map p276 (www.naartjiekids.com; Shop 119, Victoria Wharf, Breakwater Blvd, Waterfront; ⊙9am-9pm; P; ☐Waterfront) This attractive range of designer cotton children's clothing has grown from a stall on Greenmarket Sq to a global brand. There are also branches in Cavendish Square, Canal Walk and a factory shop in Hout Bay.

CARROL BOYES
HOMEWARES
Map p276 (www.carrolboyes.co.za; Shop 6180, Victoria Wharf, Breakwater Blvd, Waterfront; ⊙9am-9pm; P; ☐Waterfront) Carrol Boyes' sensuous designs in pewter and steel give a fun feel to cutlery, kitchen products and homewares. You'll also find some rainbow-hued beadworks from Monkeybiz on sale here and Barbara Jackson's ceramics.

SHIMANSKY
JEWELLERY
Map p276 (www.shimansky.co.za; 1st fl, Clock Tower Centre; ⊙9am-9pm; P; ☐Breakwater) Diamonds are synonymous with South Africa and here you'll find plenty of them set in a range of jewellery designs. They also have a small museum and a workshop where you can take a peek at how all that bling is put together.

CAPESTORM
OUTDOOR GEAR
Map p276 (www.capestorm.co.za; Shop 123 Victoria Wharf, Breakwater Blvd,Waterfront; P; ☐Waterfront) Gear up for your outdoor adventures, from rock climbing to long-distance cycling, at this outdoor leisurewear shop specialising in garments made from technical fabrics and fleece. The products are all locally designed and made.

 # SPORTS & ACTIVITIES

HARBOUR CRUISES CRUISES
See p101.

HELICOPTER TOURS SCENIC FLIGHTS
See p101.

TABLE BAY DIVING DIVING
Map p276 (☎021-419 8822; www.tablebaydiving. com; Shop 7, Quay 5, Waterfront; P; 🚇Breakwater) This reputable operator offers shore dives for R200, boat dives for R300 and full equipment hire for R300. Its openwater PADI course is R3250 and it can also arrange shark-cage diving trips to Gansbaai.

TWO OCEANS AQUARIUM DIVING
Map p276 (☎021-418 3823; www.aquarium.co.za; Dock Rd, Waterfront; dives R485; P; 🚇Breakwater) A guaranteed way to swim with sharks is to dive in the tanks at the Two Oceans Aquarium. No great whites, but several ragged-tooth sharks, other predatory fish and a turtle make for a delightful diving experience. The cost includes gear hire, and you need to be a certified diver. If not, one-day resort courses can be arranged. Experienced divers can also dive in the aquarium's kelp forest tank.

OCEAN SAILING ACADEMY SAILING
Map p276 (☎021-425 7837; www.oceansailing. co.za; West Quay Rd, Waterfront; P; 🚇Waterfront) Contact the only Royal Yachting Association (RYA) school in South Africa to find out about its sailing courses, tailored to all skill levels.

METROPOLITAN GOLF CLUB GOLF
Map p276 (☎021-430 6011; metropolitangolfclub. co.za/index.php; Fritz Sonnenberg Rd, Mouille Point; 9/18 holes R250/425; P; 🚇Stadium) As part of the revamp of the sports facilities on Green Point Common this course also got an upgrade with four species of local grasses planted to give it a more natural look. The wind-sheltered position between Cape Town Stadium and Green Point Park, with Signal Hill in the background, can't be beat.

Sea Point to Hout Bay

SEA POINT | CLIFTON | CAMPS BAY | HOUT BAY

Neighbourhood Top Five

1 No need to climb over rocks or down steps to reach the golden crescent of the palm-fringed beach at **Camps Bay** (p110), which is one of the reasons – along with the ritzy suburb's trendy sea-facing bars and restaurants – for its popularity.

2 Gazing down on **Hout Bay Harbour** (p111) from thrilling **Chapman's Peak Drive** (p110).

3 Shedding your clothes at secluded **Sandy Bay** (p111) and exploring its giant rock formations.

4 Checking out the tanned and toned flesh on the quartet of beaches at **Clifton** (p110).

5 Strolling along **Sea Point Promenade** (p110) and swimming at its art deco **Pavilion** (p115).

For more detail of this area, see Map p280, p278 and p279 ➡

Explore Sea Point to Hout Bay

Long popular with Cape Town's Jewish, gay and Chinese communities, Sea Point sports numerous art deco apartment blocks, lending it an almost Miami Beach elegance. Main Rd and Regent Rd form its commercial spine, lined with increasingly good restaurants, cafes and shops.

Moving south, the exclusive and wealthy residential neighbourhoods of Bantry Bay, Clifton and Camps Bay follow hard and fast on each other in a tumble of mansions with to-die-for sea views: this is prime beach territory.

Follow the coastal Victoria Rd over the pass beside Little Lion's Head (436m) to drop down into the fishing community of Hout Bay. Hout means 'wood' in Afrikaans: this is where Jan van Riebeeck found the plentiful supplies of timber in the forests that once blanketed the valley around the Disa River to build his original fort in Cape Bowland to fire the kilns to make bricks. The forests are long gone, but Hout Bay's stunning geography – a natural harbour and horseshoe sweep of white sand nestled between the almost vertical Sentinel and the steep slopes of Chapman's Peak – remains eternal.

With its township of Imizamo Yethu (also known as Mandela Park) inland and its coloured district of Hangberg facing the harbour, Hout Bay is like a microcosm of South Africa, and is facing the same post-apartheid integration challenges. Its village atmosphere and handy location midway along the Cape make it a good base.

If you're not planning on staying in the area, a day is fine to see the sights here.

Local Life

➡ **Markets** Join locals on Friday night grazing at Hout Bay's Bay Harbour Market (p113) and listening to music.

➡ **Beaches** Search out less high-profile beaches to escape the crowds such as Glen Beach (p110) or the beach at Llandudno (p111).

➡ **Constitutionals** Jog or stroll along Sea Point's promenade p110) in the late afternoon and early evening and meet legions of locals doing likewise.

Getting There & Away

➡ **Buses** Golden Arrow buses shuttle from the city to Hout Bay. There are plans to extend MyCiTi services to Camps Bay and Hout Bay.

➡ **City Sightseeing Cape Town** The hop-on, hop-off tour buses make stops in Camps Bay and Hout Bay.

➡ **Shared taxis** Run regularly from the city to Sea Point and Camps Bay.

Lonely Planet's Top Tip

In Camps Bay, the playground of the rich and beautiful, making a booking at restaurants and bars is essential if you wish to get a prime spot for sunset drinks and nibbles.

 Best Places to Eat

➡ Roundhouse (p111)
➡ La Boheme (p111)
➡ The Duchess of Wisbeach (p111)
➡ The Mussel Bar (p112)
➡ La Perla (p112)

For reviews, see p111 ➡

 Best Places to Drink

➡ The Bungalow (p112)
➡ La Vie (p112)
➡ Dunes (p113)
➡ Salt (p113)
➡ Café Caprice (p113)

For reviews, see p112 ➡

Best Places to Shop

➡ Bay Harbour Market (p113)
➡ Hout Bay Craft Market (p113)
➡ Ethno Bongo (p114)
➡ T-Bag Designs (p114)

For reviews, see p113 ➡

SEA POINT TO HOUT BAY

◉ SIGHTS

CLIFTON BEACHES
BEACH

Map p278 (Victoria Rd, Clifton; sun lounge & umbrella R80) Giant granite boulders split the four linked beaches at Clifton, accessible by steps from Victoria Rd. Almost always sheltered from the wind, these beaches are top sunbathing spots. No 3 is the gay beach, though plenty of straights frequent it, too, and No 4 is popular with families. Vendors hawk drinks and ice creams along the beach, and at No 3 there's usually a massage tent set up. Before hopping in the sea, remember the water comes straight from the Antarctic and swimming here is exhilarating (ie freezing).

SEA POINT PROMENADE
WALK, SWIMMING

Map p280 (Beach Rd, Sea Point) A stroll or jog along Sea Point's wide paved and grassy promenade is a pleasure shared by Capetonians from all walks of life – it's a great place to come at sunset and see how multicultural the city is. There are play areas for the kids and, at the northern end, a not very well-maintained outdoor gym.

The coast here is rocky and swimming is dangerous, although you can get in the water at Rocklands Beach and at a couple of tidal rock pools: **Milton's Pool**, which is OK for kids, and **Graaff's Pool**. If you're too thin-skinned for the frigid sea, there's **Sea Point Pavilion**, towards the promenade's southern end.

CHAPMAN'S PEAK DRIVE
DRIVING ROUTE

Map p279 (www.chapmanspeakdrive.co.za; Chapman's Peak Drive; cars/motorcycles R31/20; P) Whether you choose to drive, pedal or walk along 'Chappies', a 5km toll road linking Hout Bay with Noordhoek, take your time as it's one of the most spectacular stretches of coastal road in the world. There are picnic spots to admire the view and it's certainly worth taking the road at least one way en route to Cape Point. If you don't plan to go all the way, ask for a free day pass as you enter at the Hout Bay end (where the toll booths are) to allow you to drive to the viewpoint overlooking the bay.

Perched on a rock near the Hout Bay end of the drive is a bronze **leopard statue**. It has been sitting there since 1963 and is a reminder of the wildlife that once roamed

◉ TOP SIGHTS
CAMPS BAY BEACH

With the spectacular mountain buttresses known as the Twelve Apostles as a backdrop, and soft white sand, the ritzy suburb of Camps Bay is home to one of the city's most popular beaches. The non-native palm trees that line beachside Victoria Rd were planted here way back to give the suburb more of a 'Mediterranean' ambiance. As it's within 15 minutes' drive of the city centre, the beach can get crowded, particularly on weekends. Don't come if it's windy as the sand storm will give you an instant exfoliation. There are no lifeguards and the surf is strong, so take care if you do swim. At the north end of the bay, climb over the boulders or down the stairs from the main road to get to more sheltered and less busy Glen Beach.

The name of the Twelve Apostles is said to have been coined by British governor Sir Rufane Donkin in 1820. However, there are well over 12 buttresses and none is individually named after an apostle. The Dutch called them De Gevelbergen, which means Gable Mountains. They're best viewed towards sunset from Lower Kloof Rd. A nice spot to escape the crowds is The Glen, a shady picnic spot and part of Table Mountain National Park that's directly below the Roundhouse restaurant.

DON'T MISS

➡ Glen Beach
➡ Drinks at sunset along Victoria Rd
➡ Sunset views of the Twelve Apostles

PRACTICALITIES

➡ Map p278
➡ campsbay.com
➡ Victoria Rd
➡ admission free

the area's forests (which has also largely vanished).

LLANDUDNO & SANDY BAY BEACH
off Map p279 (off Victoria Rd/M6); The exclusive real estate of Llandudno has a giant boulder-strewn beach that's a beauty. It's a popular spot with families. There's surfing here on the beach breaks (mostly rights), best at high tide with a small swell and a southeasterly wind.

South of Llandudno follow the signs to Sandy Bay, Cape Town's unofficial nudist beach. It's a gay stamping ground but plenty of straights frequent this particularly beautiful stretch of sand and there's no pressure to take your clothes off. There are incredible rock formations and trails through shrubby *fynbos* (literally 'fine bush', primarily proteas, heaths and ericas) to explore, too. From the Sunset Rocks parking area, the beach is roughly a 15-minute walk to the south.

HOUT BAY HARBOUR BOAT TOUR
Map p279 (Harbour Rd, Hout Bay) Although increasingly given over to tourism with complexes such as **Mariner's Wharf** (www.marinerswharf.co.za), Hout Bay's harbour still functions and the southern arm of the bay is an important fishing port and processing centre.

The best thing you can do here is board a **cruise to Duiker Island** (also known as Seal Island because of its large colony of Cape fur seals, but not to be confused with the official Seal Island in False Bay). Three companies run near identical cruises, lasting between 40 minutes and an hour, usually with guaranteed sailings in the mornings: **Circe Launches** (☏021-790 1040; www.circelaunches.co.za; adult/child R45/18) **Drumbeat Charters** (☏021-791 4441; www.drumbeatcharters.co.za; adult/child R65/25) **Nauticat Charters** (☏021-790 7278; www.nauticatcharters.co.za; adult/child R60/30).

WORLD OF BIRDS AVIARY
off Map p279 (www.worldofbirds.org.za; Valley Rd; adult/child R75/40; ☺9am-5pm; P) Barbets, weavers, flamingos and ostriches are among the 3000 birds and small mammals, covering some 400 different species, that can be found here. A real effort has been made to make the aviaries, which are South Africa's largest, as natural looking as possible with the use of lots of tropical landscaping. In the **monkey jungle** (☺11.30am-1pm & 2-3.30pm) you can interact with the cheeky squirrel monkeys.

OUDERKRAAL PARK, DIVING
Map p278 (Victoria Rd/M6; adult/child R20/10; ☺7am-6pm) There's an attractive picnic spot maintained by Table Mountain National Park on this clump of granite boulders jutting into the Atlantic. The protected coves, teeming with marine life, plus the oldest known wreck in South Africa (dating from 1670) also make this a prime dive location.

 EATING

⌖ ROUNDHOUSE CONTEMPORARY $$$
Map p278 (☏021-438 4347; theroundhouserestaurant.com; The Glen, Camps Bay; restaurant 4/6 course menu R450/595, Rumbullion mains R65-85; ☺restaurant 6-10pm Tue-Sat year-round, also openMay-Sep noon-4pm Wed-Sat, noon-3pm Sun; Rumbullion Oct-Apr 9am-11.30pm Fri-Sun, May-Sep noon-8pm; P) Overlooking Camps Bay, this 18th-century heritage-listed building, in wooded grounds, is perfect for the elegant restaurant it now houses. Their menu can also be configured to provide a delicious vegetarian meal. If they're full for dinner, then a relaxed lunch or breakfast (weekends only) on the lawns at their Rumbullion operation, where you can snack on gourmet pizza and salads, is a pleasure.

⌖ LA BOHEME SPANISH $$
Map p278 (☏021-434 8797; www.labohemebistro.co.za; 341 Main Rd, Sea Point; 2/3 courses R95/120; ☺8.30am-10.30pm Mon-Sat; ☏) With twinkling candles on the tables and fake Picassos on the walls, this superb value wine bar and bistro is a lovely place to dine at night. At their daytime operation La Bruixa you can stoke up on espresso and their delicious tapas.

THE DUCHESS OF WISBEACH FRENCH $$
Map p280 (☏021-434 1525; The Courtyard Bldg, 1 Wisbeach Rd, Sea Point; mains R70-120; ☺7-10.30pm Mon-Sat) Under the stewardship of a celebrated Jo'burg chef, this Duchess is one romantic-looking lady raising Sea Point's dining bar several notches. They serve classic French bistro food with a modern South African spin. All the ingredients are fresh with the only thing frozen being the house made icecreams and sorbets.

THE MUSSEL BAR
MUSSELS $$

Map p278 (☑021-438 4612; themusselbar.co.za; Camps Bay; mussels R75-150; ☺1pm-11pm daily) Keeping it simple pays off at this street-side operation serving fresh and plump Saldhana Bay mussels in a creamy wine sauce, and chunky chips with aioli and rosemary salt. Wash them down with the quaffable Darling Slow Brew beer.

TOP CHOICE LA PERLA
ITALIAN $$

Map p280 (☑021-439 9538; www.laperla.co.za; cnr Church & Beach Rds, Sea Point; mains R95-160; ☺10am-midnight) This eternally-stylish restaurant, with its waiters in white jackets, has been a fixture of Sea Point's promenade for decades. Enjoy something from the menu of pasta, fish and meat dishes on the terrace shaded by stout palms, or retreat to the intimate bar.

MASSIMO'S
ITALIAN $

off Map p279 (☑021-790 5648; www.pizzaclub.co.za; Oakhurst Farm Park, Main Rd, Hout Bay; mains R56-110; ☺5pm-11pm Wed-Fri, noon-11pm Sat & Sun) They do pasta and spuntini (tapas style bites) but it's the thin crust wood-fired pizzas that are Massimo's speciality – and very good they are too. It's all served up with warmth and humour by Italian Massimo and his Liverpudlian wife Tracy.

LA MOUETTE
FRENCH $$

Map p280 (☑021-433 0856; http://lamouette-restaurant.co.za; 78 Regent Rd, Sea Point; mains R110-145, tasting menu R240; ☺noon-3pm Tue-Sun, 6-10.30pm daily) Finally this charming building, notable for its lush outdoor courtyard with fountain, gets the chef and pleasant service it deserves. They serve well-executed classics such as bouillabaisse and linefish Niçoise and inventive new dishes like salt and pepper prawns with chorizo popcorn.

KITIMA
ASIAN $$

Map p279 (☑021-790 8004; www.kitima.co.za; Kronendal, 140 Main Rd, Hout Bay; mains R90-190; ☺6pm-10.30pm Tue-Sat, noon-3.30pm Sun) The Kronendal, a Cape Dutch farmhouse with parts dating back to 1713, has been sensitively restored to house this excellent panAsian restaurant specialising in Thai food and sushi. Smiling Thai staff and chefs ensure that dishes such as chicken pad thai are not mucked up.

FISH ON THE ROCKS
SEAFOOD $

Map p279 (www.africasfavourite.com; Harbour Rd, Hout Bay; mains R39; ☺10.30am-8.15pm) Dishing up some of Cape Town's best fish and chips in a breezy bayside location. Watch out for the dive-bombing seagulls if you eat on the rocks, though.

CEDAR
LEBANESE $

Map p280 (☑021-433 2546; 100 Main Rd, Sea Point; mains R50-80; ☺11am-1pm & 5pm-9.30pm Mon-Sat; ☑) It's nothing fancy, but this family-run operation rates highly for its scrumptious range of meze and Middle Eastern dishes, such as falafel, baba ganoush and hummus.

HESHENG
CHINESE $

Map p280 (☑021-434 4214; 70 Main Rd, Sea Point; mains R40-60; ☺11am-11pm Mon & Wed-Sun, 5-11pm Tue) Sea Point is stacked with Chinese restaurants, but this inauspicious-looking hole in the wall is the real deal, run by a friendly Chinese couple and frequented by Chinese expats. They make their dumplings and noodles by hand.

HARVEY'S
INTERNATIONAL $$

Map p280 (☑021-434 2351; www.winchester.co.za; Winchester Mansions Hotel, 221 Beach Rd, Sea Point) Book for their Sunday Jazz brunch (R225; ☺11am-2pm) with live music. The chic sea-facing bar and bistro is also good for lunch, drinks and nibbles.

🍷 DRINKING & NIGHTLIFE

TOP CHOICE THE BUNGALOW
BAR, RESTAURANT

Map p278 (☑021-438 2018; www.thebungalow.co.za; Glen Country Club, 1 Victoria Rd, Clifton; ☺noon-2am daily; ℗) This restaurant and lounge bar, with a Euro-chic vibe, is a great place for beers, cocktails and a boozy meal after which you can crash in the day bed section and under a billowing white awning or dangle your feet in the tiny bar-side splash pool. A DJ creates a more clubby atmosphere by night. Bookings advised.

LA VIE
BAR, CAFE

Map p280 (☑021-439 2061; 205 Beach Rd, Sea Point; ☺7.30am-midnight; ☎) Next to the South African Broadcasting Company's studios, this is one of the very few places you can have anything from breakfast to late-night cocktails within sight of Sea Point's promenade. Lounge on the outdoor terrace and enjoy the thin-crust pizza (R40-90).

DUNES BAR, RESTAURANT
Map p279 (www.dunesrestaurant.co.za; 1 Beach Rd, Hout Bay; ☺10am-10pm Mon-Fri, 8am-10pm Sat & Sun; ♠) You can hardly get closer to the beach than this – in fact, the front courtyard *is* the beach with a safe kids' play area. Up on the terrace or from inside the restaurant-bar there's a great view of Hout Bay with decent pub grub and tapas.

SALT BAR, RESTAURANT
Map p280 (✆021-439 6170; www.saltrestaurant. co.za; Ambassador Hotel, 34 Victoria Rd, Bantry Bay) The floor-to-ceiling windows at this minimalist restaurant and bar provide a vertigo-inducing vista over the crashing waves and rocks below. Perfect for cocktails and nibbles on the way back from Clifton.

CAFÉ CAPRICE CAFE, BAR
Map p278 (✆021-438 8315; www.cafecaprice. co.za; 37 Victoria Rd, Camps Bay; ☺9am-2am) The bronzed and beautiful gather at this cafe-bar, which is as popular for breakfast as it is for sundown drinks. Reserve a pavement table for the best view.

LEOPARD BAR COCKTAIL BAR
Map p278 (✆021-437 9000; www.12apostleshotel. com; Victoria Rd, Ouderkraal) The Twelve Apostles Hotel's bar has a dress-circle view over the Atlantic and is an ideal spot to escape the hoi polloi of Camps Bay for a classy cocktail or – better yet – deliciously decadent afternoon tea (R165) served from 2pm to 6pm.

GESELLIG CAFE, BAR
Map p280 (✆021-433 1515; www.gesellig.co.za; 1 Mayphil Court, cnr Regent & Church Rd, Sea Point; ☺9am-10pm Tue-Sat, 10am-10pm Sun & Mon; ♠) The food is so-so but this convivial, gay-friendly space also has comfy sofas, board games, free wi-fi and a deck (with a glimpse of the distant promenade), so it's fine for kicking back with a drink.

ST YVES DANCE CLUB
Map p278 (www.styves.co.za; The Promenade, Victoria Rd, Camps Bay) The latest incarnation of this slick Camps Bay nightspot has a groove going on with a class line up of DJs and live acts, including local sensations

Goldfish, most Sundays during the summer season (tickets available for R110 via www. webtickets.co.za).

DECODANCE DANCE CLUB
Map p280 (www.decodance.co.za; 120 Main Rd, Sea Point; men/women R20/free before 10pm, men/women R60/30 after 10pm; ☺8.30pm-4am Fri & Sat) Music 'you forgot to remember' from the '60s to the '90s is what gets people jiving at this fun club, which has two dance floors, one reserved for non-smokers. Check the website for themed parties and for details of their new club on Canterbury St in The Fringe.

 ENTERTAINMENT

THEATRE ON THE BAY THEATRE
Map p278 (✆021-438 3300; www.theatreonthe bay.co.za; 1 Link St, Camps Bay) The program here sticks with conventional plays or one-person shows. A new addition is the chic Sidedish Theatre Bistro.

CINE 12 CINEMA
Map p278 (www.12apostleshotel.com/dining/ dining/dinner-movie/cinema-times; Victoria Rd, Ouderkraal; admission free with a meal; P) There are just 16 luxurious red-leather upholstered seats in the Twelve Apostles Hotel's cinema, where different movies are screened four times a day; check the website for the schedule.

SHOPPING

TOP CHOICE BAY HARBOUR MARKET MARKET
Map p279 (bayharbour.co.za/home.html; 31 Harbour Rd, Hout Bay; ☺5-10pm Fri, 9am-5pm Sat, 10am-4pm, Sun) At the far western end of the harbour this imaginatively designed indoor market has been a rip-roaring success. There's a good range of gifts and crafts as well as very tempting food and drink options and live music. The market only runs on Fridays from November to end of February, but the weekend opening times are year round.

HOUT BAY CRAFT MARKET MARKET
Map p279 (Baviaanskloof Rd, Hout Bay; ☺10am-5pm Sun) Browsing the stalls at this little

LIVE MUSIC GUIDE

Patrick Craig, musician, manager of a cappella group D7 (www.d7live.com) and creator of **Studio 7** (www.studio7.org.za) in Sea Point, filled us in on the 'jazz cats' and breaking bands of the Capetonian scene.

Best indoor venues?

Assembly and Mercury Live can always be relied on; the former is mainly DJs and electronic music. Zula Sound Bar has a great line up for live music and fun DJ floor. There's an acoustic night most Mondays at The Waiting Room, Wednesday at &Union and Polana on Friday and Saturday is always a good party, plus they have jazz on Sunday. There's also Mike Campbell Big Band playing jazz on Mondays at the end of month at Trinity.

Best outdoor venues?

In summer you can't miss the concerts in Kirstenbosch. Although it's a 45-minute drive out of town, the Paul Cluver Forest Ampitheatre (www.cluver.com/amphitheatre) in Elgin is really beautiful, a very different environment in which to catch a gig. Also look for outdoor shows at other wine estates.

Artist to watch?

Electro-jazz combo GoodLuck; Aking, the most accessible of the many Afrikaans rock bands banging out lately; killer blues guitarist Natasha Meister; and the band DieselVanilla – but they may change their name!

What's Studio 7?

It's a members-only music club I started in my living room. It's taken off and I've managed to score some top local and international artists to play acoustic sets in a very intimate environment. For most shows there's around 10 to 20 tickets for the public sold online so, if you're lucky, you may be able to get one.

village green market is a lovely way to while an hour or so away on a Sunday. You'll find crafts made by locals including the impressive beadwork of Lizzy & Vince who can arrange custom orders.

ETHNO BONGO   JEWELLERY

Map p279 (www.ethnobongo.co.za; 5 Main Rd, Hout Bay; ⊙9.30am-5.30pm Mon-Fri, 9.30am-4pm Sat, 10am-4pm Sun) A court order may have stopped them using the name Dolce & Banana for their bead jewellery but it hasn't put a dent in this long-running shop, in an original fisherman's cottage, selling fun fashion items made by local craftspeople. Their products include home decor using materials such as reclaimed wood and drift wood.

T-BAG DESIGNS   HANDMADE CRAFTS

Map p279 (www.tbagdesigns.co.za; Mainstream Mall, Main Rd, Hout Bay; ⊙9am-5.30pm Mon-Fri, 9am-3pm Sat, 9.30am-4pm Sun) Recycled tea bags are used to produce an attractive range of greetings cards, stationery and other quality hand-made paper products; it's a worthwhile project employing 13

people from the neighbouring township of Imizamo Yethu. They also have a stall at the Blue Shed in the V&A Waterfront.

SHIPWRECK SHOP   ANTIQUES

Map p279 (www.marinerswharf.com; Hout Bay Harbour; ⊙9am-5.30pm) If you're after anything to do with ships from scrimshaw (old carved ivory) to charts and models then this treasure trove, containing over 20,000 pieces of memorabilia salvaged from ocean-going vessels, should be on your visit list.

IZIKO LO LWAZI   ARTS & CRAFTS

Map p279 (www.izikoll.co.za; Hout Bay Community Cultural Centre, Baviaanskloof Rd, Hout Bay; ⊙9.30am-1pm Mon-Fri) What began as an adult literacy program has morphed into a craftwork collective producing creative recycled-paper products from, among other things, elephant, horse and camel dung! Their beaded cards are delightful.

PEACH   FASHION

Map p280 (www.peachsa.com; 2 Marine House, Main Rd, Sea Point) A well-curated selection of quality imported clothing, scarves, costume jewellery, underwear, bags and other accessories are on display at this colourful boutique, a favourite of local fashionistas.

NAARTJIE KIDS
CHILDREN'S CLOTHING

Map p279 (www.naartjiekids.com; 46 Victoria Ave, Hout Bay; ⊙9am-6pm Mon-Fri, 9am-5pm Sat, 10am-4pm Sun) Factory shop of the designer children's clothing brand.

SPORTS & ACTIVITIES

SEA POINT PAVILION
SWIMMING

Map p280 (Beach Rd, Sea Point; adult/child R16/7.50; ⊙7am-7pm Oct-Apr, 9am-5pm May-Sep) This huge outdoor pool complex is a Sea Point institution and has some lovely art deco decoration. It gets very busy on hot summer days, not surprisingly, since the pools are always at least 10°C warmer than the always-frigid ocean.

IN THE BLUE
DIVING

Map p280 (⊉021-434 3358; www.diveschool capetown.co.za; 88B Main Rd, Sea Point; open-water PADI courses from R3450, shore/boat dives R200/300 per dive, gear hire R380 per day) Conveniently located near Sea Point's hostels and guesthouses this operator runs courses and has regular dives on a variety of themes scheduled around the Cape, including shark-cage dives.

THE BOARDROOM ADVENTURE CENTRE
KAYAKING, SURFING

Map p279 (⊉021-790 8132; 072-763 4486; www. theboardroomadventures.co.za; 37 Victoria Rd, Hout Bay; kayaking/surf lessons from R350) Kayaking out to Duiker Island or around Hout Bay, as well as various surfing trips, are offered by the guys at this surf gear rental shop. They also have bikes for rent (hour/day R50/160), a small cafe making crepes, and sell Re-Sail (www.resails.com) jackets and bags made from recycled old yacht sails.

Southern Suburbs

MOWBRAY | RONDEBOSCH | NEWLANDS | BISHOPSCOURT | WYNBERG | CONSTANTIA

Neighbourhood Top Five

1 Immerse yourself in the diverse splendour of the Cape Floral Kingdom at **Kirstenbosch Botanical Gardens** (p118), and be sure to attend one of their outdoor summer concerts.

2 Taste wines along the **Constantia Valley Wine Route** (p119) visiting his-

toric estates such as Groot Constantia.

3 Take a stroll around the lovely urban conservation area of **Wynberg Village** (p121).

4 Admire the view from the grand **Rhodes Memorial** (p121)

5 Step into the world of one of South Africa's top 20th-century painters at the **Irma Stern Museum** (p123).

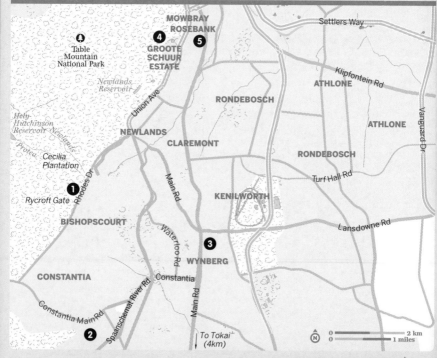

For more detail of this area, see Map p282 ➡

Explore Southern Suburbs

If you want to see how the other half in Cape Town lives – the rich half – take a trip into the Southern Suburbs, the residential areas clinging to the eastern slopes of Table Mountain. Heading south out of the City Bowl and around Devil's Peak you'll first hit Mowbray and Rondebosch; this is the territory of the University of Cape Town (UCT). It's also where you'll find one of Cape Town's premier arts spaces, the Baxter Theatre Centre.

Leafy Newlands and Bishopscourt are clearly affluent and where you'll find several of the area's highlights, including the Kirstenbosch Botanical Gardens and the city's major cricketing and rugby venues. The area around Claremont station is a fascinating study in contrasts, with black and coloured traders crowding the streets around the ritzy Cavendish Square mall. It's a similar story in Wynberg, another place where the haves rub shoulders with the have-nots. The thatched-roof Cape Georgian homes of Wynberg Village are worth a look.

Immediately to the west is Constantia, home to South Africa's oldest wineries, where the super-wealthy live in huge mansions behind high walls. It's a verdant area that culminates in Tokai, with its shady forest reserve.

Local Life

➡ **Sports** Join the fans cheering on South African cricket and rugby teams at Sahara Park Newlands (p128) and Newlands Rugby Stadium (p128).

➡ **Beer** Sample microbrews at Banana Jam (p125), tour South Africa's oldest commercial brewery (p123) or drop by the ever-popular boozer the Forrester's Arms (p126)

➡ **Markets** The commons in front of Kirstenbosch get used for various markets, including a monthly craft market (p127); also head to the Porter Estate (p127) on Saturday for its farm-fresh produce and craft market.

Getting There & Away

➡ **Car** From the city follow the M3, which runs parallel to the east side of Table Mountain with turn-offs for UCT, the Rhodes Memorial, Newlands and Kirstenbosch. Stay on the M3 for Constantia and Tokai.

➡ **Bus** The City Sightseeing Cape Town Blue Route bus stops at Kirstenbosch; you can add a free extension bus tour to the Groot Constantia and Eagle's Nest wineries.

➡ **Shared taxi** Minibus taxis shuttle along Main Rd from Mowbray to Wynberg.

➡ **Train** Cape Metro Rail has stops at Rondebosch, Newlands, Claremont, Kenilworth, Wynberg, Rosebank and Mowbray.

Lonely Planet's Top Tip

Arderne Gardens (www.ardernegardens.org.za; 222 Main Rd, Claremont; ⊘9am-6pm) were planted by botanist Ralph Arderne in 1845 and represent the oldest collection of trees in the southern hemisphere, including bamboo, fir, gum and enormous Moreton Bay fig trees. It's a lovely place for a quiet wander and is especially colourful on weekends when many Capetonian wedding parties come to have their photos taken.

SOUTHERN SUBURBS

✗ Best Places to Eat

➡ La Colombe (p124)
➡ Bistro Sixteen82 (p124)
➡ River Café (p124)
➡ Gardener's Cottage (p124)
➡ A Tavola (p124)

For reviews, see p124

🍷 Best Places to Drink

➡ Banana Jam (p125)
➡ Martini Bar (p126)
➡ Caveau at the Mill (p126)
➡ Forrester's Arms (p126)
➡ O'ways Teacafe (p125)

For reviews, see p125 ➡

🔒 Best Places to Shop

➡ Montebello (p127)
➡ Art in the Forest (p127)
➡ Porter Estate Produce Market (p127)
➡ Cavendish Square (p127)

For reviews, see p127 ➡

TOP SIGHTS
KIRSTENBOSCH BOTANICAL GARDENS

Covering over 500 hectares of Table Mountain, overlooking False Bay and the Cape Flats, these beautiful landscaped gardens – the largest in South Africa – merge almost imperceptibly with the surrounding natural *fynbos* (fine bush) vegetation. They're a wonderful place to relax, take in the scenery and learn about the magnificent Cape Floral Kingdom. There is always something flowering, but the gardens are at their best between mid-August and mid-October.

History of the Gardens

In 1657 Jan van Riebeeck appointed a forester to the area. A group of shipwrecked French refugees on their way to Madagascar were employed during 1660 to plant a wild almond hedge as the boundary of the Dutch outpost (a remnant of it is still here). Van Riebeeck called his private farm Boschheuwel, and it wasn't until the 1700s, when the gardens were managed by JF Kirsten, that they got the name Kirstenbosch. Cecil Rhodes owned the land from 1895 until his death in 1902 when he bequeathed his estate to the nation. It officially became a botanical garden in 1913.

What to See

Apart from the almond hedge, some magnificent oaks, and the Moreton Bay fig and camphor trees planted by Rhodes, the gardens are devoted almost exclusively to indigenous plants. About 9000 of Southern Africa's 22,000 plant species are cultivated here.

You'll find a *kopje* (hill) that has been planted with pelargoniums; a sculpture garden; a section for plants used for *muti* (traditional medicines) by *sangomas* (traditional African healers); and a fragrance garden with raised beds and plants that can be smelt and felt, which were developed so that sight-impaired people could enjoy the garden – the plant labels here are also in Braille.

The main entrance at the Newlands end of the gardens is where you'll find plenty of parking, the information centre, an excellent souvenir shop and the atmosphere-controlled **conservatory** (⊙9am-6pm). The conservatory displays plant communities from a variety of terrains, the most interesting of which is the Namaqualand and Richtersveld section, with baobabs and quiver trees.

Make an effort to attend the series of Summer Sunset concerts, usually held on Sundays; some of the biggest names in South African music perform here.

Guided Walks & Hiking Routes

The gardens run free guided walks, or hire the My Guide electronic gizmo (R40) to hear recorded information about the various plants on the three signposted circular walks.

There are also two popular routes up Table Mountain from Kirstenbosch along either Skeleton Gorge, which involves negotiating some sections with chains, or Nursery Ravine. These can be covered in three hours by someone of moderate fitness. The trails are well marked and steep in places, but the way to the gardens from the cableway and vice versa is not signposted.

DON'T MISS...

➡ Summer Sunset Concerts

➡ Fragrance Garden

➡ Conservatory

➡ Van Riebeeck's Hedge

PRACTICALITIES

➡ ☑021-799 8783

➡ www.sanbi.org/ gardens/kirstenbosch

➡ Rhodes Dr, Newlands

➡ adult/child R40/10

➡ ⊙8am-7pm Sep-Mar, to 6pm Apr-Aug, conservatory ⊙ 9am-6pm

➡ 🚍 Stop on City Sightseeing Cape Town Blue Route; Golden Arrow buses run here from Mowbray train station 7am-4pm Mon-Fri.

TOP SIGHTS
CONSTANTIA VALLEY WINE ROUTE

South Africa's wine-farming industry began here back in 1685 when Governor Simon van der Stel was granted around 763 hectares of land behind Table Mountain. He chose the area for its wine-growing potential and named his farm Constantia. By 1709 there were 70,000 vines producing 5630L of wine. Four years after Van der Stel's death in 1712 the estate was split up. The area is now home to a route covering nine vineyards – the key ones to visit are covered below.

Groot Constantia

Simon van der Stel's manor house, a superb example of Cape Dutch architecture, is maintained as a museum at **Groot Constantia** (☏021-794 5128; www.grootconstantia.co.za; Groot Constantia Rd, Constantia; tastings R33; museum adult/child R20/free; cellar tours R45; ⊘9am-5pm; Ⓟ). Set in beautiful grounds, the estate can become busy with tour groups but is big enough for you to escape the crowds. In the 18th century, Constantia wines were exported around the world and were highly acclaimed; try their sauvignon blanc and Gouverneurs Reserve bordeaux-style blend.

The large tasting room is first on your right as you enter the estate. Further on is the free orientation centre, which provides an excellent overview of the estate's history, and the beautifully restored homestead. The interiors have been appropriately furnished; take a look at the tiny slave quarters beneath the main building. The Cloete Cellar, with a beautiful moulded pediment, was the estate's original wine cellar. It now houses old carriages and a display of storage vessels. Hour-long tours of the modern cellar depart at 2pm.

DON'T MISS...

➡ Groot Constantia
➡ Steenberg Vineyard
➡ Buitenverwachting
➡ Klein Constantia

PRACTICALITIES

➡ www.constantia valley.com
➡ Follow M3 from city; Constantia turn-off for most of wineries; Tokai turn-off for Steenberg Vineyards
➡ Tasting fees often waived on purchase
➡ City Sightseeing Cape Town has a bus to Groot Constantia and Eagle's Nest; Downhill Adventures (www. downhilladventures. com) visits Steenberg and Klein Constantia on their Cape Point and Winelands tour.

WHAT THE...?

At the entrance to Klein Constantia is the karamat (saint's tomb) of Sheik Abdurachman Matebe Shah; he was buried here in 1661 and the tomb is one of several that encircle Cape Town, supposedly providing protection against natural disasters.

There's no shortage of places to dine while out visiting the wine farms. Groot Constantia has two restaurants, and Constantia Uitsig three. Steenberg Vineyards has an excellent new bistro and Buitenverwachting an elegant formal restaurant overlooking its vineyards. At both the Groot Constantia and Eagle's Nest estates, you can pre-order picnics to enjoy in the grounds – just bring your own blanket.

WALKING TRAILS

The website of the **Zandvlei Trust** (www. zandvleitrust.org.za) has maps of nine easy walking trails, each no more than 45 minutes long, in the Constantia Valley, some running through shady old forests and beside rivers.

Steenberg Vineyards

Acquired by Graham Beck in 2005 but dating back to 1682, **Steenberg Vineyards** (☎021-713 2211; www. steenberg-vineyards.co.za; Steenberg Rd; tastings free & R50; ⊙10am-6pm; ℗) have since been revitalised with a contemporary tasting bar and lounge in which you can sample their great merlot, sauvignon blanc reserve, sémillon and cap classique sparkler. Picnics (R300 for two) include a bottle of wine. Also here is the five-star **Steenberg Hotel** (www.steenberghotel. com) in the original manor house, Catharina's Restaurant and an 18-hole golf course.

Buitenverwachting

Buitenverwachting (☎021-794 5190; buitenverwachting.co.za; Klein Constantia Rd; tastings free; ⊙9am-5pm Mon-Fri, 10am-3pm Sat; ℗) means 'beyond expectation', which is certainly the feeling one gets on visiting this 100-hectare estate. Beg, steal or borrow to snag a bottle of its delicious, but limited release, Christine claret. The chardonnay and Rhine riesling are standout whites. Order ahead to enjoy a blissful **picnic lunch** (☎083 257 6083; lunch R125; ⊙noon-4pm Mon-Sat Nov-April) in front of the 1796 manor house.

Klein Constantia

Part of the original Constantia estate, **Klein Constantia** (☎021-794 5188; www.kleinconstantia.com; Klein Constantia Rd; tastings free; ⊙tastings from 9am-5pm Mon-Fri, 9am-3pm Sat; ℗) is famous for its vin de Constance, a sweet muscat wine (R330). It was Napoleon's solace on St Helena, and Jane Austen had one of her heroines recommend it for having the power to heal 'a disappointed heart'. Klein Constantia doesn't offer the frills and bonuses of other wineries, but it's worth visiting for its excellent tasting room.

Other Wine Farms

Constantia Glen (☎021-795 6100; www.constantiaglen. com; Constantia Main Rd; tasting R30; ⊙10am-5pm Mon-Fri, 10am-4pm Sat & Sun; ℗) is known for its sauvignon blanc but also does two bordeaux-style blends.

Stuart Botha, the young winemaker at **Eagle's Nest** (☎021-794 4095; www.eaglesnestwines.com; Constantia Main Rd; tasting R30; ⊙10am-4.30pm; ℗), is one of the stars of an SABC reality TV series *Exploring the Vine*. Picnics are R300 for two.

Call at **Constantia Uitsig** (☎021-794 1810; www. constantia-uitsig.com; Spaanschemat River Rd; tastings R25; ⊙tastings from 9am-4.30pm Mon-Fri, 10am-4.30pm Sat & Sun; ℗) to sample their crisp sémillon, luscious MCC blanc de blanc brut or limited-release muscat D'Alexandrie in the tasting room next to the River Café.

TOP SIGHTS
CONSTANTIA VALLEY WINE ROU

SIGHTS

**KIRSTENBOSCH
BOTANICAL GARDENS**   GARDENS
See p118.

**CONSTANTIA VALLEY
WINE ROUTE**   WINERIES
See p121.

WYNBERG VILLAGE   HISTORIC DISTRICT
(Durban Rd, Wynberg; ⓡWynberg) Declared an urban conservation area in 1981, Wynberg Village is also known as Little Chelsea or Chelsea Village, a nickname it gained in the 1950s in reference to London's Chelsea. Like that arty quarter, the village's stock of Cape Georgian buildings (the densest collection in South Africa) houses the homes and shops of artists, designers and interior decorators.

Midway between Cape Town and Simon's Town, this charming village of thatched-roof cottages was developed mainly in the 19th century as a garrison for the British army, but there are also older buildings here; it's best explored on a walking tour. The main focus is **Maynardville Park**, once the estate of Victorian property magnate James Maynard. His 1870s mansion was demolished when the city took over the grounds in the 1950s, but the old swimming pool remains as a pond and the archery lawn has been replaced by the Maynardville Open-Air Theatre.

FREE **RHODES MEMORIAL**   MONUMENT
Map p282 (www.rhodesmemorial.co.za/memorial.aspx; off M3, below Devil's Peak, Groote Schuur Estate, Rondebosch; ◷7am-7pm; Ⓟ) This impressive and monumental granite memorial stands on the eastern slopes of Table Mountain at a spot where the mining magnate and former prime minister used to admire the view. Rhodes bought all the surrounding land in 1895 for £9000 as part of a plan to preserve a relatively untouched section of the mountain for future generations.

Partly modelled on the arch at London's Hyde Park Corner, the memorial has 49 steps, one for each year of Rhodes' life. Despite providing sweeping vistas to the Cape Flats and the mountain ranges beyond – and, by implication, right into the heart of Africa – the statue of Rhodes himself has the man looking rather grumpy. The exit for the memorial is at the Princess Anne Interchange on the M3.

Behind the memorial is a restaurant, a tea garden and a steep path leading up to the **King's Blockhouse**, a defensive position built by the British between 1795 and 1803. From here it's possible to follow the contour path above Newlands Forest to Skeleton Gorge and down into Kirstenbosch.

SOUTHERN SUBURBS SIGHTS

CECIL RHODES: EMPIRE BUILDER

Empire builder Cecil John Rhodes (1853–1902) was a legend in his own lifetime. When he arrived in South Africa in 1870, he was a sickly, impoverished son of an English vicar. The climate obviously agreed with Rhodes, as he not only recovered his health but went on to found the De Beers mining company (which in 1891 owned 90% of the world's diamond mines) and become prime minister of the Cape in 1890 at the age of 37.

As part of his dream of building a railway from the Cape to Cairo (running through British territory all the way), Rhodes pushed north to establish mines and develop trade. He established British control in Bechuanaland (later Botswana) and the area that was to become Rhodesia (later Zimbabwe). His grand ideas of empire went too far, though, when he became involved in a failed uprising in the Boer-run Transvaal Republic in 1895. An embarrassed British government forced Rhodes to resign as prime minister in 1896, but Rhodesia and Bechuanaland remained his personal fiefdoms.

Rhodes never married (there's been much debate over whether he was gay); late in his life he became entangled in the schemes of the glamorous and ruthless Princess Randziwill, who was later jailed for her swindles. His health again in decline, Rhodes returned to Cape Town in 1902, only to die from his ailments at the age of 49 at his home in Muizenberg. Rhodes' reputation was rehabilitated by his will. He devoted most of his fortune to the Rhodes scholarship, which sends recipients to Oxford University, and his land and many properties in Cape Town now belong to the nation.

START WYNBERG STATION
END WYNBERG STATION
DISTANCE 2.5KM
DURATION ONE HOUR

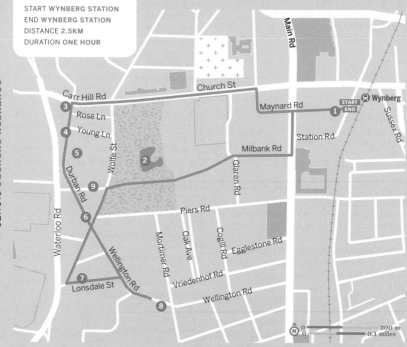

Neighbourhood Walk
Wynberg Village Walk

This conservation area is packed with Cape Georgian and Victorian buildings, some of them thatched, and many with lovely flower gardens. However, the area around **Wynberg Station**, always jammed with shared taxi cabs and traders, contrasts starkly with the genteel village less than 10 minutes' walk west. Opposite the station is the recently restored ① **Town Hall**, designed at the turn of the 19th century by W Black in Flemish revival style.

Cross Main Rd and head down Maynard Rd. Across from the car park (an alternative start/finish point if you're driving) is ② **Maynardville Park**. Walk through the park, emerging at the junction of Wolfe St and Carr Hill Rd. The neo-Gothic ③ **Dutch Reformed Church**, up the hill on the corner of Durban Rd, dates back to 1831; inside are four granite supporting pillars donated by Cecil Rhodes.

Turn left (south) at the church down Durban Rd. There are many pretty thatched-roof cottages lining this street, including ④ **Winthrop House**, which was once the British army officers' mess, and ⑤ **Falcon House**, said to be the village's first courthouse.

Where Durban Rd meets Wolfe St, there's a small square shaded by a pair of oak trees. Around here are interior-design shops, including ones that surround the hidden ⑥ **Chelsea Courtyard,** a delightful garden.

Return to Wolfe St and continue south to the junction with Lonsdale St to admire the ⑦ **old bakery** (c. 1890) with its fish-scale slate turret flanked by gryphons; it's now an interior-design shop.

Turn left (east) into Lonsdale St and continue to the junction with Durban Rd. Detour right to peek through the wire fence at the late 18th-century mansion ⑧ **Tenterden**. The Cape Dutch revival–style veranda was added in the 20th century. The Duke of Wellington slept at the now destroyed coach house which was once also part of the property. Retrace your steps back along Durban Rd until you reach the village square again and the ⑨ **Wolfe St** parade of shops. Return to Wynberg Station via Maynardville Park.

IRMA STERN MUSEUM
ART MUSEUM

Map p282 (www.irmastern.co.za; Cecil Rd; adult/child R10/5; ☺10am-5pm Tue-Sat; ⩗Rosebank) The pioneering 20th-century artist Irma Stern (1894–1966) lived in this house for almost 40 years and her studio has been left virtually intact, as if she'd just stepped out into the verdant garden for a breath of fresh air. Her ethnographic art-and-craft collection from around the world is as fascinating as her art, which was influenced by German expressionism and incorporated elements of traditional African art. In March 2011, a Stern painting was sold for R34 million (US$4.94 million) at auction in London, creating a record for a South African artist.

GROOTE SCHUUR
ARCHITECTURAL MONUMENT

Map p282 (☎083 414 7961, 021-686 9100; Klipper Rd, Rondebosch; admission R50; ☺tours 10am-noon Mon-Fri; ⩗Rondebosch) Cecil Rhodes bequeathed this historic house and its surrounding estate to the nation. It was home to a succession of prime ministers, culminating with FW de Klerk. The beautifully restored interior, all teak panels and heavy colonial furniture, antiques and tapestries of the finest calibre, is suitably imposing. The best feature is the colonnaded veranda overlooking the formal gardens, which slope uphill towards an avenue of pine trees and sweeping views of Devil's Peak. Advance booking is necessary and you must bring your passport to gain entry to this high-security area; the entrance is unmarked but easily spotted on the left as you take the Princess Anne Ave exit off the M3.

⭐ TOKAI FOREST
PARK, ARBORETUM

(http://sanparks.org.za/parks/table_mountain/tourism/attractions.php; Tokai Rd, Tokai; adult/child R10/5, car/mountain bike R10/35; ☺8am-5pm Apr-Sep, 7am-6pm Oct-Mar; Ⓟ) This wooded section of Table Mountain National Park, south of Constantia, is a favourite spot for picnics, mountain biking and walks, the most challenging of which is the 6km hike up to Elephant's Eye Cave within the Silvermine section of the park. The zigzag path is fairly steep and offers little shade as you climb higher up Constantiaberg (928m), so bring a hat and water.

At the walk's base you'll find the **Tokai Arboretum**, a planting of 1555 different trees representing 274 species, begun in 1885 by Joseph Storr Lister, the conservator of forests for the Cape Colony. Here, too, is the very pleasant **Lister's Place Tea Garden** (☎021-715 4512; ☺9am-5pm Tue-Sun), where you can pick up a map of walks in the area. There is also excellent accommodation at **Wood Owl Cottage** (see p31). To reach the forest, take the Tokai exit from the M3 highway.

NEWLANDS BREWERY
BREWERY, TOUR

Map p282 (☎021-658 7440; www.newlandsbrewery.co.za; 3 Main Rd; admission R30; ☺tours 10am, noon, 2pm Mon-Fri, 10am Sat; Ⓟ; ⩗Newlands) In the early 19th century Jacob Letterstedt built the Mariendahl Brewery in Newlands, a handsome building granted National Monument status that is now part of Newlands Brewery, owned by South African Breweries. Fascinating tours of the complex, including the chance to sample the various beers made here (which include Castle and Black Label), will give you an insight into large-scale beer making. The brewery hosted the inaugural **Oktober Bierfest** (www.oktoberbierfest.co.za) in 2011 and plans to make it an annual event.

JOSEPHINE MILL
WATER MILL

Map p282 (www.josephinemill.co.za; Boundary Rd, Newlands; donation R10, milling demonstration R20; ☺10am-7pm Mon-Fri, 10am-2pm Sat; Ⓟ; ⩗Newlands) Beside the Liesbeek River, Cape Town's only surviving water mill is still used in this now museum, restaurant and wine-bar setting to grind flour: demonstrations are held during the week at 11am and 3pm. The giant iron wheel was originally built sometime after 1819 by Jacob Letterstedt, who went on to become a wealthy brewer and miller. In the attached shop you can buy stone-ground flour and various baked goods made from it as well as other deli treats.

UNIVERSITY OF CAPE TOWN
UNIVERSITY, ARCHITECTURE

Map p282 (UCT; www.uct.ac.za; Ⓟ; ⩗Rondebosch) For the non-academic there's no pressing reason to visit the University of Cape Town, but it's nonetheless an impressive place to walk around. UCT presents a fairly cohesive architectural front, with ivy-covered neoclassical facades, and a fine set of stone steps leading to the temple-like Jameson building. Visitors can usually get parking permits at the university – call in at the information office on the entry road, near the bottom of the steps.

TABLE MOUNTAIN RESERVOIRS

On the area of Table Mountain known as the Back Table are five dams and reservoirs created in the late 19th and early 20th centuries to provide a secure water supply for the booming population of Cape Town. Work commenced on the first dam in 1890 and the 995-megalitre reservoir, **Woodhead Reservoir** was named after the mayor of the time Sir John Woodhead when it was eventually completed in 1897. At the same time the independent municipality of Wynberg began working on a series of dams: **Victoria Reservoir** was completed in 1896, **Alexandra Reservoir** was finished in 1903 and the **De Villiers Reservoir** in 1907. In 1904 the city of Cape Town also added the 924-megalitre **Hely-Hutchinson Reservoir**, named after Sir Walter Hely-Hutchinson, the last governor of Cape Colony.

In hikes around the Back Table you can admire the construction skill and detail of these dams and learn something of their history at the **Waterworks Museum** (☑021 686 3408). Call ahead as this small building at the northern corner of the Hely-Hutchinson Reservoir is often closed. Inside, various bits of machinery used to build the dams are displayed, including the Barclay locomotive made in Scotland in 1898, dismantled and reconstructed on top of the mountain. A straightforward way up here is from Constantia Nek, where there's parking, and through the Cecilia Plantation; the route to Hely-Hutchinson dam is around 4km one way.

As you're following the M3 from the city, just after the open paddocks on Devil's Peak, you'll pass the old **Mostert's Mill**, a real Dutch windmill dating from 1796, on the left. Just past the old windmill, also on the left, is the exit for the university. Turn right at the T-intersection after you've taken the exit.

Alternatively, if you approach UCT from Woolsack Dr, you'll pass the **Woolsack**, a cottage designed in 1900 by Sir Herbert Baker for Cecil Rhodes; it's now a student residence. It's said that Rudyard Kipling wrote the poem *If* during his residence here between 1900 and 1907.

✖ EATING

TOP CHOICE LA COLOMBE   FRENCH $$$
(☑021-794 2390; www.constantia-uitsig.com; Constantia Uitsig, Spaanschemat River Rd, Constantia; mains R100-215, 6-course menu R600; ◷12.30-2.30pm & 7.30-9.30pm; ℗) The shady garden setting makes this wine estate restaurant one of the most pleasant places to dine in Cape Town. British chef Scott Kirkton rustles up skilful dishes such as trout sous vide, beetroot cannelloni and smoked tomato risotto.

BISTRO SIXTEEN82   TAPAS, INTERNATIONAL $$
(☑021-713 2211; www.steenberg-vineyards. co.za; Steenberg Vineyard, Tokai; mains R60-100; ◷9am-8pm; ℗) Perfectly complementing the dazzlingly contemporary wine-tasting lounge is Steenberg Vineyard's highly appealing bistro, serving everything from breakfast with a glass of bubbly to an early supper of tapas with their quaffable merlot. Seating is both indoor and outdoor with beguiling views of the gardens and mountain.

RIVER CAFÉ   INTERNATIONAL $$
(☑021-794 3010; www.constantia-uitsig.com; Constantia Uitsig, Spaanschemat River Rd, Constantia; mains R60-100; ◷8.30am-5pm; ℗) A back-up if La Colombe is full or beyond your budget, this delightful and popular cafe at the entrance to the estate is worthy of a visit in its own right. It can be relied on for big portions of food made with organic and free-range products. Booking is essential, especially for weekend brunch.

A TAVOLA   ITALIAN $$
Map p282 (☑021-794 3010; www.atavola.co.za; Library Square, Wilderness Rd, Claremont; mains R65-120; ◷noon-3pm Mon-Fri, 6-10pm Mon-Sat; ℗; ℝClaremont) This spacious, classy neighbourhood joint, with walls hung with photos of people tucking into food, makes a near-perfect Caesar salad as well as delicious pasta and other mains – no wonder the people are smiling in those photos.

GARDENER'S COTTAGE   CAFE $
Map p282 (☑021-689 3158; Montebello Craft Studios, 31 Newlands Ave, Newlands; mains R45-70; ◷8am-2.30pm Mon-Fri, 8.30am-3pm Sat & Sun;

Newlands) After exploring the Montebello craft studios, relax at this lovely cafe and tea garden in the grounds. It serves simple, hearty meals in the shade of leafy trees.

O'WAYS TEACAFE
TEA

Map p282 (☏021-617 2850; www.oways.co.za; 20 Dreyer St, Claremont; mains R47-150; ☺7.30am-5pm Mon-Fri, 9am-2pm Sat; ☝; ⒭Claremont) Pronounced 'always', this stylish, relaxing place offers 60-odd loose-leaf teas as well as coffee. The menu is fully vegetarian, including tasty dishes such as dim sum dumplings, and portobello mushrooms filled with couscous.

ORCHID CAFÉ
INTERNATIONAL $

(☏021-761 1000; 23 Wolfe St, Wynberg Village; mains R60-70; ☺8.30am-5pm Mon-Fri, 8.30am-2pm Sat; ⒭Wynberg) To the rear of a boutique is this enchanting place, a favourite of the ladies who lunch in Little Chelsea. Sit in the courtyard draped with bougainvillea and enjoy scrumptious egg dishes, sandwiches, salads and cakes, and consider taking the nearby Wynberg Village Walk.

JONKERSHUIS
CAPE MALAY $$

(☏021-794 6255; www.jonkershuisconstantia.co.za; Groot Constantia; mains R50-80, 2/3 courses R140/160; ☺9am-10pm Mon-Sat, 9am-5pm Sun; ℗) This casual brasserie-style restaurant in the grounds of Groot Constantia has a pleasant vine-shaded courtyard and tables looking onto the manor house. Sample Cape Malay dishes, including a tasting plate for R128, cured meats with a glass or two of the local wines, or satisfy your sweet tooth with the desserts.

CHART FARM
FARM CAFE

(☏021 762-0067; www.chartfarm.co.za; Klaasens Rd, Wynberg; mains R28-50; ☺9am-4.30pm; ℗; ⒭Wynberg) Roses, chestnuts, lemons and grapes are among the tasty things grown on this small farm tucked away on the west side of the M3. At their coffee shop, with a panoramic view across the farm to the mountains, enjoy homemade cakes, breakfasts and lunch treats such as chicken pie. Pick your own roses afterwards for R4 a stem. There's a produce market here on Sundays.

LA BELLE
BAKERY, INTERNATIONAL $$

(☏021-795 6336; www.alphen.co.za; Alphen Drive, Constantia; mains R70-140; ☺7am-7pm; ℗☎) In front of the Alphen hotel, this is an appealing dining spot both inside and out for breakfast, lunch or a snack. Treat yourself to a five-star brekkie with champers (R250) or one of their speciality leaf teas (R20).

TASHAS
BAKERY, INTERNATIONAL $

(www.tashascafe.com; shop 55, Constantia Village, Constantia Main Rd, Constantia; mains R55-80; ☺7am-6pm; ℗) Muffins that could feed a small family and other delectable baked goods and desserts are the forte of this luxe-design cafe offering 'easy eating' – a hit Jo'burg concept imported to the Mother City.

KIRSTENBOSCH TEA ROOM
INTERNATIONAL $

(☏021-797 4883; www.ktr.co.za; Gate 2, Kirstenbosch Botanical Gardens, Rhodes Dr, Newlands; mains R36-100; ☺8.30am-5pm; ℗) Kirstenbosch's best dining option. Picnics and English tea for two (R120), including cucumber and cream-cheese sandwiches, mini-quiches and homemade scones with strawberry jam and clotted cream, can be ordered up to enjoy anywhere you please in the gardens.

RHODES MEMORIAL RESTAURANT
CAPE MALAY $$

Map p282 (www.rhodesmemorial.co.za; Off M3, below Devil's Peak, Groote Schuur Estate, Rondebosch; mains; ☺7am-5pm; ℗) Behind the memorial is the pleasant restaurant in a 1920 thatched-roof cottage and al-fresco tearoom. It's family run and they specialise in Cape Malay dishes such as curries, *bredies* (pot stews of meat or fish and vegetables) and *bobotie* (delicately flavoured ostrich meat curry with a topping of beaten egg baked to a crust). Booking advised on the weekends.

🍷 DRINKING & NIGHTLIFE

 BANANA JAM
CRAFT BEER

(www.bananajamcafe.co.za; 157 2nd Ave, Harfield Village, Kenilworth; ☺11am-11pm Mon-Sat, 5pm-11pm Sun; ℗☎; ⒭Kenilworth) Real beer lovers rejoice – this convivial Caribbean restaurant and bar is like manna from heaven, with a host of on tap and bottled ales from local microbrewers including Jack Black, Triggerfish, Darling Brew, Camelthorne and Boston Brewery. Try a taster set of six types for R45.

MARTINI BAR
COCKTAIL BAR

(www.cellars-hohenort.com; 93 Brommerslvei Rd, Constantia; ⊙11am-11.30pm; P) Ponder which from the 200-strong list of cocktails on the menu you'll try (we recommend the Liz McGrath Rose Martini, which is flavoured with rose petals from the hotel's famous gardens) while admiring the magnificent pink, lemon, burgundy and teal colours of the lounge decoration. Peacocks wander around in the grounds outside.

CAVEAU AT THE MILL
WINE BAR

Map p282 (☑021-685 5140; www.caveau.co.za; 13 Boundaries Rd; ⊙7am-midnight Mon-Sat; P; ⧆Newlands) Some 400 different wines, 70 by the glass, are served at this pleasant wine bar and restaurant in the historic Josephine Mill.

FORRESTER'S ARMS
PUB

Map p282 (52 Newlands Ave, Newlands; ⊙11am-11pm Mon-Sat, 10am-6pm Sun; P⧆) The English-style pub Forries has been around for well over a century. It offers up a convivial atmosphere, good pub meals including wood-fired pizza, and a very pleasant beer garden with a play area for the kids.

BARRISTERS
PUB, GRILL

Map p282 (☑021-674 1792; www.barristers grill.co.za; cnr Kildare Rd & Main St; ⊙9.30am-10.30pm; P⧆) A local's favourite watering hole with a series of cosy rooms hung with an eye-catching assortment of items in ye-olde-country-pub style. It's also an excellent spot for warming pub grub on a chilly night.

CAFFÉ VERDI
CAFE-BAR

(21 Wolfe St; ⊙9.30am-12.30am Mon-Thu, to 1.30am Fri, to midnight Sat; ⧆Wynberg) This handsome cafe-bar, set in a 110-year-old house with a pretty courtyard, is a pleasant place to retire for a drink after exploring Chelsea Village.

☆ ENTERTAINMENT

TOP CHOICE **BAXTER THEATRE**
THEATRE

Map p282 (☑021-685 7880; www.baxter.co.za; Main Rd, Rondebosch; P; ⧆Rosebank) Since the 1970s the Baxter has been the focus of

Capetonian theatre. There are three venues – the main theatre, the concert hall and the studio – and between them they cover everything from kids' shows to African dance spectaculars. They have an ongoing relationship with the Royal Shakespeare Company thanks to Capetonian Sir Anthony Sher, who has performed here.

ALMA CAFÉ
LIVE MUSIC

Map p282 (☑021 685 7377; www.facebook. com/pages/The-Alma-Cafe/159089414146612; 20 Alma Rd, Rosebank; ⊙8am-4pm Mon-Thu, 6-10pm Wed, 8am-5pm Fri, 8am-1pm Sat & Sun, 6-11pm Sun; ⧆Rosebank) This cosy venue, also serving food and drinks, usually has live music Wednesday (free) and Sunday (cover charge; bookings necessary).

MAYNARDVILLE OPEN-AIR THEATRE
THEATRE

(☑021-421 7695; www.artscape.co.za; cnr Church & Wolfe Sts; ⧆Wynberg) It wouldn't be summer in Cape Town without a visit to Maynardville's open-air theatre to see Shakespeare. Bring a blanket, pillow and umbrella, though, as the weather can be dodgy and the seats are none too comfy. At other times of the year, dance, jazz and theatre performances also take place here.

STARDUST
BAR

Map p282 (☑021-686 6280; www.stardust capetown.com; 165 Main Rd; ⊙4-11pm Mon-Sat; ⧆Rondebosch) This cheesy but hugely popular 'theatrical diner' gets packed with groups who come to enjoy their tagines (R80 to R100) and other dishes while listening to their waiters – all professional singers – who periodically hop up on stage to belt out tunes. There's a spacious bar here so you don't need to eat if you want to watch the show.

CAVENDISH NOUVEAU
CINEMA

Map p282 (www.sterkinekor.com; Cavendish Square, Dreyer St, Claremont; tickets R45; P; Claremont) Classy multiplex showcasing independent and art-house movies as well as digital screenings of international opera and theatre productions.

 # SHOPPING

TOP CHOICE MONTEBELLO
ARTS & CRAFTS

Map p282 (www.montebello.co.za; 31 Newlands Ave; 9am-5pm Mon-Fri, 9am-4pm Sat, 9am-3pm Sun; P) This development project has helped several great craftspeople and designers along the way. In the leafy compound, check out the colourful bags made from recycled materials; the fashions of **Mielie** (www.mielie.co.za); **Sitali Jewellers** (www.sitalijewellers.com), hand-making gold and platinum pieces in old stables; **David Krut Projects** (www.davidkrutprojectscape town.com), a gallery specialising in prints and works on paper; and more creative jewellery by **Beloved Beadwork** (http://be lovedbeadwork.co.za). There's also an organic deli, the excellent cafe Gardener's Cottage and car-washers!

TOP CHOICE ART IN THE FOREST
CERAMICS, ART

(021-794 0291; www.lightfromafrica.com; Cecilia Forest, Constantia Nek, Rhodes Dr, Constantia; 10am-4pm Mon-Sat; P) Profits from this gallery, hidden away in the Cecilia Forest, go towards supporting Fikelela, a childcare centre in Khayelitsha. But that's not the sole reason for visiting: there's the ceramic art on sale, many pieces created by top Capetonian potters and up-and-coming talents; the handsome 1950s building with its panoramic aspect towards Constantia; and a by-donation cafe. Workshops, lectures and art classes are held here, too.

PORTER ESTATE PRODUCE MARKET
MARKET

(www.pepmarket.co.za; Chrysalis Academy, Tokai Manor, Tokai Rd, Tokai; 9am-1pm Sat; P) If you can tear yourself away from the other Saturday markets, this outdoor farm-fresh produce and craft market held in the leafy surrounds of Tokai is well worth attending. Grab breakfast here and let the little ones run wild in the various activity areas.

CAVENDISH SQUARE
SHOPPING MALL

Map p282 (021-657 5620; www.cavendish. co.za; Cavendish Square, Dreyer St, Claremont; 9am-7pm Mon-Sat, 10am-5pm Sun; P; Claremont) This top-class shopping mall has outlets of many of Cape Town's premier fashion designers, as well as supermarkets, department stores and two multiplex cinemas. Call them for info about their free shuttle bus from the city.

KIRSTENBOSCH CRAFT MARKET
ARTS & CRAFTS

(021-671 5468; cnr Kirstenbosch & Rhodes Drs, Newlands; 9am-5pm last Sun of month) Lots to choose from at this large craft market spread across the commons outside Kirstenbosch. One good aspect is that it's possible to use a credit card to pay for most purchases here: payments are made in one of the stone cottages on the site. Proceeds from the market go to the development fund for Kirstenbosch.

HIP HOP
FASHION

Map p282 (www.hiphopfashion.co.za; 12 Cavendish St, Claremont; 9am-5.30pm Mon-Fri, 9am-4pm Sat, 10am-2pm Sun; Claremont) Hip Hop is one of Cape Town's fashion success stories. The women's clothes look good on all shapes and sizes and are suitable for a range of occasions. Drop by their **factory outlet** (Map p270; 35B Buitenkant St, The Fringe; 9am-5pm Mon-Fri, 9am-1pm Sat) for bargains.

HABITS
FASHION

Map p282 (www.habits.co.za; 1 Cavendish Close, Cavendish St, Claremont; 9am-5pm Mon-Fri, 9am-1.30pm Sat; Claremont) Women's clothes, made from linen, cotton and silk by Jenny le Roux, are classical and practical. Her Bad Habits label is for younger women. Bored partners can crash on the sofa, watch TV and sip complimentary drinks.

SPACE
FASHION

Map p282 (www.thespace.co.za; Cavendish Square, Dreyer St, Claremont; 9am-6pm Mon-Thu & Sat, 9am-9pm Fri, 10am-4pm Sun; P; Claremont) Celebrating individual style, this groovy boutique in the bowels of Cavendish Square stocks creative local fashion designs and accessories, as well as fun gift items.

YDE
FASHION

Map p282 (www.yde.co.za; Cavendish Square, Dreyer St, Claremont; P; RClaremont) Standing for Young Designers Emporium, this place is all a bit of a jumble, but you'll most likely find something reasonably inexpensive and disposable to suit among the clothes and accessories for both sexes by South African streetwear designers. There are branches at **Victoria Wharf** at the V&A Waterfront and **Canal Walk**.

COCO KAROO
INTERIOR DESIGN

(www.cocokaroo.co.za; 32 Durban Rd, Wynberg Village; RWynberg) Victorian oil portraits, antique copper baths and wood-carved fish from Malawi are among the eclectic products available at this great interior design store in the heart of Wynberg's Little Chelsea.

ACCESS PARK
OUTLET SHOPS

(www.accesspark.co.za; Chichester Rd, Kenilworth; ⊙9am-5pm Mon-Fr, 9am-3pm Sat, 10am-2pm Sun; P; RKenilworth) Bargain hunters converge on the 70-odd outlet and factory shops here selling everything from Adidas trainers to computers and luggage.

SPORTS & ACTIVITIES

SAHARA PARK NEWLANDS
CRICKET

Map p282 (☑021-657 3300, ticket hotline 021-657 2099; www.capecobras.co.za; 146 Campground Rd, Newlands; RNewlands) If it weren't for a nearby brewery messing up the view towards the back of Table Mountain, Newlands would be a shoo-in for the title of world's prettiest cricket ground. Under a sponsorship deal its official name is Sahara Park Newlands, but everyone still knows it as Newlands Cricket Ground. With room for 25,000, it's used for all international matches. The season runs from September to March, with the one-day matches drawing the biggest crowds. Grab a spot on the grass to soak up the festive atmosphere. Tickets cost around R50 for local matches – the Nashua Mobile Cape Cobras play here – and up to R200 for internationals.

NEWLANDS RUGBY STADIUM
RUGBY

Map p282 (☑021-659 4600; www.wprugby.com; 8 Boundary Rd, Newlands; RNewlands) This hallowed ground of South African rugby is home to the **Stormers** (www.iamastormer. com). Tickets for Super 12 games cost from R50, and for international matches around R350.

KENILWORTH RACE COURSE
HORSE RACING

(☑700 1600; Rosemead Ave, Kenilworth; RKenilworth) There's year-round racing here. The main event to put down in your diary is the glitzy **J&B Met**, South Africa's equivalent of Ladies Day at Ascot and often more of a fashion show than a horse race. In the centre of the course is the **Kenilworth Racecourse Conservation Area** (www.krca. co.za), 52 hectares of protected Cape Flats sands *fynbos* where nature walks and other events are sometimes organised; see the website for details.

SPORTS SCIENCE INSTITUTE OF SOUTH AFRICA
GYM, SWIMMING

Map p282 (www.ssisa.com; Boundary Rd, Newlands; per day R90; ⊙5.30am-9pm Mon-Fri, 6.30am-7pm Sat, 8am-12.30pm & 4-7pm Sun; RNewlands) Many of the country's top professional sports-people train here. Amenities include a 25m pool, an indoor running track and a crèche. Day visitors are welcome. It's sandwiched between the Newlands cricket and rugby stadiums.

Simon's Town & Southern Peninsula

MUIZENBERG | KALK BAY & AROUND | SIMON'S TOWN | SOUTHERN PENINSULA

Neighbourhood Top Five

❶ Drive, cycle or trek out to the rugged tip of the peninsula at the **Cape of Good Hope** (p131), a nature reserve where you can encounter local fauna and flora as well as serene beaches.

❷ Snap photos of the colony of African penguins waddling around **Boulders** (p137).

❸ Go shopping in **Kalk Bay** (p134) and enjoy a meal or drink overlooking its harbour.

❹ Check out the cultural events at Muizenberg's beautiful **Casa Labia** (p133) or learn to surf (p142).

❺ Explore caves and walk around the reservoir in the **Silvermine** (p133) section of Table Mountain National Park.

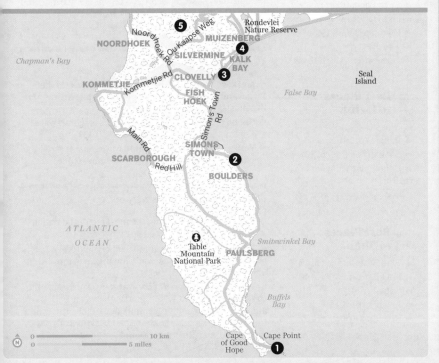

For more detail of this area, see Map p286 and p284 ➡

Lonely Planet's Top Tip

From late May to early December, False Bay is a favourite haunt of whales and their calves, with October and November the peak viewing season. Southern right, humpback and bryde (pronounced 'bree-dah') whales are the most commonly sighted. Good viewing spots include the coastal walk from Muizenberg to St James, the Brass Bell at Kalk Bay, and Jager's Walk at Fish Hoek. You can also take whale-watching cruises with Simon's Town Boat Company from Simon's Town's harbour.

Best Places to Eat

➡ Foodbarn (p138)
➡ Casa Labia (p137)
➡ Live Bait (p138)
➡ Olympia Café & Deli (p138)

For reviews, see p137 ➡

Best Places to Drink

➡ Brass Bell (p139)
➡ Polana (p139)
➡ Skebanga's Bar (p139)
➡ Cape Point Vineyards (p139)

For reviews, see p139 ➡

Best Places to Shop

➡ Blue Bird Garage (p140)
➡ Kalk Bay Modern (p140)
➡ Sobeit (p140)
➡ Artvark (p140)
➡ Red Rock Tribal (p140)

For reviews, see p140 ➡

Explore Simon's Town & Southern Peninsula

The Cape's deep south is practically a world unto itself, far divorced from the big-city bustle of the northern end of town. You'll be amply rewarded for taking a few days to explore the area's sights, the principal of which is the magnificent Cape of Good Hope (Cape Point).

Other places to check out include the regenerating seaside suburb of Muizenberg, home to the gorgeous Casa Labia; Kalk Bay packed with antique and craft shops, good cafes and a lively daily fish market; the naval base of Simon's Town, where the frigates are now joined by pleasure boats that depart for thrilling cruises to Cape Point; and Boulders, home to the famous colony of African penguins.

On the Atlantic Coast side of the peninsula, life is even quieter at Noordhoek, famous for its wide, sandy beach, and the surfing mecca of Kommetjie (pronounced 'kom-ickey', but also known as just 'Kom'), a quiet and isolated crayfishing village, marked by the cast-iron Slangkop Lighthouse. Scarborough is the last coastal community before you round the peninsula to the entry to Cape Point.

The beaches on the False Bay (eastern) side of the coast are not quite as spectacular as those on the Atlantic side, but the water is often 5°C or more warmer, and can reach 20°C in summer. This makes swimming far more pleasant.

Local Life

➡ **Markets** Much of Muizenberg decamps to the Blue Bird Garage on Friday night (p140) for eats, drinks and live music.
➡ **Surfing** Suit up and join the surfies catching waves at Kommetjie (p137) and Muizenberg (p133).
➡ **Walks** Watch out for crashing waves as you stroll the coastal trail from Muizenberg to St James (p135).

Getting There & Away

➡ **Car** Essential for getting the most out of the region.
➡ **Taxi** Try **Noordhoek Taxis** (☎021-234 7021).
➡ **Train** There are stops at Muizenberg and Kalk Bay before the terminus at Simon's Town. Cape Metro Rail offers a good-value day ticket.
➡ **Water Taxi Mellow Yellow Water Taxi** (www.watertaxi. co.za; single/return R100/150) shuttles between Kalk Bay and Simon's Town. It's recommended to take the train to Simon's Town and the water taxi back to Kalk Bay rather than the other way around.

TOP SIGHTS
CAPE OF GOOD HOPE

Commonly called Cape Point, this 77.5 sq km section of Table Mountain National Park includes awesome scenery, fantastic walks and often deserted beaches. Some 250 species of birds live here, including cormorants and a family of ostriches that hang out near the Cape of Good Hope, the southwesternmost point of the continent. Although the reserve also has bonteboks, elands and zebras, it's rare to spot them – the most common large animals you'll see are baboons and dassies. The reserve is particularly beautiful in spring, when the wild flowers are in bloom.

Flying Dutchman Funicular

It's not a hard walk uphill, but if you're feeling lazy the **Flying Dutchman Funicular** (www.capepoint.co.za; one way/return adult R37/47, child R15/20; ⊙10am-5.30pm) runs up from beside the restaurant to the souvenir kiosk next to the old lighthouse. Dating from 1860, this lighthouse was built too high up (238m above sea level) so was often obscured by mist and fog. The new lighthouse built at Dias Point in 1919 is 87m above the water.

Beaches

There are some excellent beaches, which you may even have to yourself (this can make them dangerous if you get into difficulties in the water, so take care). The best beaches for swimming or walking are **Platboom Beach**, and the pretty one at **Buffels Bay** is also safe for swimming. **Maclear Beach**, near the main car park, is good for walks or diving but is too rocky for enjoyable swimming. Further down towards Cape Point is the beautiful **Diaz Beach**. Access is on foot from the car park.

DON'T MISS

➡ Cape of Good Hope
➡ Cape Point Lighthouses
➡ Cape of Good Hope & Hoerikwaggo Trails
➡ Buffels Beach
➡ Platboom Beach

PRACTICALITIES

➡ ☑021-780 9204
➡ www.sanparks.org/parks/table_mountain
➡ adult/child R85/30
➡ ⊙6am-6pm Oct-Mar, 7am-5pm Apr-Sep

TOURS

Numerous tour companies include Cape Point on their itineraries. Most whip into the reserve, pause at the Buffelsfontein Visitor Centre, then allow you just enough time to walk to Cape Point, grab lunch and get your picture snapped at the Cape of Good Hope on the way back.

Portuguese navigator Bartholomeu Dias coined the name Cabo da Boa Esperança (Cape of Good Hope); a cross carved into the rock near here could indicate the spot where Dias stepped onto the Cape in 1488.

EATING & SLEEPING

If you've not packed a picnic, snacks can be bought at the Buffelsfontein Visitor Centre and a shop next to the funicular, where you'll also find the Two Oceans Restaurant, set up to deal with tour-bus crowds. Its terrace does have terrific views. Camping is not allowed, but there are three self-catering cottages – Olifantsbos, Eland and Duiker – that can be rented, as can the Smitswinkel Tented Camp just outside Cape Point's main entrance gate (see p30 for more details).

Beware the Baboons

The signs warning you not to feed the baboons are there for a reason. After years of interacting with tourists, the baboons will grab food from your hands or climb in the open windows of your car to get at it. *Never* challenge them as they will turn aggressive. The damage inflicted might end up being far more serious than baboon crap over your car seats.

Hiking & Cycling

The best way to explore the reserve is on foot or by bike – several tour companies include biking in their itineraries, including Awol, Daytrippers and Downhill Adventures. A basic map is provided with your ticket at the entrance gate. Serious hikers are advised to pick up the more detailed Slingsby Maps. Bear in mind that the weather can change quickly; for basic hiking safety guidelines see p28.

Cape of Good Hope Trail

Bookings are required for the two-day, one-night **Cape of Good Hope Trail** (R200, not including the reserve entry fee), which traces a spectacular 33.8km circular route through the reserve. Highlights along the way include spotting many species of proteas and other *fynbos* (literally 'fine bush', primarily proteas, heaths and ericas) and enjoying sweeping vistas on the section between Paulsberg and Judas Peak on the False Bay side of the trail.

Accommodation is at the basic erica, protea and restio huts on the north side of De Gama Peak. The huts' elevated position allows you to see both sunset and sunrise. The dormitory sleeps six in bunk beds and you need to bring your own sleeping bag. Cutlery and crockery are provided and there's a hot shower. Contact the **Buffelsfontein Visitor Centre** (✆021-780 9204) in the park.

Other Trails

Other hikes in the reserve include the first (or last) day of the **Hoerikwaggo Trail**. This 15km section of the trail begins at the Cape Point Lighthouse and runs down the False Bay coast to Smitswinkel Bay; there are some steep sections but from late August to October you may be rewarded with sightings of whales in the bay.

A trail runs from the Cape of Good Hope up to the Cape Point Lighthouse via Diaz Beach. There's also the straightforward 3.5km walk from Buffels Bay to the spectacular Paulsberg peak.

The easiest walk is the 1km trail linking the old and new lighthouses. It takes less than 30 minutes to walk along a spectacular ridgeway path to look down on the new lighthouse and the sheer ocean cliffs.

TOP SIGHTS
CAPE OF GOOD HOPE

SIGHTS

Muizenberg was established by the Dutch as a staging post for horse-drawn traffic in 1743. Its heyday was the early 20th century when it was a seaside resort favoured by the wealthy. Kalk Bay is named after the lime (*kalk* in Afrikaans) used for painting buildings in the 17th century, which was produced by burning seashells in kilns. During apartheid it was neglected by government and business as it was mainly a coloured area. Simon's Town is named after Governor Simon van der Stel. The winter anchorage for the Dutch East India Company (Vereenigde Oost-Indische Compagnie; VOC) from 1741, and a naval base for the British since 1814, it remains a naval town.

Muizenberg, Kalk Bay & Around

FREE CASA LABIA
CULTURAL CENTRE   CULTURAL CENTRE
Map p284 (☑021-788 6068; www.casalabia.
co.za; 192 Main Rd, Muizenberg; ☉10am-4pm

Tue-Sun; ⊠Muizenberg) This magnificent seaside villa dating from 1930 was the palatial home of Count Natale Labia and his South African wife. Labia was the Italian ambassador to South Africa at the time, so this grand building – designed by Capetonian architect Fred Glennie and furnished by a Venetian interior designer with antique fixtures and fittings – doubled as the embassy residency and legation.

After a varied history, the rights to oversee the building were handed back to the Labias' son in 2008. It has since undergone a loving restoration to emerge as a beautiful building that hosts a program of concerts, lectures and events, as well as housing works from the family's art collection (including paintings by Irma Stern and Gerald Sekoto) and regularly changing contemporary art exhibitions. There's a branch of the Africa Nova arts and crafts shop here as well as an excellent cafe.

MUIZENBERG BEACH   BEACH
Map p284 (Beach Rd, Muizenberg; ⊠Kalk Bay) Popular with families, this surf beach is famous for its row of primary-colour-painted Victorian bathing chalets. Surfboards can

TOP SIGHTS
SILVERMINE

Off the main tourist trail, but still a spectacular section of Table Mountain National Park, Silvermine can be accessed from the cross-peninsular road Ou Kaapse Weg as well as hiking trails from Boyes Dr. It's named after the fruitless attempts by the Dutch to prospect for silver in this area from 1675 to 1685. The park is popular with locals who come here to hike, mountain bike, rock climb and go caving. The focal point is the **Silvermine Reservoir**, constructed in 1898. It's a beautiful spot for a picnic or a leisurely 20-minute walk on a wheelchair-accessible boardwalk. It's also possible to swim in the tannin-stained waters of the reservoir. The **Silvermine River Walk** (45 minutes one way) from the main car park is well worth doing.

On the southeastern edge of the reserve is **Peers Cave**: a trail leads here from a marked parking spot on the Ou Kaapse Weg. The cave is named after Victor Peers, who with his son Bertie, started excavating the site in 1927, collecting evidence of the habitation of the Khoe-San dating as far back as 10,000 years, including a skull: it's thought this was an ancient burial site. Declared a National Monument in 1941, the cave provides a dramatic viewpoint towards Noordhoek and the sea.

DON'T MISS

➡ Silvermine Reservoir
➡ Silvermine River Walk
➡ Peer's Cave

PRACTICALITIES

➡ Map p284
➡ www.sanparks.org/parks/table_mountain
➡ Main entrance & car park Ou Kaapse Weg
➡ adult/child R25/10
➡ ☉7am-6pm Oct-Mar, 8am-5pm Apr-Sep

SUNPATHS OF THE CAPE

In his research into the Khoe-San and even older people who lived on the Cape, Dean Liprini, an archaeoastronomer, has developed an astonishing theory. He believes that the Cape is crisscrossed by a grid of sight lines and key points comprising caves, sound chambers, geometrical marker stones, and sun and moon shrines, some in the uncanny shape of giant human faces. Sunrise and sunset are exactly aligned with these points at the summer and winter solstices and the spring and autumn equinoxes, thus indicating that they formed a way for the ancient people to measure the passing of the year and record auspicious dates.

As whacky as it may sound, there may be something in Liprini's theory, as you'll discover if you go for a hike in the hills of the Southern Peninsula with him or one of his colleagues. Observed from certain angles, unmistakable profiles of faces appear in the rocks, some with 'eye' holes that catch the light – one such rock is a granite boulder on Lion's Head, while another is the Pyramid All Seeing Eye, just off the M6 between Glencairn and Sunnydale. There's also what Liprini calls the Cave of Ascension, above the ancient burial site of **Peers Cave**. To find out more about the sunpaths and see when walks are scheduled, check the website www.sunpath.co.za.

be hired and lessons booked at either Roxy Surf Club or Gary's Surf School, and lockers are available in the pavilions on the promenade. The beach shelves gently and the sea is generally safer than elsewhere along the peninsula. At the eastern end of the promenade is a fun **water slide** (1hr/day pass R35/65; ☉9.30am-5.30pm Sat & Sun, daily in school holidays).

RONDEVLEI NATURE RESERVE
NATURE RESERVE

(☎021-706 2404; www.rondevlei.co.za; Fisherman's Walk Rd; adult/child R10/5; ☉7.30am-5pm daily year-round, 7.30am-7pm Sat & Sun Dec-Feb; ℗) Hippos hadn't lived in the marshes here for 300 years until they were reintroduced in 1981 to this small, picturesque nature reserve northeast of Muizenberg. There are eight hippos, but they're shy creatures and it's unlikely that you'll spot them unless you stay overnight (R800 per person). For further details contact **Imvubu Nature Tours** (☎082-847 4916, 021-706 0842; www.imvubu. co.za), which is based at the reserve and also runs one-hour-long **guided walks** (R300 per person, minimum 4 people) during which you can spot some 237 species of birds from the waterside trail, viewing towers and hides.

KALK BAY HARBOUR
HARBOUR

Map p284 (Main Rd, Kalk Bay; ℝKalk Bay) Visit this picturesque harbour in the late morning when the community's few remaining fishing boats pitch up with their daily catch and a lively quayside market ensues. This is an excellent place to buy fresh fish for a braai (barbecue) or to spot whales during the whale-watching season. Nearby, next to Kalk Bay station and the Brass Bell pub, are a couple of tidal swimming pools.

RHODES COTTAGE MUSEUM
MUSEUM

Map p284 (246 Main Rd; admission by donation; ☉10am-1pm Wed, Fri & Sat, 10am-4pm Tue; ℝMuizenberg) Staffed by dedicated volunteer guides from the Muizenberg Historical Conservation Society, this thatched-roof cottage, designed by Sir Herbert Baker (p219), is now an engaging museum where you can find out all about Cecil Rhodes, who died in the front bedroom in 1902. The cottage has pleasant mountainside gardens, which are a lovely place to rest and spot whales during the season.

FREE SAVE OUR SEAS SHARK CENTRE
EDUCATION CENTRE

Map p284 (www.saveourseas.com; 28 Main Rd; ☉10am-4pm Mon-Fri, 10am-3pm Sat; ℝKalk Bay) This laudable education centre aims to encourage awareness, protection, conservation and the sustainable fishing of sharks worldwide. There's a mini-aquarium and other good displays on the global organisation's work. You can also find out about the pioneering **Shark Spotters** (www.sharkspotters.org.za) program, which monitors key beaches and raises the alarm if sharks are spotted swimming near them.

FISH HOEK & CLOVELLY
WALKS

(Main Rd/M4; ℝFish Hoek) South around False Bay from Kalk Bay, the communities of Fish

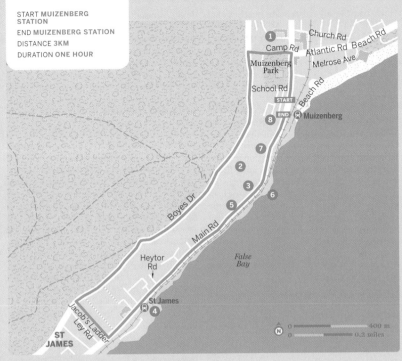

SIMON'S TOWN & SOUTHERN PENINSULA NEIGHBOURHOOD WALK

Neighbourhood Walk

Muizenberg–St James Walk

This invigorating coastal walk provides spectacular views of False Bay and gives you a sense of the history and once-grand nature of this seaside suburb.

From Muizenberg Station, head north past Muizenberg Park to Camp Rd, passing the red-and-white painted ❶ **synagogue**; Muizenberg had a large Jewish population in the 1920s and '30s. Concrete steps lead up to Boyes Dr from where you'll have a commanding view across Muizenberg and its broad, flat beach.

A wrought-iron gate on your left-hand side has steps leading down to the ❷ **grave of Sir Abe Bailey** (1864–1940), 'soldier, former sportsman, philanthropist, mining pioneer'. You should also be able to glimpse Bailey's house, ❸ **Rust-en-Vrede**, with its red tiles and high gables, on Main Rd below. Rust-en-Vrede was commissioned by Cecil Rhodes, but he never lived in it.

Keep walking along Boyes Dr until you reach the Jacob's Ladder steps leading down towards ❹ **St James Station**. Next to the station are a set of the primary-colour-painted Victorian-style bathing huts that this area is best known for, and a tidal rock pool – ideal for a cooling dip. A coastal walking path starts here and heads back towards Muizenberg.

As you approach a grand Spanish-style mansion with green-glazed roof tiles (called Gracelands after Elvis' pad), you'll see another underpass that will allow you to nip across to busy Main Rd and visit ❺ **Rhodes Cottage**, where Rhodes passed away in 1902.

Back on the coastal path, on the right-hand side, is the thatched ❻ **Bailey's Cottage**, once Sir Abe Bailey's guest cottage. Closer to Muizenberg, on Main Rd, you'll also pass ❼ **Casa Labia**, which belongs to the family of an Italian count who built the property in 1930.

Further along is the whitewashed ❽ **Posthuys**. Dating from the 1670s, this one-time lookout post for ships entering False Bay is one of Cape Town's oldest European-style buildings. It's a minute's walk from here to Muizenberg Station.

Hoek and Clovelly have wide beaches that are safe for swimming. At the southern end of Fish Hoek Beach, **Jager's Walk** is a paved walk that provides a pleasant stroll of around 1km south to Sunny Cove (which is on the train line). If you're feeling energetic, a coastal path continues 5km from here to Simon's Town.

Nature lovers may want to follow the **Silvermine River Wetland Route**. This self-guided trail, which is wheelchair- and blind-friendly, starts at the Clovelly car park near the electricity substation and follows the flood plain of the Silvermine River. Along the way, if you're lucky, you may spot a wide range of wildlife, from kingfishers, clawless otters and porcupines to the endangered leopard toad. There's a bird-watching platform – 63 species have been spotted in the area.

Simon's Town & Rest of Southern Peninsula

CAPE OF GOOD HOPE · NATIONAL PARK
See p131.

NOORDHOEK BEACH · BEACH
This magnificent 5km stretch of beach is favoured by surfers and horse riders. It tends to be windy, and dangerous for swimmers. The Hoek, as it is known to surfers, is an excellent right beach break at the northern end that can hold large waves (only at low tide); it's best with a southeasterly wind. In the middle of the beach the rusted shell of the steamship *Kakapo* sticks out of the sand like a weird sculpture. It ran aground here on its maiden voyage in 1900 from Britain to Australia.

SIMON'S TOWN BOAT COMPANY · CRUISE
Map p286 (☑021 786 2136; www.boatcompany. co.za; Town Pier, Simon's Town; harbour cruise adult/child R40/20; ⓡSimon's Town) This company runs the popular *Spirit of Just Nuisance* cruise around the harbour, as well as longer boat trips to Cape Point (adult/child R350/200) and Seal Island (adult/child R250/150). During the whale-watching season they also offer cruises that allow you to get up close to these magnificent animals.

SIMON'S TOWN MUSEUM · MUSEUM
Map p286 (www.simonstown.com/museum/ stm_main.htm; Court Rd; adult/child R5/2; ⓣ10am-4pm Mon-Fri, 10am-1pm Sat; ⓡSimon's

Town) Housed in the old governor's residence (1777), the exhibits in this rambling museum trace Simon's Town's history. Included is a display on Just Nuisance, the Great Dane that was adopted as a navy mascot in WWII, and whose grave, off Red Hill Rd above the town, makes for a long walk from the harbour. There's also a **statue of Just Nuisance** in Jubilee Sq, by the harbour.

HERITAGE MUSEUM · MUSEUM
Map p286 (www.simonstown.com/museum/ sthm.htm; Almay House, King George Way; admission R5; ⓣ11am-4pm Tue-Thu & Sun; ⓡSimon's Town) Simon's Town's community of Cape Muslims was 7000 strong before apartheid forcibly removed most of them, mainly to the suburb of Ocean's View across on the Atlantic side of the peninsula. This interesting small museum, with a lovely front garden, is dedicated to the evictees and based in Almay House (dating from 1858). It's curated by Zainab Davidson, whose family was kicked out in 1975. Nearby, Alfred Lane leads to the handsome **mosque**, built in 1926.

IMHOFF FARM · FARM
(www.imhofffarm.co.za; Kommetjie Rd; admission free; ⓣ10am-5pm Tue-Sun; ⓟ) There's plenty to see and do at this historic and very attractive farmstead just outside Kommetjie. Among the attractions are craft shops and studios, the good Blue Water Café, a **snake and reptile park** (adult/child R35/30), a farmyard stocked with animals, **camel rides** (bookings on ☑021-789 1711; adult/child R50/30;

LOCAL KNOWLEDGE

TO SIMON'S TOWN BY STEAM TRAIN

Atlantic Rail (☑021 556 1012; www. atlanticrail.co.za; ⓣoffice 8am-12.30pm Mon-Fri; ⓓ), Cape Town's only private vintage steam train operator runs day trips, usually on Sundays, from the city to Simon's Town (adult/ child R220/110). The wooden-bodied coaches dating from the 1920s and '30s are pulled by a Class 24 steam loco built in 1949. One of the coaches is a lounge bar. With prior arrangement, drop-offs and pick-ups in Kalk Bay are also possible.

TOP SIGHTS
BOULDERS

Some 3km southeast of Simon's Town, Boulders, a picturesque area with a number of enormous boulders dividing small, sandy coves, is home to a colony of 2800 delightful African penguins. A boardwalk runs from the Boulders Visitor Centre at the Foxy Beach end of the protected area (another part of Table Mountain National Park) to Boulders Beach, where you can get down on the sand and mingle with the waddling penguins. Don't be tempted to pet them: the penguins have sharp beaks that can cause serious injuries.

The bulk of the colony, which has grown from just two breeding pairs in 1982, seems to prefer hanging out at Foxy Beach where, like nonchalant stunted supermodels, they blithely ignore the armies of camera-touting tourists snapping away from the viewing platform. The aquatic birds, which are an endangered species, were formerly called jackass penguins on account of their donkey-like braying – you'll have a chance to hear it if you turn up during the main breeding season, which peaks from March to May. Parking is available at either end of the reservation on Seaforth Rd and Bellevue Rd, where you'll also find accommodation and places to eat.

DON'T MISS

➡ Penguins
➡ Boulders Beach

PRACTICALITIES

➡ Map p286
➡ ☏021 701 8692
➡ www.sanparks.org/parks/table_mountain
➡ adult/child R45/20
➡ ⊙7am-7.30pm Dec-Jan, 8am-6.30pm Feb-May & Sep-Nov, 8am-5pm Jun-Aug

---

⊙noon-4pm Tue-Sun) and a farmyard shop selling tasty cheeses and other provisions.

KOMMETJIE BEACHES BEACH
(Kommetjie Rd/M65; **P**) A focal point for surfing on the Cape, Kommetjie offers an assortment of reefs that hold a very big swell. Outer Kommetjie is a left point out from **Slangkop Lighthouse**, at the southern end of the village. Inner Kommetjie is a more protected, smaller left with lots of kelp (only at high tide). They both work best with a southeasterly or southwesterly wind. For breezy beach walks, it doesn't get much better than the aptly named **Long Beach**, accessed off Benning Dr.

CAPE POINT OSTRICH FARM FARM
(www.capepointostrichfarm.com; guided tour adult/child R45/20; ⊙9.30am-5.30pm; **P**🐾) There's ostriches aplenty at this family-run farm, restaurant and tourist complex just 600m from Cape Point's main gate. Tours of the breeding facilities are conducted at regular intervals. The well-stocked shop is notable if for nothing else than the myriad artistic ways that ostrich eggs can be turned into decorative objects.

FREE **SOUTH AFRICAN NAVAL MUSEUM** MUSEUM
Map p286 (St George's St; ⊙9.30am-3.30pm; ☒Simon's Town) Definitely one for naval enthusiasts, this museum nonetheless has plenty of interesting exhibits. The highlight is arranging a tour out to the **SAS Assegaai** (☏021-786 5243; www.navy.mil.za/museum_submarine/Default.htm; adult/child R40/20; ⊙10.30am-3pm Dec-Jun, 11.30am-2.30pm Jul-Nov), which served the navy from 1971 to 2003. Groups of up to 12 are guided through the floating vessel and given an explanation of what life onboard was like. The plan is to bring the sub ashore at the museum in 2013.

 EATING

Muizenberg & Kalk Bay

TOP CHOICE **CASA LABIA** INTERNATIONAL $
Map p284 (☏021-788 6068; www.casalabia.co.za; 192 Main Rd, Muizenberg; mains R45-70;

AVOIDING TRAFFIC & CROWDS

Main Rd is the coastal thoroughfare linking Muizenberg with Fish Hoek, although a prettier (and often less congested) alternative route between Muizenberg and Kalk Bay is mountainside Boyes Dr, which provides fantastic views down the peninsula.

If you can only spare a day for the southern peninsula, a strategy for beating the crowds is to head down the Atlantic Coast via Chapman's Peak Dr, then follow Main Rd/M65 to the entrance to Cape Point. Start early and you'll arrive at the tip of the Cape well before the bulk of the coach buses, which tend to stop off at Boulders first: you can see this on the way back.

⊙10am-4pm Tue-Thu, 9am-4pm Fri-Sun; 🚂Muizenberg) Some of the ingredients at this exceedingly pleasant cafe in the gorgeous cultural centre come from the adjoining garden. They plan to make wine and olive oil from the vines and olive trees that grow on the slopes, too. Enjoy home-baked treats and delicious breakfasts and open sandwiches.

TOP CHOICE LIVE BAIT SEAFOOD $$

Map p284 (☑021-788 5755; www.harbourhouse. co.za; Kalk Bay harbour; mains R70-120; ⊙noon-4pm & 6-10pm; 🚂Kalk Bay) Sit within arm's reach of the crashing waves and the bustle of Kalk Bay harbour at this breezy, Greek island–style fish restaurant – it's one of the best options for a relaxed seafood meal. The same company runs the fancy Harbour House restaurant upstairs, the cheap-as-chips Lucky Fish take-away and the bar Polana.

OLYMPIA CAFÉ & DELI BAKERY, INTERNATIONAL $$

Map p284 (☑021-788 6396; 134 Main Rd; mains R60-100; ⊙7am-9pm; 🚂Kalk Bay) Still setting the standard for relaxed rustic cafes by the sea, Olympia bakes its own breads and pastries on the premises. It's great for breakfast, and its Mediterranean-influenced lunch dishes are delicious, too.

ANNEX INTERNATIONAL $$

Map p284 (☑021-788 2453; www.theannex.co.za; 124 Main Rd, Kalk Bay; mains R60-100; ⊙7am-3pm daily, 6-9.30pm Mon-Sat; 🚂; 🚂Kalk Bay) Behind Kalk Bay Books, Annex is yet another great option for all-day-dining, offering a tempting menu running from French toast, croissants, bacon and maple syrup to quiches, salads and more substantial mains.

EMPIRE CAFÉ INTERNATIONAL $

Map p284 (☑021-788 1250; www.empirecafe. co.za; 11 York Rd; mains R40-50; ⊙7am-4pm Mon-Sat, 8am-4pm Sun; 🚂; 🚂Muizenberg) The local surfers' favourite hang-out is a great place for a hearty eggs on toast–type breakfast or lunch. Local art exhibitions enliven the walls and there's a dramatic chandelier dangles from the ceiling.

KNEAD BAKERY, INTERNATIONAL $

Map p284 (http://kneadbakery.co.za; Surfer's Corner, Beach Rd, Muizenberg; mains R30-70; ⊙10am-5pm Mon, 7am-5pm Tue-Sun; 🚂Muizenberg) Breads, brioches, bagels, buns, pastries, pies and pizzas – anything involving dough, these guys have it covered. The chandelier and mirror tiles add glamour to this hit seaside venue, but their product can also be relied on at their branches at the Lifestyle Centre and Wembley Square, both in Gardens.

CLOSER VEGAN $

Map p284 (42 Palmer Rd, Muizenberg; mains R45; ⊙9am-4pm Mon-Fri, 10am-4pm Sat & Sun; 🚂; 🚂Muizenberg) One of the very few places you can eat vegan in Cape Town. Fortunately, the food – mainly creative veggie burgers such as sun-dried tomato and basil or curried butternut and beetroot – is pretty tasty, nicely presented and pleasantly served.

Simon's Town & Rest of Southern Peninsula

TOP CHOICE FOODBARN INTERNATIONAL $$$

(☑021 789 1390; www.thefoodbarn.co.za; Noordhoek Farm Village, cnr Noordhoek Main Rd & Village Ln; 3/7-course menu R220/380, cafe mains R50; ⊙restaurant noon-2.30pm daily, 7-9.30pm Wed-Sat, deli 8am-9pm Tue-Sat, to 5pm Sun-Mon, cafe 8am-4.30pm daily, tapas bar 6-9.30pm Tue-Sat; 🅿🚂) Masterchef Franck Dangereux might have opted for the less stressful life in Noordhoek, but that doesn't mean this operation skimps on quality. Expect rustic, delicious bistro dishes. The separate book-lined deli-bakery-cafe and tapas bar is just as good and stocks their freshly baked goodies, chocolates and other locally sourced food and drinks.

MEETING PLACE
INTERNATIONAL $$

Map p286 (☎021 786 1986; www.themeetingplaceupstairs.co.za; 98 St George's St; mains R65-120; ⊙9am-9pm Mon-Sat, to 3pm Sun; ⓡSimon's Town) A foodie's delight, there's a casual deli-cafe on the ground floor and an arty restaurant upstairs with a balcony overlooking Simon Town's main drag. Sample gourmet sandwiches or their homemade ice creams.

BLUE WATER CAFÉ
INTERNATIONAL $

(☎021 783 2007; www.bluewatercafe.co.za; Imhoff Farm, Kommetjie Rd, Ocean View; mains R50-90; ⊙9am-5pm Tue, to 9pm Wed-Sun) There's a stunning view of Chapman's Peak from the stoop of this historic property at the heart of Imhoff Farm. It's a lovely place to enjoy an all-day breakfast (R68.50) or other simple but good dishes, including pasta and pizza.

CAPE FARMHOUSE RESTAURANT
INTERNATIONAL $

(☎021 780 1246; www.capefarmhouse.co.za; M66 & M65 Junction, Red Hill; mains R50-90; ⊙9am-5pm) This 250-year-old farmhouse has a scenic setting beside interesting craft stalls and a kids' playground, and serves everything from breakfast to fillet steak. In summer it hosts music concerts (R60) on Saturdays from 3.30pm; see the website for details.

SOPHEA GALLERY & TIBETAN TEAHOUSE
VEGETARIAN $

Map p286 (www.sopheagallery.com; 2 Harrington Rd, Seaforth; mains R50-70; ⊙10am-5pm Tue-Sun; ⓩ) Tasty vegetarian and vegan teahouse food, based on recipes from Tibet, are served in part of this colourful gallery stocking artefacts and jewellery from the East. From its raised perch there's a nice view out to sea.

SWEETEST THING
BAKERY, INTERNATIONAL $

Map p286 (☎021 786 4200; 82 St George's St, Simon's Town; mains R20-30; ⊙8am-5pm Mon-Fri, 9am-5pm Sat & Sun; ⓡSimon's Town) Quiches, cakes and biscuits are all freshly made at this adorable patisserie, which also serves gourmet sandwiches. It's an ideal place for afternoon tea with scones.

CAFÉ PESCADOS
PIZZA $

Map p286 (☎786 2272; www.pescados.co.za; 118 St George's St; mains R40-60; ⊙9.30am-10pm; ⓡSimon's Town) Occupying Simon's Town's one-time Criterion Cinema, this pub-like place serves up a mean pizza and a good range of seafood at reasonable prices. Live music on weekends adds to the atmosphere.

🍷 DRINKING & NIGHTLIFE

⬛TOP CHOICE BRASS BELL
RESTAURANT-BAR

Map p284 (www.brassbell.co.za; Kalk Bay Train Station, Main Rd, Kalk Bay; ⊙11am-10pm; ⓡKalk Bay) Take the tunnel beneath the train tracks to reach this Kalk Bay institution overlooking the fishing harbour. On a sunny day there are few places better to drink and eat (mains R50 to R80) by the sea. Before or after you could take a dip in the adjacent tidal pools.

⬛TOP CHOICE POLANA
RESTAURANT-BAR

Map p284 (☎021-788 7162; www.harbourhouse.co.za; Kalk Bay harbour; ⓡKalk Bay) Providing an excellent reason to hang out in Kalk Bay rather than rush back to the city is this chic bar, right over the rocks at the edge of the harbour. It serves Portuguese-style seafood – sardines, mussels and delicious peri peri prawns. There's often live music, mainly jazz, Friday to Sunday.

SKEBANGA'S BAR
BAR

(cnr Beach & Pine Rds, Noordhoek; ⊙11am-11.30pm) If you're down this way, say after a drive along Chapman's Peak Dr, the bar above the Red Herring restaurant is a pleasant place for a drink or a bite to eat (kitchen closes at 10pm). There's a good view of the beach from the terrace.

CAPE POINT VINEYARDS
WINERY

(☎021-789 0094; www.capepointvineyards.co.za; 1 Chapmans Peak Drive, Noordhoek; tastings from R15; ⊙9am-5pm Mon-Fri, 10am-5pm Sat, to 4pm Sun) Known for its sauvignon blanc, this small vineyard regularly wins awards. The setting overlooking Noordhoek Beach is lovely and the tastings, conducted in a room hung with an 18th century European tapestry are elegantly done. Enjoy the wines with a picnic (noon to 3pm, R260 for two, bookings essential) or from 5pm to 8pm with a cheese platter (R150).

TOAD IN THE VILLAGE
PUB

(thetoad.co.za; Noordhoek Farm Village, cnr Noordhoek Main Rd & Village Ln, Noordhoek) This thatched-roof pub with indoor and outdoor seating is the convivial heart of the Noordhoek Farm Village. They serve pretty good pizza, too.

☆ ENTERTAINMENT

MELTING POT
LIVE MUSIC

Map p284 (☎021-709 0785; www.facebook.com/themeltingpotsocialclub; 15 Church St, Muizenberg; cover charge varies; ⊘concert usually from 8pm; ☒Muizenberg) There's plenty of variety in the performances at this cosy 'social club', but they major in live music gigs. You can catch some up-and-coming Capetonian acts here.

KALK BAY THEATRE
THEATRE

Map p284 (☎073 220 5430; http://kbt.co.za; 52 Main Rd, Kalk Bay; ☒Kalk Bay) One of the city's several intimate dinner and show venues, this theatre is housed in a converted church. You don't need to eat there beforehand to see the productions which are often reasonably short. The improvisational troupe Theatresports plays here Tuesday at 8.30pm.

MASQUE THEATRE
THEATRE

Map p284 (☎021-788 6999; www.masquetheatre.co.za; 37 Main Rd, Muizenberg; ☒Muizenberg) The program at this small theatre (seating 174) changes on a pretty regular basis, veering from one-man comedy shows to musical reviews and more serious plays.

🛍 SHOPPING

Muizenberg's Palmer Rd has a handful of interesting small boutiques and cafes. Kalk Bay's Main Rd is a shopper's delight, stacked with fashion, gift and antique retailers; on Sunday there's a small market opposite Kalk Bay Theatre. Simon's Town's St George's St has several antique shops, many stocked with naval memorabilia.

TOP CHOICE KALK BAY MODERN
ARTS & CRAFTS

Map p284 (www.kalkbaymodern.com; 136 Main Rd, Kalk Bay; ⊘9.30am-5pm; ☒Kalk Bay) This wonderful gallery is stocked with an eclectic and appealing range of arts and crafts. There are often exhibitions by local artists showing here. Check out the collection of Ekoka print cloths, a fair-trade product made by the !Kung Bushmen in Namibia.

TOP CHOICE SOBEIT
ARTS & CRAFTS

Map p284 (www.sobeitstudio.com; 51 Main Rd, Muizenberg; ⊘8am-5pm Mon-Sat; ☒Valsbaai) Occupying the top floor of a turquoise-and-pink painted art deco building, this mayhem space is a modern curiosity shop of crazy creatives including wax artists, graphic and furniture designers and jewellery makers. Pick up a distinctive souvenir, such as their skull candles. Downstairs, **David Bellamy** (⊘9am-5pm Thu-Sat) is a cornucopia of beautiful imported fabrics and items made from them.

BLUE BIRD GARAGE FOOD & GOODS MARKET
MARKET

Map p284 (39 Albertyn Rd, Muizenberg; ⊘4-10pm Fri, 10am-3pm Sat; ☒False Bay) This hit artisan food and goods market is based in a 1940s hangar, once the base for the first southern hemisphere airmail delivery service and then a garage in the 1950s. It's a fun place to shop and graze, particularly on Friday nights when there's live music. On the corner of the building is the associated cafe **Bluebird Pantry** (⊘8am-5pm Tue-Sat).

RED ROCK TRIBAL
ARTS & CRAFTS

(www.redrocktribal.co.za; Cape Farm House, cnr M65 & M66, Redhill; ⊘9am-5pm Tue-Sun) Join owner Juliette as she hula-hoops outside her quirky collection of crafts and African tribal artefacts from tin can planes made in KwaZulu Natal to old Ethiopian silver and Coptic crosses. Opposite is a giant metal zebra made for an advertisement.

ARTVARK
ARTS & CRAFTS

Map p284 (www.artvark.org; 48 Main Rd, Kalk Bay; ⊘9am-6pm; ☒Kalk Bay) This contemporary folk-art gallery is a great place to find attractive souvenirs. It stocks a wide range of interesting arts and crafts by local artists, including paintings, pottery and jewellery, as well as goods from India and Central America.

GINA'S STUDIO
ARTS & CRAFTS

Map p284 (journeyinstitches.co.za; 38 Palmer Rd, Muizenberg; ◎10am-4pm Wed & Fri, to 1pm Sat; ⓡMuizenberg) Gina Niederhumer is the crafter behind this small boutique packed with appealing items from crocheted jewellery to patchwork bags and quilts, and origami made from old Afrikaans Braille paper.

BELLE OMBRE
ARTS & CRAFTS

Map p284 (19 Main Rd, Kalk Bay; ◎9.30am-5.30pm; ⓡKalk Bay) Carries a tasteful collection of traditional woven baskets and carved wooden pieces, including work from Ethiopia and Namibia. In a shady garden at the rear, you'll find a French crêperie – a rustic place for a snack while you're doing the shopping rounds.

KALK BAY BOOKS
BOOKS

Map p284 (www.kalkbaybooks.co.za; 124 Main Rd; ◎9am-6pm; ⓡKalk Bay) Where the southern peninsula's book lovers gather. Check their website for details of regular book launches and readings.

QUAGGA ART & BOOKS
BOOKS

Map p284 (www.quaggabooks.co.za; 84 Main Rd; ◎9.30am-5pm Mon-Sat, 10am-5pm Sun; ⓡKalk Bay) It's hard to pass this appealing bookshop by if you're looking for old editions and antiquarian books; they also have local art, and tribal art and artefacts.

POTTERSHOP
POTTERY

Map p284 (☑788 8737; 6 Rouxville Rd; ◎9.30am-4.30pm Mon-Sat, 11am-4.30pm Sun; ⓡKalk Bay) Pick up works by local ceramicists, including very good rejects of hand-painted plates and cups by the **Potter's Workshop** (www.pottersworkshop.co.za) and the jungle fantasy art of **Ardmore** (ww.ardmoreceramics.co.za).

FRANKI'S VILLAGE CHIC
FASHION

Map p284 (http://frankis-vintage.co.za; 70 Main Rd, Kalk Bay; ⓡKalk Bay) Get the floaty boho look at this boutique that stocks vintage and vintage-inspired chic – much of it is local brands, including Take Care, Jessica Harwood and Savvy. There's also a smaller branch in Muizenberg, near the station.

BIG BLUE
FASHION

Map p284 (www.bigblue.co.za; 80 Main Rd, Kalk Bay; ⓡKalk Bay) A good boutique for picking up quirky, affordable T-shirts, fun clubbing gear or beachwear by South African designers.

REDHILL POTTERY
POTTERY

(☑021-780 9297; www.redhillpotterycape.com.za; Kilfinan Farm, Scarborough) Specialising in pottery that mimics old enamelware in its glaze and incorporating bright African colours in the designs. It's possible to decorate your own pot and pick it up later (or have it shipped to your home).

WHATNOT & CHINA TOWN
ANTIQUE CHINA

Map p284 (70 Main Rd; ◎10am-5pm Mon-Sat, to 3pm Sun; ⓡKalk Bay) As if a thousand mad aunts have combined their prize china collections, this emporium – occupying a maze of rooms – offers all manner of plates, cups, bowls and decorative objects crafted from clay, including rare collectables by the likes of Clarice Cliff.

LARIJ WORKS
ARTS & CRAFTS

Map p286 (www.larijworks.com; 2 Alfred Ln, Simon's Town; ◎10am-4pm Mon-Fri, to 2pm Sat; ⓡSimon's Town) Contemporary, nautical-themed artwork and decor are sold in this upstairs gallery alongside cotton sleepwear. The woven rope mats are particularly appealing.

🏃 SPORTS & ACTIVITIES

Awol Tours (p25) can arrange cycling tours around the township of Masiphumelele (Xhosa for 'we will succeed').

TOP CHOICE SEA KAYAK SIMON'S TOWN
KAYAKING

Map p286 (☑082 501 8930; www.kayakcapetown.co.za; 62 St Georges St, Simon's Town; ⓡSimon's Town) Paddle out to the African penguin colony at Boulders (R250) with this Simon's Town–based operation. It also offers a variety of other tours, including one to Cape Point (R950).

SLEEPY HOLLOW HORSE RIDING
HORSE RIDING

(☑021 789 2341, 083 261 0104; www.sleepyhollowhorseriding.co.za; Sleepy Hollow Ln, Noordhoek) This reliable operation can arrange horse riding along the wide, sandy Noordhoek beach, as well as in the mountainous hinterland.

SUNSCENE OUTDOOR ADVENTURES
SANDBOARDING, SURFING

(☎021 783 0203, 084 352 4925; sunscene.co.za; Cape Farm House, cnr M65 & M66) As well as offering sandboarding lessons at Atlantis (R395), with expert guides and refreshments (essential!) included, they also run traditional surfing courses and a host of other adrenaline-pumping activities for adults and kids.

GARY'S SURF SCHOOL
SURFING

Map p284 (☎021-788 9839; www.garysurf.co.za; Surfer's Corner, Beach Rd; ☺8.30am-5pm; ®Muizenberg) If genial surfing coach Gary Kleynhans can't get you to stand on a board within a day, you don't pay for the two-hour lesson (R500). His shop, the focus of Muizenberg's surf scene, hires out boards and wetsuits (per hour/day R100/300). It also runs sandboarding trips to the dunes at Kommetjie (R300).

ROXY SURF CLUB
SURFING

Map p284 (☎021-788 8687; www.roxysurfschool.co.za; Surfer's Corner, Beach Rd; ☺8am-5pm; ®Muizenberg) Roxy started in 2003 as a women-only surf club to encourage more girls to get into this male-dominated sport. If you join the club, it's R400 per month for four lessons of 1½ hours each. A private lesson including board is R330.

PISCES DIVERS
DIVING

(☎021-782 7205; www.piscesdivers.co.za; 12 Glen Rd, Glencairn; ®Glencairn) Just metres from the water's edge, this recommended PADI dive centre offers a range of courses and scheduled dives.

Cape Flats & Northern Suburbs

LANGA | PINELANDS | GUGULETHU | KHAYELITSHA | BLOUBERGSTRAND | MILNERTON | CENTURY CITY

Neighbourhood Top Five

1 Learn about the tragedies of South Africa's past and the hopes for the future on a **township tour** (p26) or stay at a **township B&B** (p199).

2 Get your fingers sticky eating delicious barbecued meats at **Mzoli's** (p146) in **Gugulethu** or **Nomzamo** (p147) in Langa.

3 Marvel at kite surfers riding the waves and soaring into the skies off **Bloubergstrand** (p145).

4 Follow the **Durbanville Wine Route** (p148) around a dozen wineries.

5 Take a ferry ride around the wetlands of **Intaka Island** (p145).

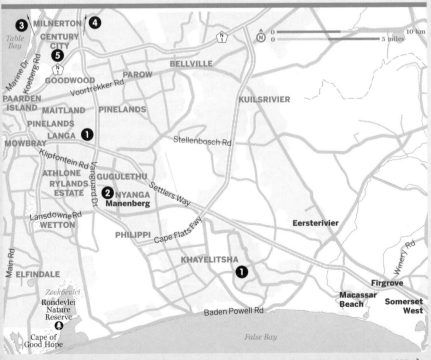

For more detail of this area, see Map p287 ➡

Lonely Planet's Top Tip

Visiting a township might well be one of the most illuminating and life-affirming things you do while in Cape Town. You'll see how the vast majority of Capetonians really live and learn a hell of a lot about South African history and the cultures of black and coloured South Africans. The easiest, and safest, way to organise this is by taking a tour. Better still is to stay overnight at one of several B&Bs.

Best Places to Eat

➡ Mzoli's (p146)
➡ Lelapa (p147)
➡ Nomzamo (p147)
➡ Millstone (p147)

For reviews, see p146 ➡

Best Places to Drink

➡ Blue Peter (p147)
➡ Kefu's (p147)
➡ Deon Nagel's Gat Party (p147)
➡ Galaxy (p148)

For reviews, see p147 ➡

Best Places to Shop

➡ Canal Walk (p148)
➡ Milnerton Flea Market (p149)
➡ Philani Nutrition Centre (p149)

For reviews, see p148 ➡

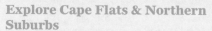 Explore Cape Flats & Northern Suburbs

Sprawling across the sandy plains east of Table Mountain, the Cape Flats seldom get good press, stricken as they are with crime, poverty and disease. The down-at-heel coloured communities and informal settlements (ie shacks) of the largely black townships would seem unlikely candidates as tourist destinations. However, a visit here might end up providing your fondest memories of Cape Town.

Langa, founded in 1927, is the oldest planned township in South Africa and has areas of affluence as well as poverty – a pattern repeated in the other main townships of Gugulethu and Khayelitsha (the largest with an estimated population of over 1.5 million). It's not all one-note misery. The infrastructure in the townships has improved since 1994, with the rows of concrete Reconstruction and Development Programme (RDP) houses being the most visible examples. We highlight some of the sights and projects you might like to arrange to visit on your own or on a township tour. While most of the places we list here will be safe for you to visit on your own, be sure to call your destination first and get clear directions or arrange for a local to meet you – a wrong turn in the townships can have dire consequences.

The lush garden suburb of Pinelands lies cheek by jowl with Langa; come here to visit the Oude Molen Eco Village. North of the city centre alongside Table Bay there's Bloubergstrand, a beach with a grand view of Table Mountain, and Milnerton, best visited for its weekend flea market and the gigantic Canal Walk shopping centre at Century City. Give yourself a day to see the sights in the townships and another day for the northern suburbs.

Local Life

➡ **Markets** Join the antique, bargain and curio hunters at the weekend Milnerton Flea Market (p149)
➡ **Pubs** Enjoy a beer and a slice of pizza on the grass in front of Blue Peter (p147), a Bloubergstrand institution.

Getting There & Away

➡ **Car** Take the N2 to Langa, Gugulethu and Khayelitsha, the N1 to Century City, and Marine Drive (R27) to Milnerton and Bloubergstrand.
➡ **Tour bus** The best way to see the townships. There are set itineraries but tour guides can be flexible in where they go, depending on the wishes of the group.
➡ **Bus** MyCiTi buses run through Milnerton to Table Bay.
➡ **Train** Metro trains run to Langa, Gugulethu (closest stop Nyanga) and Khayelitsha.

◉ SIGHTS

CAPE FLATS & NORTHERN SUBURBS SIGHTS

FREE GUGA S'THEBE ARTS
& CULTURAL CENTRE   CULTURAL CENTRE
Map p287 (☎021-695 3493; cnr Washington
& Church Sts, Langa; ⊙8am-4.30pm Mon-Fri,
8.30am-2pm Sat & Sun; P) Brilliantly decorated with colourful ceramic murals, this
is one of the most impressive buildings in
the townships. A host of community classes
are held here, including beadwork and the
making of traditional garments and pottery. Performances by local groups are often staged in the outdoor amphitheatre. It's
a good place to shop for local crafts and you
can meet artists such as Odon, who teaches
sand-painting classes here and sells his
own canvases.

There's a Cape Town Tourism office here,
too: enquire with them about whether the
planned apartheid pass laws museum for
the nearby old Native Affairs Office has
opened.

BLOUBERGSTRAND   BEACH, VILLAGE
The British won their 1806 battle for
the Cape on this beach facing Table Bay.
The panoramic view it provides of Table
Mountain is its most famous feature, although the seemingly eternal wind makes
it popular with kite-surfers and windsurfers; watching them ride the waves on the
weekends is a very impressive sight. The
village of Bloubergstrand itself is attractive,
with picnic areas, some long, uncrowded,
windy stretches of sand, the good pub Blue
Peter, and several other places to dine with
ocean views. From the city follow Marine
Dr and West Coast Rd for 18km to reach
Bloubergstrand.

INTAKA ISLAND   WETLAND RESERVE
(www.intaka.co.za; 2 Park Lane, Intaka Island,
Century City; adult/child R10/5, entrance & ferry
ride adult/child R30/20; ⊙7.30am-7pm daily
Oct-Apr, 7.30am-5.30pm daily May-Sep; P) Intaka means 'bird' in Xhosa and you can
see plenty of these feathered creatures at
this 16-hectare wetland reserve that's part
of the Century City complex (where you'll
also find the Canal Walk mall). Some 120
bird species have been spotted here, living
among 212 species of fynbos (literally 'fine
bush', primarily proteas, heaths and ericas).
Learn about it all at the Eco-Centre, built
and run to the best environmental princi-
ples and from where you can take a **ferry
ride** (⊙10am-4pm) through the canals that
flow around the island, or follow the 2km
walking trail around the reserve.

On the first Sunday of the month a Natural Goods Market is held in the park opposite Intaka Island. The N1 from the city
leads to Century City.

OUDE MOLEN ECO VILLAGE   ORGANIC FARM
Map p287 (Alexandra Rd, Pinelands; P) Many
grassroots-style operations occupy this
once-abandoned section of the buildings
and grounds of the Valkenberg psychiatric
hospital. You can volunteer to work at the
village's organic farm through the Will-
ing Workers on Organic Farms scheme, go
horse riding with Oude Molen Stables, eat

LOCAL KNOWLEDGE

TOWNSHIP MOSAICS, MURALS & MONUMENTS

Langa
Along Washington St near the Guga S'Thebe Arts & Cultural Centre are four colourful mosaic-decorated plinths. Each side of the plinths has a different theme: one is
the only memorial to the *Mendi,* a troop ship that sank in the English Channel in 1917,
drowning 607 members of the South African Native Labour Corps. The huge mural
painted on the building opposite the cultural centre was done by Philip Kgosana, the
man held aloft in the composition – it commemorates the defiance campaign against
apartheid laws of 1960.

Gugulethu
On the corner of NY1 and NY111 is the Gugulethu Seven Memorial commemorating
seven young black activists from the townships who were killed by the police here in
1986. Nearby is the Amy Biehl Memorial celebrating the life of the US anti-apartheid
activist who died under tragic circumstances in Gugulethu in 1993, and a mosaic-
covered bench, one in a series around Cape Town installed by Rock Girl (www.rock
girlsa.org) as part of a project to create safe spaces for girls and women.

GREENING THE CAPE FLATS *Simon Richmond*

'Alex, this is your tree,' says Mr Pretorius, the principal of Heathfield Primary School in the Cape Flats suburb of Elfindale.'When you are old, come back and look at your tree. Bring your children.' Alex is one of a group of kids who helped plant 30 indigenous trees around their school grounds in a program organised by **Greenpop** (www. greenpop.org). I was among the adult volunteers who had come along to assist and find out more about the work of this innovative local social enterprise.

'So far we've planted some 9000 trees in schools, communities and deforested areas across the Cape Flats and further afield,' says Lauren O'Donnell who with Misha Teasdale and Jeremy Hewitt founded Greenpop in 2010. Apart from being able to gift trees via their website (from R100), they regularly run tree-tour planting days (R450), as well as major events such as the Heritage Day of a Thousand Trees on 24 September 2011. Organised in conjunction with the community organisation **Proudly Mannenberg** (proudlymannenberg.org), this saw 1000 trees planted in Mannenberg, one of the most deprived and crime-ridden areas in the Cape Flats. Every Wednesday is usually a tree-tour day (but they do plant trees on other days; for details email treetours@greenpop.org) and pickups can be arranged.

The schools and other places, such as retirement homes and community centres, where Greenpop have planted are carefully vetted to ensure that the trees have the best chance of survival with consistent aftercare. Heathfield Primary is in a relatively well off part of the Cape Flats, but, as the principal explains, the vast majority of the kids studying there travel in from far more disadvantaged suburbs; some families are so poor their children don't eat breakfast before school, so the school now has a programme to provide 180 of its students with a decent meal each day.

And why plant trees? Misha explains to the kids before the planting begins: they provide oxygen; they're a source of food; they aid biodiversity and create shelter for other plants and animals to thrive; and – perhaps most importantly – as they grow on previously barren land they provide a sense of pride for the community.

If planting trees doesn't appeal, there are plenty of other ways to volunteer and get involved with various social projects and Capetonian charities: see p238 for further information.

at the cafe and farm stall Millstone or go for a swim in the village's outdoor pool. However, we've had too many reports of robberies occurring to recommend the backpacker accommodation also on the site.

RATANGA JUNCTION   AMUSEMENT PARK
(www.ratanga.co.za; Century Boulevard, Century City; adult/child R152/75; ⊙10am-5pm Sat & Sun Jan-Mar, daily in school holidays; P) Offering some 20 odd rides and attractions – ranging from stomach churning, looping roller coasters to an animal petting zoo – this African-themed amusement park is next to Canal Walk shopping centre. If you don't want to board any of the rides there's still a R50 entrance charge to the park. The N1 from the city leads to Century City.

FREE **LOOKOUT HILL**   VIEWPOINT
(cnr Mew Way & Spine Rd, Khayelitsha; P) Climb the wooden staircase leading to the top of this sand hill for a sweeping view of the Khayelitsha township. For access it's best to go into the cultural and tourism centre at its base, where you'll find the restaurant Malibongwe and a craft market. Ask there for one of the guards to accompany you, as there have been incidents of muggings.

✖ EATING

You don't go to the townships for fine dining, but there are a few small restaurants where you can try traditional Xhosa cuisine or enjoy a braai (barbecued meat).

TOP CHOICE **MZOLI'S**   BRAAI **$**
(☑021-638 1355; 150 NY111, Gugulethu; meal R50; ⊙9am-6pm) Tourists, TV stars and locals gather at this busy butchery serving Cape Town's tastiest grilled meat. It's all DIY. First buy your meat and make sure you

get them to add their special sauce. Take it to the kitchen to be braaied (barbecued) and then find a table outside. It gets super hectic here at weekends so arrive early. Beers and other drinks are available from vendors nearby. Bring plenty of napkins as cutlery is nonexistent.

LELAPA
AFRICAN $$

Map p287 (021-694 2681; 49 Harlem Ave, Langa; buffet R120) Sheila has been so successful with her delicious African-style buffets that she's taken over the neighbour's, extending the once-cosy home restaurant into a space for big tour groups. Book, as there are no set opening hours at this place.

NOMZAMO
BRAAI $

Map p287 (021-695 4250; 15 Washington St, Langa; meal R50; ⊘9am-7pm daily) This spotlessly clean butchers is the Langa equivalent of Mzoli's but with a more relaxed, peaceful vibe since they don't sell alcohol. The cuts of meat – beef, lamb, pork, sausages and chicken wings – are top class. Call ahead if you want to add side dishes such as bread, salads etc to make a full meal.

MILLSTONE
INTERNATIONAL, BAKERY $

Map p287 (021-447 8226; eastern-comfort.com/Millstone; Valkenberg East, Oude Molen Eco Village, Pinelands; meals R50-60; ⊘9am-5pm Tue-Sun; P) This rustic cafe and farm stall specialises in organic produce and hand-crafted breads, preserves and jams. Kids will love the tree house in its garden and the pony rides next door.

MZANSI
AFRICAN $$

Map p287 (021-694 1656; www.mzansi45.co.za; 45 Harlem Ave, Langa; buffet R120) Next door to Lelapa, a similar buffet deal is offered by this convivial place with a roof top dining area that has a great view of Table Mountain. They can also arrange a mariba band and African drumming lessons.

EZIKO
AFRICAN $

Map p287 (021-694 0434; www.ezikores taurant.com; cnr Washington St & Jungle Walk, Langa; mains R30-45; ⊘9am-5pm Mon-Sat; P) Eziko offers simple, good food in a pleasant setting; try the chef's special fried chicken or the breakfast. If you're feeling adventurous go for the 'delectable' tripe. Dishes are served with sides of *samp* (a mixture of maize and beans), *pap* (maize porridge), bread and vegetables.

MALIBONGWE
AFRICAN $

(021-361 6259; malibongwerestaurant.co.za; cnr Mew Way & Spine Rd, Khayelitsha; mains R40-60; ⊘8am-6pm Mon-Sat; P) Tripe curry and grilled meats are among the traditional dishes served at this pleasantly decorated, spacious restaurant and bar at the base of Lookout Hill. For a more local vibe, head down Spine Rd to the street braai joints opposite Kefu's; Ziba's Chicken is recommended.

 # DRINKING & NIGHTLIFE

BLUE PETER
RESTAURANT, BAR

(021-554 1956; www.bluepeter.co.za; Popham St, Bloubergstrand; ⊘11am-11pm) At this perennial favourite, around 15km north of the city centre, the deal is grab a beer, order a pizza and plonk yourself on the grass outside to enjoy the classic views of Table Mountain and Robben Island. It's also a hotel.

KEFU'S
JAZZ, PUB

(021-361 0566; www.kefus.co.za; 39-41 Mthawelanga St, Ilitha Park, Khayelitsha; ⊘10am-midnight Mon-Thu, 10am-2am Fri & Sat) Ms Kefuoe Sedia has come a long way since she started a six-seater pub in her front lounge in 1990. This spiffy, two-level, 140-seater place with mellow jazz as background music and also serving food is where Khayelitsha's 'black diamonds' like to relax. Call ahead Monday to Thursday to check they're open.

DEON NAGEL'S GAT PARTY
GAY CLUB

(082 821 9185; www.facebook.com/groups/117474602037; Theo Marais Park, Koeberg Rd, Milnerton; cover R30; ⊘9pm-2am, first, second & last Sat of month; P) A uniquely Capetonian gay event are *gat* parties. *Gat* means 'hole' in Afrikaans, and the name comes from the original location of the party at the old Parrow Athletic Club based in a former quarry – literally a hole in the ground. The Afrikaans name is also a clue that these are parties at which mainly Afrikaans queers can indulge in their culture's love of *langarm*-style ballroom dancing to country-and-western-style tunes. People go in groups and bring their own food and drink (although there's always a bar); if you're solo it won't take you long to make friends and the DJs usually

WORTH A DETOUR

DURBANVILLE WINE ROUTE

About 25km or a 30-minute drive north of the City Bowl and still within Cape Town's metropolitan borders, fine wines and good food can be enjoyed along the **Durbanville Wine Route** (www.durbanvillewine.co.za). Vines have been grown here since 1698; the area's signature grape is sauvignon blanc, which benefits from the cooler winds the hills receive off the coast. Among the 11 wineries on the route are:

Durbanville Hills (☎021-558 1300; www.durbanvillehills.co.za; M13, Durbanville; tastings R40-60; ⊙9am-4.30pm Mon-Fri, 10am-3pm Sat, 11am-3pm Sun) In an ultramodern hilltop building, commanding splendid views of Table Bay and Table Mountain, the range of tastings here include ones paired with tapas or chocolates.

Meerendal (☎021-975 1655; www.meerendal.co.za; M48 Visserhok, Durbanville; tastings R10; ⊙9am-6pm Tue-Sat, 8am-5pm Sun) Established in 1702 and with some of the oldest pinotage and shiraz vineyards in South Africa, Meerendal has a pedigree for its wines. It has a couple of restaurants including the bistro Barn & Lawn; book for the Sunday buffet (adult/child R195/85).

Nitida (☎021-976 1467; www.nitida.co.za; Tygerberg Valley Rd, Durbanville; tastings R20; ⊙9.30am-5pm Mon-Fri, 9.30am-3pm Sat, 11am-3pm Sun) Excellent tastings of these award-winning wines are held in the wine cellar. Also here is the excellent **Tables @ Nitida** (☎021-975 9357; www.tablesatnitida.co.za; h9am-3pm Tue-Sun) where you can pre-book delicious gourmet picnics (R225 for two) or enjoy one of their luscious cakes.

play a range of music that anyone can dance to. From the city it's a 10km drive to Theo Marais Park along Marine Drive.

GALAXY CLUB

(superclubs.co.za; College Rd, Ryelands Estate; admission R50; ⊙9pm-4am Thu-Sat) This legendary Cape Flats dance venue is where you can get down to R&B, hip hop and live bands with a black and coloured crowd. Women often get in for free. The plush live music venue **West End** (⊙5pm-4pm Fri & Sat) is next door. Follow the N2 out of Cape Town, take the M17 exit to Klipfontein Rd and then drive to Rylands, about a 14km journey.

ENTERTAINMENT

GRANDWEST CASINO CASINO

(☎021-505 7174; www.suninternational.com; 1 Vanguard Dr, Goodwood) Cape Town's long-gone Victorian post office served as the model for the florid facade of this casino. Even if gambling isn't your thing, there's plenty to keep you entertained, including a six-screen cinema, many restaurants, a food court, an Olympic-sized ice rink, a kids' theme park, music shows, nightclub Hanover Street and a bowling alley. Major international singing stars often perform here. Follow Voortrekker Rd for 12.5km east of the city centre to find the casino.

SWINGERS BLUES, JAZZ

(☎021-762 2443; 1 Whetton Rd, Whetton; 🚉Whetton) Book a table at the renowned Monday-night jam sessions hosted by guitarist Alvin Dyers, leader of the house band. The music is a mix of music at this smoky, atmospheric place is of all kinds of jazz often with guest artists.

IBUYAMBO MUSIC & DANCE

Map p287 (☎021-694 3113, 083 579 0853; www.ibuyambo.co.za; Washington St, Langa) Dizu Plaatjies and his award-winning group of Xhosa musicians and dancers perform at this cultural centre by arrangement. Drumming sessions can be arranged and traditional bead work explained.

SHOPPING

CANAL WALK SHOPPING MALL

(www.canalwalk.co.za; Century Blvd, Century City; ⊙9am-9pm) With over 400 shops, 50-odd restaurants, 18 cinema screens and parking for 6500 cars, you'd be a fool to argue with this mall's claim of being the largest in Africa. The food court is so big that acrobatics shows are often held over the diners. Check the website for details of a shuttle bus service (R50) from the city.

MILNERTON FLEA MARKET — MARKET

(R27, Paarden Island; ⊙7am-3pm Sat & Sun) Hunt for antiques and other collectables among the junk at this car-boot sale that fills up a car park on the edge of Table Bay. Follow Marine Dr out of the city for a couple of kilometres to find the market.

SIVUYILE TOURISM CENTRE — CRAFTS

(☑021-637 8449; cnr NY1 & NY4, College of Cape Town, Gugulethu; ⊙8am-5pm Mon-Fri, 8am-2pm Sat) Sivuyile means 'we are happy' in Xhosa. Inside a local technical college, this tourism centre has an interesting photographic display on the townships, artists at work and a good craft shop.

PHILANI NUTRITION CENTRE — CRAFTS

(☑021-387 5124; www.philani.org.za) This long-running community-based health organisation has six projects in the townships, including a weaving factory in Khayelitsha's Site C and a printing project. Women are taught how to feed their families adequately on a low budget, and the crèche and various projects enable them to earn an income through producing rugs, wall hangings and other crafts. Philani goods are available in shops around the Cape.

SPORTS & ACTIVITIES

SKYDIVE CAPE TOWN — PARACHUTING

(☑082 800 6290; www.skydivecapetown.za.net; R1500) Based about 20km north of the city centre in Melkboshstrand, this experienced outfit offers tandem skydives – needless to say the views, once you stop screaming, are spectacular.

MOWBRAY GOLF CLUB — GOLF

Map p287 (☑021-685 3018; www.mowbray golfclub.co.za; 1 Raapenberg Rd, Mowbray; ℗) Established in 1910, Mowbray is considered by some to be the best in-town course for its rural setting and abundant birdlife. It certainly has a lovely view of Devil's Peak.

MILNERTON GOLF CLUB — GOLF

(☑021-552 1351; www.milnertongolf.co.za; Bridge Rd, Milnerton) About 12km north of the city centre along the R27, the 18-hole, par-72 Milnerton has a magnificent position overlooking Table Bay and great views of Table Mountain. Wind can be a problem, though.

OUDE MOLEN STABLES — HORSE RIDING

Map p287 (☑073 199 7395; Oude Molen Eco Village, Alexandra Rd, Pinelands; per hr R120) Ride around this eco-village, with a magnificent view of the back of Table Mountain, where you'll also find pony rides next to the Millstone farm stall and cafe.

WINDSWEPT — WINDSURFING, KITE BOARDING

(☑082 961 3070; www.windswept.co.za) Philip Baker runs windsurfing and kite-surfing camps out of his base in Bloubergstrand. Two-hour group lessons are R495 (R990 for individuals), or if you know the ropes you can hire a kite and board for R395. Packages including accommodation are available.

ATHLONE STADIUM — SOCCER

(Cross Blvd, Athlone) Upgraded for the World Cup, this stadium is mainly used for soccer matches. To find out about upcoming matches go to www.psl.co.za.

CAPE FLATS & NORTHERN SUBURBS SPORTS & ACTIVITIES

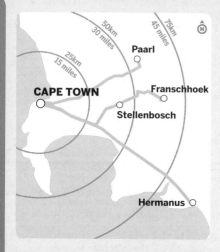

Day Trips & Wineries

Stellenbosch p151
At the heart of hundreds of vineyards, Stellenbosch is an elegant town with Cape Dutch, Georgian and Victorian architecture.

Franschhoek p156
Lush vineyards surround Franschhoek's compact town centre, and its main road is dotted with excellent restaurants.

Paarl p160
The largest town in the Winelands, Paarl lies on the banks of the Berg River and has Cape Dutch architecture and vineyards within the town limits.

Hermanus p163
Clinging to the clifftops, Hermanus has pretty beaches, *fynbos*-covered hills and some of the best land-based whale-watching in the world.

Stanford p166
This picture-perfect village on the banks of the Klein River offers fabulous foodie experiences off the beaten track.

Darling p168
Darling is known for its wine, arty community and inimitable drag shows.

Langebaan p169
Coastal Langebaan is a place to come for open-air seafood restaurants, phenomenal sunsets and kite-surfing lessons on the lagoon.

Stellenbosch

Explore

If you only have a day to spend, start at the excellent Village Museum before turning to the reason most people visit this vibrant university town – wine. Choosing vineyards to visit can be a daunting task, so stop first at the tourist office to pick up a free copy of *Stellenbosch and its Wine Routes*. You'll need your own wheels (bicycle wheels will do) to explore the vineyards, which are scattered far and wide around the town. Better still, join a tour and enjoy sipping rather than spitting. Tours usually visit up to four vineyards and include lunch – eating at one of the estates is a Stellenbosch must. Those staying overnight will appreciate the town's after-dark vibe, largely revolving around bustling student bars.

The Best...

→ **Sight** Villiera
→ **Place to Eat** Apprentice@Institute of Culinary Arts (p155)
→ **Place to Drink** Brampton Wine Studio (p155)

Top Tip

If you don't want to drive, and being tied to a tour group doesn't appeal, try the Vinehopper (www.vinehopper.co.za), a hop-on, hop-off service that visits 12 vineyards in the Stellenbosch area.

Getting There & Away

Bus Baz Bus (☎021-439 2323; www.bazbus. com) runs daily to and from Cape Town (R160, 30 minutes).

Train Metrorail (☎0800 656 463) operates frequent trains from Cape Town (1st/economy class R13/7.50, about one hour).

Need to Know

→ **Area Code** ☎021
→ **Location** Stellenbosch is 50km east of Cape Town
→ **Tourist Office** (☎883 3584; www.stellenboschtourism.co.za; 36 Market St; ◉8am-5pm Mon-Fri, 9am-2pm Sat & Sun)

◉ SIGHTS & ACTIVITIES

VILLIERA WINERY
(☎865 2002; www.villiera.com; Rte 101; tastings free; ◉8.30am-5pm Mon-Fri, 8.30am-3pm Sat) Villiera produces several excellent Méthode Cap Classique wines and a highly rated and very well-priced shiraz. You can sample their wines in the revamped tasting room or outside under oak trees. Excellent two-hour wildlife drives (R150 per person) with knowledgeable guides take in the antelopes, zebras and birds on the farm.

WARWICK ESTATE WINERY
(☎884 4410; www.warwickwine.com; Rte 44; tastings R25; ◉10am-5pm) Warwick's red wines are legendary, particularly their bordeaux blends. They offer an informative 'Big Five' wine safari through the vineyards (think major grape varieties, not large mammals) which pauses at the estate's highest point for a glass of crisp sauvignon blanc with a view. Afterwards put together a gourmet picnic to enjoy on comfy cushions strewn across the lawn or try your hand at drinking from the 'wedding cup'.

DELAIRE GRAFF ESTATE WINERY
(☎885 8160; www.delaire.co.za; Rte 310; tastings R10; ◉10am-6pm Mon-Sat, 10am-4pm Sun) The views are stunning from this 'vineyard in the sky' at the top of Helshoogte Pass. In fact, the views inside are impressive too,

DAY TRIPS & WINERIES STELLENBOSCH

A WALKING TOUR OF STELLENBOSCH

If you need to walk off all those wine tastings, you could take a **guided town walk** (per person R90; ◉11am & 3pm) from Stellenbosch Tourism. Bookings are essential for weekend walks. If you prefer to go it alone, pick up the excellent brochure *Historical Stellenbosch on Foot* (R5), which has a walking-tour map and information on many of the town's historic buildings.

Stellenbosch

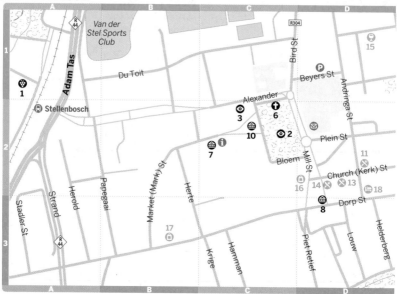

Stellenbosch

thanks to the ultra-modern overhaul this winery has received. Across the board their wines are superb – sip them on comfy couches as a grand piano is played in the background. The main restaurant serves bistro-style cuisine, while **Indochine** offers Asian-inspired dishes. There's also a spa and two elegant lodges.

TOKARA WINERY
(☎808 5900; www.tokara.co.za; Rte 310; tastings free; ☉9am-5pm Mon-Fri, 10am-3pm Sat & Sun) Tokara is renowned for its excellent wines – particularly chardonnay and sauvignon blanc – as well as its upmarket restaurant, fine art collection and sleek design. In summer you can enjoy intricate dishes outside with mountain views; in winter, snuggle up by the fire with a taster of the noble late harvest (dessert wine) or pot still brandy (R10). There's a fantastic deli/sculpture gallery for less fancy lunches and you can taste the olive oil made on the estate.

HARTENBERG ESTATE WINERY
(☎865 2541; www.hartenbergestate.com; tastings free; ☉9am-5.15pm Mon-Fri, 9am-3pm Sat, 10am-3.30pm Sun) Thanks to a favourable microclimate, this estate, founded in 1692, produces superlative red wines, particularly cabernet, merlot and shiraz. Lunch

is served at the estate from noon to 2pm (bookings essential). Picnics are also available to take on a wetland walk through the estate. Hartenberg is located off Bottelary Rd, 10km northwest of Stellenbosch.

L'AVENIR WINERY

(☎889 5001; www.lavenir-south-africa.com; Rte 44; tastings R25; ⊙9am-5pm Mon-Fri, 10am-4pm Sat & Sun) Here a visit is not about facilities, but simply about splendid wine: the chenin blancs are superb and the pinotage (a cross between pinot noir and hermitage) highly

awarded. Ask about staying overnight in the cottages. The estate is 5km out of Stellenbosch on the way to Paarl.

BLAAUWKLIPPEN WINERY

(☎880 0133; www.blaauwklippen.com; Rte 44; tastings R35; ⊙9am-5pm Mon-Fri, 10am-5pm Sat, 10am-4pm Sun; ⓘ) This rustic, 300-year-old estate with several Cape Dutch buildings is known for its red wines, particularly its cabernet sauvignon. It is also one of very few vineyards in South Africa that produces zinfandel. There's a wine and cheese tasting option (R65), cellar tours are available by appointment and lunch is offered at the **Barouche** restaurant. A food and craft market is held here on Sunday mornings and there are horse rides (R10) around the estate for children on weekends. Midweek, they can enjoy the playground instead.

SPIER WINERY

(☎809 1100; www.spier.co.za; Rte 310; tastings from R35; ⊙10am-5pm; ⓘ) Spier has some excellent shiraz, cabernet and red blends, though a visit to this vast winery is less about wine and more about the other activities available. There's something for everyone at this mega-estate, including bird of prey displays, horse rides through the vines, golf, beautifully restored Cape Dutch buildings, several restaurants and a hotel.

VAN RYN BRANDY CELLAR WINERY

(☎881 3875; www.vanryn.co.za; Rte 310; tastings from R30; ⊙8am-5pm Mon-Fri, 9am-2pm Sat) One of 14 stops on the **Western Cape Brandy Route** (www.sabrandy.co.za). It generally runs three tours a day (except for Sunday),

---

SLEEPING IN STELLENBOSCH

As well as a wealth of sleeping options for all budgets in the town itself, there is the possibility of sleeping over at one of the wine estates.

➡ **Banghoek Place** (☎887 0048; www.banghoek.co.za; 193 Banghoek Rd; dm/r R150/450; @⊠) The owners of this stylish suburban hostel are keen to organise tours of the district. The recreation area has satellite TV and a pool table.

➡ **Lanzerac Hotel** (☎887 1132; www.lanzerac.co.za; Jonkershoek Valley; s/d/ste incl breakfast R2560/3410/5780; ✳@⊠) This opulent place consists of a 300-year-old manor house and winery. Some suites have private pools and stunning views.

➡ **Stellenbosch Hotel** (☎887 3644; www.stellenbosch.co.za/hotel; 162 Dorp St; s/d incl breakfast from R835/1040; ✳@) A comfortable country-style hotel with a variety of rooms, including some with self-catering facilities and others with four-poster beds. A section dating from 1743 houses the Jan Cats Brasserie, a good spot for a drink.

WORTH A DETOUR

HELDERBERG WINERIES

There are around 30 wineries in the Helderberg region, including **Vergelegen** (☑021-847 1334; www.vergelegen.co.za; Lourensford Rd, Somerset West; adult/child R10/5, tastings R30; ☉9.30am-4.30pm), arguably the most beautiful estate in the Cape. The buildings and elegant grounds have ravishing mountain views and a 'stately home' feel to them. Tasting the flagship Vergelegen wines costs an extra R10. On the dining front you can choose from the casual Rose Terrace, the upmarket Stables at Vergelegen or a picnic hamper (per person R165, November to April) – bookings are essential for the last two options.

For a total contrast, climb the hill towards Sir Lowry's Pass where the stunning contemporary architecture of **Waterkloof** (☑021-858 1292; www.waterkloofwines. co.za; Sir Lowry's Pass Village Rd, Somerset West; tasting R30; ☉10am-5pm) commands a breathtaking panorama of False Bay. The estate specialises in biodynamic wines and ecofriendly farming methods, while their restaurant is worth the trip alone for brilliantly conceived, intensely flavoursome dishes.

including a choice of tastings pairing brandy with coffee, chocolate or cured meats.

BERGKELDER
WINERY

(☑809 8025; www.bergkelder.co.za; off Adam Tas Rd; ☉8am-5pm Mon-Fri, 9am-2pm Sat; tours 10am, 11am, 2pm & 3pm Mon-Fri; 10am, 11am & noon Sat) For wine lovers without wheels, this cellar is a short walk from the train station and town centre. Hour-long tours (R30) are followed by an atmospheric candle-lit tasting in the cellar. Informal tastings are also available throughout the day.

NEETHLINGSHOF
WINERY

(☑021-883 8988; www.neethlingshof.co.za; off the M12; tastings R30; ☉9am-5pm Mon-Fri, 10am-4pm Sat & Sun) A beautiful tree-lined avenue leads to this charming estate with a rose garden and **restaurant** (mains R40 to R140; ☉breakfast, lunch & dinner). There are cellar and vineyard tours (bookings essential), and their pinotage and cabernet sauvignon have won several awards. Food and wine pairings are available if you book ahead.

MEERLUST ESTATE
WINERY

(☑843 3587; www.meerlust.com; Rte 310; tastings R30; ☉9am-5pm Mon-Fri, 10am-2pm Sat) Hannes Myburgh is the eighth generation of his family to have run this historic wine estate since 1756. They are most famous for Rubicon, a wine that John Platter's guide once called a 'preeminent Cape claret'. Its tasting room, decorated with the owner's collection of posters and a fine history of the winery, is worth a look.

VILLAGE MUSEUM
MUSEUM

(☑887 2902; 18 Ryneveld St; adult/child R30/5; ☉9am-5pm Mon-Sat, 10am-4pm Sun) A group of exquisitely restored and period-furnished houses dating from 1709 to 1850 make up this **museum**, which occupies the entire city block bounded by Ryneveld, Plein, Drostdy and Church Sts and is a must-see. Also included are charming gardens and, on the other side of Drostdy St, stately **Grosvenor House**.

JONKERSHOEK NATURE RESERVE
PARK

(☑866 1560; adult/child R30/15) This small **nature reserve** is 8km southeast of town along the WR4 and set within a timber plantation. There are walking and cycling trails ranging from 2.9km to 18km. A hiking map is available at the entrance.

SASOL ART MUSEUM
GALLERY

(☑808 3695; 52 Ryneveld St; admission by donation; ☉9am-4.30pm Tue-Sat) Featuring one of the country's best selections of local art, both famous and emerging, this **museum** also contains an irreplaceable collection of African anthropological treasures. The exhibition displays the different ecological, social and cultural contexts of the human experience in Africa, and is not to be missed.

TOY & MINIATURE MUSEUM
MUSEUM

(☑079-981 7067; Rhenish Parsonage, 42 Market St; adult/child R10/5; ☉9am-4pm Mon-Fri, 9am-2pm Sat) This surprising **museum** features a remarkable collection of detailed toys ranging from railway sets to dollhouses – ask curator Philip Kleynhans to point out some of the more interesting pieces.

BRAAK
PARK

At the north end of the **Braak** (Town Sq), an open stretch of grass, you'll find the neo-Gothic **St Mary's on the Braak Church**, completed in 1852. To the west of the church is the **VOC Kruithuis** (Powder House; adult/child R5/2; ⊙9am-4.30pm Mon-Fri), which was built in 1777 to store the town's weapons and gunpowder and now houses a small military museum. On the northwest corner of the square is **Fick House**, also known as the Burgerhuis, a fine example of Cape Dutch style from the late 18th century. Most of this building is now occupied by Historical Homes of South Africa, established to preserve the country's important architecture.

FREE UNIVERSITY OF STELLENBOSCH ART GALLERY
GALLERY

(⊠808 3489; cnr Bird & Dorp Sts; ⊙9am-5pm Mon-Fri, 9am-1pm Sat) In a nearby old Lutheran Church, the university's **art gallery** focuses on contemporary works by South African artists and art students. It's well worth a visit.

LYNEDOCH ECOVILLAGE
CULTURAL TOUR

On Rte 310, some 15km southwest of Stellenbosch and on the railway line from Cape Town, Lynedoch EcoVillage is the first ecologically designed, socially mixed community in South Africa. Home of the Sustainability Institute (www.sustainability institute.net), there are energy efficient houses here as well as a preschool and primary school for farm workers' children. Its aim is to promote a sustainable lifestyle based on good governance and alternative energy strategies. Book in advance for a tour (R150 per group).

EATING & DRINKING

APPRENTICE@INSTITUTE OF CULINARY ARTS
FUSION **$$**

(⊠887 8985; Andringa St; mains R45-130; ⊙breakfast & lunch Sun & Mon, breakfast, lunch & dinner Tue-Sat) This is a stylish restaurant with a small, inspired menu. The restaurant is operated by students attending the

Institute of Culinary Arts and service is excellent.

DE OUDE BANK
DELI **$**

(⊠883 2187; 7 Church St; platters R45-60; ⊙breakfast & lunch Tue-Sun, dinner Wed & Sat) A vibrant bakery and deli priding itself on locally sourced ingredients. The menu changes weekly but always features salads, sandwiches and meze-style platters that you can put together yourself. There's live music on Saturday evenings and if you're all wined out they also serve superlative craft beer from a nearby brewery, **Triggerfish**.

BRAMPTON WINE STUDIO
MEDITERRANEAN **$**

(⊠883 9097; 11 Church St; mains R40-80; ⊙10am-7pm Mon-Sat) Play board games and scribble on tables while munching on gourmet pizzas and sipping shiraz at this trendy pavement cafe that also serves as Brampton winery's tasting room.

BOTANICAL GARDEN RESTAURANT
CAFE **$**

(⊠021-808 3025; Van Riebeeck St; mains R50-90; ⊙9am-5pm) Surrounded by exotic plants, this is a lovely spot for coffee, cake or a light lunch.

MYSTIC BOER
PUB

(3 Victoria St) Cool kids hang out here in surroundings that can best be described as post-transformation era retro-Boer chic. Pizzas and steaks are on the menu.

ENTERTAINMENT

OUDE LIBERTAS AMPHITHEATRE
ARTS

(⊠809 7380; www.oudelibertas.co.za; cnr Adam Tas & Oude Libertas Rds; ⊙Nov-Apr) Performing-arts festivals are held here and at Spier wine estate (see p153) between January and March.

⌂ SHOPPING

OOM SAMIE SE WINKEL
SOUVENIRS

(Uncle Sammy's Shop; 84 Dorp St; ⊙8.30am-5.30pm Mon-Fri, 9am-5pm Sat & Sun) This place was on the Stellenbosch map before Stellenbosch was on the map. Unashamedly touristy but still worth visiting for its curious range of goods – from high kitsch to genuine antiques and everything in between.

WINING AND DINING

The Cape Winelands boast many of South Africa's top restaurants and enjoying a spot of fine dining at one of the vineyards is a worthy splurge. Many places offer set gourmand menus offering three to six smallish courses. There's often a wine pairing option, where each dish comes with a glass of wine chosen by the sommelier to complement the food. Some superb winery restaurants include:

Rust en Vrede (☏021-881 3757; www.rustenvrede.com; ⏱dinner Tue-Sat) Chef John Shuttleworth prepares a four-course à la carte menu (R480) as well as a six-course tasting menu with/without wines R880/585) with a contemporary take on the classics. Also a winery, it's at the end of Annandale Rd, off Rte 44 south of Stellenbosch.

Overture Restaurant (☏021-880 2721; Hidden Valley Wine Estate, off Annandale Rd, Stellenbosch; 4 courses with/without wines R490/R350; ⏱lunch Tue-Sun, dinner Thu & Fri) A very modern wine estate and restaurant where chef Bertus Basson focuses on local, seasonal produce paired with Hidden Valley wines.

96 Winery Rd (☏021-842 2020; Zandberg Farm, Winery Rd; mains R105-155; ⏱lunch & dinner Mon-Sat, lunch Sun) Off Rte 44 between Stellenbosch and Somerset West, this restaurant at the Zandberg winery is one of the most respected in the area, known for its dry aged beef. It is a relaxed place with simply cooked food.

Haute Cabrière Cellar (☏021-876 3688; Franschhoek Pass Rd; mains R75-145; ⏱lunch Tue-Sun, dinner Wed-Mon) As well as the delectable à la carte option offering imaginative dishes, there is a six-course set menu with accompanying wines (R750). The setting is dramatic: a dining room is in a cellar cut into the mountainside.

La Petite Ferme (☏021-876 3016; www.lapetiteferme.co.za; Franschhoek Pass Rd; mains R90-145; ⏱noon-4pm) In a stupendous setting overlooking the valley, this is a must for foodies. Sample the boutique wines and the smoked, deboned salmon trout, its delicately flavoured signature dish. There are some luxurious rooms if you can't bear to leave.

Bread & Wine (☏021-876 3692; Môreson Wine Farm, Happy Valley Rd; mains R65-105; ⏱lunch) Hidden away down a dirt road as you approach Franschhoek along Rte 45, Bread & Wine is known for its breads, pizzas, cured meats and tasty Mediterranean-style cuisine.

Backsberg Restaurant (☏021-875 5952; www.backsberg.co.za; Simondium Rd, Klapmuts; mains R75-110; ⏱breakfast & lunch daily; 🚻) The leafy terrace is a great location for summer lunches and there's a fire indoors for winter days. There are simple home-style South African dishes on the menu and it's known for its Sunday lamb spit-braai (R170). There's a children's playground and a menu designed for little ones.

CRAFT MARKET MARKET
(⏱9am-5pm Mon-Sat) Near the Braak, this small market is a great place to haggle for African carvings, paintings and costume jewellery.

Franschhoek

Explore

The most compact of the Winelands towns, Franschhoek is the best option for those without wheels – presuming you don't mind taking a taxi from Stellenbosch to get here. Begin your explorations at the Huguenot Memorial Museum to discover Franschhoek's French roots and how it came to be a prime winemaking town. From here you can amble along Huguenot St, perusing menus and shopping for arts and crafts. Enjoy lunch at one of the country's top restaurants before delving into the myriad wine tasting options – many are within walking distance of the main road. If you have a car – and a designated driver – explore either the vineyards west of the town or the Franschhoek Pass to the east.

The Best...

➡ **Sight** Boschendal (p157)
➡ **Place to Eat** The Tasting Room (p159)
➡ **Place to Drink** Chamonix (p157)

Top Tip

Franschhoek is considered the gastronomic capital of the Cape and a number of local restaurants offer cooking courses led by award-winning chefs. Enquire at the tourist office for details.

Getting There & Away

Trains from Cape Town run to Stellenbosch (1st/economy class R13/7.50, about one hour). From here you can get a shared minibus taxi (R20) or a private taxi (☑083 951 1733).

Need to Know

➡ **Area Code** ☑021
➡ **Location** Franschhoek is 85km east of Cape Town along the N1 and Rte 45
➡ **Tourist Office** (☑876 2861; www. franschhoek.org.za; 62 Huguenot St; ☺8am-6pm Mon-Fri, 9am-5pm Sat, 9am-4pm Sun)

◉ SIGHTS

BOSCHENDAL   WINERY
(☑870 4210; www.boschendal.com; Rte 310, Groot Drakenstein; tastings R20; ☺9am-5.30pm) You'll need transport to reach this quintessential Winelands estate, with lovely architecture, food and wine. Its reds, including cabernet sauvignon and shiraz, get top marks. The tours of the vineyard (R35) and cellars (R25) are well worth it; booking is essential. For a dose of history with your wine, take the self-guided tour of the **manor house** (R15). Boschendal has three eating options: the huge buffet lunch (R240) in the main restaurant, light lunches in **Le Café** or 'Le Pique Nique' hamper (adult/child R150/59; bookings essential), served under parasols on the lawn from September to May – bookings essential.

 SOLMS-DELTA   WINERY
(☑874 3937; www.solms-delta.com; Delta Rd, off R45; tastings R10; ☺9am-5pm Sun & Mon, 9am-6pm Tue-Sat) This enlightened wine farm – a joint venture between South African Mark Solms, Richard Astor from the UK and their farm workers – goes from strength to strength. In addition to their excellent **Museum Van de Caab**, which tells the story of the wine farm from the perspective of farm workers throughout the years, there's also the **Dik Delta Fynbos Culinary Gardens** of indigenous plants; **Fyndraai** restaurant serving delicious food with inventive Cape Malay influences, as well as picnics that can be enjoyed along an enchanting trail beside the Dwars River (look for the towering bamboo grove); and a second museum, **Music Van der Caab**, tracing the origins and development of the Cape's Creole style of music.

LA MOTTE   WINERY
(☑876 8000; www.la-motte.com; Main Rd; tastings R30; ☺9am-5pm Mon-Sat) There's enough to keep you occupied for a full day at this vast estate just west of Franschhoek. As well as tasting their superb shiraz range, wine-pairing lunches and dinners are served at the **Pierneef à la Motte** restaurant. The restaurant is named for South African artist Jacob Hendrik Pierneef and a collection of his work is on show at the onsite museum. This is also the starting point for historical walks through the estate, taking in four national monuments and a milling demonstration and ending with a bread tasting (Wednesday 10am, bookings essential). If you've over-indulged, walk off a few calories on the 5km circular hike that starts from the farm.

CHAMONIX   WINERY
(☑876 8426; www.chamonix.co.za; Uitkyk St; tastings R20; ☺9.30am-4.30pm) Chamonix has cellar tours at 11am and 3pm by appointment (R10). The tasting room is in a converted blacksmith's; there's also a range of schnapps and grappa to sample. The pretty, bistro-style restaurant, **Mon Plaisir** (mains R135-200; ☺lunch Tue-Sun, dinner Wed-Sat), has a French menu featuring seasonal produce. There are also well-priced cottages in which visitors can self-cater amid the vineyards.

MONT ROCHELLE   WINERY
(☑876 3000; www.montrochelle.co.za; Dassenberg Rd; tastings R20; ☺tastings 10am-7pm, tours 11am, 12.30pm & 3pm Mon-Fri, 11am & 3pm Sat & Sun) Combine wine tasting with a cheese platter (R75) or enjoy lunch (mains R50-90) with a superb view of the town and the mountains beyond. The white wines, particularly the chardonnay, are sublime.

Franschhoek

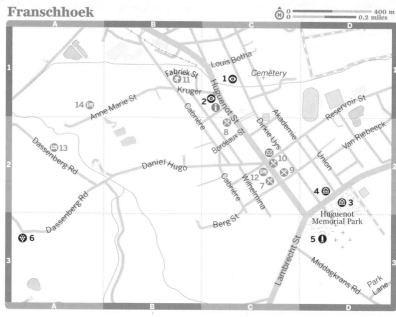

Franschhoek

HAUTE CABRIÈRE   WINERY
(☎021-876 8500; www.cabriere.co.za; Fran-schhoek Pass Rd; tastings from R30; ☺9am-5pm Mon-Fri, 10am-4pm Sat, 11am-3pm Sun) Tasting options include their MCC and the excellent range of white and red wines plus a brandy. During the Saturday session, stand by for the proprietor's party trick of *sabrage:* slic-ing open a bottle of bubbly with a sword. Cellar tours (R50) at 11am and 3pm.

GRANDE PROVENCE   WINERY
(☎876 8600; www.grandeprovence.co.za; Main Rd; tastings R20; ☺10am-6pm) A beautifully revamped, 18th-century manor house

that is home to a stylish restaurant and a splendid gallery showcasing contemporary South African art. Tasting the flagship Grande Provence red costs an extra R80.

**HUGUENOT FINE
CHOCOLATES**   CHOCOLATIER
(☎876 4096; www.huguenotchocolates.com; 62 Huguenot St; ☺8am-5pm Mon-Fri, 9am-5.30pm Sat & Sun) An empowerment program gave the two local guys who run this chocolatier a leg up and now people are raving about their confections. Call in advance to ar-range a tour and chocolate-making demon-stration, which includes a tasting (R35).

CERAMICS GALLERY   GALLERY
(☑876 4304; 24 Dirkie Uys St; ⊙10am-5pm) You can watch David Walters, one of South Africa's most distinguished potters, at work in the beautifully restored home of Franschhoek's first schoolteacher. There are also exhibits of work by other artists.

HUGUENOT MEMORIAL MUSEUM   MUSEUM
(☑876 2532; Lambrecht St; adult/child R10/5; ⊙9am-5pm Mon-Sat, 2-5pm Sun) This **museum** celebrates South Africa's Huguenots and houses the genealogical records of their descendants. Some of the names of the original settlers, such as Malan, de Villiers and Roux, are among the most famous Afrikaner dynasties in the country. Behind the main complex is a pleasant cafe; in front is the **Huguenot Monument** (admission free; ⊙9am-5pm), opened in 1948; and across the road is the **annexe**, which offers displays on the Anglo-Boer War and natural history.

 EATING & DRINKING

COMMON ROOM   MODERN SOUTH AFRICAN **$$**
(☑876 2151; 16 Huguenot St; mains R45-85; ⊙breakfast, lunch & dinner) The recently revamped bistro option at Le Quartier Français still offers South African ingredients like wildebeest and crayfish in modern, original dishes. Also here is the **Tasting Room** (5-course meal R620; ⊙dinner), consistently rated as one of the world's 50 top restaurants by *Restaurant Magazine* UK. If you're really serious about food, chef

Margot Janse will whip up the gourmet, nine-course menu for R770 (R1150 with wine pairings).

REUBEN'S   FUSION **$$**
(☑876 3772; 19 Huguenot St; mains R80-220; ⊙breakfast, lunch & dinner) The flagship restaurant for local celebrity chef Reuben Riffel has a deli-style eatery and courtyard for breakfast and lunch. Dinner is served in the restaurant.

KALFI'S   MODERN SOUTH AFRICAN **$**
(☑021-8876 2520; 17 Huguenot St; mains R55-190; ⊙breakfast, lunch & dinner; ☑ ⊞) You can watch the world go by from the shady verandah of this family-oriented restaurant. There's a children's menu and a number of vegetarian options.

**FARM KITCHEN
AT GOEDERUST**   MODERN SOUTH AFRICAN **$**
(☑876 3687; Main Rd, La Motte; mains R60-105; ⊙breakfast & lunch Tue-Sun) A new take on Cape farm-kitchen food is served in this charming old-fashioned farm-restaurant that's set in a pleasant garden. On Sundays there's a spit-braai (barbecue) lamb buffet (bookings essential). The farm stall sells local, seasonal produce.

FRENCH CONNECTION   INTERNATIONAL **$$**
(☑021-876 4056; 48 Huguenot St; mains R70-125; ⊙lunch & dinner) No-nonsense bistro-style food using only fresh ingredients is dished up at this deservedly popular place.

DAY TRIPS & WINERIES FRANSCHHOEK

SLEEPING IN FRANSCHHOEK

➡ **Reeden Lodge** (☑876 3174; www.reedenlodge.co.za; Anne Marie St; cottage from R600per night; ☒ ⊞) A good-value, terrific option for families, with well-equipped cottages sleeping up to eight self-catering people, situated on a farm about 10 minutes' walk from town. Parents will love the peace and quiet and their kids will enjoy the sheep, tree house and open space.

➡ **Otter's Bend Lodge** (☑876 3200; www.ottersbendlodge.co.za; Dassenberg Rd; campsite R100 per site, s/d R250/450) A delightful budget option in a town lacking in affordable accommodation. Double rooms lead onto a shared deck shaded by poplar trees or there's space for a couple of tents on the lawn. It's a 15-minute walk from town and close to the Mont Rochelle winery.

➡ **Le Quartier Français** (☑876 2151; www.lequartier.co.za; 16 Huguenot St; d from R3900; ☒ @ ☒) One of the best places to stay in the Winelands. Set around a leafy courtyard and pool, guest rooms are very large with fireplaces, huge beds and stylish decor. There's a bistro here as well as arguably the country's top restaurant, the Tasting Room.

🏃 SPORTS & ACTIVITIES

PARADISE STABLES
HORSE RIDING

(☏876 2160; www.paradisestables.co.za; per hr R200; ☺Mon-Sat) As well as hourly rides through Franschhoek's surrounds, there are four-hour trips taking in two vineyards (R600 including tastings).

MANIC CYCLES
CYCLING

(☏876 4956; www.maniccycles.co.za; Fabriek St; half/full day R120/200) You can rent bikes or join a guided cycling tour visiting three different wine estates (R315).

Paarl

Explore

The main drawback to the oft-overlooked Paarl is how spread out the town is – the main road stretches for 11km, making your own transport necessary if you want to explore in depth. If you're interested in history, start at the northern end of town, where the two small museums sit a couple of blocks apart. Paarl's restaurants are all in the centre of town, while two wineries flank the southern entrance as you approach from the N1. If you're arriving by train, these are both an easy walk from the station. Paarl's main attractions, though, all lie out of the town itself. There's a cluster of wine estates on the Suid-Agter-Paarl Rd, west of the centre, and another group due south on the WR1.

The Best...

➡ **Sight** Fairview (p160)
➡ **Place to Eat** Bosman's Restaurant (p162)
➡ **Activity** A balloon ride over the Winelands (p161)

Top Tip

In February and March look out for harvest festivals at the wineries, where you get chance to pick and stomp grapes to a backdrop of live entertainment.

Getting There & Away

Train Metrorail (☏0800 656 463) operates frequent trains from Cape Town (1st/economy class R16/10, 1¼ hours).

Need to Know

➡ **Area Code** ☏021
➡ **Location** Paarl is 63km east of Cape Town along the N1
➡ **Tourist Office** (☏872 4842; www.paarlonline.com; 216 Main St; ☺8am-5pm Mon-Fri, 10am-1pm Sat & Sun)

👁 SIGHTS & ACTIVITIES

FAIRVIEW
WINERY

(☏863 2450; www.fairview.co.za; Suid-Agter-Paarl Rd; wine & cheese tasting R25; ☺9am-5pm) This hugely popular estate on the Suid-Agter-Paarl Rd, off Rte 101 6km south of Paarl, is a wonderful winery but not the place to come for a calm tasting. It is great value though, since tasting options cover some 30 wines *and* a wide range of goats'- and cows'-milk cheeses.

SPICE ROUTE
WINERY

(☏863 5200; www.spiceroutewines.co.za; Suid-Agter-Paarl Rd; tastings with/without cellar tour R35/25; ☺9am-5pm Sun-Thu, 9am-6pm Fri & Sat) Owned by Charles Back of Fairview, Spice Route is known for its complex red wines, particularly the flagship syrah. Aside from wine there is a lot going on here, including glass-blowing demonstrations, food and wine pairings and a restaurant (mains R90–135). Plans to open a chocolate factory, distillery and microbrewery were underway when this guide was being researched.

BACKSBERG
WINERY

(☏875 5141; www.backsberg.co.za; Simondium Rd, Klapmuts; tastings R15; ☺8am-5pm Mon-Fri, 9.30am-4.30pm Sat, 10.30am-4.30pm Sun) Backsberg is an immensely popular estate thanks to its reliable label and lavish outdoor lunches (see boxed text p156). This was South Africa's first carbon-neutral wine farm and its wines include the easy-drinking Tread Lightly range, packaged in lightweight, environmentally-friendly bottles.

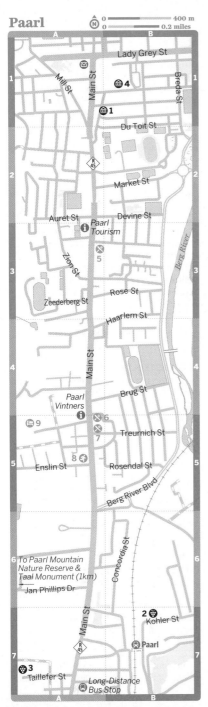

Paarl

◎ **Sights**	**(p160)**
1 Afrikaans Language Museum	B1
2 KWV Emporium	B7
3 Laborie Cellar	A7
4 Paarl Museum	B1

✪ **Eating**	**(p163)**
Harvest at Laborie	(see 3)
5 Kikka	A3
6 Marc's Mediterranean Cuisine & Garden	A5
7 Noop	A5

✪ **Sports & Activities**	**(p163)**
8 Wineland Ballooning	A5

🛏 **Sleeping**	**(p163)**
9 Grande Roche Hotel	A5

NEDERBURG WINES WINERY

(☏862 3104; www.nederburg.co.za; Sonstraal Rd; tastings R20-85; ⊙8am-5pm Mon-Fri year-round, plus 10am-4pm Sat, 11am-4pm Sun Nov-Mar) This is one of South Africa's most well known labels, a big but professional and welcoming operation featuring a vast range of wines. Inventive tasting options include a brandy, coffee and biscotti experience and the Burgermaster Tasting – pairing reserve wines with a range of mini burgers. Nederburg is off the N1, 7km east of Paarl.

KWV EMPORIUM WINERY

(☏807 3007; www.kwvwineemporium.co.za; Kohler St; cellar tour with tastings R35; ⊙9am-4pm Mon-Sat, 11am-4pm Sun) This is a good first stop when exploring the Paarl region. Its fortified wines, in particular, are among the world's best. **Cellar tours** take place at 10am, 10.30am and 2.15pm and there is a range of tasting options, including chocolate and brandy (R40). It's a two-minute walk from the train station – ideal if you're arriving on public transport.

LABORIE CELLAR WINERY

(☏807 3390; Taillefer St; tastings R15; ⊙9am-5pm Mon-Fri, 10am-5pm Sat) Best known for its award-winning shiraz, Laborie also produces good MCC and dessert wines. Tasting options including wine and olives (R22), chocolate (R35) or combining their vintages with an estate tour (R30). There's an excellent artisanal food market held here on Saturday mornings. It's just off Main St

BABYLONSTOREN

This 250 hectare wine and fruit farm, on the north slope of the Simonsberg mountain between Klapmuts and Paarl, has existed for over 300 years, but never used to figure on the Winelands tourism trail. All that began to change in 2007, when **Babylonstoren** (☑863 3852; www.babylonstoren.com; Simondium Rd, Klapmuts; entry R10; ◷10am-4pm daily; ℗) passed to new owners with the vision to transform it into one of the region's must-see destinations.

The estate's highlight is an eight-hectare, formally designed garden of edible and medicinal plants containing everything from lotus ponds and espaliered quince trees to chicken coops and a maze of prickly-pear cacti. Inspired by Cape Town's Company's Gardens and French medieval monastery gardens it is an incredible undertaking; reserve a place on one of their **garden tours** (10am and 4pm daily) or, better yet, check into one of the super-chic guest rooms (from R4270), crafted from the old workers' cottages, so that once the day visitors have left you can enjoy the gardens – not to mention the spa and pool in one of the farm's old reservoir tanks.

There's no need to reserve if you'd like refreshments in the tea garden with its lovely glasshouse. However, bookings are essential for the restaurant **Babel** (mains R140; ◷9am-4pm Wed-Sun), which serves delicious meals made with produce from the garden and quaffable wines that the farm has recently resumed making. The new wine cellar (of which tours are available) is a model of contemporary design with interesting exhibits related to the wine-making process. And the tasting room/deli/bakery showcases a selection of wines from estates around Simonsberg which is said to have some of the best terroir in the Cape.

and not far from the train station and the long-distance bus stop.

GLEN CARLOU
WINERY

(☑875 5528; www.glencarlou.co.za; Simondium Rd, Klapmuts; tastings R25-35; ◷8.30am-5pm Mon-Fri, 10am-4pm Sat & Sun) Sitting south of the N1, the tasting room here has a panoramic view of Tortoise Hill. Enjoy a glass of their sumptuous chardonnay or renowned bordeaux blend, Grand Classique, over lunch (mains R85–150). There's an art gallery here housing works of world-famous artists such as Andy Goldsworthy, Ouattara Watts and Deryck Healey.

LANDSKROON
WINERY

(☑863 1039; www.landskroonwines.com; Suid-Agter-Paarl Rd; tastings R10; ◷8am-5pm Mon-Fri, 9am-1pm Sat) Next door to Spice Route, this estate represents five generations of the De Villiers family. Overlooking the vines there's a nice terrace on which you can quaff their impressive cinsaut and port.

WINELAND BALLOONING
SCENIC FLIGHTS

(☑021-863 3192; 64 Main St; per person R2580) You'll need to get up very early in the morning, but a hot-air balloon trip over the Winelands will be unforgettable. Trips run between November and May when the weather conditions are right.

DRAKENSTEIN PRISON
HISTORIC SITE

On 11 February 1990, when Nelson Mandela walked free from incarceration for the first time in more than 27 years, the jail in question was not Robben Island, but here. There's a superb statue of him, fist raised in *viva* position, at the entrance. Then called the Victor Verster, this prison on Rte 310 was where Mandela spent his last two years of captivity in the relative comfort of the warder's cottage, negotiating the end of apartheid. It's still a working prison so there are no tours, but there is a grill-style **restaurant** (reservations ☑864 8095).

PAARL MOUNTAIN NATURE RESERVE
PARK

The three giant granite domes that dominate this popular reserve and loom over the western side of town glisten like pearls when washed by rain – hence the name 'Paarl'. The reserve has mountain *fynbos* (literally 'fine bush'; primarily proteas, heaths and ericas), a cultivated wildflower garden in the middle that's a delightful picnic spot, and numerous walks with excellent views over the valley. A map showing walking trails is available from Paarl Tourism.

While up this way you could also visit the **Taal Monument** (☑872 3441; adult/child R15/5; ☺8am-5pm), a giant needlelike edifice that commemorates the Afrikaans language (*taal* is Afrikaans for 'language'). On a clear day there are stunning views all the way to Cape Town.

PAARL MUSEUM   MUSEUM
(☑872 2651; 303 Main St; admission R5; ☺9am-5pm Mon-Fri, 9am-1pm Sat) Housed in the Oude Pastorie (Old Parsonage), built in 1714, this museum has an interesting collection of Cape Dutch antiques and relics of Huguenot and early Afrikaner culture. There's a bookcase modelled on King Solomon's temple and displays about the 'road to reconciliation', the old mosques of the local Muslim community and slavery.

AFRIKAANS LANGUAGE MUSEUM   MUSEUM
Paarl is considered the wellspring of the Afrikaans language, a fact covered by this interesting **museum** (☑872 3441; www.taal museum.co.za; 11 Pastorie Ave; adult/child R15/5; ☺9am-4pm Mon-Fri). It also shows, thanks to a multimedia exhibition, how three continents contributed to the formation of this fascinating language. Follow up a visit here with a visit to the somewhat phallic Taal Monument.

✕ EATING & DRINKING

HARVEST AT
LABORIE   MODERN SOUTH AFRICAN $$
(☑807 3095; Taillefer St; mains R70-115; ☺breakfast Sat, lunch Mon-Sun, dinner Wed-Sat) Eat on a patio overlooking vines at this elegant

wine estate a short walk from Main Street. Local produce dominates the menu, including West Coast mussels, Karoo lamb and seasonal game steaks.

NOOP   FUSION $$
(☑863 3925; 127 Main St; mains R95-135; ☺lunch & dinner Mon-Fri) Recommended by locals all over the Winelands, this restaurant and wine bar has a small but excellent menu and fresh salads.

MARC'S MEDITERRANEAN
CUISINE & GARDEN   MEDITERRANEAN $$
(☑863 3980; 129 Main St; mains R90-140; ☺lunch & dinner Mon-Sat, lunch Sun) Another favourite, and with good reason. Patron Marc Friedrich has created a light and bright place with food to match and a Provence-style garden to dine in.

KIKKA   CAFE $
(☑872 0685; 217 Main St; mains R20-70; ☺7.30am-5pm Mon-Fri, 7.30am-3pm Sat) Watch florists at work in this delightful deli and cafe with its funky, retro decor. It's a great spot for breakfast and people watching.

Hermanus

Explore
On arrival, make a beeline straight for the Old Harbour – still the hub of the town. In whale season (June–December) you're likely to spot whales from here while all year it's the site of the town's museums, a permanent craft market and many superb restaurants, cafes and hotels. From here, the

---

SLEEPING IN PAARL

➡ **Berg River Resort** (☑863 1650; www.bergriverresort.co.za; off Rte 45; campsites from R55, d chalets from R425; ✖⛲) An attractive camping ground beside the Berg River, 5km from Paarl on the N45 towards Franschhoek. Facilities include canoes, trampolines and a cafe. It gets very crowded during school holidays and is best avoided then.

➡ **Grande Roche Hotel** (☑863 2727; www.granderoche.co.za; Plantasie St; d from R3025; ✖@☀) A super-luxurious hotel set in a Cape Dutch manor house, offering wonderful mountain views, a heated swimming pool and the award-winning **Bosman's Restaurant** (mains from R130), whose wine list runs for more than 40 pages! There's a tasting menu of eight courses for R660.

Cliff Path Walking Trail takes you either southwest to the restaurants, bars and boat trips of the New Harbour or east to Grotto Beach, a 4km walk. In whale season, Hermanus quickly gets overcrowded, but it's easy enough to escape. Try the beaches to the east or the mountains to the north or, if you're keen to follow a lesser-trodden wine-tasting path, seek out the Hemel-en-Aarde Valley (see boxed text p165).

The Best...

➡ **Sight** Cliff Path walking trail (p163)
➡ **Place to Eat** Fisherman's Cottage (p164)
➡ **Place to Drink** Gecko Bar (p164)

Top Tip

In whale season keep your eyes – and ears – peeled for the whale crier, who belts out a Morse code signal on his kelp horn whenever he spots a whale.

Getting There & Away

Taxi Trevi's Tours (☏072 608 9213) offers daily shuttles to and from Cape Town (R800 one-way, 1½ hours).

Need to Know

➡ **Area Code** ☏028
➡ **Location** Hermanus is 122km east of Cape Town along the N2 and Rte 43.
➡ **Tourist Office** (☏312 2629; www.hermanus.co.za; Old Station Bldg, Mitchell St; ⏱8am-6pm Mon-Fri, 9am-5pm Sat, 11am-3pm Sun)

◉ SIGHTS

CLIFF PATH WALKING TRAIL   HIKING

The path meanders for 10km from the New Harbour, 2km west of town, along the sea to the mouth of the Klein River, though you can join it anywhere along the cliffs.

Along the way you'll pass Grotto Beach, the most popular beach, which has excellent facilities, Kwaaiwater, a good whale-watching lookout, and Langbaai and Voelklip Beaches.

OLD HARBOUR   MUSEUM

The old harbour clings to the cliffs in front of the town centre; the **museum** (☏312 1475;

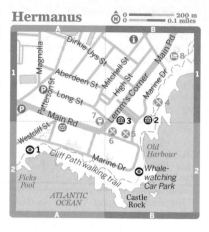

adult/child R15/5; ⏱9am-1pm & 2-5pm Mon-Sat, noon-4pm Sun) doesn't really have a lot going for it, but outside there's a display of old fishing boats. The admission fee includes entrance to the more interesting **Whale House Museum** (⏱9am-4pm Mon-Sat, whale shows 10am & 3pm) and the **Photographic Museum** (⏱9am-4pm Mon-Fri, 9am-1pm Sat) located on Market Square. There's a permanent craft market in the square as well.

FREE **FERNKLOOF NATURE RESERVE**   PARK

(☏313 8100; fernkloof.com; Fir Ave; ⏱9am-5pm) This 1400-hectare reserve is wonderful if you're interested in *fynbos*. Researchers have identified 1474 species so far. There's a 60km network of hiking trails for all fitness levels and the views over the sea are spectacular.

✕ EATING & DRINKING

FISHERMAN'S COTTAGE   SEAFOOD $$
(☎312 3642; Lemm's Corner; mains R55-120; ☺lunch & dinner Mon-Sat) The emphasis is on excellent seafood at this 1860s thatched cottage draped with fishing nets, though they also serve steaks and traditional meals.

BURGUNDY RESTAURANT   SEAFOOD $$
(☎312 2800; Marine Dr; mains R60-140; ☺breakfast, lunch & dinner) Booking is recommended at this eatery, one of the most acclaimed and popular in the area. The menu is mostly seafood with a different vegetarian dish each day.

BIENTANG'S CAVE   SEAFOOD $$
(☎028-312 3454; www.bientangscave.com; Marine Dr; mains R80-150; ☺breakfast & lunch) You can get closer to the whales here than on any boat trip. This really is a cave, occupied by the last Strandlopers (coastal indigenous people) at the turn of the 19th century. Its remarkable setting obscures the fact that the restaurant is only so-so. Access is only via a steep flight of cliffside stairs.

GECKO BAR   BAR
(☎312 4665; New Harbour; mains R45-75; ☺lunch & dinner) With wood-fired pizzas, beer from Birkenhead brewery in Stanford and a deck hanging over the ocean, this is a top spot for sundowners that tend to turn into late night drinks. There's live music on weekends.

ZEBRA CROSSING   PUB
(☎312 3906; 121 Main Rd; mains R40-90; ☺breakfast, lunch & dinner) This bar with a funky zebra theme is a great late-night party spot on weekends, and popular with backpackers.

🏃 SPORTS & ACTIVITIES

WHALE WATCHING   BOAT TRIPS
While Hermanus is renowned for its land-based whale watching, boat trips are also available. Approaching whales in the water is highly regulated and the boats must stay a minimum of 50m from the whales. There are only two licensed boat operators, **Southern Right Charters** (☎082 353 0550; www.southernrightcharters.co.za) and **Hermanus Whale Cruises** (☎313 2722; www. hermanus-whale-cruises.co.za). Two-hour trips with both companies cost R600 (R250 for children) and leave from the New Harbour. Out of season, other boat trips are available.

WALKER BAY ADVENTURES   WATER SPORTS
(☎082 739 0159; www.walkerbayadventures. co.za; kayaking R300, canoeing R450, boat-based whale-watching R650) A vast range of activities is on offer, including sea-kayaking tours that give you the opportunity to see whales up close and personal. The company also rents kayaks and boats.

SLEEPING IN HERMANUS

There is a huge amount of accommodation in Hermanus, but you might still find yourself searching in vain for a bed in the holiday season, so book ahead.

➡ **Potting Shed** (☎312 1712; www.thepottingshedguesthouse.co.za; 28 Albertyn St; s/d incl breakfast R525/700; @☒) An excellent-value guest house enjoyed by readers. The neat rooms are comfortable and have bright, imaginative decor. A unit, in which four people can self-cater, is also available.

➡ **Hermanus Backpackers** (☎312 4293; www.hermanusbackpackers.co.za; 26 Flower St; dm R130, d with shared bathroom R350, d R380; @☒) This is a great place with upbeat decor, good facilities and clued-up staff who can help with activities. Free breakfast is served in the morning, and evening braais are R90.

➡ **Marine** (☎313 1000; www.marine-hermanus.co.za; Marine Dr; s/d incl breakfast from R2500/4000; ✳@☒) Right on the sea with immaculate grounds and amenities. The hotel has two restaurants, both sea-facing. The **Pavilion** (mains R95 to R175, ☺breakfast and dinner) serves contemporary South African cuisine while the **Seafood Restaurant** (☺lunch and dinner) offers two-/three-course meals for R195/240.

WORTH A DETOUR

OCEAN DRIVE

If you have an extra half an hour to spare, taking the ocean road to Hermanus is a spectacular way to arrive and only adds 30 minutes to your trip. As you reach Strand, veer off the N2 onto Rte 44, a road that hugs the coast once you reach Gordon's Bay. Known as Clarence Drive, this coastal route is a very worthy alternative to Cape Town's Chapman's Peak Drive but without the toll. Allow time to stop at the many lookout points for photos and between June and December keep an eye on False Bay for frolicking whales. There are a few worthy stops en route, starting with the **Kogelberg Nature Reserve** (028-271 4792; www.capenature.co.za; adult/child R30/15). The reserve has the most complex biodiversity on the planet, including over 1880 plant species. Day walks are available as well as mountain-biking routes, but all activities must be prebooked. Do take the time to stop at the **Stony Point African Penguin Colony** (028-271 8400; admission R10; 8am-5pm). It's a much quieter place to watch the diminutive penguins than at the infinitely more famous Boulders Beach, on the other side of False Bay. After driving through Betty's Bay, you'll find the **Harold Porter National Botanical Gardens** (028-272 9311; adult/child R17/7; 8am-4.30pm Mon-Fri, 8am-5pm Sat & Sun), worth a quick visit. There are paths exploring the indigenous plant life in the area and, at the entrance, a tearoom and plenty of places to picnic. Pretty **Kleinmond** is a good place for a seafood lunch on the water.

Stanford

Explore

As you approach along the Rte 43 from Hermanus, look out for Stanford's uncrowded wineries, stopping off for tastings, tours or lunch. Once in Stanford, it's best to park and explore the often-deserted streets on foot. Skirt the Village Green and make your way down to the star attraction – the Klein River. Here you'll find boat trips, canoes for hire and plenty of spots for a picnic or birdwatching. End your explorations at the brewery just outside the village, or exploring more vineyards to the east of Stanford.

The Best...

➡ **Sight** Klein River (p166)
➡ **Place to Eat** Mariana's (p166)
➡ **Place to Drink** Birkenhead Brewery (p166)

Top Tip

Stock up on meat and drinks before boarding one of Stanford's river cruises. The African Queen and River Rat both have braai facilities on board and BYO is encouraged.

Getting There & Away

You really need your own car to reach Stanford. It's 24km east of Hermanus.

Need to Know

➡ **Area Code** 028
➡ **Location** Stanford is 145km east of Cape Town
➡ **Tourist Office** (341 0340; www.stanfordinfo.co.za; 18 Queen Victoria St; 8.30am-5pm Mon-Fri, 9am-4pm Sat, 9am-1pm Sun)

◉ SIGHTS

RIVER CRUISES BOAT TRIPS

There are three companies offering cruises along the Klein River. **African Queen** (082 732 1284) is the largest boat, while **River Rat** (083 310 0952) and **Platanna** (073 318 5078) offer a more intimate experience. All charge R100 per person for a three-hour trip and allow swimming from the boat. River Rat also offers canoe hire and specialised birdwatching boat trips.

ROBERT STANFORD ESTATE WINERY

(341 0441; tastings free; 9am-4pm Thu-Mon) You could easily spend a morning at this gracious estate, tasting their excellent sauvignon blanc, visiting the on-site grappa distillery and enjoying a host of family-friendly activities including horse or tractor rides through the vines and picnics to enjoy in the grounds. There's a restaurant

here too, serving dishes made with fresh farm produce.

KLEIN RIVER CHEESE FARM FARM

(📞341 0693; www.kleinrivercheese.co.za; ⊗9am-5pm Mon-Fri, 9am-1pm Sat; 🖻) There are various cheeses available to sample, including a wonderful gruyère, and staff will explain the cheese-making process. Picnics are available from November to May (for two/children's basket R220/45) to enjoy on the riverbank and children will love the petting zoo and playground.

RAKA WINERY

(📞341 0676; www.rakawine.co.za; tastings free; ⊗9am-5pm Mon-Fri, 10am-2.30pm Sat) There's no restaurant or other activities here, but Raka is worth a stop for their highly awarded cool-weather red wines, including the Biography Shiraz, Bordeaux-style Figurehead blend and their merlot, malbec and cabernet sauvignon.

EATING & DRINKING

TOP CHOICE BIRKENHEAD BREWERY BREWERY $

(📞341 0183; www.birkenhead.co.za; brewery tours 11am & 3pm Wed-Fri; ⊗11am-5pm Wed-Sun) Sitting just outside the village, Birkenhead boasts the prettiest grounds of any of the Western Cape breweries. Tastings (R20) of their varied range of craft brews can take place out on the lawns in summer or in front of a roaring log fire in winter. Meals (R60–90) are also available and there is a winery on site as well.

MARIANA'S SOUTH AFRICAN $$

(📞341 0272; 12 Du Toit St; mains R60-110; ⊗lunch Thu-Sun; 🖋) This long-running country restaurant is as popular as ever so bookings are essential. Much of the menu features produce grown in the restaurant's garden and there's plenty for vegetarians.

LOCAL KNOWLEDGE

ELGIN VALLEY – CATHY MARSTON

Around 70km southeast of Cape Town, en route to Hermanus and just over the spectacular Sir Lowry's Pass is **Elgin**, part of the world's first biodiversity wine route, the **Green Mountain Eco Route** (www.greenmountain.co.za). Apart from delicious wines there are plenty of scenic walks in the area as well as a mountain-biking route through Oak Valley along well-marked trails.

We asked Cathy Marston, wine journalist and educator, about the area's best wineries and places to eat:

'Much lauded for its cool-climate whites such as sauvignon blanc and chardonnay, Elgin has also produced some of the country's top pinot noirs from the likes of **Catherine Marshall Wines** (📞083 258 1307; www.cmwines.co.za), **Shannon Vineyards** (📞021-859 2491; www.shannonwines.com), **Oak Valley** (📞021-859 2510; www.oakvalley. co.za) and **Paul Cluver Wines** (📞021-844 0605; www.cluver.com), where, if you're lucky, you might catch top local and international performers at the Paul Cluver Amphitheatre set among the trees – they offer picnic baskets and exquisite wines.

Turn off past the **Peregrine Farmstall**, meander down scenic lanes through stunning scenery, and taste at will. There's also great food to be had at **South Hill Wines** (📞021-844 0033; www.southhill.co.za) and black empowerment wine farm **Thandi** (📞021-844 01247; www.thandiwines.com), while a **Highlands Road** (📞021-849 8699; www.highlandsroadestate.co.za) pizza night is not to be missed!'

If you choose to stay over, **Old Mac Daddy** (📞021-844 0245; www.oldmacdaddy. co.za; 112 The Valley Rd, Grabouw; d Sun-Thu/Fri & Sat R750/1200; 🅿✳@🛜🌊) is a luxury trailer park, each Airstream caravan boasting a different themed interior design. Rustically stylish attached lounges and bathrooms give space to spread out. There's a wonderful playroom and kids aged six to 16 are charged just R175 a night, making it a brilliant place to bring the family.

!KHWA TTU

Billed as the San Culture & Education Centre, **!Khwa ttu** (☎022-492 2998; www.khwattu.org; Rte 27, Yzerfontein; ☺9am-5pm) is a joint venture by the San people and a Swiss philanthropic foundation (Ubuntu Foundation) and is the only San-owned and operated culture centre in the Western Cape.

Set within the ancestral lands of the San, !Khwa ttu is based on an 850-hectare nature reserve. There's a good **restaurant** (mains R50-95; ☺breakfast & lunch) serving traditional South African cuisine and a wonderful craft shop. Excellent **tours** (2hr R250; ☺10am & 2pm) with a San guide involve a nature walk, a wildlife drive and learning about San culture.

You can stay and self-cater on the reserve in well-equipped **accommodation** (4-person bush camp tents R400, 4-person bush cottage R770, 6-person guest house R880). !Khwa ttu is off Rte 27 just south of Yzerfontein, 70km from Cape Town.

Darling

Explore

For many, the main reason to visit Darling is to watch the poignant and very funny political show performed by satirist Pieter-Dirk Uys. If you want to catch the cabaret, book ahead – shows are generally held on weekend lunchtimes, with the occasional evening show. There's a small museum in the tourism office, which serves as a good starting point for a day in Darling and there are a few nice spots for lunch. Once you've explored this dusty dorp, take time to check out the wineries in its outskirts and to visit the superb !Khwa ttu, south of Darling on Rte 27.

The Best...

⇒ **Sight** Evita se Perron (p168)
⇒ **Place to Eat** Marmalade Cat (p168)
⇒ **Place to Drink** Slow Quarter (p168)

Top Tip

In early and mid-spring (August to September), Darling is the perfect place to witness South Africa's famous flowers burst into bloom, with over a dozen flower reserves around the town and a wildflower festival in mid-September.

Getting There & Away

Car Rte 27 is the quickest route from Cape Town. For a scenic detour, replace the northern stretch of Rte 27 with the prettier, quieter Rte 307.

Need to Know

⇒ **Area Code** ☎022
⇒ **Location** Darling is 73km north of Cape Town.
⇒ **Tourist Office** (☎492 3361; cnr Hill Rd & Pastorie St; ☺9am-1pm & 2-4pm Mon-Thu, 9am-3.30pm Fri, 10am-3pm Sat & Sun)

◉ SIGHTS

EVITA SE PERRON   COMEDY
(Darling Station; ☎492 2831; www.evita.co.za; tickets R90; ☺performances 2pm & 7pm Sat & Sun) This uniquely South African cabaret featuring Pieter-Dirk Uys as his alter ego Tannie Evita is based in the old train station. It touches on everything from South African politics to history to ecology. Nothing is off limits – including the country's racially charged past and the AIDS epidemic. Although the shows include a smattering of Afrikaans, they're largely in English and always hilarious and thought-provoking.

The splendidly kitsch **restaurant** (mains R40-65; ☺lunch Tue-Sun) serves traditional Afrikaner food including *bobotie*. Uys also set up the **Darling Trust** (☎021-492 2851; www.thedarlingtrust.org) to assist Swartland communities to empower themselves through participation in education, skills development and health programs. The **A en C Shop** at the complex stocks beading, clothes, wire-art and paintings.

DARLING WINE & ARTS EXPERIENCE WINERY
There are five wineries within easy reach of Darling. **Groote Post** (☎492 2825;

www.grootepost.com; tastings free; ⊙9am-5pm Mon-Fri, 10am-4pm Sat & Sun) has the most to offer the visitor, with wildlife drives, nature walks, a superb restaurant and, of course, free tastings of their excellent chardonnays and sauvignon blancs. **Ormonde Private Cellar** (✆492 3540; www.ormonde.co.za; tastings R25; ⊙9am-4pm Mon-Fri, 9am-3pm Sat) is a short walk from the town centre and offers cheese and wine pairings (R55) and olive tasting as well as standard wine tastings.

✕ EATING & DRINKING

MARMALADE CAT   CAFE **$**
(✆492 2515; 19 Main Rd; mains R30-60; ⊙breakfast & lunch daily, dinner Fri & Sat) For afternoon coffee or all-day breakfast, this is the place. It also serves sandwiches, delicious cheeses and homemade sweet treats, and Friday night is pizza night – bookings essential.

SLOW QUARTER   BAR **$**
(✆492 3798; 5 Main Rd; light meals R55-85; ⊙11am-7pm Mon-Sat, closed Tue) The home base of the popular local beer, Darling Brew, is a chic place to munch on ale-inspired tapas and sip one of their four flagship beers.

GROOTE POST RESTAURANT   INTERNATIONAL **$$**
(✆492 2825; www.grootepost.com; mains R90-110; ⊙lunch Wed-Sun) Perhaps Darling's most upmarket place to dine, with a constantly changing menu that is designed to pair with Groote Post's wines.

Langebaan

Explore

When you get to Langebaan, make a beeline for the beach, whether it's for sailing, windsurfing, kitesurfing or just lounging on the white sand. The lagoon can be further explored in the West Coast National Park, which also boasts a pretty beach at Kraalbaai. For most of the year the park's main attractions are ostriches and views of the ocean and lagoon, but in August and September the park gets a temporary facelift when the spring flowers bloom. Entrance fees and visitor numbers increase considerably at this time, but it's still well worth a trip. Langebaan can easily be explored in a day, unless you're keen to take a multiday water sports course. If you stay over, pick a place close to the beach where everything is within easy walking distance.

The Best...

➡ **Sight** West Coast National Park (p169)
➡ **Place to Eat** Die Strandloper (p169)
➡ **Place to Drink** Club Mykonos (p169)

Top Tip

As well as the eateries mentioned here, there is a small strip of restaurants on Bree St, some on the beachfront with awesome sunset views.

WORTH A DETOUR

HEAVENLY WINES

If you're all whaled out and seeking some tranquillity, Hermanus is also home to a lesser-known wine route. The Hemel-en-Aarde Valley has a lot to live up to – its name translates as 'Heaven and Earth'. Luckily though, there are divine wines to be found as well as strikingly beautiful scenery. The road, Rte 320, has 15 wineries, largely known for their superlative pinot noirs and sauvignon blancs. Peter Finlayson of **Bouchard Finlayson** (✆028-312 3515; www.bouchardfinlayson.co.za; tastings free; ⊙9am-5pm Mon-Fri, 9.30am-12.30pm Sat) is known for his pioneering pinot. Taste this and the award-winning chardonnays in the atmospheric cellar. Another stand-out is **Creation Wines** (✆028-212 1107; www.creationwines.com; tastings free; ⊙10am-5pm daily), who offer a 90-minute walking tour of the farm (R350), food and wine pairing experiences (from R100) and personal cellar tours with the chance to create your own blend from their superlative wines (R350). There's a restaurant here too, open for lunch.

GANSBAAI

Gansbaai's star has risen in recent years thanks to shark-cage diving, though most people just visit on a day trip from Cape Town. The unspoilt coastline is perfect for those wishing to explore more out-of-the-way Overberg nature spots.

The road from Hermanus leads you past the village of De Kelders – a great spot for secluded whale watching – straight into Main Rd, which runs parallel to the coastline. Kleinbaai, 7km further east along the coast, is the launch point for **shark-cage diving** tours. There are a number of operators offering similar trips, though **Marine Dynamics** (028-384 1005; www.sharkwatchsa.com; R1400) has a marine biologist on board and the company works with the **Dyer Island Conservation Trust** (028-384 0406; www.dict.org.za), funding marine research in the area.

Continuing south from Kleinbaai is the **Danger Point Lighthouse** (028-384 0530; adult/child R16/8; 10am-3pm Mon-Fri) dating from 1895 and the **Walker Bay Reserve** (028-314 0062; adult/child R30/15; 7am-7pm). There's birdwatching here, some good walks and the Klipgat Caves, site of an archaeological discovery of Khoe-San artefacts.

If you're looking for lunch, try **Coffee on the Rocks** (028-384 2017; Cliff Street, De Kelders; mains R40-80; 10am-5pm Wed-Sun). All breads here are baked daily on-site and everything is homemade. The ocean-facing deck is a great place for a sandwich, a salad or just a coffee while you watch the sea during whale season.

If you don't have your own wheels, try **Trevi's Tours** (072 608 9213/028-312 1413), which has daily shuttles to and from Cape Town (R1000, two hours).

Getting There & Away

Minibus Taxi There are daily services to and from Cape Town (R70 one way, 1¼ hours).

Need to Know

→ **Area Code** 022

→ **Location** Langebaan is 127km north of Cape Town along Rte 27

→ **Tourist Office** (772 1515; www.langebaaninfo.com; Bree St; 9am-5pm Mon-Fri, 9am-2pm Sat)

◉ SIGHTS

WEST COAST NATIONAL PARK PARK
(772 2144; www.sanparks.org; adult/child Aug-Oct R88/44, Nov-Jul R44; 7am-7.30pm). Encompassing the clear, blue waters of the Langebaan Lagoon and home to an enormous number of birds, this park covers around 31,000 hectares and protects wetlands of international significance as well as important seabird breeding colonies. Wading birds flock here by the thousands in summer. The most numerically dominant species is the curlew sandpiper, which migrates north from the sub-Antarctic in huge flocks. The offshore islands are home to colonies of African penguins.

The vegetation is predominantly stunted bushes, sedges and many flowering annuals and succulents. There is some coastal *fynbos* vegetation in the east, and the park is famous for its wildflower display, usually between August and October. The park is only about 120km from Cape Town, 7km south of Langebaan. The return trip from Langebaan to the northern end of the Postberg section is more than 80km; allow plenty of time. The rainy season is between May and August.

The **Geelbek Visitors' Centre & Restaurant** (772 2134; West Coast National Park; mains R65-105; breakfast & lunch) has a broad menu specialising in traditional fare. It's also an information centre for the park and can help with accommodation options, including the houseboats moored at Kraalbaai.

WEST COAST FOSSIL PARK ARCHAEOLOGICAL SITE
The first bear discovered south of the Sahara, lion-sized sabre-toothed cats, three-toed horses and short-necked giraffes are all on display at this excellent **fossil park** (766 1606; www.fossilpark.org.za; adult/child R50/15; 8am-4pm Mon-Fri, 10am-1pm Sat & Sun) on Rte 45 about 16km outside Langebaan. Fas-

cinating tours depart hourly from 10am to 3pm (until 1pm on weekends) and take you to the excavation sites – among the richest fossil sites in the world. There are also mountain-biking and walking trails, and a coffee and gift shop.

EATING & DRINKING

TOP CHOICE **DIE STRANDLOPER** SEAFOOD **$$**
(☎772 2490; buffet R205; ⊘lunch Sat & Sun, dinner Fri & Sat, lunch & dinner daily Dec-Jan) This is the West Coast life exemplified – a *10*-course outdoor fish and seafood braai right on the beach. There's also freshly made bread, bottomless *moerkoffie* (freshly ground coffee) and a local crooner who plays West Coast ballads at your table. You can BYO (corkage free) or get drinks from the rustic bar, from which the view is sensational. Bookings are essential.

CLUB MYKONOS RESORT **$$$**
(☎0800 226 770; www.clubmykonos.co.za) This Greek-themed, pseudo-Mediterranean resort might not appeal as a place to stay over, but it is a fun spot to spend an evening. There are eight restaurants to choose from as well as numerous bars and a casino, all open to nonguests.

SPORTS & ACTIVITIES

CAPE SPORTS CENTRE WATER SPORTS
(☎772 1114; www.capesport.co.za; 98 Main Rd) Langebaan is a water sports mecca, particularly for windsurfing and kitesurfing. This cheery office offers kitesurfing courses (three-day course R2185) and windsurfing lessons (two hours R500) and rents out surfboards and kayaks (R185/295 per day).

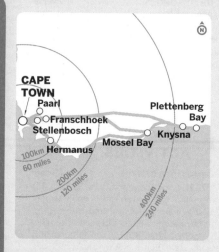

The Garden Route

High on the must-see list of most visitors is the Garden Route, named for the year-round greenery of its forests and lagoons along the coast. It stretches some 300km from Mossel Bay to just beyond Plettenberg Bay.

Mossel Bay p173

Beyond the world's largest gas-to-oil refinery you'll find beaches, gnarly surfing spots and activities including shark-cage diving and coastal hikes.

George p176

The largest town along the Garden Route boasts attractive old buildings, world-class golf courses and superb mountain drives.

Wilderness p178

Living up to its name, Wilderness is blessed with gorgeous beaches, bird-rich estuaries and sheltered lagoons backed by densely forested hills.

Knysna p179

Embracing an exquisitely beautiful lagoon and surrounded by ancient forests, Knysna is a place for hiking, sailing, mountain biking or sampling the home-grown oysters and local beer.

Plettenberg Bay p183

The verdant mountains, white sand and crystal-blue waters make 'Plett' one of the country's top tourist spots, loved by locals and foreign visitors alike.

Mossel Bay

Explore

Start your explorations at the excellent Dias Museum Complex to gain insight into Mossel Bay's role in South African history. From here it's a short hop to the harbour to take a dolphin-watching boat trip or enjoy a seafood braai at the water's edge. Head to Santos Beach to swim or relax, or peruse the restaurants and bars of Marsh Street, slowly ambling to The Point. Here you'll find a laid-back vibe and restaurants overlooking the ocean as well as the Cape St Blaize caves and lighthouse. Spend a second day shark-cage diving, surfing or sky-diving.

The Best...

➡ **Sight** Dias Museum Complex (p174)

➡ **Place to Eat** Kaai 4 (p174)

➡ **Place to Drink** Big Blu (p175)

Top Tip

Send a postcard home from South Africa's oldest 'postbox' – a tree inside the Dias Museum Complex where sailors left messages. All letters get a special postmark.

Getting There & Away

Bus Translux (☑0861 589 282; www.translux. co.za), **Greyhound** (☑011-611 8000; www.grey hound.co.za) and **Intercape** (☑0861 287 287; www.intercape.co.za) each operate regular services from Cape Town (R280, six hours, twice daily).

Need to Know

➡ **Area Code** ☑044

➡ **Location** Mossel Bay is 390km east of Cape Town along the N2.

➡ **Tourist Office** (☑691 2202; www. mosselbay.net; Market St; ☺8am-6pm Mon-Fri, 9am-4pm Sat, 9am-2pm Sun)

Mossel Bay

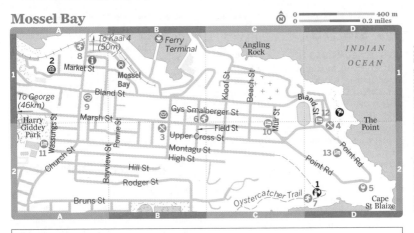

THE GARDEN ROUTE MOSSEL BAY

Garden Route

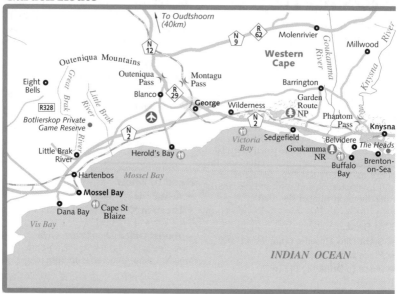

To Oudtshoorn
(40km)

Outeniqua Mountains

Western
Cape

Molenrivier

Millwood

Eight
Bells

Outeniqua
Pass

Montagu
Pass

Barrington

Garden
Route
NP

Phantom
Pass

Knysna

R328

Blanco

George

Wilderness

Botlierskop Private
Game Reserve

Little Brak
River

Herold's Bay

Victoria
Bay

Sedgefield

Belvidere

The Heads

Goukamma
NR

Buffalo
Bay

Brenton-
on-Sea

Hartenbos

Mossel Bay

Mossel Bay

Dana Bay

Cape St
Blaize

Vis Bay

INDIAN OCEAN

○ SIGHTS

DIAS MUSEUM COMPLEX MUSEUM

This excellent **museum** (☑691 1067; Market St; adult/child R20/5; ☺9am-4.45pm Mon-Fri, 9am-3.45pm Sat & Sun) includes the spring where Dias watered the postal tree, the 1786 Dutch East India Company (Vereenigde Oost-Indische Compagnie; VOC) granary, a **shell museum** (with some interesting aquarium tanks) and a local **history museum**.

The highlight of the complex is the replica of the caravel that Dias used on his 1488 voyage of discovery. Its small size brings home the extraordinary skill and courage of the early explorers. The replica was built in Portugal and sailed to Mossel Bay in 1988 to commemorate the 500th anniversary of Dias' trip. Boarding the caravel costs an extra R20.

BOTLIERSKOP PRIVATE
GAME RESERVE WILDLIFE RESERVE

This **game reserve** (☑696 6055; www.bot lierskop.co.za; Little Brak River; s/d with dinner, breakfast & game drive R2500/3340) offers the chance to stay on a ranch and view a vast range of wildlife, including lions, elephants, rhinos, buffalos and giraffes. Day visitors are welcome for a variety of activi-

ties including wildlife drives (adult/child R395/198), horseback safaris (per hour R200) and elephant rides (adult/child over six years R595/300). The reserve is about 20km east of Mossel Bay along the N2 (take the Little Brak River turnoff and follow the signs towards Sorgfontein). Booking ahead is essential.

✕ EATING & DRINKING

TOP CHOICE KAAI 4 BRAAI $

(☑079 980 3981; Mossel Bay Harbour; mains R25-60; ☺lunch & dinner) Boasting one of Mossel Bay's best locations, this low-key seafood spot has picnic tables on the sand overlooking the ocean. Food is cooked on massive fire pits and the hungry can take the all-you-can-eat option (R125).

CAFÉ HAVANA INTERNATIONAL $

(☑690 4640; 38 Marsh St; mains R50-110; ☺lunch & dinner) About as Cuban as Mossel Bay can get, this restaurant and cocktail bar has a great vibe. The stews and steaks are a nice antidote to all the seafood in Mossel Bay – though of course there's plenty of that as well. Sit inside or on the candlelit verandah and watch the world go by.

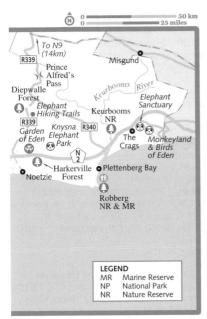

BIG BLU
BAR $$

(☎691 2010; Point Rd; mains R40-135) This ramshackle place right on the rocks at The Point draws a young crowd. It's great for a sundowner and serves burgers, seafood, steaks and tapas (R15 to R25) of a kind not found in Spain.

KINGFISHER
SEAFOOD $$

(☎690 6390; Point Rd; mains R45-120; ⊙lunch & dinner) Locals love the seafood and ocean views dished up here. You can choose between sushi, seafood platters, fish and salads, with a bit of meat too, and a children's menu.

PAVILION
INTERNATIONAL $$

(☎690 4567; Santos Beach; mains R50-150; ⊙lunch & dinner) In a 19th-century bathing pavilion modelled on the one in Brighton, this is a good choice for a beachside meal. The menu offers just about everything.

🏃 SPORTS & ACTIVITIES

ROMANZA
BOAT TRIPS

(☎690 3101) This company offers regular boat trips to view the seal colony, birds and dolphins that frequent the waters around Seal Island. **Seven Seas** (☎082-297 7165) runs similar trips and both charge R125 for an hour-long jaunt. In late winter and spring the *Romanza* also runs whale-watching trips (R600, 2½ hours).

OYSTERCATCHER TRAIL
HIKING

(☎699 1204; www.oystercatchertrail.co.za) If you have time to stick around, you can tackle this four-day (R7690) trail from Mossel Bay to Dana Bay via Cape St Blaize, where you're likely to see an endangered bird, the black oystercatcher. Included in the price are excellent accommodation and meals as well as luggage transportation en route. While out here, it's worth a stop at the **Cape St Blaize Lighthouse** (☎690 3015; adult/child R16/8; ⊙10am-3pm).

ELECTRODIVE
DIVING

(☎082 561 1259; 2 Field Street; gear hire per day R200, shore-/boat-based dives R190-230) A family-run operation offering a number of options. In addition to Professional Association of Diving Instructors (PADI) courses, it does a snorkelling trip (R190, two hours) and a short scuba course (R550, two to three hours). Although diving in Mossel Bay offers the opportunity to see quite a lot of coral, fish and other sea creatures, remember that these aren't tropical waters and you're not going to have perfect visibility.

WHITE SHARK AFRICA
WATER SPORTS

(☎691 3796; www.whitesharkafrica.com; cnr Church & Bland Sts; dives R1350) Full-day cage-diving trips to view great white sharks include breakfast, lunch and afternoon tea.

SKYDIVE MOSSEL BAY
EXTREME SPORTS

(☎082 824 8599; www.skydivemosselbay.com; Mossel Bay Airfield; from R1600). Tandem sky-dives over the bay start either from 10,000 or 12,000 feet and when the weather and tides cooperate you get to land on Diaz Beach.

BACK ROAD SAFARIS
GUIDED TOURS

(☎690 8150; www.backroadsafaris.co.za) A vast range of tours is on offer, including **Meet the People** (4hr tour per person R450), which offers home visits with traditional meals on request (R30) in nearby Friemersheim and KwaNonqaba townships – preferable to the sometimes voyeuristic township tours offered in larger cities.

THE GARDEN ROUTE MOSSEL BAY

SLEEPING IN MOSSEL BAY

There are three municipal **caravan parks** (690 3501; campsites from R190, chalet from R430) in town. Bakke and Santos are next to each other on pretty Santos Beach; Bakke is the one with chalets. Punt is on the Point and very close to the surf. Prices rise steeply in the high season.

➡ **Point Village Hotel** (690 3156; www.pointvillagehotel.co.za; 5 Point Rd; s/d R420/720; @) The quirky, fake lighthouse on this well-priced hotel's exterior is a sign of what's inside: a range of fun, funky, bright rooms and exceptionally friendly service. Rooms have a kitchenette and some have balconies.

➡ **Park House Lodge & Travel Centre** (691 1937; www.park-house.co.za; 121 High St; dm R150, d with/without bathroom from R520/400; @) This place, in a gracious old sandstone house next to the park, is friendly, smartly decorated and has beautiful gardens. Breakfast is R40, and staff can organise activities.

➡ **Mossel Bay Backpackers** (691 3182; www.gardenrouteadventures.com; 1 Marsh St; dm R120, d with/without bathroom R450/340; @ ✉) Close to the beach at the Point and the bars on Marsh St, this long-established place is reliable and well run. It offers comfortable rooms, a pool and bar and an impressive fully equipped kitchen. Staff can arrange all sorts of activities.

George

Explore

For many people, George is little more than a transport hub but there are gems to be found in the Garden Route's largest town. Start at the museum for a little historical perspective, then take a stroll down York Street to the diminutive St Mark's Cathedral and the 'Slave Tree'. Guided historical walks take place on weekdays at 10am or you can pick up a brochure for a self-guided walk from the tourist office. Spend the afternoon playing golf or exploring the surrounding Outeniqua Mountains on foot, by car or on the quirky Outeniqua Power Van.

The Best...

➡ **Sight** Outeniqua Power Van (p177)
➡ **Place to Eat** Old Townhouse (p177)
➡ **Activity** Golf (p177)

Top Tip

Take a drive south of George to the picturesque beaches at Herold's Bay and Victoria Bay, both surfing hot spots (see boxed text, p184). The latter has a tidal pool for kids.

Getting There & Away

Bus Greyhound (011-611 8000; www.greyhound.co.za), **Translux** (0861 589 282; www.translux.co.za) and **Intercape** (0861 287 287; www.intercape.co.za) operate frequent buses from Cape Town (R320, seven hours).

Plane Airlink (011-978 1111; www.flyairlink.com) and **SA Express** (011-978 9905; www.flyexpress.aero) fly from Cape Town to George Airport (50 minutes), 7km west of town.

Need to Know

➡ **Area Code** 044
➡ **Location** George is 430km east of Cape Town, along the N2.
➡ **Tourist Office** (801 9295; www.visitgeorge.co.za; 124 York St; 7.45am-4.30pm Mon-Fri, 9am-1pm Sat)

 **SIGHTS**

GEORGE MUSEUM MUSEUM
(873 5343; Courtenay St; admission by donation; 9am-4pm Mon-Fri, 9am-12.30pm Sat) George was once the hub of the indigenous timber industry and the museum contains a wealth of artefacts related to the town's past.

OUTENIQUA TRANSPORT MUSEUM MUSEUM
(801 8288; cnr Courtenay & York Sts; adult/child R20/10; 8am-4.30pm Mon-Fri, 8am-2pm

Sat) Although the Choo-Tjoe steam train is sadly no longer running, the museum is still the starting point and terminus for scenic local journeys on the **Outeniqua Power Van**. It's well worth a visit if you're interested in trains. Some 11 locomotives and 15 carriages, as well as many detailed models, have found a retirement home here, including a carriage used by the British royal family in the 1940s.

EATING & DRINKING

OLD TOWNHOUSE STEAKHOUSE **$$**
(☑874 3663; Market Street; mains R50-115; ☺lunch & dinner Mon-Fri, dinner Sat) Situated in the one-time town administration building dating back to 1848, this longstanding restaurant is known for its excellent steaks and ever-changing game meat options.

LA CAPANNINA ITALIAN **$**
(☑874 5313; 122 York St; mains R50-100; ☺lunch Mon-Fri, dinner daily) La Capannina is a deservedly popular Italian restaurant, located next to the tourist bureau, with an award-winning wine list and knowledgeable waiters.

SPORTS & ACTIVITIES

GOLF
George is the golfing capital of the Western Cape, and perhaps the entire country. There are a dozen courses – including short courses – scattered around the town's outskirts as well as three golf schools if you're not quite up to par. The most elite and famous is **The Links at Fancourt** (☑804 0000; www.fancourt.co.za), designed by Gary Player. **Little Eden** (☑881 0018; www.edenforest.co.za) is a secluded nine-hole course while **Oubaai** (☑851 1234; www.oubaai.regency.hyatt.com) is an opulent spot offering ocean vistas from the greens.

SCENIC DRIVES
The Montagu Pass is a quiet dirt road that winds away from George through the mountains; it was opened in 1847 and is now a national monument. Take some sustenance, because there are great picnic sites along the way, then head back on the Outeniqua Pass, where views are even better; but, because it's a main road, it's more difficult to stop when you want to.

Alternatively, you could opt for the **Outeniqua Power Van** (☑082 490 5627; adult/child R110/90; on demand Mon-Sat), a motorised trolley van that will take you from the

THE GARDEN ROUTE GEORGE

GARDEN ROUTE RETREATS

As one of the most popular tourist spots in the country, parts of the Garden Route can get pretty crowded, especially during South African school holidays. Escape to one of these hidden lodges to avoid the throngs.

Phantom Forest Eco-Reserve (☑044-386 0046; www.phantomforest.com; s/d from R2375/3750; ☒) This 137-hectare private ecoreserve, 6km west of Knysna along the Phantom Pass road, overlooks the lagoon and comprises 14 cleverly designed and elegantly decorated tree houses built with sustainable materials. Various activities, including conducted nature walks and a spa, are available. If nothing else, visit for the award-winning six-course African dinner (R300) served in the Forest Boma daily; booking is essential.

Hog Hollow (☑044-534 8879; www.hog-hollow.com; s/d incl breakfast R2190/2900) Hog Hollow, 18km east of Plett along the N2, provides delightful accommodation in African-art-decorated units, which are around an old farmhouse overlooking the forest. Each unit comes with a private wooden deck and hammock. You can walk to Monkeyland (p185) from here; staff will collect you if you don't fancy the walk back.

Eight Bells Mountain Inn (☑044-631 0000; www.eightbells.co.za; s/d R900/1020; ☒ ⓚ) This country inn is 35km north of Mossel Bay on Rte 328 to Oudtshoorn (50km) and makes a good lunch stop, even if you're not staying here. It's in a lovely mountain setting at the foot of the Robinson Pass and its 160 hectares offer squash, hiking, horse riding, a tea garden and plenty for kids to do. You'll find a variety of rooms with TV and safes; the *rondavels* are fun.

Outeniqua Transport Museum on a 2½-hour trip into the Outeniqua mountains. You can even take a bike and cycle back down the Montagu Pass.

Wilderness

Explore

After a brief stop at the tourist office, head straight for that which gives Wilderness its soul – the outdoors. Start with a gentle hike in the Garden Route National Park or a canoeing stint on one of the lagoons. Wilderness is a quieter, more laid-back alternative to Knysna and Plettenberg Bay, but its ultra-compact town centre has a surprising number of decent eateries. From here it is a short stroll under the N2 to the beach – but be warned: a strong riptide means swimming is not advised. After a spot of sun-worshipping, drive out to Timberlake Organic Village, a great place to shop for crafts and organically grown fresh produce or to eat at the recommended Zucchini.

The Best...

➡ **Sight** Garden Route National Park
➡ **Place to Eat** Zucchini (p179)
➡ **Activity** Canoeing on the lagoon

Top Tip

On Saturday mornings, head 24km east to Sedgefield, host to an excellent farmers' market and a great place for brunch.

Getting There & Away

Bus Greyhound (☑011-611 8000; www.greyhound.co.za) and **Translux** (☑0861 589 282; www.translux.co.za) operate services from Cape Town twice a day (R250, 7 hours).

Need to Know

➡ **Area Code** ☑044
➡ **Location** Wilderness is 445km east of Cape Town and sits right on the N2.
➡ **Tourist Office** (☑877 0045; Milkwood Village, George Rd; ◷7.45am-4.30pm Mon-Fri, 9am-1pm Sat)

◉ SIGHTS

GARDEN ROUTE NATIONAL PARK   PARK
Formerly the Wilderness National Park, this section has now been incorporated into the vast and scattered **Garden Route National Park** (☑877 1197; http://sanparks.org.za/parks/garden_route; adult/child R88/44; ◷24hr) along with the Knysna Forests and Tsitsikamma. The park covers a unique system of lakes, rivers, wetlands and estuaries that are vital for the survival of many species.

There are several nature trails in the national park for all levels of fitness, taking in the lakes, the beach and the indigenous forest. The **Kingfisher Trail** is a day walk that traverses the region and includes a boardwalk across the intertidal zone of the Touws River. The lakes offer anglers, canoeists, windsurfers and sailors an ideal venue. Canoes (R250 per day) can be hired from **Eden Adventures** (☑877 0179; www.eden.

SLEEPING IN WILDERNESS

➡ **Interlaken** (☑877 1374; www.inter laken.co.za; 713 North St; r per person incl breakfast R495; @) Rave reviews from readers, and we can't argue: this is a well run and very friendly guest house offering magnificent lagoon views. Delicious dinners are available on request.

➡ **Fairy Knowe Backpackers** (☑877 1285; www.wildernessbackpackers.com; Dumbleton Rd; dm R120, d with/without bathroom R450/350; @) Set in spacious, leafy grounds overlooking the Touws River, this 1874 farmhouse was the first in the area. The bar and cafe are in another building some distance away, so boozers won't keep you awake. It's a great place to relax, but numbers are limited so book ahead. The Baz Bus comes to the door. If you're driving, head into Wilderness town from the N2 and follow the main road east for 2km to the Fairy Knowe turn-off.

co.za; Wilderness National Park), which also offers abseiling (R375) and canyoning (R495).

There are two similar camping grounds in the park with basic but comfortable accommodation, including in *rondavels* (round huts with conical roofs): **Ebb & Flow North** (campsites from R150, d rondavel without/with bathroom R280/325), which is the smaller, and **Ebb & Flow South** (campsites from R150, forest cabins R540, 4-person log cottage R1015).

 EATING & DRINKING

ZUCCHINI EUROPEAN **$$**
(☑882 1240; Timberlake Organic Village; mains R40-125; ☻lunch & dinner; ☑) Stylish decor combines with home-grown organic produce, free-range meats and lots of vegetarian options at this delightful place. It sits in the Timberlake Organic Village, which has small shops selling organically grown fresh produce and crafts. There's live music on Sundays, and activities such as quad biking and zip-line tours available. The complex is off the N2 between Wilderness and Sedgefield.

SERENDIPITY MODERN SOUTH AFRICAN **$$$**
(☑877 0433; Freesia Ave; 5-course set menu R300; ☻dinner Mon-Sat) Readers and locals alike recommend this elegant restaurant with a deck overlooking the lagoon. The South African–inspired menu changes monthly but always features original takes on old classics. Accommodation is available here as well.

GIRLS RESTAURANT INTERNATIONAL **$$**
(☑877 1648; 1 George Rd; mains R50-175; ☻dinner Tue-Sun) It doesn't look much from afar – a restaurant tucked down the side of a petrol station – but the Girls gets rave reviews. Try the fresh prawns in a range of divine sauces. There's internet access here too.

BEEJUICE CAFE **$**
(☑073 975 9614; Sands Rd; light meals R40-80; ☻breakfast, lunch & dinner) Although no trains ply the tracks any more, this cafe filling the old station building is still a great spot for freshly made salads and sandwiches. In the evenings, traditional South African fare is served.

Knysna

Explore
Timber played a vital role in Knysna's history so there is no better place to start exploring than in the forests surrounding the town. Hikes range from short strolls to multi-day treks. Main Street has a plethora of shops and cafes, as well as the quaint Old Gaol Museum. Read up on local history, then head to the bustling if touristy Knysna Quays for a seafood lunch and a boat trip on the lagoon. Enjoy craggy ocean views from the Eastern Head and dine in one of the chic new eateries on Thesen's Island. If you're sticking around, take a township tour and indulge in one of the many outdoor activities this region is known for.

The Best...
➡ **Sight** Knysna Forests (p182)
➡ **Place to Eat** Phantom Forest Eco-Reserve (p177)
➡ **Place to Drink** Mitchell's Brewery (p180)

Top Tip
If you want to stay overnight in either the Rastafarian community or in the township, contact Knysna Tourism and ask for their brochure, *Living Local*.

Getting There & Away
Bus Translux (☑0861 589 282; www.translux.co.za), **Intercape** (☑0861 287 287; www.intercape.co.za) and **Greyhound** (☑011-611 8000; www.greyhound.co.za) have regular buses from Cape Town (R350, eight hours, twice daily)

Minibus taxi Catch a minibus taxi from the Shell petrol station on Main St. Routes include Plettenberg Bay (R20, 30 minutes, daily) and Cape Town (R150, 7½ hours, daily).

Need to Know
➡ **Area Code** ☑044
➡ **Location** Knysna is 490km east of Cape Town.
➡ **Tourist Office** (☑382 5510; www.visitknysna.co.za; 40 Main St; ☻8am-5pm Mon-Fri, 8.30am-1pm Sat year-round, plus 9am-1pm Sun Dec-Jan & Jul)

👁 SIGHTS

KNYSNA ELEPHANT PARK   WILDLIFE RESERVE
(Map p174; ☎532 7732; www.knysnaelephant
park.co.za; 1hr tours adult/child R190/100;
⏲8.30am-4.30pm) While you're highly unlikely to see any wild elephants in Knysna's
forests, you are sure to see some if you head
to this sanctuary, 22km east of Knysna off
the N2. Here, small groups of visitors go on
walking tours with the elephants, or you
can take a short ride (adult/child R815/390).
The tours might not be authentic wildlife
encounters, but are guaranteed to bring
out the child in any visitor. There is luxury
accommodation here too, with a shared
lounge overlooking the elephant stables.

KNYSNA LAGOON   PARK
Although regulated by **SAN Parks** (Map
p181; ☎302 5606; www.sanparks.org; Long St,
Thesen's Island), Knysna Lagoon, covering
13 sq km, is not a national park or wilderness area. Much is still privately owned,
and the lagoon is used by industry and for
recreation. The protected area starts just
to the east of Buffalo Bay and follows the
coastline to the mouth of the Noetzie River.
The lagoon opens up between two sandstone cliffs, known as the Heads – once
proclaimed by the British Royal Navy the
most dangerous harbour entrance in the
world. There are good views from a lookout on the eastern head, and the privately
owned **Featherbed Nature Reserve** on the
western head.

The best way to appreciate the lagoon is
to take a cruise. The **Featherbed Company**
(Map p181; ☎382 1697; www.featherbed.co.za;
Waterfront) has several vessels, including the
MV John Benn (Map p181; adult/child R130/60;
⏲departs 12.30pm & 5pm in winter, 6pm in sum-
mer), that take you to Featherbed Nature
Reserve.

MITCHELL'S BREWERY   BREWERY
South African's oldest microbrewery (Map
pmap:Around Knysna; ☎382 4685; Arend St; tastings R30, tours R50; ⏲11am-4pm Mon-Fri, tours
11am, 12.30pm & 2.30pm Mon-Fri) is in an industrial area to the east of town. The Eng-
lish-style beers and one cider can be found
all over Western Cape. There's also a beer
and oyster pairing option (R125 including
tour). Bookings essential.

FREE OLD GAOL MUSEUM   MUSEUM
(Map p179; ☎302 6320; cnr Main & Queen Sts;
⏲9.30am-4.30pm Mon-Fri, 9.30am-12.30pm Sat)
Since this region has plenty of wet weather,
a rainy-day option is welcome. The main
museum is a pleasant complex in a mid-
19th century building that was once the
gaol. There's a gallery showcasing local art,
a display on the Knysna elephants and a
community art project. Around the corner
on Queen Street with the same opening hours is **Millwood House**, a mini complex of museums detailing Knysna's history.
It's a quaint set of buildings dating back to
the town's booming timber era. This is the
main focus of the museum, though it also

SLEEPING IN KNYSNA

Low-season competition between the several backpackers and many guest houses
in town keeps prices down, but in high season expect steep rate hikes (except at the
backpackers), and book ahead.

➡ **Brenton Cottages** (Map p183; ☎381 0082; www.brentononsea.net; 2-person cabin
R890, 6-person chalet R1940) On the seaward side of the lagoon, the *fynbos*-covered
hills drop to Brenton-on-Sea, overlooking a magnificent 8km beach. The cottages
here have a full kitchen while cabins have a kitchenette; some have ocean views.
There are plenty of braai areas dotted around the manicured lawns.

➡ **Island Vibe** (Map p181; ☎382 1728; www.islandvibe.co.za; 67 Main St; dm R120, d with/
without bathroom R385/330; @✉) This funky backpackers has excellent communal
areas, cheery staff and nicely decorated rooms. There's a bar, free internet and a
great view from the deck.

➡ **Inyathi Guest Lodge** (Map p181; ☎044-382 7768; www.inyathiguestlodge.co.za; 52
Main St; s/d from R500/720) This is an imaginatively designed guesthouse with a real
African flair that avoids the kitsch. Accommodation is in decorated timber lodges –
some with Victorian bath tubs, others with stained-glass windows. It's in a very
convenient spot and is worth a stay.

Knysna

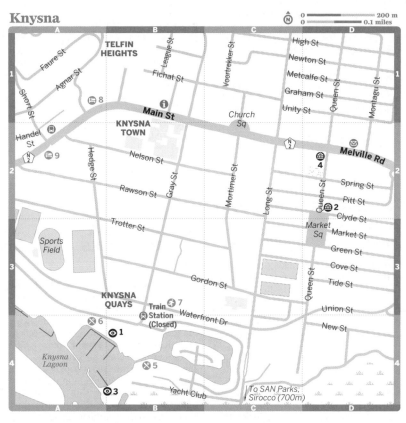

houses information on Knysna's involvement in the Anglo-Boer War and details on the town's founder George Rex.

GOUKAMMA
NATURE RESERVE   NATURE RESERVE
(☑383 0042; www.capenature.co.za; adult/child R30/15; ⊙8am-6pm) This nature reserve is 20km southwest of Knysna, accessible from the Buffalo Bay road. It protects 14km of rocky coastline, sandstone cliffs, dunes covered with coastal *fynbos* and forest, and Groenvlei, a large freshwater lake.

The nature reserve also extends 1.8km out to sea and you can often see dolphins (and whales, in season) along the coast. There are four day trails ranging from the short Lake Walk along Groenvlei's southern shore up to four-hour beach and dune walks. Permits can be obtained on arrival. Canoeing and fishing are great here, and canoes can be hired (R60 per day).

NOETZIE   BEACH
Reached by a turn-off along the N2 10km east of Knysna, **Noetzie** is a quirky little place with holiday homes in mock-castle

style. There's a lovely surf beach (spacious but dangerous) and a sheltered lagoon running through a forested gorge. The trail between the car park and beach is steep.

BELVIDERE & BRENTON VILLAGE
Belvidere, 10km from Knysna, is so immaculate it's positively creepy. But it's worth a quick look for the beautiful Norman-style **church** (Map p183) built in the 1850s by homesick English expats. Further on is the Featherbed Nature Reserve, and, on the seaward side, Brenton Beach.

EATING & DRINKING

EAST HEAD CAFÉ CAFE $$
(Map p183; ☑384 0933; The Heads; mains R45-110; ⊙breakfast & lunch; ☑) There's an outdoor deck here, overlooking the lagoon and ocean, and a good range of vegetarian dishes, plus wild oysters at R15 each.

OYSTERCATCHER SEAFOOD $
(Map p181; ☑382 9995; Knysna Quays; ⊙lunch & dinner) The Oystercatcher is a relaxed place in a waterside setting serving four sizes of farmed oyster and other light dishes such as fish and chips.

SIROCCO INTERNATIONAL $$
(Map p183; ☑382 4874; Thesen Harbour Town; mains R50-130; ⊙lunch & dinner) Inside it's a stylish place to dine on steaks and seafood; outside it's a laid-back bar with wood-fired pizzas and the full range of Mitchell's beers. Call to ask about daily specials.

34 SOUTH INTERNATIONAL $$
(Map p181; ☑382 7268; Waterfront; mains R50-175; ⊙lunch & dinner) With outdoor tables overlooking the water, lavish salads, deli produce and seafood platters, this is a great place for lunch. The wine selection is one of the best in town.

CRAB'S CREEK PUB $$
(Map p183; ☑386 0011; mains R50-200; ⊙lunch & dinner;☑) This is a favourite local watering hole, in a chilled-out setting right on the lagoon, off the N2. There's a buffet lunch (R65) on Sundays. Children will enjoy the sandpit and climbing frames.

SPORTS & ACTIVITIES

☑**TOWNSHIP TOURS & HOMESTAYS** CULTURAL TOUR
Follow Gray St uphill and eventually you'll emerge on the wooded slopes of the hills behind town. On top are the sprawling Knysna townships, best visited on an excellent tour (R350) run by **Emzini Tours** (☑382 1087; www.emzinitours.co.za). Readers can't get enough of these three-hour trips, with many claiming it to be a highlight of their entire South Africa stay. Township resident Ella leads the way to some of the projects that Emzini has set up in the local community. You might visit the soup kitchen, the animal welfare centre or a school – tours can be tailored to suit your interests but generally end at Ella's home for tea, drumming and a gig-

---

HIKING THE KNYSNA FORESTS

Now part of the Garden Route National Park, the Knysna Forests are the perfect place for hikers of all levels. At the easy end of the scale is the **Garden of Eden** (Map p174) where there are lovely forest picnic spots and a wheelchair-friendly walk. The gold mine at **Millwood** (Map p174) walk is also a gentle hike, while the Elephant Trails at **Diepwalle Forest** (Map p174) offer varying degrees of difficulty.

If you're looking for something more challenging, The **Harkerville Coast Trail** (☑044-302 5656; R165) is a two-day hike that leads on to the popular Outeniqua Trail. The **Outeniqua Trail** (☑044-302 5606) is 108km long and takes a week to walk, although you can also do two- or three-day sections. To stay in a basic hut on the trail costs R66 per night. You will need to bring your own bedding. For permits, maps and further information, contact SAN Parks (Map p183; ☑044-302 5656; www.sanparks.org; Long St, Thesen's Island).

There are also plenty of mountain-biking trails. **Outeniqua Biking Trails** (☑044-532 7644; www.gardenroute.co.za/plett/obt) rents bikes (R100 per day, including helmets) and will give you a map of the surrounding trails.

Around Knysna

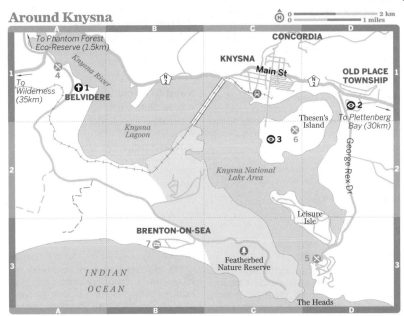

gle as you try to wrap your tongue around the clicks of the Xhosa language.

Other Activities

There are plenty of other activities on offer in the area, including abseiling, canyoning, horse riding, kayaking and quad biking.

ADVENTURE CENTRE   OUTDOOR ADVENTURE
(☏083 260 7198; www.theadventurecentre. co.za) Start by contacting this outfit based at Highfield Backpackers.

GO VERTICAL   OUTDOOR ADVENTURE
(☏082 731 4696; www.govertical.co.za) Offers rock climbing, abseiling and canoeing. 181

LIQUID GRACE   WATERSPORTS
(☏343 3245; www.liquidgrace.co.za) Watersports operator based 30km from Knysna in Sedgefield.

KNYSNA CYCLE WORKS   CYCLING
(Map p181; ☏382 5152; 20 Waterfront Dr; per day R170). There are also bike trails around the area; visit Cycle Works for bike hire and more information on cycling.

Plettenberg Bay

Explore

Plett, as the town is known, is compact and most amenities are concentrated around a single thoroughfare, Main Road. It's a pleasant place to begin, lined with restaurants and some excellent cafes, good for breakfast or brunch. Of course, the main reason people visit Plett is for its beaches. Start at Lookout Beach, close to the town, where the Keurbooms River Lagoon meets the Indian Ocean. Further stretches of sand await east of town – the main beach at Keurboomstrand is a stunner. Inland you can hike or horse-ride through the forests or get up-close with a range of African animals. Return to town for dinner either on Main Road or at one of the restaurants overlooking the water. Spend a second day exploring the cliffs and dunes of the Robberg Nature Reserve and end with a dolphin-watching trip leaving from Central Beach.

The Best...
➡ **Sight** Tenikwa
➡ **Place to Eat** Ristorante Enrico (p185)
➡ **Activity** Hiking in Robberg Nature Reserve (p185)

Top Tip
If you're getting wine-withdrawal symptoms, check out the Méthode Cap Classique (MCC) and sauvignon blanc at Bramon Wine Estate, just off the N2 at The Crags. There's a restaurant here too.

Getting There & Away
Bus Intercape (☎0861 287 287; www. intercape.co.za) operates two buses per day from Cape Town (R320, nine hours)

Need to Know
➡ **Area Code** ☎044
➡ **Location** Plett is 520km east of Cape Town.
➡ **Tourist Office** (☎533 4065; www. plettenbergbay.co.za; 5 Main St; ⏱8.30am-5pm Mon-Fri year-round, 9am-2pm Sat Apr-Oct)

◉ SIGHTS

TENIKWA WILDLIFE RESERVE
(☎534 8170; www.tenikwa.co.za; cheetah walk R500; ⏱9am-4.30pm) Considered a trip highlight by many, this is a chance to spend some quality time with cheetahs. Tenikwa is a sanctuary and rehabilitation centre for injured or abandoned animals, though

---

SURFING ALONG THE GARDEN ROUTE

With the water warming up as you round Cape Agulhas where the Indian Ocean takes over, you can be happy surfing in just baggies/boardshorts or a short suit during summer. You'll need a full suit in winter, though.

In **Mossel Bay**, there's a good right in a big swell called Ding Dangs that's best at a lowish tide, especially in a southwesterly or easterly wind. It might be a bit of a hassle paddling out, but the right is better than the left. To the right of the tidal pool, there's a soft wave called Inner Pool. Outer Pool (left of the tidal pool) is a better bet and is a great reef and point break.

You might find something at **Grootbrak** and **Kleinbrak**, but better is **Herold's Bay**. When it's on, there's a left-hand wedge along the beach, and it's unusual in that it works in a northwesterly wind.

Best of all though is **Victoria Bay** which has the most consistent breaks along this coast. It's perfect when the swell is about 1m to 2m and you get a great right-hander.

A little further along is **Buffel's Bay** where there's another right-hand point. Buffel's Bay is at one end of **Brenton Beach**; at the northern end, you'll find some good peaks, but watch out for sharks.

On to **Plettenberg Bay**: avoid Robberg Peninsula as that's home to a seal colony. But the swimming area at Robberg Beach (where the lifeguards are stationed) can have some good waves if the swell isn't too big. Central Beach has one of the best known waves, the Wedge, which is perfect for goofy-footers. Lookout Beach can have some sandbanks and the Point can be good, but there's a lot of erosion here and the beach is slowly disappearing. Watch out for rip currents, especially when there are no lifeguards on duty.

Nature's Valley has a long beach that has consistent sandbanks and is fine in a swell. When it's up, there's a left-hand sandbar that is perfect for experienced surfers.

Plettenberg Bay

N 0 ———————————— 400 m
   0 ———————————— 0.2 miles

the majority of its inhabitants are cats. The hour-long Wild Cat Experience (adult/child R160/80) visits all the lesser cats of South Africa, but it's the two-hour sunrise and sunset cheetah walks that have people sending postcards home. The cheetahs are on leads, and you're pretty much guaranteed personal contact.

ROBBERG NATURE RESERVE PARK
This **reserve** (Map p174; ✆533 2125; www.cape nature.org.za; adult/child R30/15; ◷7am-5pm Feb-Nov, 7am-8pm Dec-Jan), 9km southeast of Plettenberg Bay, protects a 4km-long peninsula with a rugged coastline of cliffs and rocks. There are three circular walks of increasing difficulty, with rich intertidal marine life and coastal-dune *fynbos,* but it's very rocky and not for the unfit or anyone with knee problems! You have to keep to the trail and watch out for freak waves. The Point and the Fountain are overnight huts (R360). The peninsula acts as a sort of marine speed bump to larger sea life, with mammals and fish spending time here before moving on. To get to the reserve head along Robberg Rd, off Piesang Valley Rd, until you see the signs.

MONKEYLAND WILDLIFE RESERVE
(Map p174; ✆534 8906; www.monkeyland.co.za; 1hr tours adult/child R135/67.50; ◷8am-5pm) This very popular attraction helps rehabilitate wild monkeys that have been in zoos or private homes. The walking safari through a dense forest and across a 128m-long rope bridge is a brilliant way to find out more about the monkeys.

BIRDS OF EDEN WILDLIFE RESERVE
(Map p174; ✆534 8906; www.birdsofeden.co.za; adult/child R135/67.50) This is the world's largest free-flight aviary with a 2-hectare dome over the forest. Combo tickets to Monkeyland and Birds of Eden cost R216/108 per adult/child. The tours are educational and popular with children.

ELEPHANT SANCTUARY WILDLIFE RESERVE
(Map p174; ✆534 8145; www.elephantsanctu ary.co.za; tours from adult/child R325/175, rides adult/child over 8 R435/220; ◷8am-5pm) There are various tour and ride options allowing up-close pachyderm encounters.

✗ EATING & DRINKING

⌂TOP CHOICE RISTORANTE ENRICO SEAFOOD $$
(✆535 9818; Main Beach, Keurboomstrand; mains R70-120; ◷lunch & dinner) Highly recommended by readers, this is *the* place for seafood in Plett. Enrico has his own boat that, weather permitting, heads out each morning. The large deck has awesome

---

SLEEPING IN PLETTENBERG BAY

⇒ **Abalone Beach House** (☎535 9602; www.abalonebeachhouse.co.za; 50 Milkwood Glen, Keurboomstrand; d with/without bathroom R450/380; @☒) This relaxing and extremely friendly backpackers is more like a budget guesthouse. A magnificent beach is two minutes away and surf and boogie boards are provided free. To reach the house follow the Keurboomstrand signs from the N2 (about 6km east of Plett), then turn into Milkwood Glen.

⇒ **Nothando Backpackers Hostel** (☎533 0220; www.nothando.com; 5 Wilder St; dm R130, d with/without bathroom R400/350) This excellent, five-star budget option, YHA-affiliated and award winning, is owner-run and it shows. There's a great bar area with satellite TV, yet you can still find peace and quiet in the large grounds. It's centrally situated behind the minibus taxi rank.

⇒ **Milkwood Manor** (☎044-533 0420; www.milkwoodmanor.co.za; Salmack Rd, Lookout Beach; d from R1100; @) A remarkable location, right on the beach and overlooking the lagoon. Rooms are smart if not spectacular, there's a restaurant on site, and kayaks are free for guests who want to explore the lagoon.

---

views of the beach. If you book ahead you can join the fishing trips.

THE TABLE   ITALIAN $
(☎533 3024; 9 Main St; mains R60-105; ⊘lunch & dinner) A funky, minimalist venue with pizzas featuring an array of unusual toppings. At lunch time there's a 'harvest table' with ever-changing local produce.

EUROPA   ITALIAN $$
(☎533 6942; cnr Church & Main Sts; mains R42-120; ⊘breakfast, lunch & dinner; ☑) This is a large, snazzy resto-bar with a great deck. There's a good range of salads and plenty of Italian fare.

LOOKOUT   SEAFOOD $$
(☎533 1379; Lookout Rocks; mains R60-130; ⊘breakfast, lunch & dinner) With a deck overlooking the beach, this is a great place for a simple meal and perhaps views of dolphins surfing the waves.

LM IN PLETT MOZAMBICAN
RESTAURANT   SEAFOOD $$
(☎533 1420; 6 Yellowwood Centre, Main St; mains R60-125; ⊘lunch & dinner) A smart restaurant concentrating on the famous 'LM' (Laurenço Marques) prawns. A dozen of the best will cost you R315.

 # SHOPPING

OLD NICK VILLAGE   SHOPPING CENTRE
(☎533 1395; www.oldnickvillage.co.za) For a bit of retail therapy after Plett's action sports, head for this complex just 3km northeast of town, with resident artists, a weaving museum, antiques and a restaurant.

 # SPORTS & ACTIVITIES

BOAT TRIPS   BOAT TRIPS
Ocean Blue Adventures (☎533 5083; www.oceanadventures.co.za; Milkwood Centre, Hopewood St) and **Ocean Safaris** (☎533 4963; www.oceansafaris.co.za; Milkwood Centre, Hopewood St; 1½hr trip R400) offer boat trips to view dolphins and whales in season. Both operators charge R650 for whale watching, R400 for dolphin trips.

OTHER ACTIVITIES   ADVENTURE SPORTS
For skydiving try **Sky Dive Plettenberg Bay** (☎533 9048; www.skydiveplett.com; Plettenberg Airport; tandem jump R1600). For surfing lessons contact **Garden Route Surf Academy** (☎082 436 6410; www.gardenroutesurfacademy.com; 2hr group lesson incl equipment R300).

Sleeping

Creatively converted Airstream caravans, township shacks, a tepee and an organic mud house are among the more unusual Capetonian places to stay. Five-star pamper palaces abound, but choose your base carefully depending on your priorities – not everywhere is close to a beach or major sights.

Reservations

There are places to suit all budgets, but if there's somewhere you particularly want to stay, it's essential to make a reservation well in advance, especially if you're visiting during the school holidays from mid-December to the end of January and at Easter. This is especially true for the best budget stays, which fill up quickly.

Cape Town Tourism runs an accommodation booking service. However, it only recommends its members and there's plenty of excellent places to stay that aren't on its books.

Facilities

As always, you get what you pay for, but you may be pleasantly surprised at how good the quality of what you do get can be. Among the few things to watch out for are:

Internet access Wi-fi is common and often complimentary. However, service may be slow, unsecure and there may be daily download limits; if you need a reliable internet connection make detailed enquiries beforehand and check additional costs carefully.

Swimming pools Often more accurate to describe these as plunge pools, particularly when found in guesthouses – although some top hotels have tiny swimming pools, too.

Secure parking Not everywhere has it and some places that do, particularly in the City Bowl area, will slap on an extra daily charge of anything between R30 and R70.

Self-catering & Serviced Apartments

For longer-term stays, a self-catering or serviced apartment or villa can work out to be a good deal. Reliable agencies include:

Cape Breaks (Map p264; ☎083-383 4888; http://capebreaks.co.za) Offers a range of studios and apartments in St Martini Gardens beside the Company's Gardens.

Cape Stay (www.capestay.co.za) Accommodation across the Cape.

Cape Town Budget Accommodation (☎021-447 4398; www.capetownbudgetaccommodation.co.za) Units in Woodstock from R270.

De Waterkant Cottages (Map p268; ☎021-421 2300; www.dewaterkantcottages.com) For places in De Waterkant.

FZP Property Investment (Map p264; ☎021-426 1634; www.fzp.co.za) Apartments in the City Bowl and beyond.

In Awe Stays (☎083 658 6975 www.inawestays.co.za) Stylish studios and cottages in Gardens and Fresnaye from R750 a double.

Nox Rentals (☎021-424 3353; www.noxrentals.co.za) Apartment and villa rentals mainly in Camps Bay.

Platinum Places (☎021-425 5922; www.platinumplaces.co.za) Luxury options.

Village & Life (Map p268; ☎021-430 4444; www.villageandlife.com) Focused mainly on properties in De Waterkant and Camp's Bay. There are several self-catering cottages and 'tented camps' scattered through the Table Mountain National Park; see p30 for details.

Where to Stay

Neighbourhood	For	Against
City Bowl, Foreshore, Bo-Kaap & De Waterkant	Ideal for exploring city on foot with plenty of transport to other regions. Bo-Kaap & De Waterkant have characterful guesthouses and hotels.	No beaches. City Bowl is dead on Sundays when most businesses close. Mosques in the Bo-Kaap and the nightlife of De Waterkant can disturb peace and tranquility.
East City Corridor	The hip urban vibes of these edgy, slowly gentrifying areas.	Safety can still be an issue; short on both greenery and beaches.
Gardens & Surrounds	Tons of lovely boutique guesthouses; easy access to Table Mountain.	The hikes up and down the hills will keep you fit; pack earplugs for the howling wind factor.
Green Point & Waterfront	Direct access to V&A Waterfront; breezy promenade walks and Green Point Park.	Coping with the crowds at the Waterfront.
Sea Point to Hout Bay	Good seaside bases with Camps Bay one of the city's ritziest suburbs. Hout Bay is handy for both Atlantic Coast beaches and Constantia Vineyards.	Sea Point has its grungy areas; Camps Bay's popularity pushes up prices and the crowd factor. From Hout Bay it's a longish drive to main city-centre sights.
Southern Suburbs	Leafy and upmarket areas; near Kirstenbosch and vineyards of Constantia.	No beaches; city-centre sights also a drive away.
Simon's Town & Southern Peninsula	Good for families and surfers wanting nice beaches; vibey village atmosphere. Simon's Town is historic and has easy access to quiet beaches and the rugged landscapes of Cape Point.	Nearly an hour's drive from the City Bowl. Lack of big-city atmosphere and attractions.
Cape Flats & Northern Suburbs	Close to airport and on way to Stellenbosch. First hand experience of black African culture.	Cape Flats suffers wind and dust storms. The surrounding poverty. Distance from city centre.

Lonely Planet's Top Choices

Tintswalo Atlantic (p195) Spot whales from your balcony at this luxurious lodge on the edge of Hout Bay.

Mannabay (p192) Superbly decorated boutique hotel not too high up the slopes of Table Mountain.

Backpack (p192) Slickly run, fun operation with spotless rooms to suit all budgets.

Villa Zest (p194) Retro groovy pad in a Bauhaus-style villa in Green Point.

POD (p196) Super cool property overlooking Camps Bay, decorated with natural materials.

Dutch Manor (p190) Stocked with antiques, this historic building is on the edge of the colourful Bo-Kaap.

Best by Budget

$
Ashanti Gardens (p193)
La Rose B&B (p190)
Blencathra (p194)
District Six Guesthouse (p192)
Rose Lodge (p191)

$$
Hippo Boutique Hotel (p193)
Vineyard Hotel & Spa (p197)
Chartfield Guest House (p197)
Four Rosmead (p193)

$$$
Ellerman House (p196)
Mount Nelson Hotel (p193)
Taj Cape Town (p190)
Cape Grace (p195)
One & Only Cape Town (p195)

Best for Backpackers

Ashanti Gardens (p193)
Atlantic Point Backpackers (p195)
Long St Backpackers (p191)
Green Elephant (p192)

Best Boutique Stays

Cape Heritage Hotel (p190)
Kensington Place (p193)
Cape Cadogan (p193)
Cape Standard (p195)
Rouge on Rose (p190)

Best Designer Stays

Daddy Long Legs Hotel (p190)
Grand Daddy Hotel (p190)
Hippo Boutique Hotel (p193)
Hout Bay Manor (p196)
An African Villa (p194)

Best B&B

Chartfield Guest House (p197)
La Rose B&B (p190)
Bella Ev (p197)
Scalabrini Guest House (p191)
Kopanong (p199)

Best for Greenery

Vineyard Hotel & Spa (p197)
Camps Bay Retreat (p196)
Wood Owl Cottage (p31)
Orange Kloof Tented Camp (p30)

🛏 City Bowl, Foreshore, Bo-Kaap & De Waterkant

TOP CHOICE TAJ CAPE TOWN   HOTEL $$$

Map p264 (☏021-819 2000; www.tajhotels.com; Wale St, City Bowl; s/d/ste from R5500/5700/11,000; P✳@🛜🏊; 🚇Dorp) India's luxury hotel group has breathed brilliant new life into the old Board of Executors building on the corner of Wale and Adderley. There's plenty of heritage here but a new tower also houses the chic contemporary-styled rooms, many offering spectacular views of Table Mountain. Service and facilities, including the excellent Bombay Brasserie restaurant, are top grade.

TOP CHOICE DUTCH MANOR   BOUTIQUE HOTEL $$

Map p264 (☏021-422 4767; www.dutchmanor.co.za 158 Buitengracht St, Bo-Kaap; s/d R1200/1700; ✳🛜; 🚇Bloem) Four poster beds, giant armoires and creaking floorboards lend terrific atmosphere to this six room property crafted from a 1812 building. Although it overlooks busy Buitengracht the noise is largely kept at bay thanks to modern renovations. Dinners can be prepared on request by the staff who can also arrange Bo-Kaap walking tours (R70/non-guests R100) with a local guide.

CAPE HERITAGE HOTEL   BOUTIQUE HOTEL $$

Map p264 (☏021-424 4646; www.capeheritage.co.za; 90 Bree St, City Bowl; d/ste from R2260/3020; parking R55; P✳@; 🚇Longmarket) Each room at this elegant boutique hotel, part of the Heritage Sq redevelopment of 18th-century buildings, has its own character. Some have four-poster beds and all have modern conveniences such as satellite TV and clothes presses. There's a roof terrace and a Jacuzzi pool.

GRAND DADDY HOTEL   DESIGN HOTEL $$

Map p264 (☏021-424 7247; www.granddaddy.co.za; 38 Long St, City Bowl; r/trailerR1750; parking R30 per day; P✳@🛜; 🚇Castle) The Grand Daddy's star attraction is its roof-top trailer park of penthouse suites made from seven vintage Airstream trailers decorated by different artists and designers, in wacky themes such as John and Yoko or Goldilocks and the Three Bears. The regular rooms are also stylish and incorporate playful references to South African culture. Its Daddy Cool bar has been blinged to the max with gold paint and trinkets.

DADDY LONG LEGS HOTEL   BOUTIQUE HOTEL $$

Map p264 (☏021-422 3074; www.daddylonglegs.co.za; 134 Long St, City Bowl; r/apt from R735/830; ✳@🛜; 🚇Dorp) A stay at this boutique hotel-cum-art installation is anything but boring. Thirteen artists were given free rein to design the boudoirs of their dreams; the results range from a bohemian garret to a hospital ward! Our favourites include the karaoke room (with a mike in the shower), and the room decorated with cartoons of the South African pop group Freshlyground. They also offer super-stylish **apartments** (Map p264; 263 Long St) – an ideal choice if you crave hotel-suite luxury but want to self-cater.

WESTIN CAPE TOWN   HOTEL $$$

Map p268 (☏021-412 9999; www.westin.com/grandcapetown; Convention Sq, 1 Lower Long St, Foreshore; r from R3000; P✳@; 🚇Convention Centre) At this sleek, contemporary, business-focused hotel connected to the Cape Town International Convention Centre CT-ICC, the corporate feel is softened by warmer colours in the rooms, sweeping views and interesting pieces of art in the lobby. The rooftop **Arabella Spa** (☏021-412 8200; www.westincapetown.com/en/arabella-spa-en; ⏱8am-8pm) is one of Cape Town's best pamper locations.

ROUGE ON ROSE   BOUTIQUE HOTEL $$

Map p264 (☏021-426 0298; www.rougeonrose.co.za; 25 Rose St, Bo-Kaap; s/d R900/1200; ✳🛜; 🚇Longmarket) Yet another great Bo-Kaap option, offering nine rustically chic rooms including suites (for no extra charge) with kitchenettes, lounges and lots of workspace. The fun wall paintings are by a resident artist and all rooms have luxurious open bath spaces with stand-alone tubs.

LA ROSE B&B   B&B $

Map p264 (☏021-422 5883; www.larosecapetown.com; 32 Rose St, Bo-Kaap; s/d from R500/650; P✳🛜; 🚇Longmarket) Adheena and Yoann are the very welcoming South African–French couple running this charming B&B that has been so successful it has expanded into nearby properties. It's beautifully decorated and has a rooftop garden with the best views of the area. Yoann's speciality is making authentic crepes for the guests.

DE WATERKANT HOUSE
B&B $$

Map p268 (☎021-409 2500; www.dewaterkant. com; cnr Napier & Waterkant Sts, De Waterkant; s/d R850/1150; @🛜🌊) This pleasant B&B in a renovated Cape Georgian house comes with tiny plunge pool for hot summers and a lounge fireplace for chilly winters. The management Village & Life also run another appealing guesthouse **The Charles** (Map p268 ☎021-409 2500; www.thecharles.co.za; 137 Waterkant St; r from R790) and a wide range of apartments in the area, from R750/1100 for singles/doubles.

VICTORIA JUNCTION
HOTEL, SERVICED APARTMENTS $$

off Map p268 (☎021-418 1234; www.proteahotels. co.za; cnr Somerset St & Ebenezer Rd, De Waterkant; d/loft from R1900/2200; parking R35 per day; P🌸@🛜🌊) Vintage suitcases hang on the lobby walls like artwork at this Protea hotel offering something edgier than usual, with industrial loft-style rooms and self-catering apartments with exposed brick walls. There's a reasonably sized lap pool. Breakfast is R155 extra.

VILLAGE LODGE
B&B $$

Map p268 (☎021-421 1106; www.thevillagelodge. com; 49 Napier St, De Waterkant; d from R800; 🌸🛜🌊) The main location of this chic guesthouse is on Napier St. Rooms are smart but far from spacious. The rooftop plunge pool and bar is a prime spot for guests to check each other out – as well as the view. They also run a good Thai restaurant, Soho.

DE WATERKANT LODGE
B&B, SELF-CATERING $$

Map p268 (☎021-419 2476; www.dewaterkant place.com; 35 Dixon St, De Waterkant; s/d/apt from R600/800/1500; @🛜) This appealing guesthouse with friendly management offers good-value, antique-decorated, fan-cooled rooms plus a self-catering unit sleeping up to four.

ROSE LODGE
B&B $

Map p264 (☎021-424 3813; www.rosestreet28. com; 28 Rose St, Bo-Kaap; s/d R450/750; 🌸🛜; 🚌Longmarket) Inside a grey-painted corner house is this cute B&B. The Canadian owner likes to play the grand piano and has two adorable dogs. There are just three cosy rooms (with private bathrooms), all decorated in contemporary style. They manage several more similar properties in the Bo-Kaap.

MAREMOTO
BOUTIQUE HOTEL $$

Map p264 (☎021-422 5877; www.maremoto. co.za; 230 Long St, City Bowl; r from R700; 🌸🛜; 🚌Buitensingel) Offering six stylish rooms (all decorated differently), beds piled with pillows, decent bathrooms and earplugs: you'll need them since it's on one of Long St's noisiest corners. Breakfast is extra and available in the decent cafe/restaurant/bar downstairs graced by a giant chandelier and more plush furnishings.

TOWNHOUSE
HOTEL $$

Map p264 (☎021-465 7050; www.townhouse. co.za; 60 Corporation St, City Bowl; s/d from R1495/1845; parking R45 per day; P🌸@🛜) Sharing the good service and high standards of its big sister the Vineyard Hotel & Spa, this is a justly popular inner-city choice. Rooms have been given a contemporary makeover with wooden floors and chic black and white decor.

CAPE DIAMOND HOTEL
HOTEL $$

Map p264 (☎021-461 2519; www.capediamond hotel.co.za; cnr Longmarket & Parliament Sts, City Bowl; s/d/apt from R700/1000/1400; parking R70 per day; P@; 🚌Longmarket) Some features of this art deco building, such as the wood-panelled floors, have been retained in its conversion to an efficient business hotel. Boxed in by tower blocks, lower floors are short on natural light; in compensation there's a rooftop Jacuzzi with Table Mountain views.

SCALABRINI GUEST HOUSE
GUESTHOUSE, SELF-CATERING $

Map p264 (☎021-465 6433; www.scalabrini. org.za; 47 Commercial St, City Bowl; dm/s/d or tw R180/300/480; 🛜) The Italian monastic order Scalabrini Fathers have provided welfare service to Cape Town's poor and to refugees since 1994. In a former textile factory, they run a soup kitchen, several social programs, and a pleasant guesthouse with 11 immaculately clean en-suite rooms, plus a great kitchen for self-catering where you can watch satellite TV.

LONG ST BACKPACKERS
BACKPACKERS $

Map p264 (☎021-423 0615; www.longstreet backpackers.co.za; 209 Long St, City Bowl; dm/s/d R120/220/330; 🛜; 🚌Bloem) Little has changed at this backpackers since it opened in 1993 (making it the longest running of the many that dot Long St). In a block of 14 small flats, with four beds and a bathroom in each, accommodation is arranged around a leafy, courtyard decorated with funky mosaics and in which the cats Happy and Bubbles pad around.

PENTHOUSE ON LONG
BACKPACKERS $

Map p264 (☑021-424 8356; www.penthouseon long.com; 6th fl, 112 Long St, City Bowl; d R500, dm/d without bathroom from R140/450; ✳@☎; ☐Dorp) High above Long, this backpackers does amazing things with what was formerly office space. The cheapest dorm has 22 beds. Private rooms have colourful themes such as Hollywood, the Orient or Moroccan nights. In the rafters is a spacious bar and lounge.

ST PAUL'S B&B GUEST HOUSE
B&B $

Map p264 (☑021-423 4420; www.stpaulschurch. co.za/theguesthouse.htm; 182 Bree St, City Bowl; s/d R350/650; ☐; ☐Buitensingel) This spotless B&B in a very handy location is a quiet alternative to a backpackers. The simply furnished and spacious rooms have high ceilings and there's a vine-shaded courtyard where you can relax or eat breakfast.

🛏 East City Corridor

UPPER EASTSIDE HOTEL
HOTEL $$

Map p270 (☑021-404 0570; www.uppereastside hotel.co.za; Brickfield Rd, Woodstock; r/ste R955/2400; parking R40 per day; ☐✳@☎⛱) With factory-outlet shopping at its doorstep, bargain hunters will love this snazzily designed property crafted from the old Bonwitt clothing factory. Rooms are large and pleasant, offering either mountain or city views. Loft suites (ask for 507, the largest) have kitchenettes. There's an indoor pool and access to a gym.

GREEN ELEPHANT
BACKPACKERS/SELF-CATERING $

Map p272 (☑021-448 6359; www.greenelephant. co.za; 57 Milton Rd, Observatory; s/d R450/550, dm/s/d without bathroom R140/350/440; ☐@☎⛱; ☐Observatory) Under new management, this long-running backpackers, split between three houses, remains a popular alternative to the city-centre hostels. Camping is possible (R80 per tent) and they also can arrange climbs up Table Mountain with a qualified guide (R250 per person). Rates don't include breakfast but you get unlimited wi-fi.

33 SOUTH BOUTIQUE BACKPACKERS
BACKPACKERS $

Map p272 (☑021-447 2423; www.33south backpackers.com; 48 Trill Rd, Observatory; dm/s/d from R130/300/410, s/d with bathroom R350/470; @☎; ☐Observatory) Not exactly boutique but certainly imaginative, this cosy backpackers in a Victorian cottage has sought inspiration from different Cape Town suburbs as themes for its rooms. There's a delightful shared kitchen and a pretty courtyard. Staff conduct free tours of Observatory. Rates don't include breakfast.

DISTRICT SIX GUESTHOUSE
B&B $

Map p270 (☑021-447 0902; www.district sixguesthouse.co.za; 2 Chester Rd, District Six; s/d/q with breakfast R500/650/800; ☐☎) Occupying three cottages once attached to the historic Zonnebloem Farm House, this spacious guesthouse – surrounded by a broad stoop and with unimpeded views over the harbour – provides a taste of simple Cape Malay hospitality. The four-bed room is ideal for a family and although it's far from luxurious, the whole place is spotless and efficiently run.

DECO LODGE
BACKPACKERS $

Map p270 (☑021-447 4216; www.capetowndeco. com; 20-22 Roodebloem Rd, Woodstock; dm/d R130/450; ☐@☎⛱) You can't miss this huge purple-painted art deco house (also a pet-friendly lodge) in up-and-coming Woodstock; the entrance is around the back on Beacontree Lane. Rooms inside are just as colourful and there's a lush garden, with a cooling pool. Rates don't include breakfast.

🛏 Gardens & Surrounds

TOP CHOICE MANNABAY
BOUTIQUE HOTEL $$

Map p274 (☑021-461 1094; www.mannabay. com; 1 Denholm Rd, Oranjezicht; r/ste from R1425/4000; ☐✳@☎⛱) This gorgeous luxury property offers seven guest rooms, each uniquely decorated in different themes: Versaille, world explorer, Japan etc. It's just far enough up the mountain to provide great views, but not so far that it's a slog home should you walk. Rates include high tea, which is served in the library-lounge.

TOP CHOICE BACKPACK
BACKPACKERS/SELF-CATERING $

Map p274 (☑021-423 4530; www.backpack ers.co.za; 74 New Church St, Tamboerskloof; s/d

R550/750, dm/s/d without bathroom R160/500 /650; parking R20 per day; [P][@][☎][≋]; [💻]Buitensingel) This Fair Trade in Tourism–accredited operation offers affordable style, a buzzy vibe and fantastic staff. Its dorms may not be Cape Town's cheapest but they're among its nicest, while the private rooms are charmingly decorated. A fun new addition is their tepee tent (double occupancy R300). There's a lovely mosaic-decorated pool and relaxing gardens to chill out in with Table Mountain views. Rates don't include breakfast.

MOUNT NELSON HOTEL HOTEL $$$

Map p274 ([✆]021-483 1000; www.mountnelson.co.za; 76 Orange St, Gardens; r/ste from R3595/5395; [P][❊][@][☎][≋][♿]; [💻]Government Avenue) The sugar-pink painted 'Nellie' recalls Cape Town's colonial era with its chintz decor and doormen in pith helmets. Recently renovated rooms sport elegant silver and mossy green decorations. Service is mixed but it's very good for families since it pushes the boat out for the little ones, with kid-sized robes and free biscuits and milk at bedtime, not to mention the big pool and three hectares of gardens including tennis courts.

KENSINGTON PLACE BOUTIQUE HOTEL $$$

Map p274 ([✆]021-424 4744; www.kensingtonplace.co.za; 38 Kensington Cres, Higgovale; d from R2860; [P][❊][@][≋]) High up the mountain, this exclusive, chic property offers eight spacious and tastefully decorated rooms, all with balconies and beautifully tiled bathrooms. Fresh fruit and flowers in the rooms are a nice touch.

HIPPO BOUTIQUE HOTEL BOUTIQUE HOTEL $$

Map p274 ([✆]021-423 2500; www.hippotique.co.za; 5-9 Park Rd, Gardens; d/ste R1290/2200; [P][❊][@][☎][≋]; [💻]Michaelis) Brilliantly located and appealing boutique property offering spacious, stylish rooms each with a small kitchen for self-catering. Larger, arty suites, with mezzanine-level bedrooms and themes such as Red Bull and Mini Cooper, are worth the extra spend. Gadget-lovers will also be pleased with the DVD player, music system and in-room computers.

ASHANTI GARDENS BACKPACKERS/SELF-CATERING $

Map p274 ([✆]021-423 8721; www.ashanti.co.za; 11 Hof St, Gardens; d R640, dm/s/d without bathroom R150/320/460; [P][@][☎][≋]; [💻]Government Avenue) This is one of Cape Town's slickest operations, with much of the action focused on its lively bar and deck which overlooks Table Mountain. The beautiful old house, newly decorated with a tasteful collection of local contemporary art, holds the dorms and a lawn on which you can camp (R80 per person). There are excellent self-catering en suite rooms in two separate heritage-listed houses around the corner.

CAPE CADOGAN BOUTIQUE HOTEL $$

Map p274 ([✆]021-480 8080; www.capecadogan.com; 5 Upper Union St, Gardens; s/d/apt from R1330/2660/2670; [P][@][☎][≋]; [💻]Michaelis) This *Gone with the Wind*–style heritage-listed villa presents a very classy boutique operation with some rooms opening on to the secluded courtyard. If you'd prefer more privacy, they also offer appealing one- and two-bed self-catering apartments in the mews of nearby Nicol St.

15 ON ORANGE HOTEL $$$

Map p274 ([✆]021-469 8000; www.africanpridehotels.com/15onorange; cnr Grey's Pass & Orange St, Gardens; r/ste from R2550/3050; parking R65 per day; [P][❊][@][☎][≋]; [💻]Michaelis) The lipstick red and marble walkway to the lobby gives an indication of the luxe nature of this hotel, which is built around a soaring atrium on to which some rooms face (perfect for exhibitionists). It's all very plush and design savvy. Rates don't include breakfast.

FOUR ROSMEAD B&B $$

Map p274 ([✆]021-480 3810; www.fourrosmead.com; 4 Rosmead Ave, Oranjezicht; d/ste from R2050/2750; [P][❊][@][☎][≋]) A heritage-listed building dating from 1903 has been remodelled into this luxury B&B. Special touches include a saltwater swimming pool and a fragrant Mediterranean herb garden. The pool-house suite with lofty ceiling is great if you want extra privacy.

CAPE MILNER HOTEL $$

Map p274 ([✆]021-426 1101; www.capemilner.com; 2A Milner Rd,Tamboerskloof; s/d from R650/990, s/d ste R2095/2800; parking R40 per day; [P][❊][@][☎][≋]; [💻]Buitensingel) Silks and velvets in metallic colours add a sophisticated touch to the contemporary-style rooms here, which are good value for this area. Friendly service and sweeping views of Table Mountain from the luxurious suites and pool deck area are other pluses. Wi-fi is R50 per day.

ABBEY MANOR
B&B **$$**

Map p274 (☎021-462 2935; www.abbey.co.za; 3 Montrose Ave, Oranjezicht; s/d from R1750/2200; ⓟ✳@⊜⚛; 🚇Buitensingel) Occupying a grand Arts and Crafts–style home, built in 1905 for a shipping magnate, the interiors of this luxury guesthouse marry fine linen and antique furnishings with whimsical art nouveau flourishes. A decent-sized pool and courteous staff enhance the experience.

CACTUSBERRY LODGE
B&B **$$**

Map p274 (☎021-461 9787; www.cactusber rylodge.com; 30 Breda St, Oranjezicht; s/d from R640/1050; ⓟ⊜⚛) There are just six rooms at this red-wine-coloured lodge with a striking contemporary design, mixing arty photography, African crafts and Euro style. Their sun deck overlooks Table Mountain and there's a tiny splash pool in the courtyard to cool down in.

AN AFRICAN VILLA
B&B **$$**

Map p274 (☎021-423 2162; www.capetown city.co.za; 19 Carstens St, Tamboerskloof; s/d from R1150/1600; @⊜⚛) There's a sophisticated, colourful 'African modern' design theme at this appealing guesthouse, sheltering behind the facade of three 19th-century terrace houses. Relax in the evening in one of two comfy lounges while sipping the complimentary sherry.

DUNKLEY HOUSE
B&B **$$**

Map p274 (☎021-462 7650; www.dunkleyhouse. com; 3B Gordon St, Gardens; s/d from R650/850, s/d apt from R1450/1550; ✳@⊜⚛; 🚇Gardens) Tucked away on a quiet street, this ultrastylish guesthouse offers neutral-toned rooms featuring a mix of retro and modern furnishings, CD players, fresh fruit and flowers and a bamboo grove. There's a plunge pool in the courtyard, while the honeymoon suite has a private pool and separate Jacuzzi.

TREVOYAN
B&B **$$**

Map p274 (☎021-424 4407; www.trevoyan. co.za; 12 Gilmour Hill Rd, Tamboerskloof; s/d from R848/1060; ⓟ✳@⊜) This heritage building, with high-ceiling rooms, parquet floors and a faint art-deco style, has been transformed into a relaxed guesthouse that is smart but not too posh. A big plus is its lovely courtyard garden, partly shaded by an giant oak, with a pool big enough to swim in.

PROTEA HOTEL FIRE & ICE!
HOTEL **$$**

Map p274 (☎021-488 2555; www.proteahotels. com; 198 Bree St, Gardens; s/d R1295/1495; parking R40 per day; ⓟ✳@⚛; 🚇Buitensingel) Yes, that exclamation mark is justified! The Protea hotel chain thought outside of the box when designing this place that takes Cape Town's adventurous, party-hard spirit as inspiration. The stylish rooms are somewhat cramped, especially the standard ones. We love the hilarious range of toilets off the vibey bar. Rates don't include breakfast.

AMSTERDAM GUEST HOUSE
B&B **$$**

Map p274 (☎021-461 8236; www.amster dam.co.za; 19 Forest Rd, Oranjezicht; s/d from R895/995; ⓟ✳@⊜⚛) It's men only at this quirkily decorated gay guesthouse (think giant mounted stag's head meets mural of James Dean) that's notable for its range of comfortable rooms, decent-sized pool, Jacuzzi, sundeck and sauna, and all 169 episodes of *I Love Lucy* on video, plus hundreds of other movies.

BLENCATHRA
BACKPACKERS/SELF-CATERING **$**

off Map p274 (☎073 389 0702, 021-424 9571; cnr De Hoop & Cambridge Aves, Tamboerskloof; dm/d without bathroom R150/500; ⓟ@⊜⚛) You're well on the way up Lion's Head at this delightful family home, which offers a range of attractive rooms, mostly frequented by long-stay guests. It's the ideal spot for those looking to escape the city and the more-commercialised backpacker options. For long stays rates are negotiable.

CAPE TOWN BACKPACKERS
BACKPACKERS/SELF-CATERING **$**

Map p274 (☎021-426 0200; www.capetown backpackers.com; 81 New Church St, Gardens; dm from R150, s/d R550/650; parking R10 per day; ⓟ@⊜) This welcoming hostel offers both pleasant dorms and en-suite rooms facing onto neighbouring Kohling St; rooms 20 and 22 have the best views. Note the cheapest 10-bed dorm is in the basement. Have fun trying on the many hats in their bar. Rates don't include breakfast.

🛏 Green Point & Waterfront

🏆TOP CHOICE VILLA ZEST
BOUTIQUE HOTEL **$$**

Map p276 (☎021-433 1246; www.villazest.co.za; 2 Braemar Rd, Green Point; s/d R1390/1690, ste s/d R2290/2590; ⓟ✳@⚛) This Bauhaus-style villa has been converted into a quirkily decorated boutique hotel that wittily avoids the clichés of the genre. The lobby is lined with an impressive collection of '60s and '70s groovy electronic goods, including radios, phones, Polaroid cameras and eight-track cassette players. The seven guest rooms have bold retro-design furniture and wallpapered walls accented with furry pillows and shagpile rugs.

CAPE GRACE HOTEL $$$

Map p276 (📞021-410 7100; www.capegrace. com; West Quay, V&A Waterfront; s/d or tw from R5290/5450, ste s/d from R10,680/10,840; 🅿️🌸@🛜♨️; 🚇Breakwater) Fair Trade in Tourism accredited, this is one of the Waterfront's most appealing hotels. An arty combination of antiques and crafts decoration – including hand-painted bed covers and curtains – provides a unique sense of place and Cape Town's history. They also have a good spa and a private yacht should you wish to sail out into the bay.

ONE & ONLY CAPE TOWN HOTEL $$$

Map p276 (📞021-431 5888; www.oneandonly capetown.com; Dock Rd, V&A Waterfront; r/ste from R5990/11,940; 🅿️🌸@🛜♨️; 🚇Breakwater) Little expense seems to have been spared creating this luxury resort. Take your pick between enormous, plush rooms in the main building (with panoramic views of Table Mountain) or the even more exclusive island, beside the pool and spa. Their bar turns out inventive cocktails and is a nice place to plonk yourself before a meal at celeb-chef restaurants Nobu or Reuben's.

CAPE STANDARD BOUTIQUE HOTEL $$

Map p276 (📞021-430 3060; www.capestandard. co.za; 3 Romney Rd, Green Point; s/d R1050/1380; 🅿️@🛜♨️) Hidden away in Green Point, this chic property offers whitewashed beachhouse rooms downstairs or contemporary rooms upstairs. The mosaic-tiled bathrooms have showers big enough to dance in.

DOCK HOUSE HOTEL $$$

Map p276 (📞021-421 9334; www.dockhouse. co.za; Portswood Close, Portswood Ridge; d from R5770; 🅿️🌸@♨️; 🚇Breakwater) Butlers dressed in white kurta-style pyjamas greet you at this super-elegant, six-bedroom property crafted out of the former harbour master's house. The luxurious bedrooms are decorated in dove grey and olive and have spacious bathrooms. It's at the heart

of the Waterfront but feels almost a world away. The same company run the appealing (and cheaper) nearby **Queen Victoria Hotel** (Map p276; www.queenvictoriahotel.co.za).

HEAD SOUTH LODGE BOUTIQUE HOTEL $$

Map p276 (📞021-434 8777; www.headsouth. co.za; 215 Main Rd, Green Point; s/d R1250/1400; 🅿️🌸🛜♨️) A homage to the 1950s, with its retro furnishings and collection of Tretchikoff prints hung en masse in the bar. Its big rooms, decorated in cool white and grey, are hung with equally striking modern art by Philip Briel.

WILTON MANOR BOUTIQUE HOTEL $$

Map p276 (📞021-434 7869; www.wiltonguest houses.co.za; 15 Croxteth Rd, Green Point; s/d from R700/1200; 🅿️🌸@🛜♨️) This charming two-storey Victorian house, featuring a wooden veranda, has been converted into a very stylish guesthouse. Rooms are individually decorated in African themes. The owners also run the more contemporary Wilton Place higher up Signal Hill.

ATLANTIC POINT BACKPACKERS BACKPACKERS/SELF-CATERING $$

Map p276 (📞021-433 1663; www.atlanticpoint. co.za; 2 Cavalcade Rd, Green Point; d R660, dm/d without bathroom from R140/495; 🅿️@🛜) Giving longer-established backpackers some serious competition is this imaginatively designed, playful and well-run place steps away from Green Point's main drag. Features include a big balcony and bar and the loft lounge covered in AstroTurf. Rates include wi-fi and parking – extra good value.

ASHANTI GREEN POINT BACKPACKERS/SELF-CATERING $

Map p276 (📞021-433 1619; www.ashanti.co.za; 23 Antrim Rd, Three Anchor Bay; d R600; dm/s/d without bathroom R130/320/460; 🅿️@🛜♨️) More chilled than their original Gardens branch, this Ashanti has a breezy hillside position with sea views and is nicely decorated with old Cape Town photos.

🛏️ Sea Point to Hout Bay

TOP CHOICE TINTSWALO ATLANTIC HOTEL $$$

off Map p279 (📞087 754 9300; www.tintswalo. com; Chapman's Peak Drive, Hout Bay; s/d/ste from R5070/7800/25,000; 🅿️🌸@🛜♨️) The only luxury lodge within Table Mountain National Park offers 10 rooms and one suite (sleeping four) on the very edge of a beautiful rocky bay, a favourite resting ground for whales. Each room is artily themed to represent one of the world's islands, with lots of use of seashells and other natural materials. The complex is sheltered by the milkwood trees and built on raised platforms to keep environmental impact to a minimum. Rack rates include dinner and breakfast.

TOP CHOICE POD
BOUTIQUE HOTEL $$$

Map p278 (☎021-438 8550; www.pod.co.za; 3 Argyle St,Camps Bay; r/ste from R2700/7100; P✳@☎☱) Lovers of clean contemporary design will adore the slate- and wood-decorated POD, which is perfectly angled to catch the Camps Bay action from its bar and spacious pool deck area. The cheapest rooms have mountain rather than sea views; luxury rooms have their own private plunge pools.

ELLERMAN HOUSE
HOTEL $$$

Map p280 (☎021-430 3200; www.ellerman. co.za; 180 Kloof Rd, Bantry Bay; d/ste/villa from R8300/17,270/53,460; P✳@☎☱) Imagine you've been invited to stay with an immensely rich, art-collecting Capetonian friend. This elegant mansion overlooking the Atlantic and its more contemporary-styled Frank Lloyd Wright–esque villa (complete with its own spa) would be the deal. It has beautiful gardens and a splendid contemporary art gallery. A second villa, showcasing a wine cellar with some 7000 bottles, was under construction at the time of research.

CAMPS BAY RETREAT
BOUTIQUE HOTEL $$$

Map p278 (☎021-437 8300; www.campsbayre treat.com; 7 Chilworth Rd, the Glen; d/ste from R4380/6700; P✳@☎☱) Based in the grand Earl's Dyke Manor (dating from 1929, although it looks older), this splendid option is set in a secluded nature reserve. There is a choice of 15 rooms in either the main house or the contemporary Deck House, reached by a rope bridge over a ravine. Take your pick from three pools, including one fed by a stream from Table Mountain. Bicycles can be hired (R50 per day) to pedal down to the beach.

HOUT BAY MANOR
HOTEL $$$

Map p279 (☎021-790 0116; www.houtbaymanor. co.za; Baviaanskloof Rd, Hout Bay; s/d from R2100/3200; P✳@☎☱) Your eyes will pop at the fab Afro-chic makeover that the 1871

Hout Bay Manor has been treated to. Tribal artefacts are mixed with brightly coloured contemporary furnishings and handicrafts in rooms which all contain the expected electronic conveniences.

O ON KLOOF
HOTEL $$

Map p280 (☎021-439 2081; www.oonkloof.co.za; 92 Kloof Rd, Sea Point; d/ste from R2130/3950; P✳@☎☱) Cross the mini bridge over the ornamental pool leading to this gorgeous contemporary-styled guesthouse. Not all of the eight spacious rooms have full sea views but the good facilities, including a big indoor pool and gym, are ample compensation.

GLEN BOUTIQUE HOTEL
HOTEL $$

Map p280 (☎021-439 0086; www.glenhotel.co.za; 3 The Glen, Sea Point; d/ste from R1450/3250; P✳@☎☱) One of Cape Town's premier gay-friendly boutique hotels occupies an elegant old house and a newer block behind. Spacious rooms are decorated in natural tones of stone and wood. In the middle is a fabulous pool and spa, the playground for their monthly Saturday-afternoon pool parties.

WINCHESTER MANSIONS HOTEL
HOTEL $$

Map p280 (☎021-434 2351; www.winches ter.co.za; 221 Beach Rd, Sea Point; s/d from R1650/2125, ste s/d from R2050/2585; P✳@☎☱) The Winchester offers a seaside location (you'll pay extra for rooms with views), old-fashioned style and some corridors lined with putting greens for a spot of golf practice. The pool is a decent size and there's a lovely courtyard with a central fountain, which is a romantic place to dine.

HUIJS HAERLEM
B&B $$

Map p280 (☎021-434 6434; www.huijshaerlem. co.za; 25 Main Dr, Sea Point; s/d from R850/1450; P@☎☱) Get a workout walking up one of Sea Point's steeper slopes to reach this excellent gay-friendly (but not exclusively gay) guesthouse. It comprises two houses decorated with antiques and joined by delightful gardens in which you'll find a decent-sized pool.

CHAPMAN'S PEAK HOTEL
HOTEL $$$

Map p279 (☎021-790 1036; www.chapmanspeak hotel.co.za; Chapman's Peak Dr, Hout Bay; s/d from R2070/2810; P✳@☎☱) Take your pick between chic, contemporary-designed rooms with balconies and to-die-for views across Hout Bay (in a new addition), or the much cheaper and smaller rooms (R660 for a mountain view, R960 for a partial sea view) in the original building, which also houses a very popular bar and restaurant with a broad outdoor deck.

THULANI RIVER LODGE
B&B $$

off Map p279 (✆021-790 7662; www.thulani.eu; 14 Riverside Terrace, Hout Bay; s/d from R950/1150; P@⊕☎) 'Thulani' is Zulu for 'peace and tranquillity' – the perfect description for this treasure, a traditional African thatched mansion tucked away in a lush valley through which the Disa River flows towards Hout Bay. Lie in the four-poster bed in the honeymoon suite and you'll be treated to a sweeping panorama of the back of Table Mountain.

AMBLEWOOD GUESTHOUSE
B&B $$

Map p279 (✆021-790 1570; www.amblewood. co.za; 43 Skaife St, Hout Bay; s/d from R780/980; P@⊕☎) Cool off in the small pool on the deck of this upmarket B&B and look out over the beautiful sweep of Hout Bay. There's a range of pleasant rooms, decorated with period furniture to match the style of the house.

🛏 Southern Suburbs

CONSTANTIA UITSIG
HOTEL $$$

(✆021-794 6500; www.constantia-uitsig.com; Spaanschemat River Rd; s/d/ste from R2400/3600/5200; P⊕@☎) Set within the vineyard of the same name, this hotel offers appealing, chintzy Victorian-styled rooms, all florals and checks. There are beautiful gardens as well as three top-notch restaurants to choose from.

VINEYARD HOTEL & SPA
HOTEL $$

Map p282 (✆021-657 4500; www.vineyard.co.za; Colinton Rd, Newlands; s/d from R1300/1750, s/d ste from R4500/4950; P⊕@☎) Built around the 1799 home of Lady Anne Barnard, the rooms at this delightful hotel have a contemporary look and are decorated in soothing natural tones. It's surrounded by lush gardens with views onto Table Mountain. Friendly staff, the fabulous Angsana Spa, a great gym and pool, and top gourmet restaurant Myoga complete the picture.

ALPHEN
BOUTIQUE HOTEL $$$

(✆021-795 6300; www.alphen.co.za; Alphen Dr, Constantia; ste from R2900; P⊕@☎) A glitzy makeover has transformed this historic estate into a bling-tastic property with 21 suites variously dubbed 'cool', 'amazing', 'stunning' and 'magic'. This translates into a fearless mix of antiques and bold contemporary styling. The property's convivial La Belle cafe and bakery and chic Rose Bar, overlooking the manicured gardens and pool, are both worth a trip on their own. Take Constantia Exit from M3 and follow signs to Alphen.

🛏 Southern Peninsula

BELLA EV
B&B $$

Map p284 (✆021-788 1293; www.bellaevguest house.co.za; 8 Camp Rd, Muizenberg; s/d R650/1200; @; ⊕Muizenberg) This charming guesthouse, with a delightful courtyard garden, could be the setting for an Agatha Christie mystery, one in which the home's owner has a penchant for all things Turkish – hence the Ottoman slippers for guests' use and the option of a Turkish-style breakfast.

CHARTFIELD GUEST HOUSE
B&B $

Map p284 (✆021-788 3793; www.chartfield.co.za; 30 Gatesville Rd, Kalk Bay; s/d from R480/550; P@⊕☎; ⊕Kalk Bay) This rambling, 1920s, wooden-floored guesthouse has been upgraded and decorated with choice pieces of contemporary local arts and crafts. There's a variety of rooms each with crisp linen, and bathrooms with a rain-style shower. They have an internet cafe (open to nonguests), and a lovely cafe-bar with a terrace and garden overlooking the harbour.

MONKEY VALLEY BEACH NATURE RESORT
HOTEL $

(✆021-789 1391; www.monkeyvalleyresort.com; Mountain Rd, Noordhoek; s/d from R1530/2250, cottage from R3380; P☎⊕⊕) Choose between sea-facing rooms or spacious self-catering cottages all with thatched open-rafter roofs at this imaginatively designed, rustic resort shaded by a milkwood forest. It's a great place if you have kids, and the wide beach is moments away. Follow signs from Noordhoek end of Chapman's Peak Rd (M6) to the resort.

SHACK STAYS

Vicky's B&B (☎082 225 2986, 021-387 0122; Site C-685A, Khayelitsha; s/d R270/540; @) in Khayelitsha was once the only shack homestay. Vicky's success as a B&B hostess has enabled her to create a rather fine two-storey structure sporting six guest rooms, three of them en suite; it's beginning to look an anachronism as more and more proper brick houses replace shacks in Site C.

Competition now comes from **Vuvu's Small Shack** (☎072-715 5721; www.township-experience.com; s/d R150/300) in Langa. Vuvu, a friendly registered guide, offers her tiny shed-like room, which stands in front of her parent's brick house, as a place for up to two people to stay. You'll need to bring a sleeping bag and be prepared to share with Vuvu.

BOULDERS BEACH LODGE B&B $$

Map p286 (☎021-786 1758; www.bouldersbeach.co.za; 4 Boulders Pl, Boulders; s/d/apt from R500/900/1875; P @ wifi; Simon's Town) Penguins waddle right up to the doors of this smart guesthouse with rooms decorated in wicker and wood and a range of self-catering units where the rates also include breakfast. Its excellent restaurant has an outdoor deck. Note: penguins are not the quietest creatures so you may want bring earplugs.

DE NOORDHOEK HOTEL HOTEL $

(☎021-789 2760; www.denoordhoek.co.za; cnr Chapman's Peak Dr & Village Ln, Noordhoek; s/d from R990/1410; P ❄ @ wifi pool) So well has this hotel been constructed that it seems as if it has always been part of the Noordhoek Farm Village. The rooms, including ones that are specially adapted for disabled use, are spacious and comfortable and surround a pretty inner courtyard planted with *fynbos* (literally 'fine bush') and lemon trees. Follow signs to Noordhoek Farm Village from Chapman's Peak Rd (M6).

THE GLEN LODGE HOTEL $

off Map p286 (☎021-782 0314; www.theglenlodgeandpub.co.za; 12-14 Glen Rd, Glencairn; dm/s/d R200/300/500; P wifi; Glencairn) This historic inn offers simply but appealingly furnished rooms, four with sea views. The dorm (with just four bunks) rates exclude breakfast. It's convenient for Glencairn beach, the station and it's not far from Simon's Town. A convivial pub and cafe are also on the premises.

SIMON'S TOWN BACKPACKERS BACKPACKERS $

Map p286 (☎021-786 1964; www.capepax.co.za; 66 St George's St, Simon's Town; d R500; dm/d without bathroom R150/440; @; Simon's Town) The shipshape rooms at this relaxed backpackers are spacious, with several overlooking the harbour. There is bike hire for R120 per day and friendly staff can help you arrange a host of activities in the area. Rates don't include breakfast.

SAMHITAKASHA COB HOUSE B&B $

Map p284 (☎021-788 6613; www.cobhouse.co.za; 13 Watson Rd, Muizenberg; s/d R350/700; P wifi; Muizenberg) It took two years for English and French speaking tour guide Simric Yarrow to build his unique organic home out of mud, wood and straw; one room above the garage is for guests. Hot water is provided via a solar-powered heater. As well as the organic breakfast included in the rates, Simric can also rustle up dinner.

ECO WAVE LODGE BACKPACKERS $

(☎073-927 5644; 11 Gladioli Way, Kommetjie; dm/s/d R150/300/340; P wifi) Perfect for surfies, this backpackers is less than 100m from the beach and offers very salubrious digs in a spacious villa-style house complete with giant dining room hung with a chandelier and big sun deck. The management can arrange surf lessons and gear. Turn on to Somerset Way off Kommetjie Rd (M65); this leads into Gladioli Way.

BEACH LODGE BACKPACKERS $

Map p284 (☎021-788 1771; www.thebeachlodge.co.za; 13-19 York Rd, Muizenberg; dm/s/d without bathroom R120/200/380; @; Muizenberg) Set in a heritage-listed building with splendid sea views, this budget guesthouse is ideal for those who don't want to be more than 30 seconds from the sand. There's a huge kitchen and satellite TV in the comfy lounge. Rates don't include breakfast.

🛏 Cape Flats & Northern Suburbs

LIZIWE GUEST HOUSE
B&B **$**

(☎021-633 7406; www.sa-venues.com/visit/liziwesguesthouse; 121 NY 111, Gugulethu; s/d R300/600; ◉) Liziwe has made her mansion into a palace with four delightful en-suite rooms all sporting satellite TV and African-themed decor. She was featured on a BBC cooking show, so you can be sure her food is delicious. Plus her place is walking distance to Mzoli's.

COLETTE'S
B&B **$**

Map p287 (☎083 458 5344, 021-531 4830; www.colettesbb.co.za; 16 The Bend, Pinelands; s/d R380/580; 🅿🛜; 🚆Pinelands) The very charming Colette runs this women-friendly B&B in her spacious and pretty Pinelands home, which she shares with ducks Isabella and Ferdinand. All rooms, including a couple in the loft, have private bathrooms.

RADEBE'S B&B
B&B **$**

Map p287 (☎021-695 0508, 082 393 3117; www.radebes.co.za; 23 Mama Way, Settlers Pl, Langa; s/d R280/500; 🅿◉) The best of Langa's B&Bs offers three delightfully decorated guest rooms (one with a private bathroom). There's a nice sitting room with TV and DVD. Enormous meals are served in the attached Coffee Shack restaurant or you can cook for yourself in the fully equipped kitchen.

KOPANONG
B&B **$**

(☎082 476 1278, 021-361 2084; www.kopanong-township.co.za; 329 Velani Cres, Section C, Khayelitsha; s/d R300/600; 🅿) Thope Lekau, called 'Mama Africa' for obvious reasons, runs this excellent B&B with her equally ebullient daughter, Mpho. Her substantial brick home offers two stylishly decorated guest rooms, each with their own bathroom. As a guide and experienced development worker, Thope will give you an excellent insight into township life, as well as cook a delicious dinner (R110). Ask about her cookery course and walking tour of the area (R120).

MAJORO'S B&B
B&B **$$**

(☎082 537 6882, tel/fax 021-361 3412; majoros@webmail.co.za; 69 Helena Cres, Khayelitsha; s/d without bathroom R350/700; 🅿) Friendly Maria Maile is the owner of this B&B, located in a small brick bungalow in an upmarket part of Khayelitsha. She can put up four people in her two homely rooms. Dinner is available for R100 and there's safe parking should you drive here.

MALEBO'S
B&B **$$**

(☎083 475 1125, 021-361 2391; malebo12@webmail.co.za; 18 Mississippi Way, Khayelitsha; s/d R350/700) Lydia Masoleng has been opening up her spacious, modern home to guests since 1998. She's upgraded three of the four comfy rooms to have en-suite bathrooms. Dinner (R95) is available and includes her self-brewed *umqombothi* (beer).

Understand Cape Town

Cape Town Today

'Live design, transform life' is the slogan that helped Cape Town win its bid for World Design Capital 2014. Ventures such as the MyCiTi bus routes and Creative Cape Town are already having a positive impact. However, the vast majority of Capetonians live in poverty on the Cape Flats, a world away from the multimillion-rand villas of Camps Bay or the protected environment of Table Mountain National Park, so the debate over priorities continues. Accusations of racism still dog a metropolis that aspires to be multicultural.

Best on Film

Black Butterflies (www.blackbut terflies.nl) Dutch biopic about the Afrikaans poet Ingrid Jonkers (a powerful performance by Carice van Houten) set in Cape Town in the 1950s and '60s.

Sea Point Days (www.seapointdays. co.za) Documentary by Francois Verster focusing on the suburb and its prom-enade as a multicultural crossroads.

Visa/Vie (www.visaviemovie.com) Charming comedy that sets its French heroine the challenge of finding a Capetonian husband in one weekend so she can avoid deportation.

Best in Print

A City Imagined (ed Stephen Watson) Top-class selection of origi-nal essays by local writers revealing different aspects of the Mother City.

Reports From Before Daybreak (Brent Meersman) Cape Town is the principal setting for this impressive novel about the turbulent, violent decade before democracy and its damaging effect on people of all races.

Refuge (Andrew Brown) Shortlisted for the Commonwealth Writers Prize in 2009, this thriller includes char-acters ripped from local headlines including Russian mobsters and Nigerian immigrants.

District Controversies

In December 2011, the city rolled out proposals to re-build District Six and invited public comment. 'I'm fearful for the planning of the area' said Rashiq Fataar, founder of Future Cape Town (www.futurecapetown. com), whose father was evicted from the demolished inner city suburb but who has given up on the slow-moving application process to reclaim a home there. 'There's none of the broader debate about what District Six could be.'

Differences of opinion also occurred between representatives of the District Six Museum, and the public-private partnership that is working to create the innovative incubation/science park area called The Fringe, adjacent to District Six. Some of the museum staff and trustees are concerned that important histori-cal elements of the area will be lost as it gentrifies.

The city is also going through a spate of road and suburb renaming. So far Nelson Mandela, Helen Suzman and Christiaan Barnard have found their democracy-friendly monikers attached to major high-ways, while up for renaming at the time of research are 27 other roads that have apartheid/colonial connec-tions such as Hendrik Verwoerd Dr. The Name Your Hood (www.nameyourhood.co.za) campaign, support-ed by the city and provincial government, has plans to roll the process out from downtown and surroundings to Gugulethu. Quite soon you may see new inner city suburb names such as The Loop, Little Camissa and Green Mile appearing on maps.

Verbal & Physical Battles

A Twitter brawl broke out in early 2012 between repre-sentatives of the black community, including the Afro-blues singer Simphiwe Dana, and the Western Cape Premier Helen Zille over whether Cape Town is racist.

'Try live in a black skin for once. You have the power to change things,' tweeted Dana, prompting Zille to tweet back, 'You're a highly respected black professional. Don't try to be a professional black.'

Such spats highlight the rift that remains between different communities of this post-apartheid, but still economically segregated, city. Tempers flared again when an Occupy Rondebosch Common movement attempted a sit-in on the Southern Suburbs' common space to highlight the plight of long-suffering shack dwellers in the townships. Cape Town mayor Patricia De Lille branded the protesters 'agents of destruction' and sent the police in, arresting high-profile leader Mario Wanza of Proudly Mannenberg before the demo got underway. In an editorial the *Cape Times* called the city's response 'hysterical' and 'shameful'.

Meanwhile, over on Chapman's Peak Dr in February 2012, another demo proceeded against the construction of a R54 million toll booth and offices within a protected area of Table Mountain National Park. One protester went on hunger strike and two others handcuffed themselves to scaffolding at the site, temporarily halting the project.

Designing the Future

De Lille drew praise, however, for using the Pecha Kucha format (www.pecha-kucha.org; 20 slides at 20 second intervals) as a creative way to present her administration's vision for the World Design Capital 2014 process at the 2012 Design Indaba. 'This is now an opportunity for the city and its residents to engage with leading design thinkers in finding solutions to Cape Town's major challenges,' she began. 'This includes an examination of how we can overcome the legacy of apartheid spatial planning to foster a more inclusive city.'

Among the projects already started that De Lille name-checked in her speech is Violence Prevention through Urban Upgrade in Khayelitsha (www.vpuu. org), which has been successful in transforming a formerly crime ridden part of the township into a safe public space. 'We will be rolling this out to other parts of the metro,' said De Lille. Also looking promising are the various winners of the 2011 Design Indaba Your Street challenge, such as the Urban Mosaic project that aims to help prevent shack fires with fire-resistant paint.

if South Africa were 100 people

9 would be coloured
79 would be black
9 would be white
3 would be Indian/Asian

if Cape Town were 100 people

48 would be coloured
31 would be black
19 would be white
2 would be Indian/Asian

population per sq km

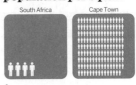

South Africa   Cape Town

≈ 10 people

History

Humans lived on the Cape for millennia before the first Europeans visited in the 15th century. The Portuguese passed up the chance to settle, but the Dutch weren't put off by the aggressive natives, savage weather and dangerous coastline – they brought slaves, forever changing the ethnic complexion of the Cape. Dutch rule lasted nearly 200 years before the British took over in 1814, prompting many Afrikaners (Boers) to trek inland. The Afrikaners came back with a vengeance during the years of apartheid. At the end of the 20th century Nelson Mandela finally walked here a free man and the new South Africa was born.

THE KHOEKHOEN & SAN PEOPLE

South Africa lays strong claim to being the cradle of mankind. At Langebaan Lagoon (north of Cape Town), the discovery of 117,000-year-old fossilised footprints prompted one researcher to speculate that 'Eve' (the very first human or common ancestor of us all) lived here.

Academics don't know whether the earliest-recorded inhabitants of South Africa – the San people – are direct descendants or if they returned to the area after aeons of travel anything between 40,000 and 25,000 years ago. For centuries, perhaps even millennia, the San and the Khoekhoen, another early Southern African people, intermarried and coexisted. The distinction is by no means clear, hence the combined term Khoe-San.

Culturally and physically, the Khoe-San developed differently from the Negroid peoples of Africa, but it's possible that they came into contact with pastoralist Bantu-speaking tribes as, in addition to hunting and gathering food, they became pastoralists, raising cattle and sheep. There's evidence that the Khoe-San lived on the Cape of Good Hope about 2000 years ago.

FIRST EUROPEAN VISITORS

The first Europeans to record a sighting of the Cape were the Portuguese, who passed by on their search for a sea route to India and spices. Bartholomeu Dias rounded the Cape in 1488, but didn't linger, as his sights were fixed on the trade riches of the east coast of Africa and the Indies.

The Cape offered the Portuguese little more than fresh water, since their attempts to trade with the Khoe-San often ended in violence. But by the end of the 16th century, English and Dutch traders were beginning to challenge the Portuguese, and the Cape became a regular stopover for

TIMELINE	c 40,000 BC	AD 1488	1510
	Middens – ancient garbage heaps packed with shells, bones and pieces of stone tools and pottery – indicate that the antecedents of the Khoekhoen and San tribes were living on the Cape.	Bartholomeu Dias, the first European to sail around the Cape, dubs it Cabo da Boa Esperança (Cape of Good Hope). Others prefer Cabo das Tormentas (Cape of Storms).	The Khoe-San fight back when Portuguese soldiers try to kidnap two of their number and Captain de Almeida and 50 of his troops are killed.

their scurvy-ridden crews. In 1647 a Dutch vessel was wrecked in Table Bay; its crew built a fort and stayed for a year before they were rescued.

This crystallised the value of a permanent settlement in the minds of the directors of the Vereenigde Oost-Indische Compagnie (VOC; Dutch East India Company). They had no intention of colonising the country, but simply wanted to establish a secure base where ships could shelter and stock up on fresh supplies of meat, fruit and vegetables.

THE DUTCH ARRIVE

The task of establishing the VOC station fell to Jan van Riebeeck (1619–77) who was Commander of the Cape from 1652 to 1662. The Dutch were not greeted with open arms by the Khoe-San and intermittent hostilities broke out. However, the locals – who are thought to have numbered between 4000 and 8000 people – hardly stood a chance against the Europeans' guns and diseases.

The Khoe-San proving uncooperative, the Cape settlement was soon suffering a chronic labour shortage. From 1657 Van Riebeeck started releasing VOC employees, allowing them to farm land independently, thus beginning the colonisation of Southern Africa and giving birth to the Boers. The following year he began to import slaves from West Africa, Madagascar, India, Ceylon, Malaya and Indonesia. By the time the slave trade ended in 1807, some 60,000 slaves had been brought to the Cape, laying the foundations for the unique mix of cultures and races.

THE SETTLEMENT GROWS

The process of colonisation kicked off a series of wars between the Khoe-San further inland and the Dutch, in which the locals were obviously no match for the well-armed and organised Europeans. The Dutch also allowed some 200 Huguenots (French Calvinists fleeing persecution by King Louis XIV) to settle on the Cape in 1688.

There was a shortage of women in the colony, so female slaves and Khoe-San women were exploited for both labour and sex. In time, the slaves intermixed with the Khoe-San, too. The offspring of these unions form the basis of sections of today's coloured population.

Under the VOC's almost complete control, Kaapstad (the Dutch name for Cape Town) provided a comfortable European lifestyle for a growing number of artisans and entrepreneurs servicing ships and crews. By the middle of the 18th century there were around 3000 people living in the riotous port, known as the 'Tavern of the Seas' by every navigator, privateer and merchant travelling between Europe and the East.

NOMADS

The San were nomadic hunters and gatherers, and the Khoekhoen (also known as Khoikhoi, possibly meaning 'Men of Men') were semi-nomadic hunters and pastoralists. European settlers later called the Khoekhoen 'Hottentots' and the San 'Bushmen'.

1652	1660	1679	1699
Jan van Riebeeck, instructed by the Vereenigde Oost-Indische Compagnie (VOC; Dutch East India Company) to establish a supply station en route to India, arrives on 6 April.	Van Riebeeck plants a wild almond hedge to protect his European settlement from the Khoe-San – a section of it remains in the Kirstenbosch Botanical Gardens.	Simon van der Stel, the son of a VOC official and a freed Indian slave, arrives in the Cape as its commander. Two years later he is promoted to governor.	After retiring to develop his estate of Constantia, the birthplace of the Cape's wine industry, Van der Stel is succeeded by his son Willem Adriaan.

WHO ARE THE BOERS?

South Africa's Afrikaner population has its roots in the Dutch and early European settlers of the Cape. The more independent of these settlers soon began drifting away from the strict regime of the Vereenigde Oost-Indische Compagnie (VOC; Dutch East India Company) into the countryside. These were the first of the Trekboers (literally 'trekking farmers'), who were later known as Boers.

Fiercely independent and with livelihoods based on rearing cattle, the Boers were not so different from the Khoe-San that they came into conflict with as they colonised the interior. Many Boers were illiterate and most had no source of information other than the Bible. Isolated from other Europeans, they developed their own separate culture and eventually their own language, Afrikaans, derived from the argot of their slaves.

THE BRITISH TAKE OVER

As the 18th century progressed, the global power of the Dutch was waning and under challenge by the British. Between 1795 and 1806 the Cape was passed like a parcel between the two colonial powers with the French also briefly drawn into the power play.

Even before the colony was formally ceded to the Crown on 13 August 1814, the British had abolished the slave trade. The remaining Khoe-San were given the explicit protection of the law in 1828. These moves contributed to Afrikaners' dissatisfaction and their mass migration, which came to be known as the Great Trek, inland from the Cape Colony.

Despite outlawing slavery, the British introduced new laws that laid the basis for an exploitative labour system little different from slavery. Thousands of dispossessed blacks sought work in the colony, but it was made a crime to be in the colony without a pass – and without work. It was also a crime to leave a job.

CAPE ECONOMY BOOMS

Under a policy of free trade Cape Town's economy flourished. During the first half of the 19th century, before the Suez Canal opened, British officers serving in India would holiday at the Cape.

In 1854 a representative parliament was formed in Cape Town, but much to the dismay of Dutch and English farmers to the north and east, the British government and Cape liberals insisted on a multiracial constituency (albeit with financial requirements that excluded the vast majority of blacks and coloureds).

1795	1806	1808	1814
The British take control of the Cape after winning the Battle of Muizenberg. Eight years later the Treaty of Amiens puts the Dutch back in power.	As part of the Napoleonic Wars, the British return and with their decisive victory at the Battle of Blouberg secure the cape for the Crown.	The new government proclaims free trade and abolishes the local slave trade. Still slaves in the Malmesbury and Tygerberg area revolt and march on Cape Town.	The Cape Colony is formally ceded to Britain, making it the empire's second possession in Africa after Sierra Leone. English replaces Afrikaans as the official language.

The opening of the Suez Canal in 1869 dramatically decreased the amount of shipping that sailed via the Cape, but the discovery of diamonds and gold in the centre of South Africa in the 1870s and '80s helped Cape Town maintain its position as the country's premier port. Immigrants flooded into the city and the population trebled from 33,000 in 1875 to over 100,000 people at the turn of the 20th century.

BOER WAR & AFTER

After the Great Trek, the Boers established several independent republics, the largest being the Orange Free State (today's Free State province) and the Transvaal (today's Northern Province, Gauteng and Mpumalanga).

When the world's richest gold reef was found in the Transvaal (a village called Johannesburg sprang up beside it), the British were miffed that the Boers should control such wealth, which precipitated war in 1899. The Boers were outnumbered, but their tenacity and local knowledge meant the war dragged on until 1902 when the British triumphed.

Cape Town was not directly involved in any of the fighting but it did play a key role in landing and supplying the half a million imperial and colonial troops who fought on the British side. The Mount Nelson Hotel was used as headquarters by Lords Roberts and Kitchener.

After the war, the British made some efforts towards reconciliation, and instituted moves towards the union of the separate South African provinces, which occurred in 1910. In the Cape, blacks and coloureds retained a limited franchise (although only whites could become members of the national parliament, and eligible blacks and coloureds constituted only around 7%), but did not have the vote in other provinces.

APARTHEID RULES

Afrikaners were economically and socially disadvantaged when compared with the English-speaking minority, which controlled most of the capital and industry in the new country. This, plus lingering bitterness over the war and Afrikaners' distaste at having to compete with blacks and coloureds for low-paying jobs, led to strident Afrikaner nationalism and the formation of the National Party (NP).

In 1948 the National Party came to power on a platform of apartheid (literally, 'the state of being apart'). Non-whites were denied the vote, mixed marriages were prohibited, interracial sex was made illegal and every person was classified by race. The Group Areas Act defined where people of each 'race' could live and the Separate Amenities Act created separate public facilities: separate beaches, separate buses, separate

1834	1835	1849	1867
Following emancipation, Cape Town's free slaves establish their own neighbourhood, the Bo-Kaap. In the same year the Cape Town Legislative Council is also founded.	Afrikaner dissatisfaction with British rule prompts the start of the Great Trek; some 10,000 families go in search of their own state, opening up the country's interior.	Governor Sir Harry Smith, anxious that the Cape not become a penal colony, bars 282 British prisoners from leaving the ship *Neptune*, forcing it to continue to Tasmania.	The discovery of the world's largest diamond deposit in Kimberley and gold in the Transvaal boosts Cape Town's economy as the port becomes the gateway for mineral wealth.

toilets, separate schools and separate park benches. Blacks were compelled to carry passes at all times and were prohibited from living in or even visiting towns without specific permission.

FICTIONAL HOMELANDS

MISSION

A system of Homelands was set up in 1951, whereby the proportion of land available for black ownership in South Africa increased very slightly to 13%. Blacks then made up about 75% of the population. The Homelands idea was that each black group had a traditional area where it belonged – and must now stay. The area around Cape Town was declared a 'coloured preference area', which meant that no black person could be employed unless it could be proved that there was no coloured person suitable for the job.

The plan ignored the huge numbers of blacks who had never lived in their 'Homeland'. Millions of people who had lived in other areas for generations were forcibly removed into bleak, unproductive areas with no infrastructure.

The Homelands were regarded as self-governing states and it was planned that they would become independent countries. Four of the 10 Homelands were nominally independent by the time apartheid was demolished (though they were not recognised as independent countries by the UN), and their leaders held power with the help of the South African military.

Meanwhile, white South Africa depended on cheap black labour to keep the economy booming, so many black 'guest workers' were admitted back to the country. But, unless a black had a job and a pass, they were liable to be jailed and sent back to their Homeland. This caused massive disruption to black communities and families. Not surprisingly, people without jobs gravitated to cities such as Cape Town to be near their husbands, wives and parents.

No new black housing was built, and as a result, illegal squatter camps mushroomed on the sandy plains to the east of Cape Town. In response, government bulldozers flattened the shanties, and their occupants were forced into the Homelands. Within weeks, inevitably, the shanties would rise again.

The Dutch Reformed Church justified apartheid on religious grounds, claiming the separateness of the races was divinely ordained, that the *volk* (literally, the 'people', but it really meant just Afrikaners) had a holy mission to preserve the purity of the white race in its promised land.

MANDELA JAILED

In 1960 the African National Congress (ANC) and the Pan African Congress (PAC) organised marches against the hated pass laws, which required blacks and coloureds to carry passbooks authorising them to

1890	1899	1902	March 1902
Two decades after first arriving in Cape Town, self-made mining magnate Cecil Rhodes, founder of De Beers, becomes the colony's prime minister at the age of 37.	Lord Kitchener dubs the British campaign to gain control of the Boer republics as a 'teatime war', but the Anglo-Boer War is fiercely fought over three years.	Bubonic plague arrives on a ship from Argentina giving the government an excuse to introduce racial segregation – 6000 blacks are forcibly sent to live on the Cape Flats.	Rhodes dies at Muizenberg; his vast estate is bequeathed to the city, providing the grounds for both the University of Cape Town and Kirstenbosch Botanical Gardens.

be in a particular area. At Langa and Nyanga on the Cape Flats, police killed five protesters. The Sharpeville massacres in Gauteng were concurrent and resulted in the banning of the ANC and PAC.

In response to the crisis, a warrant for the arrest of Nelson Mandela and other ANC leaders was issued. In mid-1963 Mandela was captured and sentenced to life imprisonment on Robben Island.

The government tried for decades to eradicate squatter towns, such as Crossroads, which were focal points for black resistance to the apartheid regime. Violent removals and killings failed and the government, forced to accept the inevitable, began to upgrade conditions. Since then, vast townships have sprung up across the Cape Flats. No-one knows exactly how many people call them home, but it is likely to be in excess of 1.5 million.

THE COLOURED EXPERIENCE

Apartheid's divide-and-rule tactics – favouring coloureds above blacks – stoked the animosity that still lingers between the Cape's coloured and black communities today. Even so, coloureds did suffer under apartheid, as the experience of those living in the poor inner-city area known as District Six shows.

In 1966 District Six was classified as a white area. Its 50,000 people, some of whose families had been there for five generations, were gradually evicted and removed to bleak and soulless Cape Flats suburbs like Athlone, Mitchell's Plain and Atlantis. Friends, neighbours and relatives were separated. Bulldozers moved in and the multiracial heart was ripped out of the city, while in the townships, depressed and dispirited youths increasingly joined gangs and turned to crime.

The coloured Muslim community of the Bo-Kaap, on the northeastern edge of Signal Hill, was more fortunate. Home to Cape Town's first mosque (the Owal Mosque on Dorp St dates back to 1798), the district was once known as the Malay Quarter, because it was where many of the imported slaves from the start of the Cape Colony lived with their masters.

In 1952 the entire Bo-Kaap region was declared to be a coloured area under the terms of the Group Areas Act. There were forced removals, but the residents of the community, which was more homogeneous than that of District Six, banded together in order to successfully fight for and retain ownership of their homes, many of which were declared National Monuments in the 1960s (also saving them from the bulldozers).

1910	1923	1939	1940
The British colonies and the old Boer republics are joined in the Union of South Africa. Cape Town is made the seat of the legislature.	The Black Urban Areas Act restricts the entry of blacks into the city centre. Three years later the prison-like settlement of Langa becomes the first planned township for blacks.	The peninsula's rugged tip is protected within the Cape of Good Hope Nature Reserve. It's 60 years before a single Cape Peninsula national park is created.	Cape Town's pier, built in 1925, is demolished as an ambitious reclamation project extends the city centre 2km from the Strand into Table Bay creating the Foreshore district.

NELSON MANDELA

His Xhosa (isiXhosa) name Rolihlahla translates as 'Trouble Maker' although today Nelson Mandela is more often called Madiba, an honorary title adopted by elders of his clan – a mark of respect for a man who was instrumental in allowing South Africa to make a peaceful transition from apartheid to democracy. A Nobel Peace Prize–winner (together with FW de Klerk in 1993), he's been awarded honorary doctorates by countless universities around the world, and even had a nuclear particle named after him.

The son of the third wife of a Xhosa chief, Mandela was born on 18 July 1918 in the small village of Mveso on the Mbashe River. A bright and determined child, he eventually overcame prejudice and poverty to qualify as a lawyer, setting up a practice with Oliver Tambo in Johannesburg (Jo'burg). In 1944 he helped form the Youth League of the African National Congress (ANC) with Walter Sisulu and Oliver Tambo. Its aim was to end the racist policies of the white South African government.

Mandela's stature as a future leader of the country grew during the 1950s when he and 156 other ANC and Communist Party members were charged with and later cleared of treason. Such was Mandela's threat to the government that he was forced to go underground to continue the struggle. He was captured and sentenced to life imprisonment in 1963.

The prison years inevitably took their toll not only on his health but also on his marriage to the increasingly renegade Winnie; in 1992 the couple separated, and were divorced in 1996. In 1998, on his 80th birthday and a year after he retired as ANC president, he married Graca Machel, the widow of a former president of Mozambique. For several years after his official retirement from the international stage in 2004 Mandela remained pretty active, but now in his early 90s he is increasingly frail and spends much of his time out of the public eye.

PATH TO DEMOCRACY

In 1982 Nelson Mandela and other ANC leaders were moved from Robben Island to Pollsmoor Prison in Cape Town. (In 1986 senior politicians began secretly talking with them.) Concurrently, the state's military crackdowns in the townships became even more pointed.

In early 1990 President FW de Klerk began to repeal discriminatory laws, and the ANC, PAC and Communist Party were legalised. On 11 February the world watched in awe as a living legend emerged from Victor Vester Prison near Paarl. Later that day Nelson Mandela delivered his first public speech since being incarcerated 27 years earlier to a massive crowd overspilling from Cape Town's Grand Parade.

From this time onwards virtually all the old apartheid regulations were repealed and, in late 1991, the Convention for a Democratic South

1948	1964	1976	1982
The National Party wins government. The right of coloureds to vote in the Cape is removed (blacks had been denied the vote since 1910) as apartheid is rolled out.	Following the Rivonia Trial, Nelson Mandela, Walter Sisulu and others escape the death penalty, but are sentenced to life imprisonment on Robben Island in the middle of Table Bay.	Students in Langa, Nyanga and Gugulethu march against the imposition of Afrikaans as the teaching medium in schools; 128 people are killed and 400 injured.	Mandela and other senior ANC leaders are moved from Robben Island to Pollsmoor Prison in Tokai, facilitating the beginning of discreet contact between them and the National Party.

Africa (Codesa) began negotiations on the formation of a multiracial transitional government and a new constitution extending political rights to all groups. Two years later a compromise was reached and an election date set. In the frustration of waiting, political violence exploded across the country during this time, some of it sparked by the police and the army.

Despite this, the 1994 election was amazingly peaceful, the ANC winning 62.7% of the vote. In Western Cape, though, the majority coloured population voted in the NP as the provincial government, seemingly happier to live with the devil they knew than with the ANC.

TRUTH & RECONCILIATION COMMISSION

One of the first acts of the new ANC government was to set up the Truth & Reconciliation Commission (TRC) to expose the crimes of the apartheid era. This institution carried out Archbishop Desmond Tutu's dictum: 'Without forgiveness there is no future, but without confession there can be no forgiveness.' Many stories of horrific brutality and injustice were heard during the commission's five-year life, offering some catharsis to individuals and communities shattered by their past.

The TRC operated by allowing victims to tell their stories and perpetrators to confess their guilt, with amnesty offered to those who made a clean breast of it. Those who chose not to appear before the commission face criminal prosecution if their guilt can be proven. Although some soldiers, police and 'ordinary' citizens have confessed their crimes, it seems unlikely that those who gave the orders and dictated the policies will ever come forward (former president PW Botha was one famous no-show), and gathering evidence against them has proven difficult.

RISE & FALL OF PAGAD

The governmental vacuum that existed between Mandela's release from jail and the election of a democratic government left Cape Town in a shaky social position. The early 1990s saw drugs and crime become such a problem in the Cape that communities began to take matters into their own hands. People against Gangsterism and Drugs (Pagad) was formed in 1995 as an offshoot of the Islamic organisation Qibla. The group saw itself as defending the coloured community from the crooked cops and drug lords who allowed gangs to control the coloured townships.

At first the police tolerated Pagad, but their vigilante tactics turned sour in 1996 with the horrific (and televised) death of gangster Rashaad Staggie. A lynch mob burned then repeatedly shot the dying gangster.

More Mandela

Long Walk to Freedom (Nelson Mandela)

Mandela: The Authorized Biography (Anthony Sampson)

The Long Walk of Nelson Mandela (www.pbs.org/wgbh/pages/frontline/shows/mandela)

Nelson Mandela Centre for Memory (www.nelsonmandela.org)

South Africa's constitution is one of the most enlightened in the world. Apart from forbidding discrimination on practically any grounds, among other things it guarantees freedom of speech and religion, and access to adequate housing and health care and basic adult education.

1986	1989	1990
An estimated 70,000 people are driven from their homes and hundreds killed as the government tries to eradicate the squatter towns of Nyanga and Crossroads in the Cape Flats.	President PW Botha suffers a stroke and is replaced by FW de Klerk who continues the secret negotiations that lead to the ANC, PAC and Communist Party becoming legalised.	Mandela walks a free man from Victor Verster Prison in Paarl and delivers his first public speech in 27 years from the balcony of the old Cape Town City Hall.

Nelson Mandela

Other gang leaders were killed, but Capetonians really began to worry when bombs, some believed to have been planted by the more radical of Pagad's members, began to go off around the city. The worst attack was in 1998 when an explosion in the Planet Hollywood restaurant at the Waterfront killed one woman and injured 27 other people. In September 2000 a magistrate presiding in a case involving Pagad members was murdered in a drive-by shooting.

Pagad leader Abdus Salaam Ebrahim was imprisoned in 2002 for seven years for public violence, but no-one has ever been convicted, let alone charged for the Cape Town bombings. Pagad, now designated a terrorist organisation by the government, keeps a much lower and quieter profile.

SHIFTING ALLIANCES

In 1999, two years after Mandela had stepped down as ANC president and was succeeded by his deputy, Thabo Mbeki, South Africa held its second free elections. Nationally, the ANC increased its vote, coming within one seat of the two-thirds majority that would allow it to alter the constitution, but in the Western Cape a pact between the old NP, restyled as the New National Party (NNP), and the Democratic Party (DP) to create the Democratic Alliance (DA), brought them victory not only in the provincial elections but also in the metropolitan elections.

In 2002 the political landscape shifted radically when the NNP completed a merger with the ANC, which gave the ANC control of Cape Town and brought the city its first black female mayor, Nomaindia Mfeketo. In national and provincial elections two years later the ANC were equally triumphant, and Ebrahim Rasool – a practising Muslim whose family had been moved out of District Six when he was 10 – was appointed premier of the Western Cape.

Conscious of their core vote in the Cape Flats, the ANC-led city council vowed to improve the lot of township folk by upgrading the infrastructure in the informal settlements and boosting investment in low-cost housing, such as the N2 Gateway Project along the motor corridor linking the city with the airport. Urban renewal projects were also announced for Mitchells Plain, one of the deprived coloured areas of the city that's blighted like so many Cape Flats suburbs by the murderous trade in drugs. Particularly deadly has been the explosion in addiction to methamphetamine, known locally as 'tik'.

For more about the TRC read the award-winning account *Country of My Skull* by journalist and poet Antjie Krog, or Desmond Tutu's balanced and honest *No Future Without Forgiveness*.

1994	1998	2002	2004
Following democratic elections, Mandela succeeds FW de Klerk as president, saying 'this is the time to heal the old wounds and build a new South Africa'.	After three years of emotionally painful testimonies the Truth & Reconciliation Commission in Cape Town delivers its verdict, condemning both sides in the liberation struggle.	Cape Town elects its first black female mayor, Nomaindia Mfeketo, as the New National Party (NNP) ditches the Democratic Party (DP) to join forces with the ANC.	Ebrahiem Murat (87) and Dan Mdzabela (82) are handed keys to new homes in District Six, the first returnees among thousands who hope to rebuild lives in the demolished suburb.

ZILLE & DE LILLE

They may sound like a pair of cops in a US crime show, but Helen Zille (pronounced Ziller, hence her nickname 'Godzille') and Patricia de Lille are the dynamic female duo dominating Capetonian politics. Zille was Cape Town's mayor for three years from 2006 during which time she was awarded the international accolade of World Mayor. In May 2009 elections she became premier of the Western Cape; the Democratic Alliance (DA) which she leads is also the official national opposition party.

Jo'burg born Zille began her career as a journalist in 1974, during which time she exposed the circumstances of the freedom fighter Steve Biko's death while in police custody. As mayor and the state's premier, she has impressed (and sometimes infuriated) locals with her no-nonsense, practical style of government, fearlessly wading into issues as thorny as drugs and gangsterism, teenage pregnancies and prevention of HIV/AIDS transmission.

De Lille has been no less fiery and controversial in her political career, which has taken her from being a union rep in her hometown of Beaufort West to one-time leader of the Independent Democrats (ID) and a campaigner to bring to light the details of a shady arms deal that still dogs the upper echelons of the ANC. The ID merged with the DA in 2010 and in 2011 De Lille was chosen as the mayoral candidate, a post she was elected to in May the same year.

XENOPHOBIA & SOCCER

Battling charges of corruption, and also taking stick for disruptive rolling power cuts caused by the Western Cape's overstretched nuclear power station at Koeberg, the ANC narrowly lost out to the Democratic Alliance (DA) in the municipal elections of March 2006. The DA's Helen Zille became Cape Town's mayor. In July 2008, Rasool – mired amid controversy over the sale of the V&A Waterfront and nearby Somerset Hospital site – was replaced as Western Cape premier by Lynne Brown.

For the poorest of Capetonians, however, the political circus counted for little against lives blighted by dire economic, social and health problems. In May 2008 frustrations in the townships, fuelled by spikes in food and fuel prices, boiled over in a series of horrific xenophobic attacks on the most vulnerable members of society – immigrants and refugees from wars and political violence. As some 30,000 people fled in panic, the vast majority of Capetonians rallied to provide assistance.

Despite controversies over the location and spiralling costs of the new Cape Town Stadium, the city's various factions united to support the hosting of the soccer World Cup in 2010. The event was judged a huge success but, facing global recession and social problems, many locals wonder if the money could not have been better spent.

History Reads

A Travellers History of South Africa (David Mason)

Beyond the Miracle: Inside the New South Africa (Allister Sparks)

Diamonds, Gold & War (Martin Meredith)

Cape Lives of the Eighteenth Century (Karel Schoeman)

2008

African immigrants are targeted in the xenophobic violence that engulfs Cape townships. Over 40 people are killed and 30,000 driven from their homes in nearly two weeks of attacks.

2010

Soccer fever grips Cape Town as over 60,000 spectators in the new Cape Town Stadium and hundreds of thousand more on the streets watch the World Cup.

The impressive Cape Town Stadium (p103)

JOHN BORTHWICK / LONELY PLANET IMAGES ©

People & Culture

Cape Town's racial mix is different from the rest of South Africa. Of its population of 3.1 million, more than half are coloured; blacks account for about a third of the total, and whites and others comprise the balance. Many South Africans proudly identify themselves with one or other of these groups – for example, you'll meet black South Africans who happily refer to themselves as black rather than South African or African (which is the African National Congress' preferred collective expression for all people of African, Indian and mixed-race origin).

RACIAL GROUPS

Coloureds

Coloureds, sometimes known as Cape coloureds or Cape Malays, are South Africans of long standing. Although many of their ancestors were brought to the early Cape Colony as slaves, others were political prisoners and exiles from the Dutch East Indies. Slaves also came from India and other parts of Africa, but their lingua franca was Malay (at the time an important trading language), which is how they came to be called Cape Malays.

Many coloureds practise Islam, and Cape Muslim culture has survived intact over the centuries, resisting some of the worst abuses of apartheid. The slaves, who moved out with the Dutch to the hinterland, many losing their religion and cultural roots in the process, had a much worse time of it. And yet practically all the coloured population of the Western Cape and Northern Cape provinces today are bound by Afrikaans, the unique language that began to develop from the interaction between the slaves and the Dutch over three centuries ago.

Although there are many people who find the old apartheid racial terms – white, black, coloured and Indian – distasteful and want to break away from the stereotypes they imply, it's a fact that in South Africa the words are used by everyone, quite often without any rancour or ill feeling.

Cape Town Minstrel Carnival

The most public secular expression of coloured culture today is the riotous Cape Town Minstrel Carnival. Also known in Afrikaans as the Kaapse Klopse, the Mother City's equivalent of Rio's Mardi Gras parade, is a noisy, joyous and disorganised affair with practically every colour of satin, sequin and glitter used in the costumes of the marching troupes, which can number over 1000 members.

Although the festival dates back to the early colonial times when slaves enjoyed a day of freedom the day after New Year, the look of today's carnival was inspired by visiting American minstrels in the late 19th century, hence the face make-up, colourful costumes and ribald song-and-dance routines. The vast majority of participants come from the coloured community.

Despite the carnival being a permanent fixture on Cape Town's calendar, it has had a controversial history with problems over funding, clashes between rival carnival organisations and allegations of gangster involvement. It has also always been something of a demonstration of coloured people power: whites who came to watch the parade in apartheid times would risk having their faces blacked-up with boot polish. Today it still feels like the Cape Flats community coming to take over the city.

THE RITES OF INITIATION

Male initiation ceremonies, which can take place from around age 16 to the early 20s, are a consistent part of traditional black African life (and coloured Muslim life where teenage boys are also circumcised, albeit with much less ritual). Initiations typically take place around the end of the year and in June to coincide with school and public holidays.

In the Eastern Cape, young Xhosa men would go into a remote area in the mountains to attend the Vkwaluka, the initiation school where they would be circumcised, live in tents and learn what it is to be a man in tribal society. Some still do return to the Eastern Cape for the ceremony, but others cannot afford to or choose not to do so, so similar initiation sites are created in makeshift tents erected amid the wastelands around the townships.

Initiations used to take several months, but these days they're likely to last a month or less. Initiates shave off all their hair, shed their clothes and wear just a blanket, and daub their faces in white clay before being circumcised. They receive a stick that symbolises the traditional hunting stick; they use it instead of their hands for shaking hands during the initiation period. Immediately after the circumcision, for about a week while the wound heals, initiates eat very little and drink nothing. No women are allowed to go near the initiation ground.

Initiations are expensive – around R6000 to R8000, mainly for the cost of the animals (typically sheep or goats) that have to be slaughtered for the various feasts that are part of the ceremony. At the end of the initiation all the items used, including the initiate's old clothes, are burned together with the hut in which he stayed, and the boy emerges as a man. You can spot recent initiates in the townships and Cape Town's city centre by the smart clothes they are wearing, often a sports jacket and a cap.

Blacks

Although most blacks in Cape Town are Xhosa, hailing from Eastern Cape Province, they are not the only group in the city. Cape Town's economy has attracted people from all over Southern Africa, including a fair few immigrants from the rest of the continent – a lot of the car-parking marshals, traders at the city's various craft markets and waiters in restaurants are from other African countries.

Xhosa culture is diverse, with many clan systems and subgroups. Within the black community there are also economic divisions and subgroups based on culture, such as the Rastafarian community in the Marcus Garvey district of the township of Philippi.

Whites

There are distinct cultural differences in the white community depending on whether people are descendants of the Boers or the British and other later European immigrants to South African. The Boers' history of geographical isolation and often deliberate cultural seclusion has created a unique people who are often called 'the white tribe of Africa'.

Afrikaans, the only Germanic language to have evolved outside Europe, is central to the Afrikaner identity, but it has also served to reinforce their isolation from the outside world. You'll find Afrikaans to be a much stronger presence in the northern suburbs of Cape Town and in the country towns of the Cape, especially around Stellenbosch, which has a prominent Afrikaans university.

Most other white Capetonians are of British extraction. Cape Town, as the seat of British power for so long, is somewhat less Afrikaner in outlook than other parts of the country. White liberal Capetonians were regarded with suspicion by more-conservative whites during the apartheid years.

DEALING WITH RACISM

Cultural apartheid still exists in South Africa. To an extent, discrimination based on wealth is replacing that based on race; most visitors will automatically gain high status. There are, however, still plenty of people who think that a particular skin colour means a particular mindset. A few believe it means inferiority.

The constant awareness of race, even if it doesn't lead to problems, is an annoying feature of travel in South Africa, whatever your skin colour. Racial discrimination is illegal, but it's unlikely that the overworked and under-resourced police force will be interested in most complaints. Tourism authorities are likely to be more sensitive. If you encounter racism in any of the places mentioned by us, please let us know.

African

If you are of African descent, you may well encounter racism from some white and coloured people. Do not assume a special bond with black South Africans either. The various indigenous peoples of South Africa form distinct and sometimes antagonistic cultural groups. Thus travellers of African descent from France or the USA will not necessarily receive a warmer welcome than anyone else.

Indian

Although Indians were discriminated against by whites during apartheid, blacks saw them as collaborating with the whites. If you are of Indian descent this could mean some low-level antagonism from both blacks and whites.

Asian

East Asians were a problem for apartheid – Japanese were granted 'honorary white' status, but Chinese were considered coloured. Grossly inaccurate stereotyping and cultural ignorance will probably be the main annoyances you will face.

RELIGION & CULTURE

Islam

Islam first came to the Cape with the slaves brought by the Dutch from the Indian subcontinent and Indonesia. Although the religion could not be practised openly in the colony until 1804, the presence of influential and charismatic political and religious figures among the slaves helped a cohesive Cape Muslim community to develop. One such political dissident was Imam Abdullah Ibn Qadi Abdus Salaam, commonly known as Tuan Guru, from Tidore, who arrived in 1780. Eight years later he helped establish the Owal Mosque, the city's first mosque, in the Bo-Kaap, thus making this area the heart of the Islamic community in Cape Town, as it still is today.

The ethnic composition of Afrikaners is difficult to quantify but it has been estimated at 40% Dutch, 40% German, 7.5% French, 7.5% British and 5% other. Some historians have argued that the '5% other' figure includes a significant proportion of blacks and coloureds.

Tuan Guru's grave is one of the 20 or so karamats (tombs of Muslim saints) encircling Cape Town and visited by the faithful on mini pilgrimages. Other karamats are found on Robben Island (that of Sayed Abdurahman Matura), at the gate to the Klein Constantia wine estate (that of Sheik Abdurachman Matebe Shah), and at Ouderkraal, where there are two (that of Sheikh Noorul Mubeen and possibly his wife or one of his followers). For a full list see www.capemazaarsociety.com/html/kramat.html.

Cape Town has managed to avoid becoming embroiled in violent Islamic fundamentalism, as seemed possible in the early 1990s. You'll encounter many friendly faces while wandering around the Bo-Kaap, where you can drop by the local museum to find out more about the community. A sizeable Muslim community also lived in Simon's Town before the Group Areas Act evictions of the late 1960s. Its history can be traced at Simon's Town's Heritage Museum.

Christianity

The Afrikaners are a religious people and the group's brand of Christian fundamentalism based on 17th-century Calvinism is still a powerful influence. Urbanised middle-class Afrikaners tend to be considerably more moderate. Whites of British descent tend to be Anglican and this along with other forms of Christianity are also popular among sections of the black and coloured communities.

Spirit Worship

Few blacks in Cape Town maintain a fully traditional lifestyle on a daily basis, but elements of traditional culture do persist, lending a distinctively African air to the townships.

Herbal medicine shops are regularly used, and *sangomas* (traditional medicine practitioners) are consulted for all kinds of illnesses. Certain *sangomas* can also help people get in touch with their ancestors, who play a crucial role in the lives of many black Capetonians. Ancestors are believed to watch over their kin and act as intermediaries between this world and that of the spirits. People turn to their ancestors if they have problems or requests. An animal may be slaughtered in their honour and roasted on an open fire as it's believed the ancestors eat the smoke.

At important junctions in life, such as birth, coming of age and marriage, various old rites and customs are followed, too.

Judaism

South Africa's oldest Jewish community is in Cape Town. Even though the rules of the Vereenigde Oost-Indische Companie (VOC; Dutch East India Company) allowed only for Protestant settlers at the Cape, there are records of Jews converting to Christianity in Cape Town as early as 1669. Jewish immigration picked up speed after the British took charge, with settlers coming mainly from England and Germany. The first congregation was established in 1841 and the first synagogue (now part of the South African Jewish Museum) opened in 1863.

Jewish immigration boomed between 1880 and 1930 when an estimated 15,000 families arrived in South Africa, mainly from Lithuania, Latvia, Poland and Belarus. During this period Jews began to make a large contribution to the city's civic and cultural life. Max Michaelis donated his art collection to the city and Hyman Liberman became the first Jewish mayor of Cape Town in 1905, the same year the Great Synagogue was consecrated.

QURAN COPIED

During his 13 years on Robben Island Tuan Guru accurately copied several copies of the Quran from memory. He's buried in Bo-Kaap's Tana Baru Cemetery.

PEOPLE & CULTURE RELIGION & CULTURE

Cape Town's Jewish population has dropped from 25,000 (second in number only to the community in Jo'burg) in 1969 to around 15,000 today. Sea Point is the most visibly Jewish area of the city.

Architecture

From the 17th-century Castle of Good Hope to the 21st-century towers rising on the Foreshore, Cape Town's range of architecture is one of its most attractive features. Much that might have been destroyed in other places has been preserved, and a walking or cycling tour of Cape Town's City Bowl is a great way to get a feel for the built history of the city.

DUTCH COLONIAL

When the Dutch colonists arrived in 1652, they brought their European ideas of architecture with them, but had to adapt to the local conditions and materials. There was plenty of stone on hand from Table Mountain to build the Castle of Good Hope between 1666 and 1679.

The first Capetonian houses were utilitarian structures, such as the thatched and whitewashed Posthuys in Muizenberg, dating from 1673. This simple rustic style of building is one that you'll still find today along the Western Cape coast.

At the other end of the architectural scale Governor Simon van der Stel's quintessential manor house, Groot Constantia, went up in 1692, setting a precedent for other glorious estates to follow further inland in the Winelands. On Strand St, the fancy facade of the late-18th-century Koopmans-de Wet House is attributed to Louis Thibault, who, as lieutenant of engineers for the Vereenigde Oost-Indische Compagnie (Dutch East India Company; VOC), was responsible for the design of most of Cape Town's public buildings in this period. Thibault also had a hand in the handsome Rust en Vreugd: completed in 1778, the house is notable for its delicately carved rococo fanlight above the main door and its double balconies and portico.

Of course, not everyone lived in such a grand manner. In the city centre, the best place to get an idea of how Cape Town looked to ordinary folk during the 18th century is to take a stroll through the Bo-Kaap. You'll notice flat roofs instead of gables, and a lack of shutters on the windows. These features are the result of building regulations instituted by the VOC in the wake of fires that swept the city.

Best Dutch Colonial

Castle of Good Hope (1679)

Groot Constantia (1685)

Vergelegen (1700)

Tuynhuis (1700)

Rust en Vreugd (1778)

BRITISH COLONIAL

When the British took over from the Dutch in the early 19th century, they had their own ways of doing things, and this extended to the architectural look of the city. British governor Lord Charles Somerset made the biggest impact during his 1814–26 tenure. It was he who ordered the restyling of Tuynhuis to bring it into line with Regency tastes for verandas and front gardens.

As the British Empire reached its zenith in the late 19th century, Cape Town boomed and a slew of monumental buildings were erected. Walk down Adderley St and through the Company's Gardens and you'll pass many, including Standard Bank with its pediment, dome and soaring columns; the Houses of Parliament; and the Byzantine-influenced Old Syna

SIR HERBERT BAKER

Like his patron Cecil Rhodes, Herbert Baker (1862–1946) was an ambitious young Englishman who seized the chance to make his mark in South Africa. Baker arrived in Cape Town in 1892 and a year later, through family connections, had gained himself an audience with Rhodes and been commissioned to remodel Groote Schuur, the prime minister's mansion on the slopes of Table Mountain. This kicked off a style known as Cape Dutch Revival.

Many more commissions followed, and Cape Town is littered with buildings of Baker's design, including several cottages in Muizenberg (where Baker lived for a while), St George's Cathedral and the First National Bank on Adderley St. In 1900 Rhodes sent Baker to Italy, Greece and Egypt to study their classical architecture in order to inspire him to design the sort of grand buildings Rhodes wished to see constructed in South Africa. Two years later, though, Rhodes was dead and Baker was designing his memorial.

Among Baker's grandest work is the imposing Union Buildings in Pretoria (1909). In 1912 he left South Africa to join Edwin Lutyens in designing the secretariat buildings in New Delhi. Back in the UK he worked on South Africa House in London's Trafalgar Sq and was knighted in 1926. He's buried in Westminster Abbey.

gogue, dating from 1863. The neighbouring and neo-Egyptian-styled Great Synagogue, with its twin towers, is from 1905.

Long St is where you can see Victorian Cape Town at its most appealing, with the wrought-iron balconies and varying facades of shops and buildings. In the adjacent suburbs of Tamboerskloof and Oranjezicht, many mansions of that era still survive.

Another building boom in the 1920s and '30s led to the construction of many fine art-deco buildings in the city centre. Prime examples include the blocks around Greenmarket Sq and the handsome 1939 Mutual Heights, the continent's first skyscraper, decorated with friezes and frescoes, all with South African themes.

TOWNSHIP ARCHITECTURE

From the early 1920s out on the empty, sandy Cape Flats, homes were being built for the coloured and black labourers. Langa was established in 1927 and is South Africa's oldest planned township; today it's home to 250,000 people – the same number who live in the city centre but squashed into a suburb some 48 times smaller.

As in many townships, the roads are wide and in good condition, thus allowing for quick access by the authorities should there be trouble. Although it's shacks (properly called 'informal settlements') that are most widely associated with the townships, this is far from the only architecture in these areas; the buildings you'll find can be broken into five main categories:

Shacks It's estimated that there are around one million people living in squatter camps of self-built shacks. Cobbled together from a variety of materials, including old packing crates, and decorated with, among other things, magazine pages and old food-tin labels, the design and structure of a shack depends on the financial situation of the owner and how long they have lived there – an example of a very fancy two-storey shack with the rare luxury of its own bathrooms is Vicky's B&B in Khayelitsha.

Hostels Built originally for migrant labourers before WWII, these two-level brick dormitories were broken up into basic units, each accommodating 16 men, who shared one shower, one toilet and one small kitchen. Tiny bedrooms housed up

Best British Colonial

Bertram House (1840)

Standard Bank (1880)

Houses of Parliament (1885)

Old Town Hall (1905)

Centre for the Book (1913)

to three men each. After the pass laws (which stated that those who didn't have a job outside the Homelands were not allowed to leave) were abolished, most men brought their families to live with them. Each unit became home to up to 16 families, each room sleeping up to three families. Although some families still live in such conditions, other hostels have been modernised to provide less-cramped and much more habitable apartments.

Terrace housing In the older townships of Langa and Gugulethu you'll come across one-storey terrace housing, built between the 1920s and '40s. Like the hostels, conditions in these 30-sq-metre 'railway carriage' houses were very basic and crowded. Since the end of apartheid these houses have been owned by the former tenants, who are now responsible for their maintenance. Residents have sometimes expanded them, when they can, into the front and back yards.

Reconstruction and Development Programme (RDP) houses In the last 10 years, tens of thousands of these low-cost houses have been built in the townships. Averaging around 28 sq metres in size, these 'matchbox' houses are little more than four concrete-block walls topped with a corrugated-iron roof. Even so, for many people they are a great improvement on the fire-prone shacks they lived in previously.

Township villas There are areas of Gugulethu, Langa and Khayelitsha that are very middle class and where you'll find spacious bungalow-style houses and villas of a high standard. The convivial Radebe's B&B is located in a part of Langa known locally as 'Beverly Hills'.

APARTHEID ERA

The election of the National Party to government in 1948 was bad news for Cape Town's architecture in more ways than one. Apartheid laws labelled Cape Town a mainly coloured city – this meant that the national government was unwilling to support big construction projects (this hampered the development of the Foreshore for decades) while the local authorities went about applying the Group Areas Act, demolishing areas such as District Six and rezoning Green Point (including De Waterkant) as a whites-only area.

Examples of rationalist architecture from this era include the hideous Artscape arts centre and the adjoining Civic Centre on the Foreshore, which demonstrate the obsession with concrete that was typical of international modernism. Such poor design wasn't necessarily a function of apartheid planning, as the Baxter Theatre proves. Designed by Jack Barnett, its flat roof is famously dimpled with orange fibreglass downlights that glow fabulously at night. Also notable is the striking Taal Monument in Paarl, with a 57m-concrete tower designed by Jan van Wijk.

The lack of planning or official architectural concern for the townships has long been criticised, although it is worth mentioning the tremendous ingenuity and resilience that residents show in creating liveable homes from scrap. A visit to the townships today reveals colourfully painted shacks and murals, homes and churches made from shipping crates, and more recent imaginative structures, such as the Guga S'Thebe Arts & Cultural Centre in Langa.

Best Modern & Contemporary

Baxter Theatre (1977)

Guga S'Thebe Arts & Cultural Centre (2000)

Green Point Stadium (2010)

The Fugard (2010)

CONTEMPORARY ARCHITECTURE

The death knell of apartheid coincided with the redevelopment of the Victoria & Alfred Waterfront in the early 1990s. More recent architectural additions to the Waterfront include the Nelson Mandela Gateway and Clock Tower Precinct, built in 2001 as the new departure point for

Robben Island, and the ritzy millionaire's playground of the V&A Marina, with some 600 apartments and 200 boat moorings.

The recent Cape Town property boom has created an environment for some interesting new residential buildings and conversions of old office blocks into apartments, such as Mutual Heights, the three old buildings that are part of Mandela Rhodes Place, and the adjacent Taj Cape Town hotel, all of which sensitively combine the original structures with new towers.

Opening in 2003, the Cape Town International Convention Centre (CTICC), with its ship-like prow and sleek glass-and-steel hotel, drew favourable nods and has helped push the City Bowl down towards the waterfront, from which it has been cut off for decades. Filling in another of the long-empty gaps here is the residential, commercial and retail centre Icon, Cape Town's first major black-empowerment development designed by DHK architects.

FUTURE DEVELOPMENTS

The CTICC is set to expand across Heerengracht. The architecture firms Louis Karol Architecture (LKA) and DHK are currently working with Old Mutual Property and FirstRand Bank to build Portside, a mixed-used development, at the Foreshore end of Bree St. At 31 storeys and 139m this will be the city's tallest building since the completion of the 123m Safmarine House in 1993 – another LKA project.

Next to Portside may eventually be the Desmond Tutu Peace Centre, a proposal by Van der Merwe Miszewski (www.vdmma.com) who have won awards for many of their residential projects around the city.

The development of District Six is finally on track, with the rebirth of Hanover St into the kind of vibrant commercial thoroughfare it once was, perhaps the most highly anticipated part of the plan. It remains a controversial process, though, with commentators such as Rashiq Fataar of Future Cape Town (www.futurecapetown.com) bemoaning the lost opportunity to bring higher density housing to this central area of the city.

Also tricky is what is to be done with the remains of the partly decommissioned Athlone Power Station which has long separated Pinelands from Langa; thousands turned up in August 2010 to watch as the twin cooling towers were blown up. The city government is running a public consultation programme on the future of the 36-hectare site.

Architecture Books

....

Cape Town: Architecture & Design (Pascale Lauber)

....

Cape Dutch Houses & Other Old Favourites (Phillida Brooke Simons)

....

Shack Chic (photographed by Craig Fraser)

Arts

Cape Town's mash-up of cultures and the sharply contrasting lives of its citizens make it a fertile location for the arts. Music is a pulsing constant in the Mother City, with jazz a particular forte. There's a surprisingly good range of performing arts, and a host of imaginative authors shed light on more obscure corners of the urban experience.

VISUAL ARTS

Exhibitions at Cape Town's public and private galleries demonstrate that the contemporary art scene is tremendously exciting and imaginative. Visual art's history on the Cape, however, stretches back to the original San inhabitants – they left their mark on the landscape in the form of rock paintings and subtle rock engravings. Despite having been faded by aeons of exposure, San works of art are remarkable; a fantastic example is the Linton Panel in the South African Museum. Today San motifs are commonly employed on tourist art such as decorative mats and carved ostrich eggs.

Among local artists of international note is Conrad Botes, who first made his mark with his weird cult comic *Bitterkomix,* founded with Anton Kannemeyer. Botes' colourful graphic images, both beautiful and horrific, have been shown in exhibitions in New York, the UK and Italy, as well as at the Havana Biennale in 2006.

Other artists to look out for include the painter Ndikhumbule Ngqinambi; Willie Bester, whose mixed-media creations of township life are very powerful; and the more conventional John Kramer (www.johnkramer. net), who captures the ordinary, serene quality of the South African landscape. At the South African National Gallery, you may find paintings by Gerard Sekoto, a black artist whose works capture the vibrancy of District Six, and Peter Clarke, a distinctive printer, poet and painter hailing from Simon's Town.

Public Art Works

....

Africa by Brett Murray

....

The Knot by Edoardo Villa

....

Nobel Square by Claudette Schreuders

....

Olduvai by Gavin Younge

MUSIC

Jazz

Cape Town has produced some major jazz talents, including the singer-songwriter Jonathan Butler and the saxophonists Robbie Jansen and Winston 'Mankunku' Ngozi. So important has the city been to the development of jazz that there is a subgenre of the music called Cape Jazz, which is improvisational in character and features instruments that can be used in street parades such as the drums and trumpets favoured in the Cape Minstrel Carnival.

The elder statesman of the scene is pianist Abdullah Ibrahim (www.abdullahibrahim.com). Born Adolph Johannes Brand in District Six in 1934, he began performing at 15 under the name Dollar Brand, and formed the Jazz Epistles with the legendary Hugh Masekela. In 1962, after moving to Zurich, he was spotted by Duke Ellington, who arranged recording sessions for him at Reprise Records and sponsored his appearance at the Newport Jazz Festival in 1965. Brand converted to Islam in 1968 and took-

THE PEOPLE'S PAINTER

Across Cape Town you'll see the striking multiracial faces that inspired the portraits of Vladimir Tretchikoff (1913–2006), the most famous of which is the iconic *Chinese Girl* – a mesmerising image of a blue-faced, red-lipped Asian beauty as instantly recognisable as the *Mona Lisa*.

Born in Petropavlovsk in present-day Kazakhstan, the twists of fate that transported Tretchikoff – via Harbin, Shanghai, Singapore and Indonesia – to Cape Town just after WWII is the stuff of high adventure. Against all odds, and with little assistance from Cape Town's established art circles, he 'succeeded in realising his "American Dream" to make money, own a home, buy a Cadillac and a fur coat for his wife,' says Natasha Mercorio, Tretchikoff's granddaughter and guardian of his legacy.

Tretchikoff, a skilled businessman and self-promoter, made a fortune marketing his art as prints around the world; his 252 exhibitions were attended by over two million people. However it wasn't until 2011 that a major retrospective of his work, including many of the originals oils, was held at the South African National Art Gallery in Cape Town. The book *Tretchikoff: The People's Painter* that accompanied the exhibition is a fine introduction to the artist's work.

Mercorio has also launched the Tretchikoff Trust (www.vladimirtretchikoff.com), with the aim of helping young creative talent realise their dreams. A percentage of sales of new prints from Tretchikoff's collection help fund the project.

the name Abdullah Ibrahim. In 1974 he recorded the seminal album *Manenberg* with saxophonist Basil Coetzee. He occasionally plays in Cape Town and his latest project is the jazz orchestra Morolong, named after another of his Jazz Epistle colleagues, Kippie 'Morolong' Moeketsi.

Goema-style jazz takes its rhythmic cues from the goema drum and has been popularised by musicians such as Mac McKenzie and Hilton Schilder. Other respected local artists to watch out for include guitarist Jimmy Dludlu, pianist Paul Hamner and singer Judith Sephuma, Afro-Indian jazz quartet Babu and the fantastic Cape Jazz Orchestra.

Dance, Rock & Pop

Few Afro-fusion groups have been as big recently as the multiracial seven-piece band Freshlyground (www.freshlyground.com), which draws huge crowds whenever performing in their hometown. Bridging the divide between jazz and electronic dance music are Goldfish (goldfishlive.com), aka the duo David Poole and Dominic Peters, who combine samplers, a groove box, keyboards, vocoder, upright bass, flute and saxophone in their live performances. Dominic's brother Ben Peters is a member of Goodluck (goodlucklive.com), who are also gaining a strong following for their similar sound.

Techno, trance, hip hop, jungle and rap are wildly popular: white trash Afrikaans rapper Jack Parow (jackparow.com) is the Capetonian answer to the national rap sensation Die Antwoord (dieantwoord.com). Also tune in to kwaito, a mix of *mbaqanga* (a Zulu style of music), jive, hip hop, house and ragga. The music of local singing superstar Brenda Fassie (1964–2004) has a strong kwaito flavour – listen to her hits such as 'Weekend Special' and 'Too Late For Mamma'. Dubbed 'Madonna of the Townships' by *Time* magazine, Fassie, who was born in Langa, struggled with drug problems throughout her brief life.

Among the many indie rock bands and singers to catch at gigs around town are Ashtray Electric (www.ashtrayelectric.co.za), Arno Carstens (www.arnocarstens.com), the one-time lead singer of the

For a preview of the Capetonian art scene check out the website Artthrob (www.artthrob.co.za), which showcases the best in South African contemporary art and has plenty of up-to-the-minute news, and the magazine ArtSouthAfrica (www.artsouthafrica.com).

NEW CAPETONIAN WRITERS *LAUREN BEUKES*

The most prolific writer on earth that I know is Sarah Lotz (sarahlotz.com). She also writes under the name Lily Herne with Savannah Lotz, her 19-year-old daughter. Their book *Deadlands* is one of a trilogy of zombie tales set in Cape Town that are razor-edge social commentaries. Under the name SL Grey she has collaborated with Louis Greenberg on the Jo'burg-set horror story *The Mall*, which has been described as '*Fight Club* meets *Saw*'.

Andrew Brown is a lawyer and reserve police officer who was once a member of the armed wing of the African National Congress. His latest novel *Refuge* is about refugees and the sex industry in Cape Town.

Winner of the Cane Prize, Henrietta Rose-Inne's *Ninnevah* is amazing – taut, beautiful writing and such a weird mind. *Cabin Fever*, by Diane Awerbuck, is a set of short stories about trauma and transformation that are urban, contemporary and avoid the clichés of African writing.

Thando Mgqolozana caused a stir with his *A Man Who Is Not a Man*, about the taboo subject of a botched circumcision; it's insightful and brave. His strange and amazing follow-up *Hear Me Alone* has caused even more controversy by retelling the nativity from an African perspective.

Cape Town-based writer and documentary maker, Lauren Beukes (laurenbeukes. com) has had international hits with her fantasy/sci-fi/social realism mashups Moxyland *and* Zoo City, *which won the 2011 Arthur C Clarke Prize. In 2012 she collaborated with Filipino artist Inaki Miranda on a story for the Vertigo–published monthly comic* Fairest. *Her next novel* The Shining Girls, *due in May 2013 and set in Chicago, is about time-travelling serial killers.*

legendary Springbok Nude Girls, and Jeremy Loops (www.jeremyloops. com), an incredible one-man-band who has opened for The Parlatones, currently South Africa's biggest act.

LITERATURE

Cape Town has nurtured several authors of international repute, including Nobel Prize–winner JM Coetzee (the first part of his Man Booker award-winning novel *Disgrace* is set in Cape Town); André Brink, professor of English at the University of Cape Town; and the Man Booker–prize nominated Damon Galgut.

Out of the coloured experience in District Six came two notable writers, Alex La Guma (1925–85) and Richard Rive (1931–89). La Guma's books include *And a Threefold Cord,* which examines the poverty, misery and loneliness of slum life, and *A Walk in the Night,* a collection of short stories set in District Six. Rive's *'Buckingham Palace', District Six* is a thought-provoking and sensitive set of stories.

Sindiwe Magona grew up in Gugulethu in the 1940s and '50s. The feisty writer's early life experiences inform her autobiographical works *To My Children's Children* (1990) and *Forced to Grow* (1992). *Beauty's Gift* (2008) deals unflinchingly with AIDS in the black community and, in particular, its impact on five women who consider themselves to be in faithful relationships.

The Cape's incredible true crime stories provide ready inspiration for a slew of thriller writers including Mike Nicol, Deon Meyer, Margie Orford and Sarah Lotz.

CINEMA

Cape Town is a major centre for South African movie-making and, increasingly, for international productions. The city acts as a magnet for many talented people in the industry and you'll frequently see production crews shooting on location around town. On the city's outskirts is the Cape Town Film Studios (www.capetownfilmstudios.co.za), where several major Hollywood productions have been shot, including *Safe House*, the Cape Town-set thriller with Denzel Washington and Ryan Reynolds.

Young local film-maker Oliver Hermanus followed up his 2009 debut feature *Shirley Adams*, a bleak Ken Loach–style drama set in Mitchells Plains on the Cape Flats, with *Skoonheid (Beauty)*; it was the first ever Afrikaans movie to play at the Cannes Film Festival (in 2011) and won the Queer Palm award. Among other recent local movies to feature Cape Town are *Long Street* directed by Revel Fox and starring his daughter and wife, and the charming *Visa/Vie* (www.visaviemovie.com) directed by Elan Ganmaker.

On DVD, keep an eye out for the American documentary *Long Night's Journey into Day*, nominated for Best Documentary at the 2001 Oscars. This very moving Sundance Film Festival–winner follows four cases from the Truth & Reconciliation Commission hearings, including that of Amy Biehl, the white American murdered in the Cape Flats in 1993. *U-Carmen e Khayelitsha*, Golden Bear–winner at the 2005 Berlin International Film Festival, is based on Bizet's opera *Carmen* and was shot entirely on location in Khayelitsha.

THEATRE & PERFORMING ARTS

One of the pleasant surprises of Cape Town is how lively and diverse the local performing arts scene is, offering everything from big-scale musicals and one-man shows to edgy dramas reflecting modern South Africa and intimate poetry reading soirees. The city has produced some notable actors, including the Sea Point–born Sir Anthony Sher who returns occasionally to the city to perform, most recently at The Fugard, the new theatre named in honour of top South African playwright Athol Fugard.

Brett Bailey's theatre company Third World Bunfight (www.third worldbunfight.co.za) specialises in using black actors to tell uniquely African stories in productions such as *Mumbo Jumbo*, which explores the interaction between the realms of theatre and ritual, and the musical extravaganza *House of the Holy Afro*. Bailey is also the curator of the annual Infecting the City arts festival (www.infectingthecity.com), which turns Cape Town's piazzas and squares into performance spaces.

Songwriter and director David Kramer (www.davidkramer.co.za) and musician Taliep Petersen (1950–2006) teamed up to work on two musicals, *District Six* and *Poison*, before hitting the big time with their jazz homage *Kat and the Kings*, which swept up awards in London in 1999 and received standing ovations on Broadway. Their collaboration *Goema* celebrates the tradition of Afrikaans folk songs while tracing the contribution made by the slaves and their descendants to the development of Cape Town.

The Labia's African Screen is the only Cape Town cinema that regularly screens South African movies. At the multiplexes you might also catch the odd South African–made feature. Otherwise, your best chance of watching home-grown product is at the city's several film festivals or by heading to local DVD rental shop DVD Nouveau (www.dvdnou veau.co.za; 166 Bree St; ☉10am to 9pm).

The Natural Environment

Cape Town is defined by its magnificent natural environment. In June 2004 the Cape Floristic Region (CFR) was awarded World Heritage status. The CFR, which covers the entire Cape Peninsula, is the richest and smallest of the world's six floral kingdoms and home to some 8200 plant species – more than three times as many per square kilometre as in the whole of South America! Table Mountain and the peninsula alone contain 2285 plant species, more than in all of Britain, and it's also home to over 100 invertebrates and two vertebrates not found anywhere else on earth.

THE LAND

Reading Up

Wild About Cape Town (Duncan Butchart)

The Rocks and Mountains of Cape Town (John Compton)

How the Cape Got Its Shape (fold-out map and chart by Map Studio)

Table Mountain's flat-top shape as we know it today probably first came about 60 million years ago, although the mountain as a whole started to be thrown up about 250 million years ago, making it the elder statesman of world mountains. By comparison, the Alps are only 32 million years old and the Himalayas 40 million years old.

The types of rock that make up the mountain and the Cape Peninsula are broken into three major geological types. The oldest, dating back 540 million years, is Malmesbury shale – this forms the base of most of the City Bowl and can be seen along the Sea Point shoreline, on Signal Hill and on the lower slopes of Devil's Peak. It's fairly soft and weathers easily. The second oldest is the tough Cape granite, which forms the foundation for Table Mountain and can also be seen on Lion's Head and the boulders at Clifton and Boulders Beaches. The third type of rock is called Table Mountain Sandstone, a combination of sandstone and quartzite.

It's thought that originally the summit of Table Mountain was a couple of kilometres higher than it is today. Over time this rock has weathered to create the distinctive hollows and oddly shaped rocks found on the mountain's summit and at Cape Point. The sandy soil on top of these rocks is very poor in nutrients. The plants that grow in this soil don't make for very good eating, hence the lack of large herbivores grazing in the region.

FLORA

The most common type of vegetation at the Cape is *fynbos* (from the Dutch meaning 'fine bush'; pronounced fain-bos) which thrives in the area's nitrogen-poor soil – it's supposed that the plants' fine, leathery leaves improve their odds of survival by discouraging predators. *Fynbos* is composed of three main elements: proteas (including the king protea, South Africa's national emblem), ericas (heaths and mosses) and restios (reeds). Examples of *fynbos* flowers that have been exported to other parts of the world include gladiolus, freesias and daisies.

On Signal Hill and the lower slopes of Devil's Peak you'll find *renoster-bos* (literally 'rhinoceros bush'), composed predominantly of a grey ericoid shrub, and peppered with grasses and geophytes (plants that grow from

BATTLING THE ALIEN INVASION

As well as guns and diseases, the European colonists also brought their plants to the Cape, some of which have proved to be aggressively invasive and damaging to the environment. Pines, oaks, poplars, wattles and three species of hakea were planted.

In the wake of the devastating forest fires that swept across the Cape in 2000 the park, in collaboration with private bodies, began a programme to rid the peninsula of invasive alien plants, to rehabilitate fire-damaged areas and to educate vulnerable communities, such as the townships, about fires. Around a third of the park's management area has so far been cleared of invasive alien plants.

But it's not just alien plants that have been destructive to the Cape environment, it's also imported animals, such as fallow deer and the Himalayan tahr. In 1936 a pair of tahrs escaped from Groote Schuur Zoo on the slopes of Devil's Peak; by the 1970s that couple had multiplied into a herd of 600, wreaking much damage throughout the park. A culling program is thought to have now eradicated the tahrs.

underground bulbs). In the cool, well-watered ravines on the eastern slopes of Table Mountain you'll also find small pockets of Afro-montane forest, such as at Orange Kloof where only 12 entry permits are issued daily.

While the biodiversity of the Cape Peninsula is incredible, it is also threatened. More than 1400 *fynbos* plants are endangered or vulnerable to extinction; some have minute natural ranges. Most *fynbos* plants need fire to germinate and flower, but unseasonal and accidental fires – such as the one that swept across the northern flank of Table Mountain in January 2006 – can cause great harm. The fires burn far longer and more fiercely, too, because of the presence of alien plants, such as the various pines and wattles that also pose a threat because of the vast amounts of water they suck up.

FAUNA

The animal most closely associated with Table Mountain is the dassie, also known as the rock hyrax. Despite the resemblance to a plump hamster, these small furry animals are – incredibly – related to the elephant. You'll most likely see dassies sunning themselves on rocks around the upper cableway station.

Among the feral population of introduced fallow deer that roam the lower slopes of Table Mountain around the Rhodes Memorial, is an animal long regarded as extinct: the quagga. This partially striped zebra was formerly thought to be a distinct species, but DNA obtained from a stuffed quagga in Cape Town's South African Museum showed it to be a subspecies of the widespread Burchell's zebra. A breeding program, started in 1987, has proved successful in 'resurrecting' the quagga. Mammals found at the Cape of Good Hope include eight antelope species, Cape mountain zebras and a troupe of Chacma baboons.

Across the Cape there's also an abundance of bird, insect and sea life. The most famous birds are the African penguins (formerly called jackass penguins because of their donkey-like squawk). You'll find some 3000 of the friendly penguins at Boulders Beach. Southern right and humpback whales, dolphins, Cape fur seals at Duiker Island (reached from Hout Bay) and loggerhead and leatherback turtles are among the other marine animals you could hope to see.

CREATING THE NATIONAL PARK

In comparison to the port that grew rapidly at the foot of Table Mountain, Europeans were slow to come to live in rugged, windswept Cape Point, the first farms being granted here in the 1780s. The areas really didn't become fully accessible until 1915 when the coastal road from Simon's Town was completed.

At over 100 sites in the national park, such as Peer's Cave in Silvermine and a cave in Smitswinkel Bay near the entrance to Cape Point, evidence has been found of the indigenous people who lived on the Cape long before the first recorded arrival of Europeans in 1503.

The campaign to designate the Cape Point area a nature reserve first got underway in the 1920s when there was a chance that the land could have been turned over to developers. At the same time, the future prime minister General Jan Smuts – a keen hiker – started a public appeal to secure formal protection for Table Mountain; today there is a track on the mountain named after him. The Cape of Good Hope Nature Reserve was eventually secured in 1939.

This was the first formal conservation on the Cape, although mining magnate and South African politician Cecil Rhodes had used a small part of his vast fortune to buy up much of the eastern slopes of Table Mountain; he gifted this land, which includes Kirstenbosch and the Cecilia Estate stretching to Constantia Nek, to the public in his will.

The Van Zyl Commission in the 1950s baulked at creating a single controlling authority for the park, but in 1958 all land on Table Mountain above the 152m-contour line was declared a National Monument. The city of Cape Town proclaimed the Table Mountain Nature Reserve in 1963 and the Silvermine Nature Reserve in 1965.

By the 1970s, 14 different bodies were in control of the publicly owned natural areas of the Cape. It wasn't until 1998 that a single Cape Peninsula National Park became a reality. In 2004 the park was renamed Table Mountain National Park. The park's area of responsibility also extends out to sea, with a single 975-sq-km Marine Protected Area being proclaimed in 2003.

Wine

Although the founder of the Cape Colony, Jan van Riebeeck, planted vines and made wine himself, it was not until the arrival of Governor Simon van der Stel in 1679 that winemaking began in earnest in Southern Africa. Van der Stel created the estate Constantia (later subdivided into the several estates in the area today), and passed on his winemaking skills to the burghers who settled around Stellenbosch.

THE FRENCH INFLUENCE

Between 1688 and 1690 some 200 Huguenots arrived in the country. They were granted land in the region, particularly around Franschhoek (which translates as 'French Corner'). Although only a few had winemaking experience, they gave the infant industry fresh impetus.

For a long time, Cape wines other than those produced at Constantia were not in great demand and most grapes ended up in brandy. The industry received a boost in the early 19th century as war between Britain and France, and preferential trade tariffs between the UK and South Africa, led to more South African wine being imported to the UK.

Apartheid-era sanctions and the power of the Kooperatieve Wijnbouwers Vereeniging (KWV; the cooperative formed in 1918 to control minimum prices, production areas and quota limits) didn't exactly encourage innovation and instead hampered the industry. Since 1992 the KWV, now a private company, has lost much of its former influence.

Many new and progressive winemakers are leading South Africa's re-emergence onto the world market. New production regions are being established in the cooler coastal areas east of Cape Town around Mossel Bay, Walker Bay and Elgin, and to the north around Durbanville and Darling. The older vines of the Swartland northwest of Paarl (and in particular the Paardeberg area) are also producing some very high-quality wines.

'Today, praise be the Lord, wine was pressed for the first time from Cape grapes.'

Jan van Riebeeck, 2 February 1659

THE HUMAN COST

The black and coloured workforce in the wine industry currently numbers over 200,000, most of whom are toiling in vineyards owned by around 4500 whites. Workers often receive the minimum monthly wage of R1375, or less if they are women. The controversial 'tot' system, whereby the wages of labourers are paid partly in wine, still occurs, and the consequences, socially and physiologically, have been disastrous.

A report released in 2011 by Human Rights Watch (HRW; www.hrw.org/reports/2011/08/23/ripe-abuse-0) damned the industry for making its workers lives 'dismal' and 'dangerous'. The report cited appalling housing conditions, lack of access to toilets or drinking water while working, no protection against pesticides, and barriers to union representation among the many things that workers have to contend with in addition to low wages.

There is labour legislation, but it's not always complied with. Besides, many workers are unaware of their rights. Su Birch, chief executive of Wines of South Africa, challenged the HRW report, pointing out the many farms that do comply with the legislation and even go beyond it. She also noted the industry's increased cooperation with the Wine Industry and Ethical Trade Association (WIETA; www.wieta.org.za), which lobbies for a better deal for those working in the wine industry.

Worker's Wine

Various wineries are leading the way in setting improved labour and fair-trade standards. Both Solms-Delta (p157) and Van Loveren (www.vanloveren.co.za) in Robertson have made their employees shareholders in joint-venture wine farms. Part of the Nelson Wine Estate (www.nelsonscreek.co.za) has been donated to the workers to produce wines under the label New Beginnings (www.fms-wine-marketing.co.za).

Other worker or black-owned and empowerment brands include:

Thandi (www.thandiwines.com) Meaning 'love' or 'cherish' in Xhosa (isiXhosa), and located in the Elgin area, this was the first winery in the world to be fair-trade certified. It's half owned by the 250 farm worker families and produces good single varietals and blends, some of which are sold at Tescos in the UK.

M'hudi (www.mhudi.com) Owned by the Rangaka family, their range includes a chenin blanc, merlot, pinotage and sauvignon blanc.

Lathithá (www.lathithawines.co.za) Made by winemakers at Blaauwklippen on behalf of Langa resident Sheila Hlanjwa. It's part of a project to popularise wine drinking in township communities.

M'zoli Wines (www.mzoliwine.co.za) The house wines for the famous township braai (barbecue) in Gugulethu. The owner is the prime mover behind the Gugulethu Wine Festival (www.gugulethuwinefestival.co.za)

Fairvalley Wines (www.fairvalley.co.za) Set on 18ha next to Fairview, this venture produces six wines – a chenin blanc, sauvignon blanc, pinotage, cabernet sauvignon, shiraz and chardonnay; sample them all at the Fairview estate.

Tukulu (www.tukulu.co.za) From the Darling area, this is the flagship Black Economic Empowerment (BEE) brand in the stable of industry giant Distell. It has won awards for its pinotage and is receiving rave reviews for its fair trade chenin blanc and cabernet sauvignon.

In the UK, Asda, Tesco, Marks & Spencer and Waitrose support WIETA, while in South Africa Woolworths is on board; check WIETA's website (www.wieta.org.za) for details.

WINE TRENDS

More than their counterparts in other 'New World' countries, South African winemakers blend grape varieties for many of their top wines. Red blends, mostly based on cabernet sauvignon, have been around for decades. Recent years have seen something of an explosion in white blends, though, in two distinct but equally exciting main styles. First, those mixing sauvignon blanc and semillon, à la white Bordeaux. Vergelegen has been the leader here, with its well-oaked and rather grand semillon-based wine. But now there are many fine versions – like Oak Valley's OV blend, Tokara White and Steenberg's Magna Carta (at R440 the 2009 is one of the most expensive local white wines).

The other strand in the white blend story is more indigenous. These wines are often from warmer inland districts, like the Swartland. Most follow the lead of the 'inventor' of this style, Eben Sadie, with his Palladius, and use plenty of chenin blanc, along with varieties like chardonnay, roussanne and viognier.

Winemakers are also moving to the coast or climbing mountains in search of cooler areas to make different styles of wine: these wines are more delicate and often have lower alcohol levels and greater freshness. Elgin, a high inland plateau, is gaining increasing recognition for its fine sauvignon blanc, chardonnay and pinot noir. Sauvignon blanc is a favourite for wineries in maritime areas too – like Lomond and Black Oystercatcher, both not far from Cape Agulhas; or Fryer's Cove up the West Coast, whose vineyards are just inland from the chilly Atlantic.

TOP TIPPLES

Tim James, wine correspondent for the *Mail & Guardian* and contributor *to Platter's South African Wines,* recommends the following:

Reds

➡ **Beyerskloof Pinotage** (R60) The Cape's own grape variety in simple, fruity guise from a specialist pinotage producer who makes everything from rosé to expensive blends and reserves, which are all recommendable.

➡ **Buitenverwachting Meifort** (R60) The estate's Christine claret is a finer and pricier (R200+) red blend; this 'second label' version is easier-going but not dumbed down.

➡ **Boekenhoutskloof Syrah** (R260) A superb, age-worthy red, both sensuous and sophisticated (but rare to find); the Chocolate Block (R185) from the same producer is a fine, warm-hearted shiraz-led blend; the 2009 was an excellent vintage.

Whites

➡ **Durbanville Hills** Sauvignon blanc (R39); widely available, which is a good thing, as it reliably and freshly delivers those green and tropical notes.

➡ **Solms-Astor Vastrap** (R49) Named for a vernacular dance, this is an appropriately cheerful but not frivolous blend.

➡ **Chamonix** Chardonnay reserve (R130); finely oaked, elegant and refined; there's also a more outgoing but still serious standard version (R50).

➡ **Graham Beck** Blanc de blancs (R150); one of the classiest, freshest bubblies you'll find in the Cape.

Rosé, the big wine success story in Europe, is making its mark on the Cape, too. Pink or copper-tinged wines, lightly fruity, crisp and dry are perfect with lunch, for sipping in the shade or while watching the sun go down. Beware some of the old-style, cheap sweet stuff, but look out for 'pinotage' on the label – not everyone admires this local variety in red wines, but all agree it's great for pink ones.

Glossary of Wine Terms

aroma The smell of a wine; 'bouquet' is usually used for the less fruity, more developed scents of older wine

balance The all-important harmony of the components in a wine: alcohol, fruitiness, acidity, tannin (and oak, when used)

blend A mix of two or more varieties in one wine, eg colombard-chardonnay – you will see 'Cape Blend' appearing on some reds' labels; it implies at least 20% pinotage

corked Not literally cork fragments in the wine, but when the cork has tainted the wine, making it (when it's extreme) mouldy-tasting and flat

estate wine This term is only permitted where the wine is grown, made and bottled on a single property

finish The impression a wine leaves in the mouth: the longer the flavour persists (and the sadder you are when it goes), the better

garage wine Wine made in minuscule quantities, sometimes by passionate amateurs, occasionally literally in a garage

oaked or wooded Most serious red wines, and a lot of smart whites, are matured for a year or two in expensive wooden barrels; it affects the texture of the wine and the flavour; a cheap way of getting oak flavour is to use wood chips or staves in a metal tank

organic It's the grapes rather than the winemaking that can be organic (naturally grown without pesticides, chemical fertilisers, etc)

tannin Mostly in red wine and derived from grape skins and pips, or oak barrels; the mouth-puckering dryness on gums and cheeks, which softens as the wine matures

vintage The year the grapes were harvested; also used to describe a port-style wine made in a particularly good year (the best are often called 'vintage reserve')

Grape (Jeanne Viall, Wilmot James & Jakes Gerwel) is a well-rounded, thought-provoking account of the development of South Africa's wine industry.

Survival Guide

TRANSPORT **234**

GETTING TO
CAPE TOWN. .234
Air 234
Train 234
Bus 235
Boat 235
GETTING AROUND CAPE TOWN . . .235
Car & Motorcycle 235
Taxi 236
Bus 237
Train 237
Bicycle 237

DIRECTORY A–Z **238**
Business Hours 238
Charities 238
Customs Regulations 238
Electricity 239
Embassies & Consulates 239
Emergency 239
Health. 239
Internet Access. 239
Medical Services 239
Money. 240
Post. 240
Public Holidays. 240
Safe Travel. 241
Taxes & Refunds. 241
Telephone 241
Time 241
Tourist Information 242
Travellers with Disabilities 242
Visas. 242
Women Travellers. 242

LANGUAGE **243**

Transport

GETTING TO CAPE TOWN

Most likely you'll arrive at Cape Town International Airport. If coming from within South Africa, it's possible that your arrival point will be Cape Town's combined rail and bus station. The city is also on the international cruise circuit with liners docking either at the Waterfront or in the docks. Flights, tours and rail tickets can all be booked online at www.lonelyplanet.com/travelservices.

Air

There are many direct international flights into Cape Town. Generally it's cheaper to book and pay for domestic flights within South Africa on the internet (rather than via a local travel agent).

Airlines

1time (☎011-086 8000; www.1time.aero)

Air Mauritius (☎087 1507 242; www.airmauritius.com)

Air Namibia (☎021-422 3224; www.airnamibia.com.na)

British Airways (☎021-936 9000; www.ba.com)

Emirates (☎021-403 1100; www.emirates.com)

KLM (☎086 0247 747; www.klm.com)

Kulula.com (☎086 1585 852; www.kulula.com)

Lufthansa (☎086 1842 538; www.lufthansa.com)

Malaysia Airlines (☎021-419 8010; www.malaysiaairlines.com)

Mango (☎021-815 4100, 086 1162 646; www.flymango.com)

Qatar Airways (☎021-936 3080; www.qatarairways.com)

Singapore Airlines (☎021-674 0601; www.singaporeair.com)

South African Airways (☎021-936 1111; www.flysaa.com)

Virgin Atlantic (☎011-340 3400; www.virgin-atlantic.com)

Airport

Cape Town International Airport (☎021-937 1200; www.acsa.co.za) The airport, 22km east of the city centre, has a tourist information office located in the arrivals hall.

GETTING INTO TOWN

Bus

MyCiTi buses (see p237) Run every 20 minutes between 5am and 10pm to Civic Centre station. The fare (adult/child 4-11/under four R53.50/26.50/free) can be paid in cash or using a myconnect card.

Backpacker Bus (☎021-439 7600; www.backpackerbus.co.za) Offers airport transfers from R160 per person (R180 between 5pm and 8am) and picks up from hostels and hotels in the city. Book in advance.

Taxi

Expect to pay around R200 for a non-shared taxi; the officially authorised airport taxi company is **Touch Down Taxis** (☎021-919 4659).

Car

All the major car-hire companies have desks at the airport. Driving along the N2 into the city centre from the airport usually takes 15 to 20 minutes, although during rush hours (7am to 9am and 4.30pm to 6.30pm) this can extend up to an hour. There is a petrol station just outside the airport, handy for refilling before drop-off.

Train

Long distance trains arrive at Cape Town Railway Station on Heerengracht in the City Bowl. There are services Wednesday, Friday and Sunday to and from Jo'burg via Kimberley on the **Shosholoza Meyl** (☎086 000 8888; www.shosholozameyl.co.za). These sleeper trains offer comfortable accommodation and dining cars, but if you require something more luxurious opt either for the elegant **Blue Train** (☎021-449 2672; www.bluetrain.co.za), which stops at Matjiesfontein on its way to Pretoria and Kimberley on the way back to Cape Town, or **Rovos Rail** (☎012-315 8242; www.rovos.com).

CLIMATE CHANGE & TRAVEL

Every form of transport that relies on carbon-based fuel generates CO_2, the main cause of human-induced climate change. Modern travel is dependent on aeroplanes, which might use less fuel per kilometre per person than most cars but travel much greater distances. The altitude at which aircraft emit gases (including CO_2) and particles also contributes to their climate change impact. Many websites offer 'carbon calculators' that allow people to estimate the carbon emissions generated by their journey and, for those who wish to do so, to offset the impact of the greenhouse gases emitted with contributions to portfolios of climate-friendly initiatives throughout the world. Lonely Planet offsets the carbon footprint of all staff and author travel.

Bus

Interstate buses arrive at the bus terminus at Cape Town Train Station, where you'll find the booking offices for the following bus companies, all open from 6am to 6.30pm daily.

Greyhound (☑083 915 9000; www.greyhound.co.za)

Intercape Mainliner (☑021-380 4400; www.intercape.co.za)

SA Roadlink (☑083 918 3999; www.saroadlink.co.za)

Translux (☑021-449 6942; www.translux.co.za)

Baz Bus (☑021-422 5202; www.bazbus.com) Aimed at backpackers and travellers, and offers hop-on, hop-off fares and door-to-door service between Cape Town and Jo'burg/Pretoria via the Northern Drakensberg, Durban and the Garden Route.

Boat

Many cruise ships pause at Cape Town. Useful contacts:

Cruise Complete (www.cruisecompete.com)

MSC Starlight Cruises (☑021-555 3005; www.starlightcruises.co.za)

Royal Mail Ship St Helena (☑020-7575 6480; rms-st-helena.com)

GETTING AROUND CAPE TOWN

Car & Motorcycle

Driving

Cape Town has an excellent road system that, outside the morning and early-evening rush hours (7am to 9pm and 4.30pm to 6.30pm), carries surprisingly little traffic. Road signs alternate between Afrikaans and English. You'll soon learn, for example, that Linkerbaan isn't the name of a town – it means 'left lane'.

Petrol stations are often open 24 hours. Petrol costs around R10.50 per litre, depending on the octane level you choose. Most petrol stations accept credit cards although some will charge you a fee, typically 10%, to do so. An attendant will always fill up your tank for you, clean your windows and ask if the oil or water needs checking – you should tip them 10% for the service.

Be prepared for erratic breaking of road rules by fellow drivers, and drive with caution. Breath testing for alcohol exists but given the lack of police resources and the high blood-alcohol level permitted (0.08%), drunk drivers remain a danger. It's highly unlikely that the police will bother you for petty breaches of the law, such as breaking the speed limit. This might sound like a pleasant state of affairs, but after you've encountered a few dangerous drivers, strict cops seem more attractive.

There's a R31 charge to drive along Chapman's Peak Dr.

Buying

Cape Town is a very pleasant place to spend the week or two that it will inevitably take to buy a car or motorbike. Many used-car dealers are clustered along Victoria Rd between Salt River and Observatory and Voortrekker Rd/R102.

You might be thinking of getting an old Land Rover for a trans-Africa trip; budget from R25,000 for a vehicle that you'll need work on to R45,000 for one ready to go. **Graham Duncan Smith** (☑021-797 3048) is a Land Rover expert who charges a consultation fee of R180 for initial inspections and R300 per hour for subsequent mechanical work.

Online classified ad sites to check include **Junk Mail** (www.junkmail.co.za/capetown) and **Auto Trader** (www.autotrader.co.za). A good car costs about R30,000; you'd be lucky to find a decent vehicle for much less than R20,000. Before buying always ask for a current roadworthy certificate. If needed, these certificates – required when you pay tax for a licence disc, and register the change-of-ownership form – can be obtained from **Dekra** (www.dekraauto.co.za) testing stations in several locations across Cape Town; they charge R340 for a test.

Whoever you're buying a car from, make sure the car's details correspond accurately with those on the ownership (registration) papers, that there is a *current* licence disc on the windscreen and that there's police clearance on the vehicle. The police clearance department can be contacted on ☑021-945 3891.

Register your newly purchased car at the City Treasurer's Department, **Motor Vehicle Registration Division** (☑021-400 4900; Civic Centre, Foreshore; ☺8am-2pm Mon-Fri); bring along the roadworthy certificate, a current licence disc, an accurate ownership certificate, a completed change-of-ownership form (signed by the seller), a clear photocopy of your ID (passport), along with the original.

Insurance for third-party damages and damage to or loss of your vehicle is a very good idea. A recommended insurance agent is **Sansure** (☑086 0786 847; www. sansure.com).

Hire

CAR
Rates range from R230 per day for a KIA Picanto to around R2800 for a convertible Porsche. It's unlikely you'll need to pay higher rates for unlimited kilometres. For meandering around, 400km a day should be more than enough, and if you plan to stop for a day here and there, 200km a day might be sufficient.

When you're getting quotes make sure that they include value-added tax (VAT), as that 14% slug makes a big difference.

One problem with nearly all car-hire deals is the excess: the amount you are liable for before the insurance takes over. Even with a small car you can be liable for up to at least R6000 (although

there's usually the choice of lowering or cancelling the excess for a higher insurance premium). A few companies offer 100% damage and theft insurance at a more expensive rate. You may also be charged extra if you nominate more than one driver. If a non-nominated driver has an accident, then you won't be covered by insurance. Always make sure you read the contract carefully before you sign.

Car-hire companies include:

Around About Cars (☑021-422 4022; www.around aboutcars.com; 20 Bloem St, City Bowl; ☺7.30am-5pm Mon-Fri, 7.30am-1pm Sat & Sun)

Avis (☑021-424 1177; www. avis.co.za; 123 Strand St, City Bowl)

Hertz (☑021-410 6800; www. hertz.co.za; 40 Loop St, City Bowl)

Status Luxury Vehicles (☑021-510 0108; http://slv. co.za)

MOTORCYCLES & SCOOTERS
The following places hire out two wheeled motors:

Cape Sidecar Adventures (☑021-434 9855; www. sidecars.co.za; 2 Glengariff Rd, Three Anchor Bay)

Harley Davidson Cape Town (☑021-446 2999; www. harley-davidson-capetown.com; 9 Somerset Rd, De Waterkant)

Scoot Dr (☑021-418-5995; www.scootdr.co.za; 61 Waterkant St, Foreshore)

Parking

Monday to Saturday during business hours there will often be a one-hour limit on parking within the city centre in a particular spot – check with the parking marshal (identified by their luminous yellow vests) who will ask you to pay for the first half-hour up front (around R5).

If there's no official parking marshal you'll almost always find someone on the

street to tip a small amount (say R2) in exchange for looking after your car. Charges for off-street parking vary, but you can usually find it for R10 per half a day.

Taxi

Consider taking a nonshared taxi at night or if you're in a group. Rates are about R10 per kilometre. There's a taxi rank on Adderley St (Map p264), or call:

Excite Taxis (☑021-448 4444; www.excitetaxis.co.za)

Marine Taxi (☑086 1434 0434, 021-913 6813; www. marinetaxis.co.za)

SA Cab (☑086 1172 222; www.sacab.co.za)

Telecab (☑021-788 2717, 082 222 0282) For transfers from Simon's Town to Boulders and Cape Point.

Rikki

A cross between a taxi and a shared taxi are **Rikkis** (☑086 1745 547; www.rikkis. co.za). They offer shared rides to most places around the City Bowl and down the Atlantic coast to Camps Bay, or in and around Hout Bay, for R15 to R30. They also do regular cab trips for R35 to R55 according to distance travelled, and airport transfers from R180 per person. See their website for locations of their free direct phones, including one at the Cape Town Tourism office on Burg St in the City Bowl. Rikkis are not the quickest way to get around the city and they are notoriously slow to turn up to a booking.

Shared Taxi

In Cape Town (and South Africa in general) a shared taxi means a minibus. These private services, which cover most of the city with an informal network of routes, are a cheap and fast way of getting around. On the downside they're usually crowded and some drivers can be reckless. Useful routes are from Adderley St, opposite the Golden Acre Centre, to Sea Point along Main Rd (R5) and up Long St to Kloof Nek (R5).

The main rank (Map p264) is on the upper deck of Cape Town Train Station and is accessible from a walkway in the Golden Acre Centre or from stairways on Strand St. It's well organised, and finding the right rank is easy. Anywhere else, you just hail shared taxis from the side of the road and ask the driver where they're going.

Bus

Golden Arrow

Golden Arrow (☑080 0656 463; www.gabs.co.za) buses run from the **Golden Acre Bus Terminal** (Map p264; Grand Parade, City Bowl) with most services stopping early in the evening. Their services are most useful for getting along the Atlantic coast from the city centre to Hout Bay (trains service the suburbs to the east of Table Mountain).

Destinations and off-peak fares (applicable from 8am to 4pm) from the city include the Waterfront (R4), Sea Point (R4), Kloof Nek (R4), Camps Bay (R5) and Hout Bay (R8). Peak fares are about 30% higher.

MyCiTi buses

The new **MyCiTi** (☑080 0656 463; www.capetown. gov.za/myciti) network of commuter buses run daily between 5am and 10pm. The main routes currently are from the airport to the city centre, from Table Bay to the city and around the City Bowl up to Gardens and out to the Waterfront. There are plans to extend routes along the Atlantic seaboard to Camps Bay and Hout Bay, up to Tamboerskloof along Kloof

Nek Rd, and east to Woodstock and Salt River.

For most city centre routes (ie from Civic Centre to Gardens and the Waterfront) the fare is R5; to Table View (18.5km north of the city centre) it is R10 and to the airport R53.50. Fares have to be paid with a stored value **myconnect card**; the exception is for the Airport-Civic Centre route on which tickets can paid for with cash.

At the time of research the myconnect card could only be purchased from the kiosks at Civic Centre and Table View stations. There is an issuing fee of R22: keep your receipt and you should be able to get the card back if you return the card to the kiosk. You then need to charge the card with credit. A bank fee of 2.5% of the value loaded (with a minimum of R1.50) will be charged; so if you load the card with R200 you will have R195 in credit. The card, issued by ABSA (a national bank), can also be used pay for low-value transactions at shops and businesses displaying the MasterCard sign.

Train

Cape Metro Rail (☑0800 656 463; www.capemetrorail. co.za) trains are a handy way to get around, although there are few (or no) trains after 6pm on weekdays and after noon on Saturday.

The difference between first- and economy-class carriages in price and comfort is negligible. The most important line for visitors is the Simon's Town line, which runs through Observatory and around the back of Table Mountain through upper-income suburbs such as Newlands, on to Muizenberg and the False Bay coast. These trains run at least every hour from 5am to 7.30pm Monday to Friday (to 6pm on Satur-

day), and from 7.30am to 6.30pm on Sunday.

Metro trains also run out to Strand on the eastern side of False Bay, and into the Winelands to Stellenbosch and Paarl. They are the cheapest and easiest means of transport to these areas; security is best at peak times.

Some economy/first-class fares are Observatory (R5/7), Muizenberg (R6.50/10), Simon's Town (R7.50/15), Paarl (R10/16) and Stellenbosch (R7.50/13). There's also a R30 ticket that allows unlimited travel between Cape Town and Simon's Town and all stations in between from 8am to 4.30pm daily.

Bicycle

If yo're prepared for the many hills and long distances between sights, the Cape Peninsula is a terrific place to explore by bicycle. Dedicated cycle lanes are a legacy of the World Cup: there's a good one north out of the city towards Table View, and another runs alongside the Fan Walk from Cape Town Train Station to Green Point. Bear in mind it's nearly 70km from the centre to Cape Point. Unfortunately, bicycles are banned from suburban trains.

Hire

The following places in Cape Town offer bicycle hire:

Bike & Saddle (☑021-813 6433; www.bikeandsaddle.com; rental per hr R30-80)

Cape Town Cycle Hire (☑021-434 1270, 084-400 1604; www.capetowncyclehire. co.za; per day from R150)

Downhill Adventures (Map p274; ☑021-422 0388; www. downhilladventures.com; cnr Orange & Kloof Sts, Gardens; ☺8am-6pm Mon-Fri, 8am-1pm Sat)

Directory A–Z

Business Hours

Exceptions to the following general hours are listed in reviews.

Banks 9am to 3.30pm Monday to Friday, 9am to 11am Saturday.

Post offices 8.30am to 4.30pm Monday to Friday, 8am to noon Saturday.

Shops 8.30am to 5pm Monday to Friday, 8.30am to 1pm Saturday. Major shopping centres, such as the Waterfront and Canal Walk, are open 9am to 9pm daily.

Cafes 7.30am to 5pm Monday to Friday, 8am to 3pm Saturday. Cafes in the City Bowl are closed on Sunday.

Restaurants 11.30am to 3pm and 6pm to 10pm Monday to Saturday.

Charities

Useful starting points for information are **Greater Good SA** (www.myggsa. co.za), with details on many local charities and development projects, and **Uthando South Africa** (ww.uthando-sa.org/projects), a tour company that supports a vast range of charitable projects. Also recommended is **How 2 Help** (www.h2h.info). If you want to donate your time

the following are bona fide projects:

Christine Revell Children's Home (www.crch.co.za/) Athlone-based kids' home caring for up to 49 babies and children.

Grassroot Soccer (www.grass rootsoccer.org) Training township kids in the field of soccer, as well as teaching them about AIDS and HIV infection.

GCU Academy (Great Commission United Academy; www. gcu.org.za) Trains young kids in Heideveld in soccer and schoolwork. Possible to visit on a Community Project Tour run in conjunction with the backpacker guesthouse The Backpack.

Habitat for Humanity (www. habitat.org.za) Helping build homes in the township of Mfuleni, 30km from Cape Town.

The Homestead (www.home stead.org.za) Set up Cape Town's first shelter for street children in 1982; runs several programs, including job-creation schemes.

Kay Mason Foundation (www. kaymasonfoundation.org) Helps talented, disadvantaged kids get a better education.

Nazareth House (www. nazhouse.org.za) Takes care of AIDS orphans.

Ons Plek (www.onsplek.org.za) Provides a shelter for girls living on the streets.

Masiphumelele Corporation & Trust (www.masicorp.org) Volunteers are needed for this trust working in Masiphumelele township in the Southern Peninsula.

Streetsmart (www.street smartsa.org.za) Check the website for a list of Cape Town restaurants signed up to this program that applies a donation of R5 to every bill to the street kids' charity.

Tourism Community Development Trust (www.tcdtrust. org.za) Focuses on supporting education projects such as crèches, school libraries, soup kitchens and respite centres.

Customs Regulations

There are the usual duty-free restrictions on entering South Africa: you're only allowed to bring in 1L of spirits, 2L of wine and 400 cigarettes. Motor vehicles must be covered by a carnet (customs permit). For more information, contact the **Department of Customs & Excise** (☎0800 007 277, 011-602 2093; www.sars.gov.za).

Electricity

The electricity system is 230V AC at 50 cycles per second. Appliances rated at 240V AC will work. Plugs have either two or three round pins.

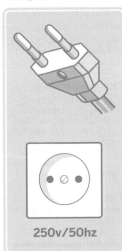

250v/50hz

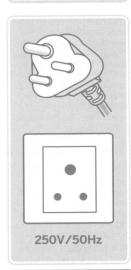

250V/50Hz

Embassies & Consulates

Most foreign embassies are based in Johannesburg (Jo'burg) or Pretoria, but a few countries also maintain a consulate in Cape Town. Most are open from 9am to 4pm Monday to Friday.

Angola (☎021-425 8700; 1st fl, Pavilion Bldg, Thibault Sq, City Bowl)

Botswana (☎021-421 1045; 5th fl, Southern Life Centre, 8 Riebeeck St, City Bowl)

France (☎021-423 1575; www.consulfrance-lecap.org; 78 Queen Victoria St, City Bowl)

Germany (☎021-464 3020; www.southafrica.diplo.de/Ver tretung/suedafrika/de/11__Ka pstadt.html; 19th fl, Triangle House, 22 Riebeeck St, City Bowl)

Italy (☎021-487 3900; www. conscapetown.esteri.it/Consol ato_Capetown; 2 Grey's Pass, Queen Victoria St, City Bowl)

Mozambique (☎021-426 2944; 7th fl, 45 Castle St, City Bowl)

The Netherlands (☎021-421 5660; http://southafrica. nlembassy.org/consulate -general-cape-town; 100 Strand St, City Bowl)

UK (☎021-405 2400; http:// ukinsouthafrica.fco.gov.uk/en; 15th fl, Norton Rose House, 8 Riebeeck St, City Bowl)

USA (☎021-702 7300; http:// southafrica.usembassy.gov; 2 Reddam Ave, Westlake)

Emergency

In any emergency call ☎107, or ☎021-480 7700 if using a mobile phone. Other useful phone numbers include the following:

Table Mountain National Park (☎086-106 417)

Sea Rescue (☎021-449 3500)

Health

Tap water is drinkable and, with the exception of HIV/ AIDS, there's little need to worry about health issues in Cape Town. The National HIV Survey in 2008 estimated that roughly 11% of the population are living with HIV. Hundreds die daily from HIV/AIDS so make sure you protect yourself while having sex. For more information on health in South Africa, read Lonely Planet's *Healthy Travel Africa* and *South Africa, Lesotho & Swaziland*.

Internet Access

Wi-fi access is available at many hotels and hostels as well as several cafes and restaurants throughout the city; we list places where it is available – at some it will be free (ask for the password), at others you'll have to pay. Rates are pretty uniform at R30 per hour. General providers include **Red Button** (www.redbutton.co.za) and **Skyrove** (www.skyrove.com).

Medical Services

Medical services are of a high standard; make sure you have health insurance and be prepared to pay for services immediately. In an emergency call ☎107, or ☎021-480 7700 if using a mobile phone, for directions to the nearest hospital. Many doctors make house calls; look under 'Medical' in the phone book or ask at your hotel.

Netcare Christiaan Barnard Memorial Hospital (☎021-480 6111; www.netcare. co.za/live/content.php?Item_ ID=250; 181 Longmarket St, City Bowl)

Netcare Travel Clinic (☎021-419 3172; www.travel clinics.co.za; 11th fl, Picbal Arcade, 58 Strand St, City Bowl; ⊗8am-4pm Mon-Fri)

Groote Schuur Hospital (Map p268; ☎021-404 9111; www.westerncape.gov.za/ your_gov/5972; Main Rd, Observatory)

PRACTICALITIES

Newspapers & Magazines

➡ **Cape Times** (www.iol.co.za/capetimes) Local morning newspaper, Monday to Friday.

➡ **Cape Argus** (www.iol.co.za/capeargus) Local afternoon newspaper, Monday to Saturday.

➡ **Mail & Guardian** (mg.co.za) National weekly, published Friday, including excellent investigative and opinion pieces and arts-review supplement.

➡ **Cape Etc** (www.capeetc.com) Bimonthly listings and features magazine.

➡ **021 Magazine** (www.021magazine.co.za) Quarterly listings and features magazine.

➡ **Big Issue** (www.bigissue.org.za) Monthly magazine; helps provide an income for the homeless; sold at many of Cape Town's busiest traffic intersections.

TV & Radio

➡ **South African Broadcasting Corporation** (SABC; www.sabc.co.za) National radio & TV channels.

➡ **Cape Talk 567MW** (www.567.co.za) Talkback radio.

➡ **Fine Music Radio** (www.fmr.co.za) 101.3FM; jazz and classical.

➡ **94.5 Kfm** (www.kfm.co.za) Pop.

➡ **Good Hope FM** (www.goodhopefm.co.za) Between 94 and 97FM; pop.

➡ **Heart 104.9FM** (www.1049.fm) Pop, soul, R&B.

➡ **Taxi Radio** (thetaxi.mobi) Woodstock-based internet radio.

Money

The unit of currency is the rand (R), which is divided into 100 cents (¢). The coins are 5¢, 10¢, 20¢ and 50¢, and R1, R2 and R5. The notes are R10, R20, R50, R100 and R200. The R200 note looks a lot like the R20 note, so check them carefully before handing them over. There have been forgeries of the R200 note; some businesses are reluctant to accept them. Rand is sometimes referred to as 'bucks'.

ATM

If your card belongs to the worldwide Cirrus network you should have no problem using ATMs in Cape Town. However, it pays to follow some basic procedures to ensure safety:

➡ Avoid ATMs at night and in secluded places. Machines in shopping malls are usually the safest.

➡ Most ATMs in banks have security guards. If there's no guard around when you're withdrawing cash, watch your back, or get someone else to watch it for you.

➡ Watch the people using the ATM ahead of you carefully. If they look suspicious, go to another machine.

➡ Use ATMs during banking hours and if possible take a friend. If your card is jammed in a machine then one person should stay at the ATM while the other seeks assistance from the bank.

➡ When you put your card into the ATM press cancel immediately. If the card is returned then you know there is no blockage in the machine and it should be safe to proceed.

➡ Politely refuse any offers of help to complete your transaction. If someone does offer, end your transaction immediately and find another machine.

➡ Carry your bank's emergency phone number, and if you do lose your card report it immediately.

Changing Money

Most banks change cash and travellers cheques in major currencies, with various commissions. You'll also find exchange bureaux at the major shopping malls including Victoria Mall at the Waterfront.

Tipping

Ten per cent is standard for most services.

Post

There are post office branches across Cape Town; see www.sapo.co.za to find the nearest. The post is reliable but can be slow. If you're mailing anything of value, consider using the private mail services such as Postnet (www.postnet.co.za), which uses DHL for international deliveries.

Public Holidays

On public holidays government departments, banks, offices, post offices and some museums are closed. Public holidays in South Africa include the following:

New Year's Day 1 January

Human Rights Day 21 March

Easter (Good Friday/Easter Monday) March/April

Family Day 13 April

Constitution Day (Freedom Day) 27 April

Worker's Day 1 May

Youth Day 16 June

Women's Day 9 August

Heritage Day 24 September

Day of Reconciliation 16 December

Christmas Day 25 December

Boxing Day (Day of Goodwill) 26 December

Safe Travel

Cape Town is one of the most relaxed cities in Africa, which can instil a false sense of security. People who have travelled overland from Cairo without a single mishap or theft have been known to be cleaned out in Cape Town – generally when doing something like leaving their gear on a beach while they go swimming.

Paranoia is not required, but common sense is. There is tremendous poverty on the peninsula and the 'informal redistribution of wealth' is reasonably common. The townships on the Cape Flats have an appalling crime rate and unless you have a trustworthy guide or are on a tour they are not places for a casual stroll.

Stick to the roads when you walk around the city, and always listen to local advice. There is safety in numbers.

Swimming at any of the Cape beaches is potentially hazardous, especially for those inexperienced in surf. Check for warning signs about rips and rocks, and only swim in patrolled areas. Parents should certainly keep an eye on their kids, bearing in mind the hypothermia-inducing water temperatures!

Taxes & Refunds

Value-added tax (VAT) is 14%. Foreign visitors can reclaim some of their VAT expenses on departure. This applies only to goods that you are taking out of the country. Also, the goods have to have been bought at a shop participating in the VAT foreign tourist sales scheme.

To make a claim, you need your tax invoice. This is usually the receipt, but make sure that it includes the following:

➡ the words 'tax invoice'

➡ the seller's name, address and VAT registration number

➡ a description of the goods purchased

➡ the cost of the goods and the amount of VAT charged

➡ a tax invoice number

➡ the date of the transaction.

For purchases over R2000, your name and address and the quantity of goods must also appear on the invoice. All invoices must be originals, not photocopies. The total value of the goods claimed for must exceed R250.

At the point of your departure, you will have to show the goods to a customs inspector. At airports make sure you have the goods checked by the inspector before you check in your luggage. After you have gone through immigration, you make the claim and then pick up your refund cheque – at the airport in Cape Town you can then cash it straight away at the currency-exchange office (usually in rand or US dollars).

You can also make your claim at the international airports in Jo'burg and Durban, at the Beitbridge (Zimbabwe) and Komatipoort (Mozambique) border crossings and at major harbours.

Telephone

South Africa's country code is ☎27 and Cape Town's area code is ☎021, as is Stellenbosch's, Paarl's and Franschhoek's; this must be included even when dialling locally. Sometimes you'll come across phone numbers beginning with ☎0800 for free calls or ☎0860 for calls shared 50/50 between the caller and receiver. Note that it's cheaper to make a call between 7pm and 7am.

Public telephones, which can be found across the city, take coins or phonecards. Local calls cost R1 for three minutes. When using a coin phone you might find that you have credit left after you've finished a call. If you want to make another call don't hang up or you'll lose the credit. Press the black button under the receiver hook.

Mobile Phones

South Africa's mobile-phone networks are all on the GSM digital system. The main three operators are Vodacom (www.vodacom.co.za), MTN (www.mtn.co.za) and Cell C (www.cellc.co.za). Both Vodacom and MTN have desks at Cape Town International Airport where you can sort out a local prepaid or pay-as-you-go SIM card to use in your phone during your visit. Otherwise you'll find branches of each company across the city, as well as many places where you can buy vouchers to recharge the credit on your phone account. Call charges average about R2.50 per minute.

Phonecards

Card phones are even easier to find than coin phones, so it's worth buying a phonecard if you're going to make more than just the odd call. Cards are available in denominations of R10, R20, R50, R100 and R200 and you can buy them at Cape Town Tourism, newsagencies and general stores.

Time

South African Standard Time is two hours ahead of Greenwich Mean Time (GMT; at noon in London, it's 2pm in Cape Town), seven hours ahead of USA Eastern Standard Time (at noon in New

York, it's 7pm in Cape Town) and eight hours behind Australian Eastern Standard Time (at noon in Sydney, it's 4am in Cape Town). There is no daylight-saving time.

Tourist Information

At the head office of **Cape Town Tourism** (☎021-426 4260; www.capetown. travel; cnr Castle & Burg Sts, City Bowl; ☺8am-6pm daily Oct-Mar, 9am-5pm Mon-Fri, 9am-1pm Sat & Sun Apr-Sep) there are advisors who can book accommodation, tours and car hire. You can also get information on national parks and reserves, safaris and overland tours.

Other Cape Town Tourism branches include:

Blaauwberg Coast Visitor Information Centre (☎021-521 1080; 1 Marine Drive, Tableview; ☺9am-5.30pm Mon-Fri, 9am-1pm Sat & Sun)

Hout Bay (☎021-790 8380; 4 Andrews Rd; ☺9am-5.30pm Mon-Fri & 9am-1pm Sat & Sun Oct-Apr, 9am-5pm Mon-Fri May-Sep)

Muizenberg Visitor Information Centre (☎021-787 9140; The Pavilion, Beach Rd; ☺9am-5.30pm Mon-Fri, 9am-1pm Sat & Sun)

Simon's Town Visitor Information Centre (☎021-786 8440; 111 St George's St; ☺8.30am-5.30pm Mon-Fri, 9am-1pm Sat & Sun)

V&A Waterfront Visitor Information Centre (☎021-408 7600; Dock Rd; ☺9am-6pm daily)

Travellers with Disabilities

While sight- or hearing-impaired travellers should have few problems in Cape Town, wheelchair users will generally find travel easier with an able-bodied companion. Very few accommodation places have ramps and wheelchair-friendly bathrooms.

The path around the reservoir in Silvermine is designed to be wheelchair accessible. It's possible to hire vehicles converted for hand control from many of the major car-hire agencies.

There are also several South African tour companies specialising in travel packages for the disabled, including a couple of Cape Town–based operations:

Endeavour Safaris (☎021-556 6114; www.endeavour-safaris.com)

Epic Enabled (☎021-785 7440; www.epic-enabled.com)

Flamingo Adventure Tours & Disabled Ventures (☎082 450 2031, 021-557 4496; flamingotours. co.za/disabled)

For further general information contact **National Council for Persons with Physical Disabilities in South Africa** (☎011-452 2774; www.ncppdsa.org.za). **Access-Able Travel Source** (www.access-able.com) lists tour operators catering for travellers with disabilities and **Linx Africa** (www.linx.co.za/trails/lists/disalist.html) has province-by-province listings of disabled-friendly trails.

Visas

Visitors on holiday from most Commonwealth countries (including Australia and the UK), most Western European countries, Japan and the USA don't require visas. Instead, you'll be issued with a free entry permit on arrival. These are valid for a stay of up to 90 days. But if the date of your flight out is sooner than this, the immigration officer may use it as the date of your permit expiry unless you request otherwise.

If you aren't entitled to an entry permit, you'll need to get a visa (also free) before you arrive. These aren't issued at the borders, and must be obtained from a South African embassy or consulate in your own country. Allow several weeks for processing.

For any entry – whether you require a visa or not – you need to have at least two completely blank pages in your passport, excluding the last two pages.

Apply for a visa extension or a re-entry visa at the **Department of Home Affairs** (☎021-465 0333; www.samigrationservices. co.za; 56 Barrack St, City Bowl; ☺7.30am-4.30pm Mon-Fri, 8.30am-12.30pm Sat).

Women Travellers

Cape Town is generally safe for women travellers. In most cases, you'll be met with warmth and hospitality. However, paternalism and sexism run strong, especially away from the city centre, and these attitudes – much more than physical assault – are likely to be the main problem.

South Africa's sexual assault statistics are appalling. Yet, while there have been incidents of female travellers being raped, these cases are relatively rare. It's difficult to quantify the risk of assault – and there is a risk – but it's worth remembering that plenty of women do travel alone safely in South Africa.

Use common sense and caution, especially at night. Don't go out alone in the evenings on foot: always take a taxi; avoid isolated areas, roadways and beaches during both day and evening hours; avoid hiking alone; and don't hitch. Carry a mobile phone if you're driving alone. Talk with local women about what and where is OK, and what isn't.

Language

South Africa has 11 official languages: English, Afrikaans, Ndebele, North Sotho, South Sotho, Swati, Tsonga, Tswana, Venda, Xhosa and Zulu. In the Cape Town area only three languages are prominent: Afrikaans, English and Xhosa.

AFRIKAANS

Afrikaans developed from the dialect spoken by the Dutch settlers in South Africa from the 17th century. Until the late 19th century it was considered a Dutch dialect (known as 'Cape Dutch'), and in 1925 it became one of the official languages of South Africa. Today, it's the first language of around six million people. Most Afrikaans speakers also speak English, but this is not always the case in small towns and among older people.

If you read our coloured pronunciation guides as if they were English, you'll be understood. The stressed syllables are in italics. Note that aw is pronounced as in 'law', eu as the 'u' in 'nurse', ew as the 'ee' in 'see' with rounded lips, oh as the 'o' in 'cold', uh as the 'a' in 'ago', kh as the 'ch' in the the Scottish *loch*, r is trilled, and zh is pronounced as the 's' in 'pleasure'.

Basics

Hello.	Hallo.	ha·*loh*
Goodbye.	Totsiens.	tot·*seens*
Yes./No.	Ja./Nee.	yaa/ney
Please.	Asseblief.	a·si·*bleef*

WANT MORE?

For in-depth language information and handy phrases, check out Lonely Planet's *Africa phrasebook*. You'll find it at **shop.lonelyplanet.com**, or you can buy Lonely Planet's iPhone phrasebooks at the Apple App Store.

| Thank you. | Dankie. | dang·kee |
| Sorry. | Jammer. | ya·min |

How are you?
Hoe gaan dit? — hu khaan dit

Fine, and you?
Goed dankie, en jy? — khut dang·kee en yay

What's your name?
Wat's jou naam? — vats yoh naam

My name is ...
My naam is ... — may naam is ...

Do you speak English?
Praat jy Engels? — praat yay eng·ils

I don't understand.
Ek verstaan nie. — ek vir·staan nee

Accommodation

Where's a ...?	Waar's 'n ...?	vaars i ...
campsite	kampeerplek	kam·peyr·plek
guesthouse	gastehuis	khas·ti·hays
hotel	hotel	hu·tel

Do you have a single/double room?
Het jy 'n enkel/ — het yay i eng·kil/
dubbel kamer? — di·bil kaa·mir

How much is it per night/person?
Hoeveel kos dit per nag/ — hu·fil kos dit pir nakh/
persoon? — pir·soon

Eating & Drinking

Can you recommend a ...?	Kan jy 'n ... aanbeveel?	kan yay i ... aan·bi·feyl
bar	kroeg	krukh
dish	gereg	khi·rekh
place to eat	eetplek	eyt·plek

Numbers – Afrikaans

1	*een*	eyn
2	*twee*	twey
3	*drie*	dree
4	*vier*	feer
5	*vyf*	fayf
6	*ses*	ses
7	*sewe*	see·vi
8	*agt*	akht
9	*nege*	ney·khi
10	*tien*	teen

I'd like ..., please.	*Ek wil asseblief ... hê.*	ek vil a·si·*bleef* ... he
a table for two	*'n tafel vir twee*	i *taa*·fil fir twey
that dish	*daardie gereg*	*daar*·dee khi·*rekh*
the bill	*die rekening*	dee *rey*·ki·ning
the menu	*die spyskaart*	dee *spays*·kaart

Emergencies

Help!	*Help!*	help
Call a doctor!	*Kry 'n dokter!*	kray i *dok*·tir
Call the police!	*Kry die polisie!*	kray dee pu·*lee*·see

I'm lost.
Ek is verdwaal. — ek is fir·*dwaal*

Where are the toilets?
Waar is die toilette? — vaar is dee toy·*le*·ti

I need a doctor.
Ek het 'n dokter nodig. — ek het i *dok*·tir *noo*·dikh

Shopping & Services

I'm looking for ...
Ek soek na ... — ek suk naa ...

How much is it?
Hoeveel kos dit? — *hu*·fil kos dit

What's your lowest price?
Wat is jou laagste prys? — vat is yoh *laakh*·sti prays

I want to buy a phonecard.
Ek wil asseblief 'n foonkaart koop. — ek vil a·si·*bleef* i *foon*·kaart koop

I'd like to change money.
Ek wil asseblief geld ruil. — ek vil a·si·*bleef* khelt rayl

I want to use the internet.
Ek wil asseblief die Internet gebruik. — ek vil a·si·*bleef* dee *in*·tir·net khi·*brayk*

Transport & Directions

A ... ticket, please.	*Een ... kaartjie, asseblief.*	eyn ... *kaar*·kee a·si·*bleef*
one-way	*eenrigting*	eyn·rikh·ting
return	*retoer*	ri·*tur*

How much is it to ...?
Hoeveel kos dit na ...? — *hu*·fil kos dit naa ...

Please take me to (this address).
Neem my asseblief na (hierdie adres). — neym may a·si·*bleef* naa (*heer*·dee a·*dres*)

Where's the (nearest) ...?
Waar's die (naaste) ...? — vaars dee (*naas*·ti) ...

Can you show me (on the map)?
Kan jy my (op die kaart) wys? — kan yay may (op dee kaart) vays

What's the address?
Wat is die adres? — vat is dee a·*dres*

XHOSA

Xhosa belongs to Bantu language family, along with Zulu, Swati and Ndebele. It is the most widely distributed indigenous language in South Africa, and is also spoken in the Cape Town area. About six and a half million people speak Xhosa.

In our pronunciation guides, the symbols b', ch', k', p', t' and ts' represent sounds that are 'spat out' (only in case of b' the air is sucked in), a bit like combining them with the sound in the middle of 'uh-oh'. Note also that hl is pronounced as in the Welsh *llewellyn* and dl is like hl but with the vocal cords vibrating. Xhosa has a series of 'click' sounds as well; they are not distinguished in this chapter.

Basics

Hello.	*Molo.*	maw·law
Goodbye.	*Usale ngoxolo.*	u·*saa*·le ngaw·*kaw*·law
Yes./No.	*Ewe./Hayi.*	e·*we*/haa·yee
Please.	*Cela.*	ke·laa
Thank you.	*Enkosi.*	e·*nk'aw*·see
Sorry.	*Uxolo.*	u·*aw*·law
How are you?	*Kunjani?*	k'u·*njaa*·nee

Fine, and you?
Ndiyaphila, unjani wena? — ndee·yaa·*pee*·laa u·*njaa*·nee we·naa

What's your name?
Ngubani igama lakho? — ngu·*b'aa*·nee ee·*gaa*·maa laa·*kaw*

My name is ...
Igama lam ngu ... — ee·*gaa*·maa laam ngu ...

Do you speak English?
Uyasithetha   u·yaa·see·*te*·taa
isingesi?   ee·see·*nge*·see

I don't understand.
Andiqondi.   aa·ndee·*kaw*·ndee

Accommodation

Where's a ...? *Iphi i ...?*   ee·*pee* ee ...

campsite	*ibala loku-khempisha*	ee·*b'aa*·laa law·k'u·ke·mp'ee·shaa
guesthouse	*indlu yama-ndwendwe*	ee·*ndlu* yaa·maa·ndwe·ndwe
hotel	*ihotele*	ee·*haw*·t'e·le

Do you have a single/double room?
Unalo igumbi   u·*naa*·law ee·*gu*·mb'ee
kanye/kabini?   k'aa·*nye*/k'aa·*b'ee*·nee

How much is it per night/person?
Yimalini   yee·*maa*·lee·nee
ubusuku/umntu?   u·*b'u*·su·k'u/*um*·nt'u

Eating & Drinking

Can you *Ugakwazi*   u·ngaa·*k'waa*·zee
recommend *ukukhuthaza ...?* u·k'u·*ku*·taa·zaa ...
a ...?

bar	*ibhari*	ee·*baa*·ree
dish	*isitya*	ee·see·*ty'aa*
place to eat	*indawo yokutya*	ee·*ndaa*·waw yaw·k'u·*ty'aa*

I'd like ..., *Ndiyafuna ...*   ndee·yaa·*fu*·naa ...
please.

a table for two	*itafile yababini*	ee·*t'aa*·fee·le yaa·b'aa·*b'ee*·nee
that dish	*esasitya*	e·*saa*·see·ty'aa
the bill	*inkcukacha ngama-xabiso*	ee·*nku*·k'aa·haa ngaa·maa·*kaa*·b'ee·saw
the menu	*isazisi*	e·*saa*·zee·see

Emergencies

Help! *Uncedo!*   u·*ne*·daw
I'm lost. *Ndilahlekile.*   ndee·laa·*hle*·k'e·le
Call a doctor! *Biza ugqirha!*   *b'ee*·zaa u·*gee*·khaa

Call the police!
Biza amapolisa!   *b'ee*·zaa aa·maa·*paw*·lee·saa

Where are the toilets?
Ziphi itoylethi?   zee·*pee* ee·*taw*·yee·le·tee

I need a doctor.
Ndifuna ugqirha.   ndee·*fu*·naa u·*giee*·khaa

Shopping & Services

I'm looking for ...
Ndifuna ...   ndee·*fu*·naa ...

How much is it?
Yimalini?   yee·*maa*·li·nee

What's your lowest price?
Lithini ixabiso   lee·*tee*·nee ee·*kaa*·b'ee·saw
elingezantsi?   e·lee·nge·*zaa*·nts'ee

I want to buy a phonecard.
Ndifuna uku thenga   ndee·*fu*·naa u·*k'u te*·ngaa
ikhadi lokufowuna.   ee·*kaa*·dee law·k'u·*faw*·wu·naa

I'd like to change money.
Ndingathanda   ndee·ngaa·*taa*·ndaa
tshintsha imali.   ch'ee·*nch'aa* ee·*maa*·lee

I want to use the internet.
Ndifuna uku   ndee·*fu*·naa u·*k'u*
sebenzisa   se·b'e·*nzee*·saa
i intanethi.   ee ee·*nt'aa*·ne·tee

Transport & Directions

A ... ticket, *Linye ...*   lee·*nye* ...
please. *itikiti*   ee·*t'ee*·k'ee·t'ee
            nceda.   ne·daa

| one-way | *ndlelanye* | *ndle*·laa·nye |
| return | *buyela* | b'u·*ye*·laa |

How much is it to ...?
Kuxabisa njani u ...?   ku·*kaa*·b'ee·saa *njaa*·nee u ...

Please take me to (this address).
Ndicela undise   ndee·*ke*·laa u·*ndee*·se
(kule dilesi).   (k'u·*le dee*·le·see)

Where's the (nearest) ...?
Iphi e(kufutshane) ...?   ee·*pee* e·(k'u·*fu*·ch'aa·ne) ...

Can you show me (on the map)?
Ungandibonisa   u·ngaa·ndee·*b'aw*·nee·saa
(kwimaphu)?   (k'wee·*maa*·pu)

What's the address?
Ithini idilesi?   ee·*tee*·nee ee·*dee*·le·see

Numbers – Xhosa
English numbers are commonly used.

1	*wani*	*waa*·nee
2	*thu*	tu
3	*thri*	tree
4	*fo*	faw
5	*fayifu*	*faa*·yee·fu
6	*siksi*	*seek'*·see
7	*seveni*	se·*ve*·nee
8	*eyithi*	e·*yee*·tee
9	*nayini*	*naa*·yee·nee
10	*teni*	*t'e*·nee

GLOSSARY

ANC – African National Congress

apartheid – literally 'the state of being apart'; the old South African political system in which people were segregated according to race

bobotie – traditional Cape Malay dish of delicate curried mince with a topping of savoury egg custard, usually served on turmeric-flavoured rice

braai – barbecue featuring lots of grilled meat and beer; a South African institution, particularly in poorer areas, where having a communal braai is cheaper than using electricity

bredie – traditional Cape Malay pot stew of vegetables and meat or fish

cafe – in some cases, a pleasant place for a coffee, in others, a small shop selling odds and ends, plus unappetising fried food; also kaffie

coloureds – South Africans of mixed race

DA – Democratic Alliance

farm stall – small roadside shop or shelter that sells farm produce

fynbos – literally 'fine bush'; the vegetation of the area around Cape Town, composed of proteas, heaths and reeds

karamat – tomb of a Muslim saint

kloof – ravine

line fish – catch of the day

mealie – an ear of maize; also see mealie meal and mealie pap

mealie meal – finely ground maize

mealie pap – mealie porridge; the staple diet of rural blacks, often served with stew

Mother City – another name for Cape Town; probably so called because it was South Africa's first colony

NP – old apartheid-era and now defunct National Party

PAC – Pan-African Congress

Pagad – People against Gangsterism and Drugs

rondavel – round hut with a conical roof; frequently seen in holiday resorts

SABC – South African Broadcasting Corporation

sangoma – traditional African healer

shared taxi – relatively cheap form of shared transport, usually a minibus; also known as a black taxi, minibus taxi or long-distance taxi

shebeen – drinking establishment in a township; once illegal, now merely unlicensed

strand – beach

township – black residential district, often on the outskirts of an otherwise middle-class (or mainly white) suburb

venison – if you see this on a menu it's bound to be some form of antelope, usually springbok

VOC – Vereenigde Oost-Indische Compagnie (Dutch East India Company)

Voortrekkers – original Afrikaner settlers of the Orange Free State and Transvaal who migrated from the Cape Colony in the 1830s

Behind the Scenes

SEND US YOUR FEEDBACK

We love to hear from travellers – your comments keep us on our toes and help make our books better. Our well-travelled team reads every word on what you loved or loathed about this book. Although we cannot reply individually to postal submissions, we always guarantee that your feedback goes straight to the appropriate authors, in time for the next edition. Each person who sends us information is thanked in the next edition – and the most useful submissions are rewarded with a selection of digital PDF chapters.

Visit **lonelyplanet.com/contact** to submit your updates and suggestions or to ask for help. Our award-winning website also features inspirational travel stories, news and discussions.

Note: We may edit, reproduce and incorporate your comments in Lonely Planet products such as guidebooks, websites and digital products, so let us know if you don't want your comments reproduced or your name acknowledged. For a copy of our privacy policy visit lonelyplanet.com/privacy.

OUR READERS

Many thanks to the travellers who used the last edition and wrote to us with helpful hints, useful advice and interesting anecdotes:

Patrick Boyce, Jon De Quidt, Lieke De Jong, Dorothée Jobert, Laura Metiary, Heather Monell, Lewis Phillips, Simric Yarrow.

AUTHOR THANKS

Simon Richmond

Cheers to the following amazing people who made my time in Cape Town such a pleasure and constant education: Lucy, James, Lee, Toni, Brent, Belinda, Sheryl, Nicole Biondi, Alison Foat, Sally Grierson, Iain Harris, Cameron and Justin, Madelen Johansen, Tamsin Turbull, Lauren, Misha and Jeremy, Tim James, Hannah Deall, Patrick Craig, Sam Walker, Oliver Hermanus, Rashiq Fataar, Lauren Beukes, Zayd Minty, Lameen Abdul-Malik, Tony Osborne and Neil Turner – the Mother City will always be extra special to me now.

Lucy Corne

Enormous thanks to Simon Richmond for all the help, guidance and suggestions and to Cathy Marston for providing tips on where to quaff in the Cape. Thank yous go to the very helpful staff at Knysna Tourism, to Denis and Debbie for their hospitality and to my husband, Shawn, for coping alone in our first month of marriage!

ACKNOWLEDGMENTS

Climate map data adapted from Peel MC, Finlayson BL & McMahon TA (2007) 'Updated World Map of the Köppen-Geiger Climate Classification', *Hydrology and Earth System Sciences,* 11, 163344.

Cover photograph: Colourful houses in Cape Town's Bo-Kaap district with a view to Lion's Head, Sebastian/Alamy

Many of the images in this guide are available for licensing from Lonely Planet Images: www.lonelyplanetimages.com.

THIS BOOK

This 7th edition of Lonely Planet's *Cape Town & the Garden Route* guidebook was researched and written by Simon Richmond and Lucy Corne. Simon also worked on the previous edition with Helen Ranger and Tim Richards, the 5th edition with Al Richards, the 4th edition alone, and the 3rd edition with Jon Murray. Jon wrote the 1st and 2nd editions. This guidebook was commissioned in Lonely Planet's Melbourne office, and produced by the following:

Commissioning Editors David Carroll, Suzannah Shwer

Coordinating Editors Paul Harding, Sophie Splatt

Coordinating Cartographer Anita Bahn

Coordinating Layout Designer Sandra Helou

Managing Editors Brigitte Ellemor, Angela Tinson

Senior Editor Andi Jones

Managing Cartographers Shahara Ahmed

Managing Layout Designer Chris Girdler

Assisting Editors Adrienne Costanzo, Laura Gibb, Sam Trafford

Assisting Cartographers Karusha Ganga, Mick Garrett, Chris Tsismetzis

Cover Research Naomi Parker

Language Content Branislava Vladisavljevic

Thanks to Ryan Evans, Samantha Forge, Larissa Frost, Errol Hunt, Trent Paton, Kirsten Rawlings, Gina Tsarouhas, Gerard Walker

See also separate subindexes for:

⚔ **EATING P257**

🍷 **DRINKING & NIGHTLIFE P259**

☆ **ENTERTAINMENT P259**

🛍 **SHOPPING P259**

🏃 **SPORTS & ACTIVITIES P260**

🛏 **SLEEPING P261**

Index

INDEX SLEEPING

Cape Town Maps

Map Legend

Sights
- Beach
- Buddhist
- Castle
- Christian
- Hindu
- Islamic
- Jewish
- Monument
- Museum/Gallery
- Ruin
- Winery/Vineyard
- Zoo
- Other Sight

Eating
- Eating

Drinking & Nightlife
- Drinking & Nightlife
- Cafe

Entertainment
- Entertainment

Shopping
- Shopping

Sleeping
- Sleeping
- Camping

Sports & Activities
- Diving/Snorkelling
- Canoeing/Kayaking
- Skiing
- Surfing
- Swimming/Pool
- Walking
- Windsurfing
- Other Sports & Activities

Information
- Post Office
- Tourist Information

Transport
- Airport
- Border Crossing
- Bus
- Cable Car/Funicular
- Cycling
- Ferry
- Metro
- Monorail
- Parking
- S-Bahn
- Taxi
- Train/Railway
- Tram
- Tube Station
- U-Bahn
- Other Transport

Routes
- Tollway
- Freeway
- Primary
- Secondary
- Tertiary
- Lane
- Unsealed Road
- Plaza/Mall
- Steps
- Tunnel
- Pedestrian Overpass
- Walking Tour
- Walking Tour Detour
- Path

Boundaries
- International
- State/Province
- Disputed
- Regional/Suburb
- Marine Park
- Cliff
- Wall

Geographic
- Hut/Shelter
- Lighthouse
- Lookout
- Mountain/Volcano
- Oasis
- Park
- Pass
- Picnic Area
- Waterfall

Hydrography
- River/Creek
- Intermittent River
- Swamp/Mangrove
- Reef
- Canal
- Water
- Dry/Salt/Intermittent Lake
- Glacier

Areas
- Beach/Desert
- Cemetery (Christian)
- Cemetery (Other)
- Park/Forest
- Sportsground
- Sight (Building)
- Top Sight (Building)

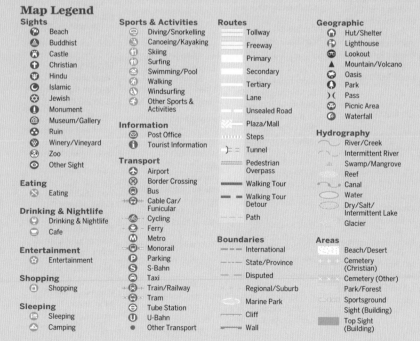

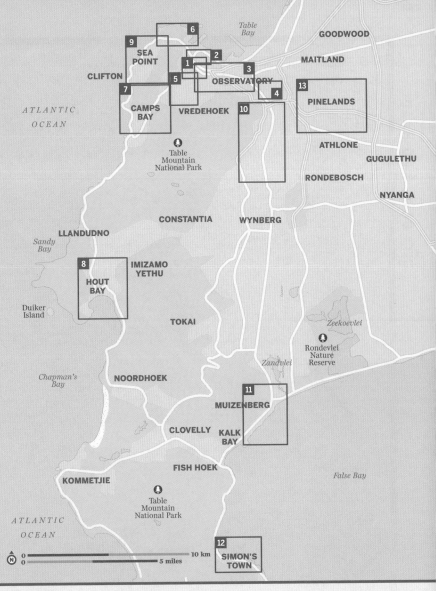

ATLANTIC OCEAN

Table Bay

GOODWOOD

MAITLAND

9 **SEA POINT**

6 *Table Bay*

CLIFTON

1 2

3 **OBSERVATORY**

13 **PINELANDS**

5

7 **CAMPS BAY**

4

VREDEHOEK

10

ATHLONE

GUGULETHU

Table Mountain National Park

RONDEBOSCH

NYANGA

CONSTANTIA

WYNBERG

Sandy Bay

LLANDUDNO

8 **HOUT BAY**

IMIZAMO YETHU

Duiker Island

TOKAI

Zeekoevlei

Rondevlei Nature Reserve

Chapman's Bay

NOORDHOEK

Zandvlei

11 **MUIZENBERG**

CLOVELLY

KALK BAY

FISH HOEK

False Bay

KOMMETJIE

Table Mountain National Park

ATLANTIC OCEAN

N
0 — 10 km
0 — 5 miles

12 **SIMON'S TOWN**

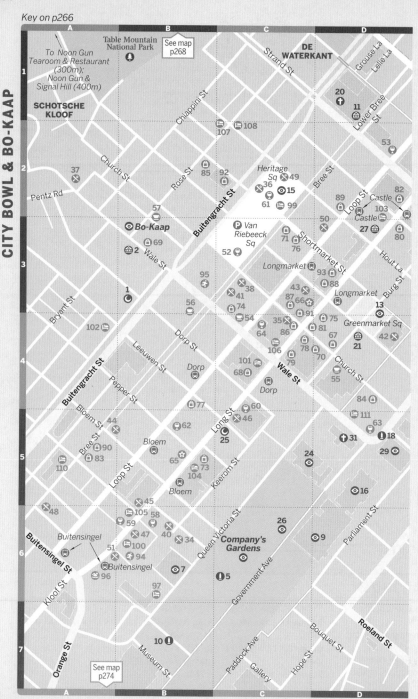

CITY BOWL & BO-KAAP

Table Mountain National Park

See map p268

DE WATERKANT

To Noon Gun Tearoom & Restaurant (300m); Noon Gun & Signal Hill (400m)

SCHOTSCHE KLOOF

Strand St

Grouse La
Leie La

Lower Bree St

Chiappini St

107   108

Church St

Rose St

85   92

Heritage Sq   49

36   15

61   99

Bree St

Loop St   Castle

89   82

Pentz Rd

37

57

Bo-Kaap

Buitengracht St

Van Riebeeck Sq

52

71   76

Shortmarket St

Castle

103

27   80

Wale St

2   69

1

95

56

Dorp St

Leeuwen St

Longmarket

Longmarket

93   88

43

87   66

91   75

35   81

67

13

Greenmarket Sq

21   42

Bryant St

102

38

41

74

54

64   86

106

78   70

79

Hout La

Burg St

Pepper St

101   68

Dorp

Wale St

55

Church St

84

77

60   46

111   63

Bloem St

44

62

Bloem

65   73

104

Bloem

Long St

25

Keerom St

24

31   18

29

16

48

45

105   58

59

47   40   34

51   100

94

Buitensingel

96

7

97

Queen Victoria St

Company's Gardens

26

9

5

Buitensingel St

Kloof St

Orange St

10

Museum St

See map p274

Government Ave

Paddock Ave

Gallery

Hope St

Bouquet St

Roeland St

A   B   C   D

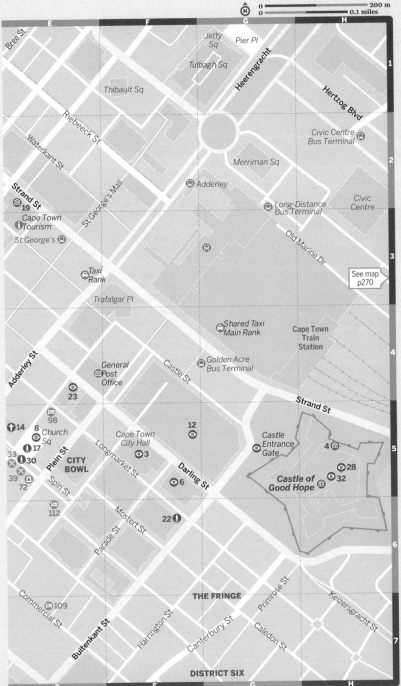

CITY BOWL & BO-KAAP *Map on p264*

FORESHORE & DE WATERKANT

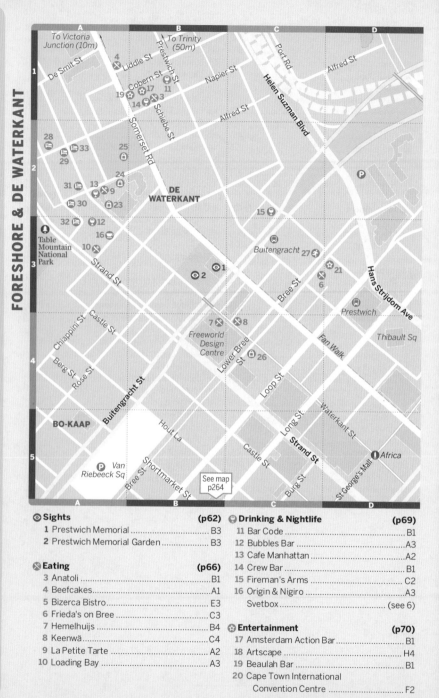

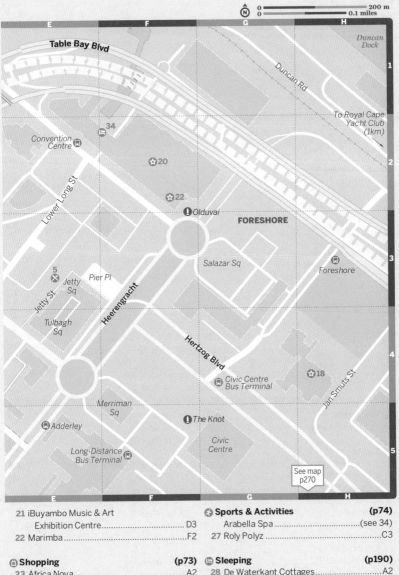

THE FRINGE, DISTRICT SIX, WOODSTOCK & SALT RIVER

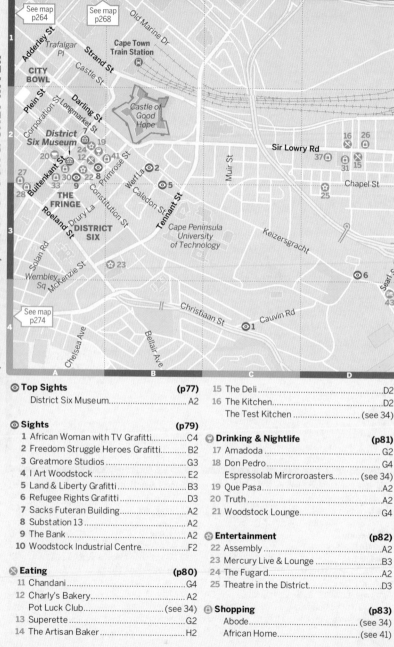

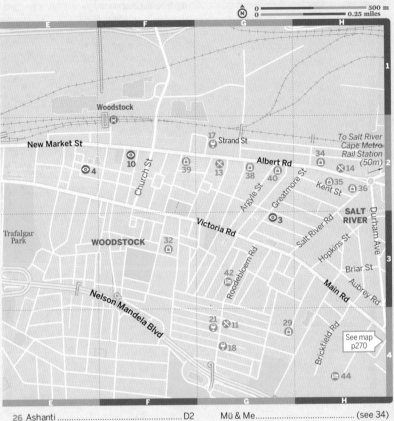

OBSERVATORY

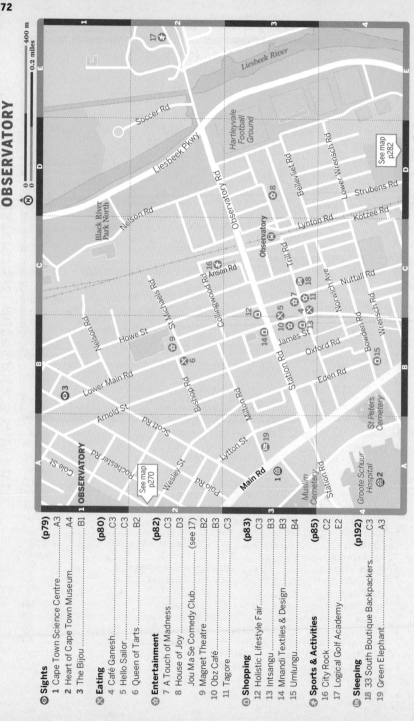

0 400 m
0 0.2 miles

See map p282

See map p270

GARDENS & SURROUNDS Map on p274

GARDENS & SURROUNDS

GARDENS & SURROUNDS

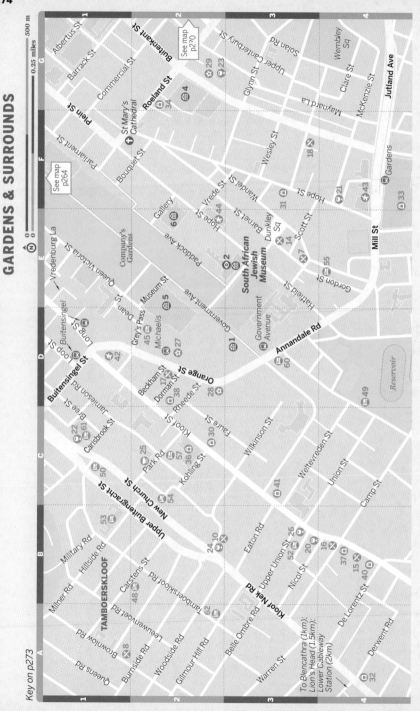

Key on p273

500 m
0.25 miles

See map p264

See map p270

TAMBOERSKLOOF

South African Jewish Museum

Company's Gardens

St Mary's Cathedral

Government Avenue

Reservoir

To Blencathra (1km);
Lion's Head (1.5km);
Lower Cableway
Station (2km)

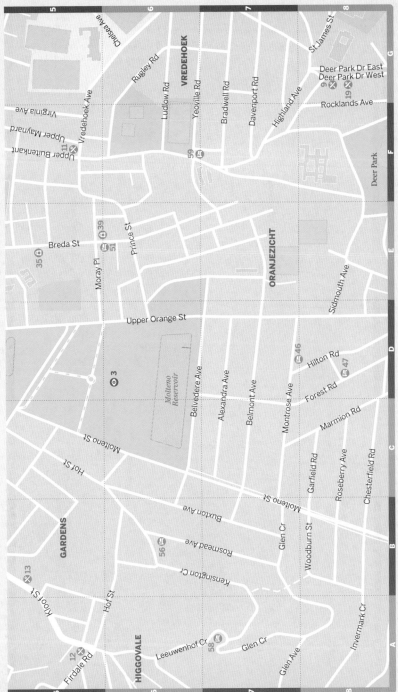

VREDEHOEK

ORANJEZICHT

GARDENS

HIGGOVALE

Deer Park Dr East
Deer Park Dr West
Rocklands Ave

Deer Park

Chelsea Ave
Rugley Rd
Ludlow Rd
Yeoville Rd
Bradwell Rd
Davenport Rd
Highland Ave
St James St

Virginia Ave
Upper Maynard
Upper Buitenkant
Vredehoek Ave

Breda St
Moray Pl
Prince St

Upper Orange St

Sidmouth Ave

Molteno
Reservoir

Belvedere Ave
Alexandra Ave
Belmont Ave
Montrose Ave
Hilton Rd
Forest Rd
Marmion Rd

Hof St
Molteno St
Molteno St
Buxton Ave
Rosmead Ave
Kensington Cr
Glen Cr
Garfield Rd
Roseberry Ave
Woodburn St
Chesterfield Rd

Kloof St
Hof St
Firdale Rd
Leeuwenhof Cr
Glen Cr
Glen Ave
Invermark Cr

GREEN POINT & WATERFRONT

Key on p277

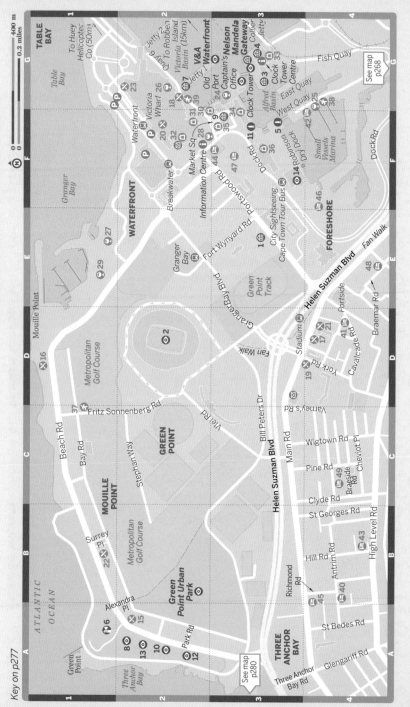

See map p268

See map p280

GREEN POINT & WATERFRONT Map on p276

CAMPS BAY

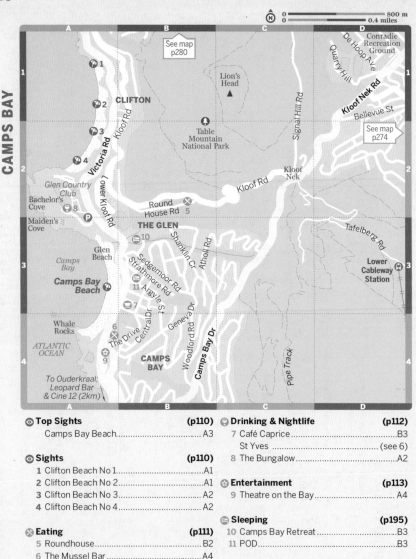

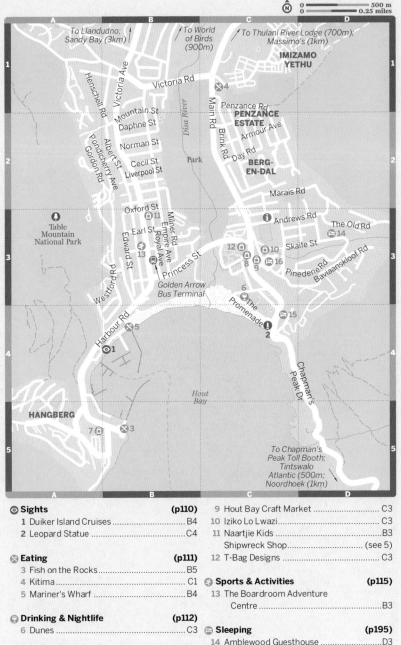

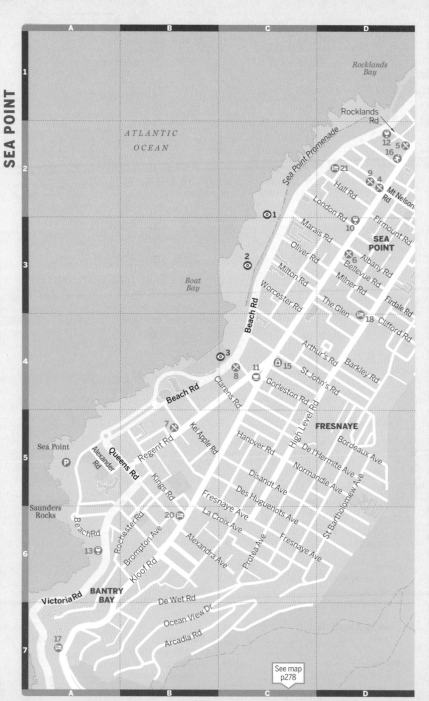

ATLANTIC
OCEAN

Rocklands
Bay

Rocklands
Rd

Sea Point Promenade

SEA
POINT

Boat
Bay

Beach Rd

Hall Rd

London Rd

Marais Rd

Oliver Rd

Milton Rd

Worcester Rd

Albany Rd
Bellevue Rd

Milner Rd

The Glen

Mt Nelson Rd

Firmount Rd

Firdale Rd

Clifford Rd

Arthur's Rd

St John's Rd

Gorleston Rd

Barkley Rd

Beach Rd

Clarens Rd

FRESNAYE

Hanover Rd

High Level Rd

De l'Hermite Ave

Bordeaux Ave

Sea Point

Alexander
Rd

Queens Rd

Regent Rd

Kei Apple Rd

Normandie Ave

Saunders
Rocks

Kings Rd

Disandt Ave

Des Huguenots Ave

Fresnaye Ave

La Croix Ave

Fresnaye Ave

St Bartholomew Ave

Beach Rd

Rochester Rd

Brompton Ave

Kloof Rd

Alexandra Ave

Protea Ave

BANTRY
BAY

Victoria Rd

De Wet Rd

Ocean View Dr

Arcadia Rd

See map
p278

SEA POINT

0 — 400 m
0 — 0.2 miles

Rocklands Beach

THREE ANCHOR BAY

See map p276

Main Rd

Three Anchor Bay Rd

Fort Rd

St Bedes Rd

Antrim Rd

Camberwell Rd

High Level Rd

Mutley Rd

Main Dr

Glengariff Rd

Ocean View Dr

Springbok Rd

Rhine Rd

Antwerp Rd

Signal Hill Rd

▲ Signal Hill

● Table Mountain National Park

Hildene Rd

See map p274

Bay View Ave

◎ **Sights**   (p110)
1 Graaff's Pool C2
2 Milton's Pool C3
3 Sea Point Pavilion C4

✕ **Eating**   (p111)
4 Cedar D2
   Harvey's ....(see 21)
5 Hesheng D2
6 La Boheme D3
7 La Mouette B5
8 La Perla C4
9 The Duchess of Wisbeach D2

◉ **Drinking & Nightlife**   (p112)
10 Decodance D3
11 Gesellig C4
12 La Vie D2
13 Salt A6

★ **Entertainment**   (p113)
14 Studio 7 .... E3

🛍 **Shopping**   (p113)
15 Peach C4

✦ **Sports & Activities**   (p115)
16 In the Blue D2
    Sea Point Pavilion .... (see 3)

🛏 **Sleeping**   (p195)
17 Ellerman House A7
18 Glen Boutique Hotel D4
19 Huijs Haerlem E2
20 O on Kloof B6
21 Winchester Mansions Hotel D2

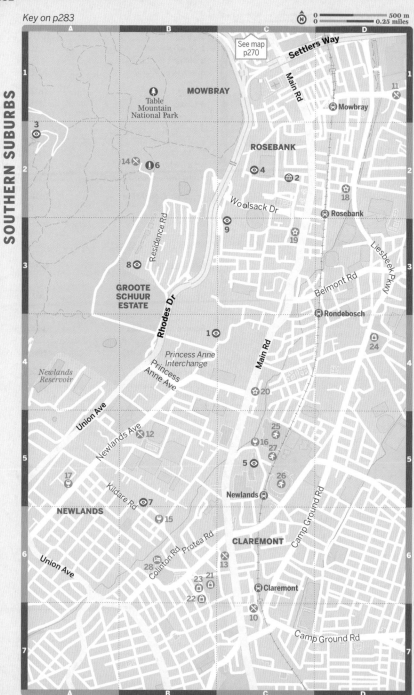

SOUTHERN SUBURBS

See map
p270

Settlers Way

MOWBRAY

Main Rd

Mowbray

Table
Mountain
National Park

3

ROSEBANK

14 6

4

2

18

Woolsack Dr

Rosebank

9

19

8

Residence Rd

GROOTE
SCHUUR
ESTATE

Belmont Rd

Rondebosch

Rhodes Dr

1

24

Princess Anne
Interchange

Main Rd

Princess
Anne Ave

Newlands
Reservoir

20

Union Ave

25

Newlands Ave

12

16

27

17

5

26

Kildare Rd

7

Newlands

15

NEWLANDS

Colinton Rd

Protea Rd

CLAREMONT

Camp Ground Rd

Union Ave

28

13

23

21

Claremont

22

10

Camp Ground Rd

Liesbeek Pkwy

SOUTHERN SUBURBS *Map on p282*

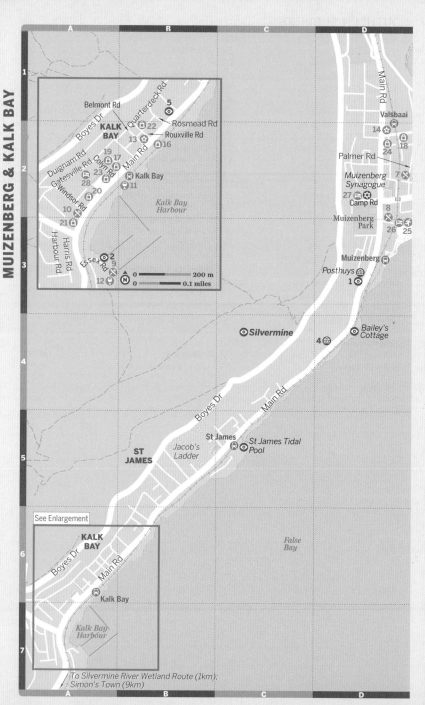

Boyes Dr
Belmont Rd
KALK BAY
Quarterdeck Rd
5
Rosmead Rd
22
13
Rouxville Rd
16
Duignam Rd
19
Gatesville Rd
17
23
Colyn Rd
Main Rd
28
Kalk Bay
20
Windsor Rd
11
Kalk Bay Harbour
10
21
Harris Rd
Harbour Rd
Essex Rd
2
9
12

0   200 m
0   0.1 miles

Main Rd
Valsbaai
14
24
18
Palmer Rd
Muizenberg Synagogue
7
27
Camp Rd
8
Muizenberg Park
26
25
Muizenberg
Posthuys
1

Silvermine
4
Bailey's Cottage

Boyes Dr
Main Rd

ST JAMES
Jacob's Ladder
St James
St James Tidal Pool

See Enlargement
KALK BAY
Boyes Dr
Main Rd

False Bay

Kalk Bay

Kalk Bay Harbour

To Silvermine River Wetland Route (1km);
Simon's Town (9km)

0	300 m
0	0.15 miles

SIMON'S TOWN

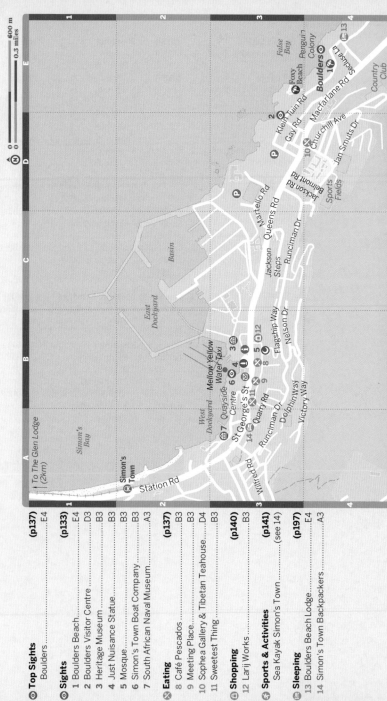

PINELANDS & LANGA

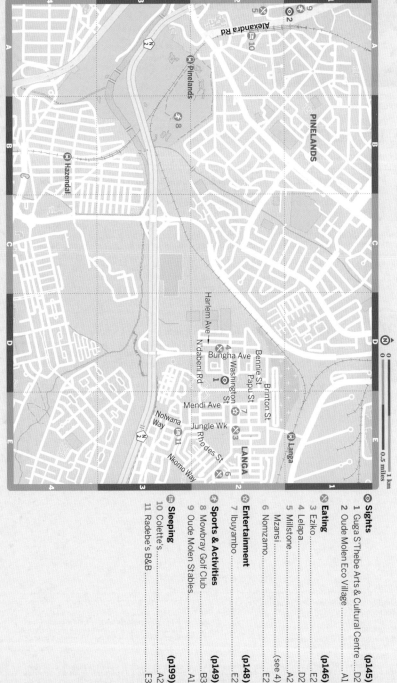

Our Story

A beat-up old car, a few dollars in the pocket and a sense of adventure. In 1972 that's all Tony and Maureen Wheeler needed for the trip of a lifetime – across Europe and Asia overland to Australia. It took several months, and at the end – broke but inspired – they sat at their kitchen table writing and stapling together their first travel guide, *Across Asia on the Cheap*. Within a week they'd sold 1500 copies. Lonely Planet was born.

Today, Lonely Planet has offices in Melbourne, London and Oakland, with more than 600 staff and writers. We share Tony's belief that 'a great guidebook should do three things: inform, educate and amuse'.

OUR WRITERS

Simon Richmond

Coordinating Author, City Bowl, Foreshore, Bo-Kaap & De Waterkant, East City Corridor, Gardens & Surrounds, Green Point & Waterfront, Sea Point to Hout Bay, Southern Suburbs, Simon's Town & Southern Peninsula, Cape Flats & Northern Suburbs Simon has been hooked on Cape Town since first visiting in 2001 to research Lonely Planet's *South Africa, Lesotho & Swaziland* guide and the *Cape Town* guide. He's returned for every edition since, exploring practically every corner of the Cape and the surrounding area, taking full advantage of a travel writer's license to indulge in eating, shopping, adventurous activities, sipping delicious wines and meeting a cast of inspirational individuals. An award-winning writer and photographer, Simon has written scores of titles for Lonely Planet and other publishers, as well as contributing features to many travel magazines and newspapers around the world. Simon also wrote Plan Your Trip, Understand Cape Town & Survival Guide. Follow his travels at www.simonrichmond.com.

Lucy Corne

Day Trips & Wineries, The Garden Route Since she first visited South Africa in 2002, Lucy has been hooked and has returned on six occasions, spending time in more than 200 towns across the country. She moved to Cape Town in 2010 and set herself the challenge of visiting every winery in the Western Cape – a task she's still working on. She was thrilled to sample the crisp Elgin sauvignon blancs and delectable pinot noirs of Hemel-en-Aarde in the name of research for this guide. Follow Lucy at www.lucycorne.com.

Read more about Lucy at:
lonelyplanet.com/members/lucycorne

Published by Lonely Planet Publications Pty Ltd
ABN 36 005 607 983
7th edition – October 2012
ISBN 978 1 74179 801 2
© Lonely Planet 2012   Photographs © as indicated 2012
10 9 8 7 6 5 4 3 2
Printed in China